Ongoing Return

CRITICAL INDIGENEITIES

J. Kēhaulani Kauanui (Kanaka Maoli) and
Jean M. O'Brien (White Earth Ojibwe), *editors*

Series Advisory Board
Chris Andersen
Emil' Keme
Kim TallBear
Irene Watson

Critical Indigeneities publishes pathbreaking scholarly books that center Indigeneity as a category of critical analysis, understand Indigenous sovereignty as ongoing and historically grounded, and attend to diverse forms of Indigenous cultural and political agency and expression. The series builds on the conceptual rigor, methodological innovation, and deep relevance that characterize the best work in the growing field of critical Indigenous studies.

A complete list of books published in Critical Indigeneities is available at https://uncpress.org/series/critical-indigeneities.

RANA BARAKAT

Ongoing Return

Mapping Memory and Storytelling in Palestine

The University of North Carolina Press *Chapel Hill*

© 2026 The University of North Carolina Press
All rights reserved
Set in Arno Pro by Westchester Publishing Services
Manufactured in the United States of America

Library of Congress Cataloging-in-Publication Data
Names: Barakat, Rana author
Title: Ongoing return : mapping memory and storytelling in Palestine / Rana Barakat.
Other titles: Critical indigeneities
Description: Chapel Hill : University of North Carolina Press, [2026] |
    Series: Critical indigeneities | Includes bibliographical references and index
Identifiers: LCCN 2025022572 | ISBN 9781469680293 cloth alk. paper | ISBN 9781469680309
    paperback alk. paper | ISBN 9781469680316 epub | ISBN 9781469680323 pdf
Subjects: LCSH: Barakat, Rana—Family | Palestinian Nakba, 1947–1948—Personal narratives |
    Palestinian Arabs—Israel—Lifta—Biography | Arab-Israeli conflict—Historiography |
    Indigenous peoples—Research—Methodology | Collective memory | Place attachment—
    Palestine | Lifta (Israel)—History | BISAC: SOCIAL SCIENCE / Ethnic Studies /
    Middle Eastern Studies | HISTORY / Middle East / General | LCGFT: Biographies |
    Autobiographies | Personal narratives
Classification: LCC DS113.6 .B367 2026 | DDC 956.04092 [B]—dc23/eng/20250807
LC record available at https://lccn.loc.gov/2025022572

Cover art: *Top*: Pathways in Lifta, 2018. Photograph by Rana Barakat. *Bottom*: 'Arifa Siam
Abuttah with Amjad Barakat, Jerusalem. Photograph in author's collection.

This book will be made open access within three years of publication thanks to Path to Open,
a program developed in partnership between JSTOR, the American Council of Learned
Societies (ACLS), the University of Michigan Press, and the University of North Carolina
Press to bring about equitable access and impact for the entire scholarly community, including
authors, researchers, libraries, and university presses around the world. Learn more at
https://about.jstor.org/path-to-open/.

For product safety concerns under the European Union's General Product Safety Regulation
(EU GPSR), please contact gpsr@mare-nostrum.co.uk or write to the University of North
Carolina Press and Mare Nostrum Group B.V., Mauritskade 21D, 1091 GC Amsterdam, The
Netherlands.

For ʿArifa

Contents

Illustrations

Preface

Where to begin in the ongoing?

I hear women talking on the street below. The sound of their voices tells me that the military must have left the neighborhood. So they gather in the wake of yet another invasion and, with their words, bring calm. Filled with curiosity and a desire to gather with them, I open the window and lean all the way out. As the dust of the invasion settles on the pavement, I stretch my body out the bedroom window—as if preparing for flight. I want to see if I can catch a glimpse of the scene or perhaps hear more of the conversation. My bedroom window does not directly overlook the street, so I have to twist around, all my senses working in unison to piece together what just happened. Sound often precedes sight, and smell is a constant indicator. No one sense alone can decipher the scene, and much has to be left to speculative imagination—a gift and a burden acquired over time and experience. In Palestine, imagination moves together with the sensory.

The post-invasion ritual has begun again. As soon as the dust and mayhem settle, women in the neighborhood gather and call on others who also managed to evade the military. Together they assess the situation in what I came to call "non–press conferences." In the summer of 2021, such gatherings occurred with greater frequency and growing intensity. But like the invasions, they are nothing new. Women have long gathered like this across Palestine to share news and assess damage.

The geography of Palestine is one, from the river to the sea. The settler military works in different ways to create a fragmented reality for Palestinians. The shores of Gaza bear the greatest brunt of this settler military. Invasion from the land, air, and sea is a kind of atmospheric violence that is unprecedented in this century, greater and more vicious in its intensity than all that came before, but this violence is nothing new for Zionist settler colonialism in Palestine. From the shores of Gaza to the bank of the River Jordan, the settler army and armies of settlers destroy, murder, and burn.

Women gather to share their news and thoughts of what just happened and what might happen next. It has been their voices that warned us all in the dark of night that the military was in the neighborhood: "Jaysh! . . . Jaysh! . . . Jaysh!" We hear the settlers' army before we see it, and we often smell invasion long before we hear it. The scent lingers long after the soldiers have left. Tear gas is atmospheric like that.

Every time I stretch my body out the bedroom window, preparing for imagined flight, I think about how I learned to use all the senses to see beyond the limits in front of me. My younger brother, Mikey, taught me that vision without the gift of sight means combining all the senses to work as one. Though he is thousands of miles away in our parents' home in Chicago, Mikey is with me as I stretch into flight mode on all the nights when the neighborhood in Ramallah al-tahta resembles, however slightly, the war zones that the settlers have brought to the land of Palestine. He helps me imagine flying, freely and beyond the settler stalkers who work to make us captive to their violent wills.

Every neighborhood is a symphony, with movements of all sorts. An experienced ear begins to learn how to hear both the whole of the symphony and the specificities of each note. I listen as I try to learn how to fly. Connecting myself to the sensory has helped me understand that stretching my arms to fly is in direct relation to grounding my feet to walk in and with Palestine. Learning how to fly and to stand solidly on the ground is no paradox: The two connect as modalities of survival.

During the late autumn months of 2023, as the skies over Ramallah were invaded by the sounds of settler machinery en route to wreaking indescribable destruction on Gaza, these gatherings carried the weight of something I could not quite name. It is surreal to bear witness to settler violence in places like Ramallah where the veil of cognitive dissonance is almost transparent but always present. And as winter turns to spring in 2024, the ladies of the neighborhood who lead these gatherings do so less frequently, though the armies invade more regularly. Given all of the neighborhoods destroyed by the settlers' military, perhaps the levels of destruction in the more recent seasons of the war on Palestine have now led people to reconsider the very notion of neighborhood gatherings.

Virtual gatherings continue through a vast network of Telegram channels. From the local to the national, Telegram hosts a virtual matrix of war mapping in the West Bank. The same menu of channels track incomprehensible destruction in the Gaza Strip. Messages on our phones warn us of the presence of the settlers' military so that people can navigate their daily movement on the ground as they follow constant updates of an ongoing genocide.

New questions arise through all of these genocidal developments in Palestine. Even though the language and the concepts of ongoing Nakba have been well established since 1948, is it now the case that Nakba needs to be reconsidered in Palestine? Consistencies in the landscape of settler violence are not difficult to understand. Destruction and elimination remain the clear intent. But the intensity and relentlessness of the violence and Nakba have changed.

By the summer of 2025, when I am writing these words, as I complete the last review of this book, every concept of the ongoing Nakba has been challenged. The genocidal intentions of an apocalypse mark all the geographies of Palestine, from the river to the sea. Survival remains a constant. We have accumulated four generations of survival. But how to survive these killing fields? This requires more fluidity in thought and practice. Although we understand settler intentions from a century of Palestinian experience and centuries of experiences of Indigenous peoples across the globe, this indescribable violence remains shocking, though not surprising.

A Family Affair: In Lieu of a Beginning, and to Be Not Exceptional

This is a book about Lifta, a village in Jerusalem. This is a book about return and this is a book about Palestine. This is a book that imagines ongoing return to and with Lifta and to and with Palestine. This is also a book that centers return as a concept and a practice in the midst of an ongoing Nakba.

This book is grounded in a mother's love—my mother's hope through despair and my fear of disappointing her because it was my mother who first taught us what it means to be Palestinian. My maternal family is from Lifta; my mother was born in Jerusalem. Because my mother gives so much, she expects so much. The surreal elevation of expectations meant that to disappoint her was to betray Palestine. The intimate and hard labor of nurturing return is ours in a world very much against us.

Being Palestinian is not an identity crisis. It is not exceptional. It is about living with expectations and navigating the constant blend of hope and disappointment. The journey of this book is a journey of return. Being Palestinian means learning that we are always returning to Palestine. Ongoing return is a commitment to vitality surrounded by death and the apocalypse. It is not a vacation or a holiday; it not a simple equation to be rehearsed and then repeated. Return as a practice is embedded in the humility of never discovering the past but instead always *uncovering* our pasts. That work is the method of this book.

We were alone in exile, because our mother was alone in exile. With a family that must have felt a million miles away in Jerusalem, she is a woman—like the whole of her generation, born after the Nakba and into the ongoing Nakba—who has held the wounds of Palestine in her body. Born in Jerusalem in a kind of afterlife of exile, after 1948, she lived in the shadow of what once was, the village of Lifta that her parents were forced to flee. In the early 1970s, after another kind of afterlife, after 1967, my mother met and married my father. My father, already having spent more than a decade building a life in the United States to escape the shadows of the Nakba, took her with him and they raised their family in Chicago, in the shadow of all of these afterlives.

My mother has tried to teach us that we must always be committed to learning, because that is what the ongoing Nakba taught her and what exile reinforced in her. Knowledge cannot be stolen. I have since come to reconsider the concept of exile, questioning its use or value as a way of being for Palestinians, but even that journey has been affected by my mother and her generation's reflections on exile. In all of her expectations grounded in learning, my mother has also imparted a sense of responsibility to each other that grew more profound over time. This sense of responsibility and knowledge are both grounded in a mother's love.

When we were children, settler soldiers were the monsters we did not see; yet my mother could not *unsee* them, so we were taught to navigate even what we did not understand. We grew up in the shadow of our mother's Palestine. We did not grow up in Palestine, but we were raised with the simultaneous pain and privilege of survival. I learned how to translate these lessons into ongoing return.

And so, this is a personal journey full of generations of intimate and familial stories. It has taken me far too long to work toward a method of sharing these stories. The hesitation of sharing the personal remains an uncomfortable imposition. Perhaps the personal might become a shadow over the collective or might somehow replace it. The danger lingers: We may fall into a trap and find that rendering a personal story can easily be twisted into a confessional or testimony of personal defeat and/or triumph. How can sharing stories actually teach us how to play with light, where the shadows are neither traps nor holes?

If a certain method of articulating the personal is a kind of confessional, how can we move beyond self-centering while not removing our personal from our collective selves? Very much mine, but not mine alone, storytelling and story sharing are a navigation of our lives through time and space.

The stories shared in this book were gathered in all kinds of modalities and languages. Bound by neither convention nor norm, these stories travel through language. Either lost or found between Arabic and English, my family gifted me a distrust of language as a practice, one that nurtured a refusal of the normative. Language came into form through practice. Long before I learned the art of deconstruction as theory, decolonial praxis, and the conceptual tools involved in both, I was taught refusal of normativity as a way of being. My brothers and I knew the world we lived in was not ours. Still, we had to learn the language of this world in order to know that to which we do not belong.

Mikey, my younger brother, coming into our lives taught us not to pathologize who we are and how we came to be. Rather than reading legibility through the binary of dis/ability, for example, my mother refused every label some so-called expert tried to impose on Mikey. Her reason was simple: Why keep Mikey captive in a box that did not know—or want to get to know—him? She applied the same principle to all of us, her children. Thus, my brothers and I were taught to refuse labels and categories, which meant a kind of refusal of language that often left me without a means through which to explain or even understand things. We were taught to refuse using categories and to refuse their use on us. Refusing categories and the language from which they emerge requires us to forge, imagine, and develop a new language that reflects our ways of being. Not an easy task, for the power of language and recognition that makes one visible or seen is enormous. Those lessons have empowered this journey, uncovering the past to find our language.

In every moment of our mother's refusal to accept or succumb to the labels of doctors or so-called experts that tried to render Mikey less whole, I stood in awe and fear. I used to wonder if that refusal of pathology prevented something. After all, Mom was navigating a world that she knew Mikey needed while trying to demand that he be seen, heard, and felt. How could Mikey make his way in a world that could not see him as anything other than incapable? For me, as a child, the myriad categories used to describe Mikey as *disabled* were as confusing as they were alienating. My mother's anger at the charts and evaluations was probably as much about refusal as it was about denial. Were we somehow preventing ourselves from understanding something because we refused the diagnosis? Or was that refusal not a rejection but instead an honoring of our bruised but never broken selves? I know now that her anger is my own, and with each generation we inherit this dignity of anger and pass it on to the next.

My mother endured and refused the labels that doctors, psychologists, social workers, or any other kind of experts tried to impose on her baby. While my older brother, Amjad, and I observed this enduring refusal as children, it seems we absorbed it as we grew and learned the same kind of refusal of language, labels, and categorical impossibilities. Over time, this has become a generative refusal. Mikey is more precious than such labels. Mikey has language, but it is his own, and he has helped to make it ours. We learn it from him. He has needs that mean that Mikey teaches us love, and how responsibility is born of that love and exists to nurture it. While this is a book about a village named Lifta in a homeland named Palestine and is an attempt to present the language of ongoing return as a conceptual offering to our collective intellectualism, I honor Mikey and my family as the means that led to this method.

Mikey made us special through being special. Part of this being special has been not only a refusal of language but also an ongoing search for language. Long before I understood hegemony in language or the brutal nature of normative discourse, Mikey showed us that practice precedes rhetoric or even ideology. Practice is far more difficult and far more meaningful. It is a way of being and a way of living.

Perhaps all of this is what has enabled and empowered this set of stories, the method that led to the methodology of this book. The form is a book, but the substance remains a flowing document of an ever-changing phenomenon momentarily captured in the pages that follow. It is a journey that, at first thought, I mistakenly considered myself alone in the taking, from historian to storyteller, from a refusal of exile to a practice of return. But the journey was never only mine; it took the imagination and the active practice embedded in the pages that follow to teach me that the contradiction of care and fear in my childhood would flourish in the hope of ongoing return, to challenge the never-ending fear of exile and relentless reality of settler colonial violence.

Our stories are not linear, and my thinking about the ongoing was a seed that was planted long before I had any kind of language or comprehension to share. It was a feeling long before it was a concept. It is the intimacy of family (of all kinds) confronting all the violence of settlers, in Palestine and across our many geographies ravaged by settlers. The stories nurtured among ourselves, with each other, are special treasures that over time evolve into a language of our own.

After learning how to refuse the fieldwork of oral history and come into the power of stories, I became obsessed with the idea of bringing my brothers with me in a grand return to Lifta. The three of us in a fantastic story of return to our grandmother. And so, I began to plot it out in my head based on what my feet learned in my own travels into Lifta that form the backbone of this book.

I would need to find a way to make Mikey hold on to me while traversing a path full of rocks on a steep incline. Mom would not be able to bring herself and Mikey up this path, because Mikey towered over her in height and her knees could only handle so much. So we would have to figure out a system by which to hold everyone together, to do this as a family. Amjad holds the role of guide and engineer because Amjad is Mikey's sight guide. I have always been the one that forges and shares a language with Mikey—I am his translation guide. Together we would guide each other into return.

But, as my obsession grew, I plotted more details because I wanted to take the lead. I am the one who knows this valley and hill. I have tried to map this out. I am the one who has imagined this gathering for a long time. I am the one who has decided to walk among and with the past, in the present, and I am the one who wants us to imagine the future together.

I then shared with my mother the dream of bringing Mikey with me to Lifta. Mom interrupted the fantasy and asked me why. What would Mikey possibly want from walking toward homes rendered empty for nearly a century by settlers? Such moments of interruption and pure disruption, courtesy of my mother, were common and necessarily humbling. While she nurtured the dreamscape that has become my life in Palestine for nearly two decades, she has also become the only person who can impose the return of harsh reality to my navigation. In ongoing return, the concept of home required more fluidity than I anticipated. I simply wanted to be with my brothers in a place I wanted us to call home. I wanted to restore that home for my mother. But what did that mean? What can that mean?

Mikey sees in his own way, his capacity for sight defying the label "blind." Mikey understands in his own way, defying another category unspoken by us as a family. And Mikey expresses himself in his special way—a means toward establishing relationality with the learning and language that he gives us. A journey often fraught with frustration and fear. When Mom interrupted my discussion of plans, I complained that she was disrupting my journey of return—to which she plainly stated, "Return is not just what *you* dream and want, it is what holds space for us all, even if it is something you do not understand or have yet to imagine." Return needed to be bigger than a singular path charted out on a map. Return is bigger than any one person.

The problem with imagination is how far removed from daily reality one's mind can wander, breeding a sense of wonder that renders the line between possible and impossible all but indistinguishable. Therein lies one of the threads of this book—how to maintain a sense of grounding to honor the past of Palestine and Palestinians while fostering a sense of hope that enables us to see beyond the barbarians who wreak our destruction.

Or try to. As summer turns to autumn again, the history of the Nakba is no longer a history lesson. Even a century of experience has not prepared us for this. The monsters of war have rendered reality an ongoing nightmare. Even the settlers have come to describe this as annihilation. They are no longer coy and no longer what passes for subtle. Words cannot describe the devastation at hand. At the time of this writing, Gaza has endured a year and a half of unrelenting and indescribable violence that even the complicit world is now finally calling a "genocide." Any invitation of conceptualizing and imagining ongoing return in the midst of all of this is perhaps the most radical of challenges.

Acknowledgments

In its dream state, this book began long before me. Hopefully, it will also find an afterlife. It was, on my part, born of equal parts frustration and rage, beauty, and hope. If there is frustration and rage in these words, they belong to our confinement to a cruel world of atmospheric violence that cannot tolerate Palestinian life. If there is beauty in these words, it belongs to the ongoing acts of love often mixed imperceptibly into the necessity of survival. If there is hope in these words, it belongs to a people who, individually and collectively, have guided us to return and to always return. Ongoing return is an act, a practice, and hopefully a new horizon.

I have endless people to thank for forming and nurturing every idea presented humbly here in the form of a book. I am grateful for the fortitude of everyone who guided, led with kindness and care, and held this project and me, in spite of my own stubborn habits. Needless to say, all that is helpful in these pages is due to their grace. My own journey began long before writing and in conversations with people from Lifta. Their voices led me back to my family: my mother, ʿAdla Nahida, and her mother, ʿArifa.

As a whole, this is a book about mothers and daughters. More concretely, it is a book about my mother, without whom neither I nor this book would exist. Long before I tried to understand Palestine and what it means to be Palestinian, my mother's love for her children taught us to always, unquestionably and without conditions, lead with love. This book is for my mother, because she is the single most important Palestinian voice my brothers, Amjad al-Din (Dean) and Mikey, know. To my brothers and my father, this book is as much yours as it is mine. ʿAdla, Daher, Amjad, Mikey, Kathy, and Omar, family is also our home and our homeland. And to my nephew, Omar, ongoing return is for you.

Each imprint matters, and each voice has been a gift. I want to thank Abdul-Rahim Al-Shaikh for sharing the beauty of belonging and longing and for helping me find hope in their connections. His poetic words define belonging in all of its grief and joy; it is the poets who write history best. I also wish to thank Sherene Seikaly, the loving historian who believed in this kind of history, even when I wavered, for listening and reading through more ideas and drafts than I could count and for never wavering for a moment in this journey; J. Kēhaulani Kauanui for her kind, patient, and always supportive voice and for seeing this project as a book before anyone else did; Jasbir Puar, who shows me how curious minds are beautifully immeasurable in brilliance and always and without hesitation gives me a sense of confidence that my voice matters; Rema Hammami, she who leads with kindness and shows me how to have grace in rage, for her thoughtful input and for always being a supportive reader and thinker; Julia Elyachar for her insane capacity to calm anxieties through her kind reading and generous editing voice; and Rashid Khalidi, a man whose intellect and demand of rigor raised a generation of Palestinian historians, for being the person who showed me just how much history can and does matter.

While the support network of beautiful souls in my life far exceeds words, I would also like to thank Kathleen Barakat, Nadine Naber, Lila Abu-Lughod, Jihad Al-Shwaikh, Jumana Dababna, Cindy Franklin, Aamer Ibraheem, Penny Johnson, Sharry Lapp, Mawakib Massad, Yasmeen Qadan, Wijdan Samara, Nadera Shalhoub-Kevorkian, Haneen Naamnih, Khaled Odetallah, Yaqub Odeh, Alejandro Paz, Stephen Sheehi, David Lloyd, Robin D. G. Kelley, and Khaled Furani. In small and big ways, each one of you teaches me love. Jean O'Brien, Mark Simpson-Vos, and Andreina Fernandez from the University of North Carolina Press have offered invaluable support and patience in seeing this book come to fruition.

Parts of this book were written while I was the Arcaptia Visiting Professor of Modern Arab Studies at Columbia University, where my work benefited from my engagements with both students and professors. Parts of this work were previously published in the *Native American and Indigenous Studies Journal* and as a chapter in a book published by the Institute for Palestine Studies titled *Lifta: Register of a People, History, Cultural Heritage and Struggle*. I have presented thoughts, pieces, and chapters of this book for several years across three continents (virtually and in-person) and am grateful to all of the organizations, institutes, and universities that have made space for my work.

This book was written in and for Palestine. I owe an enormous debt of gratitude to my students and friends at Birzeit University for all their patience in listening to the stories of Lifta; on this unique campus, everyone who supported this project came to understand how and why Lifta is the center of the universe. To my extended Lifta family, my late aunts and uncles from the Abutaah family, and everyone from Jerusalem to Ramallah who shared stories and lives, you helped make Jerusalem home and Lifta part of my return. To every person from Lifta, in all of our geographies, this book is about you and the generations who came before and shall come next. To every person who opened their homes and shared their stories, I am grateful beyond words. This is my humble attempt to continue in your generous tradition.

This book has been a long journey and was nearly entirely completed before October 2023. Since then, the idea of ongoing return has been challenged by the ever-growing violence against Palestinian life. I have struggled with concepts of return in a settler colonial genocide whose aim is to clearly obliterate Palestinian life and living in Palestine. No words can describe what Palestinians in Gaza and across the land of Palestine have endured and continue to endure. At the start of 2025, in a rare moment of ceasefire, people in Gaza, who suffered multiple and violent displacements, returned to the ruins of their homes. These heroes showed us all that ongoing return, while a challenging concept in the midst of inexplicable settler colonial violence, is never more real and alive, from 1948 to 2025. From the river to the sea, we shall continue to return.

Ongoing Return

Part I

Introduction
Walking Through History

Walking through Palestinian landscapes is the journey of return. For Palestinians, such a journey defies time; it is layered with sediments of personal experience and collective peoplehood. As I walk, I am guided by those who have walked before me. I want nothing more than to walk with them. Removed from "settler anxieties" about ghosts from the past,[1] our ancestors become our guides. We walk with each other in time and through time with stories.

Lifta, Palestine, and Return

'Arifa, my maternal grandmother, is my guide and the reason this book was conceived and how it flows: *from* and *through* and *toward*. From the academic to the personal, it all blends in this book as my search for 'Arifa and my journey with her. I am trained as a historian, and this academic discipline lays a foundation for my walking and my storytelling. But this discipline sometimes brings hesitation; it is often an obstacle and always a burden.

Our journey through place and time is shaped by the voices and experiences of those who came before as we plan for those who shall come after us. Every chapter of this book is a part of walking through the "real" to the "imagined"—toward and with 'Arifa. Walking with stories is the process—through landscapes, through time and with people, as we continue to return to Lifta and to Palestine. This book is not a blueprint for how to walk, nor is it a model for how to think about the past in Palestine or about Palestinians. It is an attempt to journey—to move in another way. To journey and to move through space are not to be taken for granted, as we remember the past and present and move into the future. Walking with stories is real and imagined, contextual and speculative, physical and abstract.

I was never good at understanding geographies through directions. I could never remember their details. But holding on to memories is different; I have learned, over time, to hold on tightly to my emotional maps and their evolutions by listening to stories. These stories are shared over time and through time; they help me move beyond and outside hegemonic "settler time."[2] Emotional maps, by way of contrast, are carved from memories of generations in the making. These are also memories I have inherited and memories I have charted. My emotional maps have evolved over time to become continuous threads in my conversations with 'Arifa's daughter, my mother, 'Adla Nahida (she has two names because her parents could not agree on one). Wherever she is in the world, my mother carries Jerusalem with her—"like the back of my hand," she often says. Her stories became the foundation for our walking.

Our walking, turning corners in the Old City of Jerusalem through our words, have become the layers of history that have been the foundation for our remembering. In our walking and sharing stories, it is difficult to pinpoint a beginning and impossible to proclaim an end, for this journey does not follow that kind of linear narrative arc. 'Arifa was born in Lifta; my mother was born in the Old City of Jerusalem, at one station of exile, and I was born in Chicago, at another station of exile. Throughout this book, I try to show how we walk together—or, rather, it was in the process of writing that I learned how much we walk together. This was not a discovery or even the making of a methodology of thinking or being. Instead, as I came to understand, this has always been and shall continue to be. Through the continuousness of walking together, we embody the ongoing.

Part of understanding this process has been learning how to listen and how to share. We comprise three generations of women who belong to Lifta and—through Lifta—to Palestine. Memories layered through generations create a landscape, past and present, that forges paths to the future. These emotional maps are the accumulation of all kinds of knowledge: lived experience, remembered experiences, the heart of storytelling and story listening, and the power of imagination—our own, as well as others'. The emotional maps I lay out in this book are a personal narrative in a collective experience. They are landscapes that lead us into and through the stories, and they are a core part of the methodology in this book. I employ these practices of mapping to share our stories of Lifta, the Nakba (the ongoing Nakba), and Palestinian history. If this methodology is removed from the confines of an academic discipline and understood as a way of being, method is no longer only a way of performing research; it becomes a means of engagement and understanding our ways of living.

Walking with stories is not new. It is an established way of being in Palestine, and it is a practice and a methodology in various other Indigenous epistemologies. As Allice Legat suggests in her work with the Tåîchô, who are among the Dene, an Athabaskan-language speaking people in northern Canada, walking, narrative and knowledge are intrinsically combined as means and methods of connecting the past into the present through establishing—and continuously reestablishing—relations with place.[3] It is not a surprise that exploring relations with and relationality to the land are foundational elements in Indigenous methodologies, where storytelling is central.[4] As settler colonialism's main feature is control of the land, the primary target of its violence is attacking Indigenous peoples' relationship to that land.[5] Palestinians share this sense of relationality to and with the land. As Raja Shehadeh beautifully explores in his *Palestinian Walks*, his relationship to place through walking defines his own personal history in the hills of Ramallah. In approaching the practice of walking, Shehadeh laments that "the curse of Palestine is its centrality to the West's historical and biblical imagination." As such, travelers would come to Palestine in search of this biblical landscape and erase all that did not fit the paradigm. "Biblical" and "Holy Land" translated in European imaginations into a drama that, as Shehadeh notes, "was not my drama." Like other kinds of settler mythologies, then, biblical stories were employed to obfuscate a relationality to the land for Palestinians. For Shehadeh, then, walking in the Ramallah hills would be about his relationship to the land, and intentionally not experienced "through the veil of words written about it, often replete with distortions."[6] In this sense, walking is a defiant act, and stories are the accompanying symphony.

Shehadeh works to see beyond the veil, or see in spite of it, which is often the case in terms of settler colonial invasion. Leanne Betasamosake Simpson, of the Mississauga Nishnaabeg / Michi Saagiig Nishnaabeg people, speaks eloquently about how Indigenous peoples not only reveal the veil but work to conquer it, noting that "four centuries of Indigenous resistance and mobilization on Turtle Island has been aimed at bringing about a decolonizing apocalypse—one that lifts the veil of colonial amnesia, amplifies Indigenous truths, and reveals the real and symbolic violence of settler colonialism."[7] Through their walks, Shehadeh and others explore not only the violence of displacement but also the possibilities for maintaining and nurturing. While Shehadeh laments the vanishing landscape of his youth, Basil al-ʿAraj worked in a slightly different vein; a martyr killed by the Israeli military in 2017, he advocated and mentored a kind of engagement with the past. Al-ʿAraj asked us to not only see a landscape of settler violence but also to consider it a landscape of Palestinian resistance.[8] Though their approaches are very different, both Shehadeh and al-ʿAraj represent how relationality to the land, space, and place of Palestine is the literal and metaphorical grounding for Palestinian life and a life told in stories. Al-ʿAraj was—both in his life and in his rich afterlife as a martyr—a notable representative of a new generation that witnessed the forced transformation of the political landscape in Palestine away from armed struggle. After 2005 his generation was supposedly raised under the low ceiling of a culture of defeat, normalization with occupation. and out-of-control consumerism as a neoliberal alternative to political emancipation. Defiance, however, trumps defeat, as Khaled Odetallah shows through his own exploration of knowledge sharing.[9] Odetallah practices walking with and through knowledge with the intention of walking beyond both colonial-produced knowledge and the borders and boundaries that such knowledge has imposed. Like (and often times with) Odetallah, al-ʿAraj worked to expose the affect of settler power on the land and colonial power on our ways of thinking to reestablish relationships with place and story. His guided walks through the landscape of resistance are now famous and widely distributed.

To be clear, this kind of relationality is not about forgetting or a fear of forgetting—which is an albatross around the neck of Palestinian history—as much as it is about how we remember. The stories that hold emotional maps nurture the vitality of living as shared methods across divergent geographies.

Walking in Jerusalem

I have a map of Jerusalem in my head; it differs from any of the maps I have seen in print. Like my maps, I also have stories, made of experiences that are grounded by the lives of those who walked throughout Jerusalem from the valley and ridges of Lifta. These stories, like our emotional maps, cannot be found in the colonial archives that hold the historical literature on Jerusalem. But how can we account for, and then hope to overcome, the alienation produced by colonial maps and settler archives? Jerusalem has been captured as the center of a global battle in the mythology of imperialism; maps of Jerusalem, consequently, incorporate this mythology. Jerusalem—and Palestine by extension—is thus confined to a discourse of control of territory that is held captive by colonial maps and settler archives. Our own emotional maps and lived stories are not merely erased from colonial maps and settler archives; they never existed within those structures. The simple explanation is played out in the daily structural violence of settler colonialism; it is bloody, destructive, and genocidal. It cannot tolerate our past, just as settlers constantly attack our present. Though countering the colonial and settler colonial narrative of Jerusalem and Palestine has been a key part of Palestinian literature, can we consider why we are working to counter that which causes us to disappear as a foundational principle? Shall we work to find ourselves in these structures of power, forcing a recognition for Palestine and Palestinians within it, or can we find another way?

Over the last decade there has been a new surge in the work on Palestine in settler colonial studies. This came about at the same time that I began the journeys in this book, and it has been useful to think with colleagues and friends about the *how* and the *why* in conversations about settler colonialism and Palestine. While much has been done in this context and even more has been said about such work, I want to position the use (and perhaps misuse) of the settler colonial analytic in the larger historical context and the vast historiography of Palestine. Most important, this return or resurgence of Palestine in settler colonial studies is a political project that makes sense and is generative. But is it about Palestine, or is it about Zionism?[10]

Zionism as a project and the settler state of Israel as a case study reveal the generative nature of a comparative analysis. Zionism was born of the same European modernity that gave birth to the settler colonial movements that have ravaged the globe. It was also a failed and nationalist response to the violence of Jewish exclusion from this modernity. Understanding settler projects in other geographical contexts, for example, reveals a great deal about the kind of violence Palestinians have endured for over a century. Using the settler colonial analytic in this way can be productive for both exposing Zionist violence and challenging the thesis of the exceptionality of the settler state. But where is Palestine, and where are the Palestinian people in this challenge? Where is ʿArifa? Can the stories of Palestine, my stories of Lifta, and our stories of the Nakba move through settler power rather than being confined by it? Asking these questions, instead of speaking to or with settlers, nurtures a conversation with fellow peoples who have endured settler colonialism.[11] Together we can account for and work to understand the settler colonial analytic even as we endure its violence. In this kind of collective and specific reckoning with settler power, our stories are the methods we follow and the voices we center.

I walk in Jerusalem in search of stories while learning how to listen to the voices that tell them. There is an inherent humility in searching—be it in archives or in stories—but there is also a power in refusing the separation from the personal and the epistemological. It is frankly frightening for me as a historian to center ʿArifa and her daughters, thus perhaps also centering myself. Am I no longer a historian if I do so? ʿArifa is not an alternative to archives; she is bigger than any settler or colonial archive. She is more profound than any military map of territory. But ʿArifa was also the victim of archives and maps and the imperial powers that produced and supported them. Countering Zionist mythology as a political project, then, is a daily necessity, a means of survival. Even so, this countering, and all of the intellectual and political necessity it entails, are not the register of this book; instead, emotional maps and lived stories are the method, the process, and the love held in all of its pages. Yet the omnipresent violence of settler anxieties cannot simply be escaped; the emotional logic of this book is in my hesitations, my inability to find a path that is somehow completely void of settler anxieties. Because of the relentless presence of settler colonial violence, even a determination to walk and share while we endure is an act of defiance, albeit one embroiled in the contradictions of survival. Nevertheless, with love, these hesitations and contradictions, and 'Arifa as my guide, this book is a journey. As such, each chapter in the first part of the book begins with a vignette that recalls, reinforces, and invites the idea and realization of this journey: walking, talking, and sharing. The second part of the book shifts from historical questions framed by stories to a place where the stories find their place in the center.

What Kind of Story? Relationality and Relational History

Seeking recognition is often a contestation in the writing of Palestinian history as a means of countering the layers of erasure that both modernity and settler colonialism have imposed on the very presence of Palestinians' past and present. As such, the hegemonic subtext in how the past is imagined has long been assigned the labor of producing a kind of counternarrative. Either to counter or respond, Palestinian history has been held captive to a colonial relationship and a framework of conflict. So much of historical writing about Palestine has been imprisoned with the notion of *relational history*, whereby we are told to seek connections, commonalities, and conversations with Zionist settlers and the structures they impose to find resolution to this conflict.[12] Presenting ourselves as part of a conflict both obfuscates the settler colonial analytical and works to keep us captive within its structures of material and epistemic power.

While the notion of the relational has been a major trap in Palestinian history, exploring relationality, when guided by Indigenous methodologies, offers new paths. Contemplating how we seek beyond or outside the "politics of recognition," re-centers a relationship to place beyond the violence of dispossession that Palestinian and other Indigenous peoples have endured. It follows, then, that exploring relationality to the land is not exceptional to Palestine or Palestinians, as this is a shared context among Indigenous peoples.

As Glen Coulthard of the Yellowknives Dene people deftly argues, recognition and dispossession are related tools in the settlers' arsenal. Settler colonialism is driven by a violent logic about stealing land and eliminating the people of that land. It is, moreover, the violent methodology of settlers across geographies. What happens when we do not work to counter this theft or do not work exclusively within a politics of recognition to expose its logic? In the context of the violence of the settler state of Canada, and its particular legacies in terms of settler state recognition politics, Coulthard offers "grounded normativity" as a theoretical and methodological intervention, by which he means "the modalities of Indigenous land-connected practices and long-standing experiential knowledge that inform and structure our ethical engagements with the world and our relationships with human and nonhuman others over time."[13] As Coulthard notes, our relation to place is obviously a target of settler colonial power, and in the context of the Dene people, Coulthard employs "grounded normativity" as a political and methodological approach by which, in part, to understand and nurture Indigenous refusal, resurgence, and resistance. Coulthard's political intervention also resonates in the Palestinian context, where cultural and political recognition have informed how we see our history under the weight of settler colonial violence.

If we follow this power of recognition, the past informs our present in how we have been forced make our own land claims. This narrative arc is based on the idea that we "were once here" and therefore we should prove ownership of what *once was*. These claims are embedded in a political project toward "achieving" a nation-state recognized by both the settlers and the imperial powers. The hold of nation-state modernity on Palestinian politics has been suffocating to the Palestinian people. In addition to the settler occupation of the land, settler frameworks have also occupied our own frames and mechanisms of relationality. Navigation, instead of exploring our own changing relationship with time and place, then becomes a kind of negotiation with the settler and within their logic. This all reduces our belonging to Palestine into an adherence to a version of the past that is nothing more than a lost paradise or a complication that cannot be lived in the present and has no future. As such, not only do we compile a list of a history of loss but our past is itself lost to this confinement. All we can do in this reductive and overdetermined framework is claim that Palestine as a place and as a land once belonged to us, a long-lost past that can at best only be memorialized.

The relationality offered in Coulthard's "grounded normativity" can be translated within the Palestinian context as we work to defy the confines of settler epistemologies even as we confront their violence. Yet this sense of grounding requires a speculative act, a relationship with memory and re-membering that is grounded in the land over time, even when our material bodies are denied this grounding in time. Zionism as a settler colonial military machine has both fragmented the land of Palestine and controlled our access to the land and to each other. That is, the settler state tries to control how we as a people can be in relation (if at all) with any part of the fragmented geographies of homeland and with each other. As such, ways of being and ways of living are not always the same because, in the material sense, fragmenting geographies involve displacement and denial of any material or physical access whereby memory serves as a replacement for present relationalities. Part of the settler violence in Palestine is ongoing displacement and the bitter reality of exile from our homeland, further reinforcing a longing for the past when we were once in relation to our land and to each other. If our ways of being fall prey to the violence of how we are forced to survive (ways of living), then we reproduce settler violence in a kind of hierarchy of belonging that is determined at its core by the settlers. At the same time, while memory holds space for those of us not able to be on the land, it cannot only remain in a contained and distant past. That is, while settler violence and modernity have caused a rupture between our ways of being and our ways of living, remembering—removed from the politics of recognition—can become the vehicle toward healing that rupture.

In Palestine, the reality of dispossession, displacement, and denial of access to land has forced a violent break not only with our collective relation with the past but also with the imaginative and real ways we can continue to be in relation to the land and each other in the present. Coulthard argues that the Marxist concept of mode of production "can be said to encompass two interrelated social processes: the resources, technologies, and labor that a people deploy to produce what they need to materially sustain themselves over time, and the forms of thought, behavior, and social relationships that both condition and are themselves conditioned by these productive forces." As such, a mode of production can equate to a mode of living and can be the basis of Indigenous sovereignty as a methodological approach that is informed by relations to the land that produces a politics rather than a politics that demarcates land. Within the Palestinian context this is an imaginative leap that combines various relationalities *to* the land through various temporalities *with* the land. Coulthard goes on to argue that "this broad understanding of mode of production as a mode of life accurately reflects what constituted 'culture' in the sense that the Dene deployed the term, and which our claims for cultural recognition sought to secure through the negotiation

of a land claim."[14] In the liberal frameworks of a settler state like Canada, negotiation of land claims are part and parcel of the politics of recognition and
the subsequent identity politics it often employs. In a less liberal framework,
like that of the Zionist settler state that continues to deny Palestinian presence in the past and continues the violent work of destroying Palestinian existence in the present, identitarian essentialism might seem like a radical
political and cultural position for Palestinians. If we can prove what a Palestinian mode of life once was, we then, at least, exist in the settlers' historical
register. What once was—when removed from the land and continually denied access to the land—is all we are left with, a past mode of life without a
present or future mode of living. In a similar register, reducing cultural politics to one of identity also plays into settler colonial power. *Grounded*, in this
sense, is a concept that holds potential possibilities outside identity politics
while we negotiate our set of realities. For all of those denied access to Palestine, there are many other Palestinians who face down the daily violence of
the military within all of the settler-designated geographies of occupied Palestine. *Grounded* is a different daily reality in each of our many geographies,
albeit with shared histories.

As the Israeli military continues its pursuit of an ongoing Nakba in a dra-
conian litany of violence, we have many battle fronts. Through a collective
navigation of all of our realities we can work to bring ways of being and ways
of living together, not as one static notion of Palestinian as an identity (in the
past or the present) but as a cornucopia of our experiences over time and
space. Rather than fall prey to a kind of identity politics that has, over time,
worked to destroy both our ways of being and our ways of living, being
grounded can offer a way for us to nurture a generative conversation among
ourselves. In this sense, Indigenous methodologies present a possibility to
turn us away from navigating settlers, their logics, and their frameworks, and
toward a way to respect ongoing survival in all the ways of being and living
that we embody.

While being careful not to collapse historical specificities in the pursuit of
an Indigenous comparative approach, exploring "grounded normativity" for
methodological cues nevertheless offers guidance. Leanne Betasamosake
Simpson argues that the practices that are held by this notion of "grounded
normativity" are centered on understanding Indigenous knowledge systems,
"the systems of ethics that are continuously generated by a relationship with
a particular place, with land, through the Indigenous processes and knowledges that make up Indigenous life."[15] Simpson goes on to describe grounded
normativity as "flight paths or fugitive escapes from the violences of settler

colonialism." In her book *Dancing on Our Turtle's Back*, Simpson employs a similar methodological approach as she uses Nishnaabeg storytelling as a means to foster modes of resistance through Indigenous resurgence.[16] Here is where storytelling is a means of grounding. Coulthard's conceptualization of ongoing dispossession for Indigenous peoples includes a forced imposition of political authority and jurisdiction of the settler state that governs relationships with Indigenous place and land. Grounded normativity, for Simpson, re-centers people and the land through storytelling, both as an ongoing past in the ongoing present, as well as being a means to resist through Indigenous resurgence in forging a future relationality to the land.[17] It is, therefore, in the Palestinian context a conceptualization of ongoing relationships with the land and, at its intellectual, cultural, and political core, can be about people's connections to and with the land over time and as a means of returning to the land. Grounding as a way of bringing together modes of being and modes of living is an opportunity to think anew about belonging.

Aware that the politics of recognition within the settler state is a form of identity politics, Coulthard's and Simpson's conceptualizations offer us a means by which to explore ways of being and ways of living that are cognizant of the obstacles presented by statist translations of peoplehood. Both Coulthard and Simpson are clearly thinking about Indigenous nationalism and peoplehood outside the nation-state. Building on the work of Gerald Alfred Taiaiake of the Mohawk Kanien'keha-ka people and George Manual of the Shuswap, among others, nationalism in this iteration is about peoplehood, and people are about a relationship with place and with each other, and distinctly not about liberal formations of colonial modernity and statehood.[18] Can engaging with peoplehood as a practice be a means toward thinking about Palestinian nationalism outside the nation-state as it is for Taiaiake in the context of the fourth world? If peoplehood and people are separated from the identity formational structures of nation-state modernity, it can be understood that this is a process of return and can affect how we read the Palestinian political past in the present while also looking toward the future. Palestinian nationalism—outside the confines of the modern nation-state and its reductive formulation of identity politics—can become a part of the process of healing the ruptures between ways of being and ways of living. That is, reducing peoplehood to a "national identity" prevents us from exploring how we were, are, and will be in an ongoing relationship with place and with each other.

Yet this is not an easy ask, and in Palestine this requires some imaginative intervention.[19] Igniting the imagination is not new to us, as it is a core feature in Arab and Palestinian literature and can potentially be a core feature in how we navigate Indigeneity in Palestine.[20] But even in the imaginative leaps we cannot lose a sense of peoplehood as practice and as belonging. Nor can we ignore the longer history of Palestinian nationalism and the political desires for a nation-state. Acknowledging this past to unpack it can enable us to understand that Palestine does not belong to us—however much frameworks of settler modernity have triggered this political response—as we work to understand that we belong to Palestine.

What Kind of Mapmaking?

Mapping Jerusalem as the heart of the so-called Holy Land has become a landscape of Oriental imaginations and military incursions. Such maps are the commodities produced by power, a way of marking the land to control it. They seek to define relations of power with place, regulating the people on/ of the land as an afterthought. As a result, cartography has a layered legacy in Palestine. Power, not people, can be read through its maps. Benedict Anderson explains that this colonial legacy of maps is connected to conquest and domination and that "maps and census shaped the grammar of colonial state power."[21] Controlling space through mapping and controlling populations through counting were and remain intrinsically connected. Edward Said asserts that, at the precipice of colonial power, we find the representations of maps as colonialism's imagined geographies: "It is Europe that articulates the Orient."[22] European imagination created the science of Orientalism, which has had long-lasting effects throughout the geographies that European colonialism invaded.[23] Long before Zionist settler colonialism's invasion of the land of Palestine, the rich and long history of the Ottoman past in the region witnessed several kinds of interests in maps. Yet, according to Salim Tamari, only with the drive toward European-styled modernity in the nineteenth century did maps take on the functional value for commercial and military purposes.[24]

Travel maps and ethnographic cartography existed, of course, long before the Ottoman Empire's Tanzimat era of bureaucratic changes toward constructing a modern state. This important reform movement in Ottoman history needs to be read in the longer historical narrative of the Ottoman past and not only or just in relation to European states. Nevertheless, the attempts by the Ottoman rulers in the mid-nineteenth century at adopting European style nation-state governance changed the value of maps for the empire.[25] In all of these iterations, Palestine was always—though sometimes marked distinctly—part of the larger geography of the region. The changes within Ottoman cartography were also coupled with a continuation of the crusader legacy of mapping for the desire of conquest in and of their version of the Holy Land.[26] In the subsequent settler colonial context of Zionist attempts at conquest in the twentieth century, controlling how the land is represented—and, quite literally, "marked and named"—has been a foundational tool in the arsenal of settler erasure in Palestine.[27]

In terms of both the colonial history of maps and settler colonial urgency in elimination, place and peoplehood have been targeted for over a century in Palestine. To overcome the imposed power of European modernity, it is key to understand the multifaceted legacy of this power in Palestine and on its people. The historical maps of the region are an archive of the contemporary legacy of Orientalism and the violence of settler invasion. The military legacy of mapmaking is part and parcel of the settler colonial logics of "discovery and conquest."[28] Given this history, the conventional duty of these maps is to measure space with the goal of controlling it, whereby distances become a metric of exclusion and power. Rather than adhere to the idea of mapping as a means to control the land, I propose the concept of emotional maps, which can work to generate proximity to the land and chart out layers of lived stories that nurture the act and idea of sharing the past to survive the present and thus imagine futures on that land.

While not ignorant of the power of European intellectual, military, and economic hegemony, the methodology proposed in this book asks a simple question: Is there a way to absorb a critical understanding of this power but not center it? While chapters 1 and 2 of this book openly struggle with the legacy of colonial and capital modernity, chapter 3 begins to chart possibilities beyond the power of imperialism—that is, I continue to ask if there is another way, of *living through* while *thinking beyond*. While these questions are bigger than me, to ask them, to walk with them, to sit with them and then to move through them, I turn to ʿArifa. Even as we journey toward and with ʿArifa, I hesitate to use the term *discovery*. I am searching for her, and perhaps I even find her, but this is distinctly not a journey of discovery. Though Palestine was not subject to the same kind of discovery doctrine that other sites of settler colonial invasion were, it has been subject to colonial and then settler colonial exceptionalism, of which the ethos of settler discovery is embedded as Zionists claim a return to a biblical homeland. In the context of Hawaii, David A. Chang asks, "What if we were to understand indigenous people as active agents of global exploration, rather than passive objects of that exploration?" Relying on the work of Kanaka Maoli historian Noenoe K. Silva,[29]

Chang is prompted to read exploration and cartography beyond colonial invasion as he works through this question. Borrowing a similar ethos, I try to hear and track those who came before me to chart a path through what is now inescapable settler colonial violence. In Palestine, then, Chang's question can, perhaps, be amended: What if we were to think about Palestinians without having to prove that Palestinians have a right to be connected to the ground in Palestine? What if we understood, in Amahl Bishara's words, that "popular sovereignty," freed from the Eurocentric notions of Sovereignty, can become about peoplehood in relation to ourselves and our futures?[30] What happens to how we think about Palestinian history without the albatross of proving that Palestinians belong in Palestine or—even more existentially dangerous— without working to prove within the framework of settler capitalism that Palestine belongs to us?

Walking with Stories and Return

Harat al-Maghariba is one location in my cartography of Jerusalem. It is where walking with my mother unintentionally began, and it seems to always now quite intentionally initiate a story: the ongoing thread. Walking with her was a way for to me to learn how to walk within layers of memories—hers, my own, and, in time, others who came before us. We were not marking territory like conquerors—far from it. We were walking through memories, creating memories through walking in the hope that moving through time—past and present—could guide us beyond settler temporalities and into imagining futures. In time and through walking with stories, I understand that we were (and are) nourishing return. Our walking through time is a kind of return.

When I first lived in Palestine, I would often get lost in the Old City of Jerusalem, and I would call my mother on the phone (an eight-hour difference in time from Chicago, where she lived) to get directions. After I would give her a brief description of where I was, to spark her own emotional map, my mother would more often than not say to me, "Just keep making a right turn; you will eventually find yourself in a familiar place." In time, my sense of the familiar grew and expanded, and my mother's "eventually" retracted. Emotional maps expand through a growing sense of the familiar.

I learned that a series of right turns in the Old City would eventually lead me to Harat al-Maghariba. Through time and shared stories over several geographies, my mother and I grew accustomed to start mapping my steps in what *once was*. But, with walking through these stories, speaking through *was* strangely connected with *is* and slowly transformed into an implicit *shall be*. Through her words and my steps, we walked through and into another register of time and the past tense blended into the present. Harat al-Maghariba was a neighborhood that once stood near the Old City walls. If you read about this *hara* (neighborhood), you will learn that it was an endowment from the son of Salah al-Din al-Ayyubi in the late twelfth century, founded to house Moroccan pilgrims after the time of the last crusaders (or, at least, those who came before the current ones).[31] In the *hara*, or where it once stood, the Buraq Wall is a border, and the gate next to it opens into the large expanse of the Haram al-Sharif, where al-Aqsa Mosque stands. Moving through this *haram* (sanctuary) and to its far side you face Bab al-Qatanin, which takes you to the *souq* (market) and through to al-Wad. At the edge of the path where the merchant storefronts punctuate the covered streets of the Old City, if you walk up the stairs to al-Hara al-S'adiya, and stay to the right, there you will find another set of descending stairs that take you into the space of Bab al-Zahra, which is named after another gate of the Old City. This *hara* is partially open, and the light of the sky leads your path.

These particular details were charted out in the calm suburbs of Chicago, back in my parents' home, far removed from the streets of Jerusalem at another moment when Palestine seemed an impossibility for me after another failed attempt to cross the colonial border—quite literally mapped on paper, through words, to arrive at stories. "Another," in this context, for denial of access to the land of Palestine had precedent for me since 2010 and has a historical legacy for Palestinians since 1948. After a semester as a visiting professor in New York, in the summer of 2019, I was once again denied access to Palestine, and could not physically return to my life and work—subjected, once again (and like so many other Palestinians) to waiting. I lingered in detail, memory, and temporary exile. Because of this, my emotional map relied on remembering and imagination as I walked through my own memories and was guided by my mother's. Though my own arrival to the bittersweet realization that emotional maps are made of layers of experiences and through the hope of return, my mother and I transformed longing into an opportunity to return to belonging. More specifically, I urged her to help me chart out my own plan for return.

Like many other parts of this book, I am grateful to my mother for her stories, which are always slow in the telling. In retrospect, I can chart out my personal need for emotional maps. The real explorations of these stories began implicitly when I was first denied entry into Palestine after a simple trip in the middle of a semester to participate in a conference in Spain, held at the airport, and then deported from our homeland in 2010. With time and serious effort, I found my way back, a return, and with this return came a newfound need for stories that flourished over the subsequent decade. This was when I actively began to seek out 'Arifa through conversations with her generation from Lifta. Over the next decade, return remained a challenge and the mere thought of travel came with a litany of questions, endless preparation, anticipatory strategy, and many cancellations, for crossing settler borders is another layer of settler violence, where boundaries and the settlers who control them serve as the militarized prison guards. Staying and return are connected like the ground is to the sky. We live with a mix of perilousness in staying and determination in returning. I realized how the action of walking generated stories that allowed for the fluidity of experience in time and space. Sharing stories tended to my own wounds as I came to understand how generations endured their own experiences. These wounds—like return—are ongoing.

I have only seen Harat al-Maghariba in photos; the Israeli state destroyed it immediately after the June War in 1967. The neighborhood safeguarded memories the settler state could not tolerate, as it was where many refugee families from villages nearby, including Lifta, made a temporary home after being violently removed by Zionist forces from their homeland in the Nakba War between 1947 and 1949.[32] Destruction of this sort is an old tool that Zionists continue to employ in the present. Not a day goes by without news of destruction in Palestine. In 2023 and 2024 the capacity for destruction and settler need of endless violence reached mind-breaking levels in Gaza. While this book was imagined and largely written before the most recent iteration of genocidal violence against Palestinians, the mere offer of ongoing return embedded in its pages seems as unrealistic as it is necessary. Even in a genocide, especially through this horror, we can center our return.

I did not live the Nakba or June War, but we live the ongoing Nakba. I walk through it—through the words of those who came before me and through the steps they have given me. We walk into, see, and hear Harat al-Maghariba. Walking through time is also walking in space; the stories have gifted a landscape that is layered through generations of experiences. The emotional maps generated through all kinds of walking are also what we hold on to when our feet cannot reach the soil of Jerusalem or Palestine. This is not a replacement for return, but rather the practice of our ongoing return.

For me, life with Palestine has been about generating emotional maps and holding on to them, because my own life in Palestine is as much about denial of place as it is about imagining space. Forced breaks with our relations to land is the long story of Zionist settler colonial violence in Palestine: The actual origin story of the settler state is a war that killed, destroyed, and forcibly removed more than three-quarters of a million Palestinians from their homeland. All of our stories are a shared narrative of an entire people born into a legacy as refugees. My story is of being constantly faced with my own personal potential rupture after rupture, and our collective story is about all the kinds of connections we have through all of kinds of ruptures.[33] Denial, constriction, and immobility have made my own feet touching the ground of Jerusalem an exercise in the "illegal," in the settler rule book of access (or lack thereof). Settlers work to make my—and others'—ability to touch the ground an impossible feat. This existential kind of violence and our need for emotional maps is but one part of our journeys. The possibilities of merging the personal with the collective is part of the journey of this book. What is imagined in the emotional map is a useful tool in a world dominated by settler disruption, but it was not born of it nor is it made of "settler time." Learning how to listen to the stories my mother tells while we walk opened up the world to the possibilities of also walking with her mother, ʿArifa. This book is the product of these ongoing journeys.

From the space of the *hara* out through Bab al-Zahra, you cross the street into what was once called Jerusalem's New City; to your right you see the post office, embedded within a police station. The post office was opened in the early 1960s as a rare investment of the state of Jordan, whose negligence of Jerusalem was an intentional political program between 1948 and 1967.[34] The settler police station is a newer addition.[35] The police state, as one apparatus of settler state surveillance, monitors you everywhere. On this corner, you can overturn the state's gaze by seeing beyond it and listening to the stories that fill this street corner that leads into the main street of Salah al-Din. Walk on the pavement of the street a bit farther away from the Old City walls and the smell of fresh roasted coffee overtakes you. If you follow the scent, you will arrive at the Sandouka Coffee Shop, a family business for generations. In the early 1960s the brothers opened a new shop on this thoroughfare as an addition to the older shop in the Old City, which they opened in 1943.

Coffee shops are one of many ways to measure time in Palestine. In my emotional map, the scent of Sandouka coffee is a regular comfort in the face of the settler police station. The lingering scent holds the emotional maps in between and over time, until we can get back to it and the streets of Jerusalem that it defines. I walk this street and hear its sounds and smell its flavors throughout this book. Three generations of the Sandouka family nurture our ongoing return in their unique art of roasting coffee beans. Walking here is both real and necessarily a part of our imaginations. Even when we cannot reach the ground, we can walk with the smell of Sandouka coffee, toward it, always charting a path of ongoing return. We can walk through the past, into the present, as we walk toward the future. Collapsing those boundaries and reconceptualizing time through space entails walking with and through history, as opposed to only looking back on it.

A few more steps and on your left are metal gates. Last I saw them, they were green, but sometime over the course of 2022, the gates were replaced and now the entrance to the cemetery is clearly marked with a large black gate with a prominent sign that reads Maqbarat al-Mujahedin. My emotional map has the green gates somewhat hidden behind the storefronts, but change is constant, so once again the past bends into the present. As when my mother shares the geography of her Jerusalem, I have to come to realize that my own geography combines her memories, my own, and those of others who share new stories that blend all of our particular details. When you arrive at the gates, you have arrived at the entrance to what is colloquially known as Bab al-Zahira Cemetery.[36] This is where many refugees from Lifta, including my own family, are buried.[37] Enter the gates—if you find them open, which is not often the case unless it is a holiday, a funeral is happening, or it is a Thursday, the regular day the gates remain open until the evening prayers. Or, could it be that, with the new entrance, the gates are open more often? Emotional maps leave space for this ongoing change. Beyond the gates, you climb the stairs to the top of the hill. You reach an edge. It feels like a cliff, overlooking a postcard landscape of Jerusalem.[38] This is the location of my grandmother's grave. And herein lies the mark of instruction and direction for this book: Every chapter is a return to ʿArifa. Her grave is neither a beginning nor and end, but an opening in space and time.

ʿArifa is part of my emotional map of Jerusalem. Perhaps she has come to define it. Where she lived, where she fled, and where she lies buried are all within sight of her home in Lifta, just northwest of her final resting place. She is buried higher up than her husband, my grandfather, ʿAta, another refugee from Lifta who passed away in 1967, nearly immediately after the June War, when the Israeli military expanded their occupation of Jerusalem that had begun in 1948. His heart, like those of many from his generation, could not hold the prospect of further dispossession. The cemetery is full of refugees from Lifta and their stories;[39] some people call it Lifta's cemetery. This map that led us here is born of imagination, experience, and layers of memories and the stories that hold them.

In the early 1960s, around the time the Sandouka brothers opened their second coffee shop, ʿArifa and her husband and children lived in a house they helped build behind Salah al-Din Street. On the walk down that street, look up and see where, in the early 1960s, my mother would sit for hours waiting to hear the flow of water. She would sit on the roof of this small building behind the street with the *lux* (flashlight) her father gave her to wait for the water. Jerusalem of the early 1960s is full of stories of waiting. Under Jordanian rule (1948–67), this part of Jerusalem was a city of people left to fend for themselves, they had a remarkable ability to do so. These stories are an untapped treasure of Palestine. When the water flow began, it would make a sound; my mother would check the flow with the flashlight and climb down from the roof to inform her mother, ʿArifa, who would jump into action with all the bottles, buckets, and pots she prepared. ʿArifa would scream at my mother to help with the buckets. Mom, who handed over the *lux* to her older sister and proclaimed her duties over, found solace in her father, who would congratulate her on a job well done. ʿArifa, giving up on my mother, summoned her two eldest daughters, those older than my mother, and they would fill everything they could with water for the days to come. In this weekly operation, ʿArifa called on the skills she acquired transporting water from the ʿayn (natural spring) in Lifta. From Lifta to Salah al-Din, water continued to connect life stories through space and time. In Ramallah al-tahta, where I now live, I follow the sound of the water flowing, waiting between Thursday night and Friday morning, listening to the building across from my *barenda* (balcony), where the owners set up a tap that goes into action once the water begins to flow. Seeking the flow of water is one of the ways we learn how to walk through and with time. When we tune into the sounds, we discover that we were made for this—generations listening for sounds, a listening that creates its own temporality. Our stories are specific and our own, but also, strangely, not only ours.

Under settler colonial capitalism and its boundaries, access to water in Palestine has been a constant struggle. Water, like land, is another target of the settler violence.[40] In the summers in Ramallah, we have water shortages directly produced and orchestrated by settler violence. Ramallah fares far better than other parts of occupied Palestine in the West Bank, but even in Ramallah, we have to be constantly aware of "the water situation." Availability of water, and severe lack thereof, demands that our lives have to be planned around how we can access it. Water is life, and preventing its flow is the work of the settlers in Palestine; it has become a commodity that can be stolen and subsequently used as a weapon to yield against the Native people. Stealing water is not new.[41] Stealing life is also not new.[42] But water is also what connects us, from the times at the ʿayn in Lifta to the times on the roofs of Jerusalem to the times of the balconies in Ramallah—a conceptualization of

continuity caused by settler violence but harvested through Palestinian survival. Ongoing return not only remembers the ʿayn in Lifta but makes plans
for a return to it.

From Documentation and Testimony to Stories

Modern Palestinian history has, in many ways, come to be defined by one
word: *Nakba*. Nakba is the "catastrophe" of Zionist settler colonialism and
the violence involved on the body and place of Palestine to create and maintain the settler state of Israel. Akin to the language of many other Indigenous
geographies and peoples, Nakba is the language of Palestinians to describe
the apocalyptic violence of settlers intent on eliminating our presence on the
land. It is Palestine's ultimate and ongoing colonial tragedy, and historians
have faced the paradox of working to remember the event that in both individual and collective terms was meant to politically and socially erase Palestine. But it was not an event that ended, or even a war that ceased. Historians
have, nevertheless, produced a great deal of literature on the Nakba as a catastrophe since the Nakba War began in late 1947. As early as August 1948, in the
midst of the brutal war that drove out three-quarters of the Palestinian people
from their homeland, Constantin Zureiq published *Mʾana al Nakba* (The
meaning of disaster), in which he gave the name to what was happening in
Palestine.[43] Since then the word has been a political cry for Palestinians as
history—like the land—has been taken over by settler colonial structures and
frameworks. In the spirit of Zureiq, a public intellectual who addressed Arabs
in a call for action, this journey with ʿArifa aspires to reframe the past and
present of the ongoing Nakba in the formation of a collective view of ongoing
return to and with Palestine.

The field of Palestinian history is certainly not monolithic, nor is it only
about the Nakba War, however apocalyptic that moment is presented in our
fields of knowledge and experience. It is important to note that this book is
not an attempt to reinvent historical writing on Palestine nor to sidestep the
rich legacy of Palestinian studies. Rather, it is series of questions accompanied by the fruit of the labor of asking, walking, listening, and sharing. In
particular, it is about how the past lives within the present as a generative
guide toward the future, and asks how other Indigenous peoples have asked
similar questions. Part of this inquiry shall necessarily rely on a critical reading of the fields of history in and about Palestine and Palestinians. As a story,
the Nakba is the interrogation of one people's destruction and the foundation of settler colonial power over the land of Palestine as manifested in the

creation of the state of Israel. It is also, in the settler colonial condition imposed on Palestine, an ongoing process, for when we use the word *Nakba* in the Palestinian context it is an event that is still happening: ongoing Nakba.[44] It is a violence that is ongoing, and survival is not a *post-* consideration to employ in retrospect because the violence is omnipresent and seemingly never ending. Part of this process invites us to understand that the historiography of Palestine as the history of Israel *and* Palestine has long imposed major obstacles preventing our imaginative power. Our ongoing stories of Palestine are, in part, the history of settler colonial violence and a settler state that works to erase us. But folding all of our stories only into a framework of settler power and presence reinforces settler erasure. This book aims to move outside dominant frameworks of settler colonialism, erasure, and loss and to focus on stories—embodied stories and grounded stories, born of storytelling as a mode of being in, with, and on the land in ongoing return.

Herein lies the historian's dilemma: Hegemonic Zionist mythology has been incorporated into the structure of settler colonial power and the brutality of the unyielding and relentless violence that is the material reality of our daily lives.[45] This violence invades our collective Palestinian memory because it is the field we must navigate in our everyday present realities. As such, settler structural violence in the past and the ongoing present creates a resonance that continues to plague our collective Palestinian national memory, as well as how people write the history of the Nakba. Given the layers of power imposed on memory and remembering, this leads to the question of how we can use the tools, politics, and analytics of Indigeneity to approach the story of destruction and dispossession outside the frameworks of the settlers' power. Linda Tuhiwai Smith, of the Ngāti Awa and Ngāti Porou, Māori peoples, shows in her work how, for the colonized, research and scholarship have been embedded in and shaped by European colonialism as an epistemic, as well as material, violence.[46] Likewise, Zionism and Zionist renditions of history have worked to invade, shape, and form Palestinian history. To reclaim control over Palestinian ways of knowing, key to this exploration is the need to understand the place of the Nakba as an event and the ongoing Nakba as the lived reality and conceptual basis for being in and of Palestine. Again, it is important to understand the local context of Palestine within this turn away from settler knowledge into a discussion of Indigeneity as a methodological approach. Walking, listening, and sharing stories is meant as a means of loosening the tight grip that the frame of narrative/counternarrative has long held on the history of Palestine.

Since any discussion about the Nakba is about history, moral culpability, and ethical accountability, how we tell this narrative is fundamental. It might, however, be useful to preface the historiographical discussion about how we have told the narrative with a quick look at the institutional history that offers us a glimpse into how this narrative was first generated and how it evolved over time. This institutional history is, in large part, held together under the implicit and explicit umbrella of the Palestine Liberation Organization (PLO). I begin this book with a long narrative of the PLO because, while there is much critique in the decision-making of the politics of the PLO that led to the disaster of negotiations with settlers, understanding Palestinian cultural and political history outside of the institutional influence of the PLO is another kind of erasure. That is, while we work to understand Palestine through an engagement with Indigenous methodologies, the local context must be taken into account; any reading of Palestine without an understanding of local institutions will result in a reading of our past and present that is removed from our people's experiences in both.

In terms of historical recording and documentation, a short look into three major Palestinian institutions— Birzeit University, the Institute for Palestine Studies, and the Palestine Research Center—reveals just how connected political engagement has been with cultural and intellectual production in the Palestinian historical context as represented by the PLO. While each is a distinct entity, these three institutions overlap and interconnect both in terms of people and knowledge production. Established as a local school in the village of Birzeit, north of Ramallah, Birzeit University is the oldest of these institutions, though its emergence as a university in 1972 actually occurred after the establishment of the Institute for Palestine Studies and the Palestine Research Center, both established in exile in Beirut in 1963 and 1965, respectively. These institutions' emergence connects directly with the political emergence of the PLO in the mid-1960s. Prior to this particular institutional political mobility, however, intellectual engagement and production paved the way forward—that is, the work of 'Arif al-'Arif and Walid Khalidi, to name two prominent figures, who, along with Constantin Zureiq, formed the legacy of Palestinian historiography of the Nakba. Though they were not the only people writing and thinking about the Nakba, these men nevertheless did in many ways form the framework for historians to follow.

Al-'Arif documented the losses of the war with the focal point of Jerusalem and within the framework of a "paradise lost."[47] Documenting the loss was and remains an intention to counter the erasure of settler colonial violence. Likewise, Khalidi followed in this frame through another documentation of destruction under the auspices of preserving the memory of what once was and is now "destroyed."[48] The intention of the work of these men, along with many others, had in part to do with recording the event of the Nakba War and its disastrous aftermath of loss and destruction. In a moment of blatant and unrelenting attempts at complete erasure by Zionist armies, this kind of documentary historiography served a fundamentally important purpose for its own time—in the words of Khalidi, "so as to not forget." Khalidi and al-'Arif worked to document destruction and lamented the vanishing history of life in Palestine before 1948 and framed the earliest iterations of Nakba history; it has since become a hegemonic frame for Palestinian history (and the history of Palestine). To be clear, without these efforts, we would have far less to work from over the succeeding generations, so the historians and the institutions that held, supported, and distributed their work serve a fundamentally important role in thinking about the past but have also come to define the confines of how generations look back. With the existential crisis and trauma of war and mass dispossession as the backdrop, documentation of this kind seems not only logical but necessary. Nevertheless, this mode of historical inquiry has had an ever-lasting effect and has become a monolithic way of thinking about the past. That is, remembering under the constant and existential threat of forgetting prevents us from imagining return as a vibrant methodology that forges space for imagination and transformation.

After these initial iterations, the Nakba as a historical "event" has been treated to two main and distinct methodological trends: archival history and oral history. While it is not the primary concern of this book, the discussion of archives in the Palestinian context is both rich and highly contested.[49] Whether in search of alternative archives or well embedded in colonial and/ or settler archives, another generation of historians has continued in the tradition of documenting the Nakba. Of note is the work of Nur Masalha, who offers a deep archival-based analysis on the war and settler intentions and implementations of Palestinian erasure in his formidable book *The Expulsion of Palestinians*.[50] Masalha studied a great number of archives in the Israeli state and was actually among the first to do so. His work preceded and exceeded the self-described "revisionist" work of Israeli historians, though he is often read in complement to their work. Masalha's thesis was a groundbreaking book that destroyed the cacophony of Zionist mythology about the Nakba War: its motivations, consequences, and aftermath. Rather than reading Masalha as a rupture (or, in some instances in complement) to Zionist literature, it is perhaps more useful to read him as an enduring part of the Palestinian historiography that worked to document the Nakba. As is the case with

Masalha's book, which was published by the Institute for Palestine Studies, the growth of Palestine and Palestinian studies in this next generation is deeply connected to the work of Palestinian institutions. Both in terms of research and publications, these institutions collectively held the ground on which Nakba studies, in particular, and Palestine studies, in general, could grow.[51] That is, they served an important role in generating and supporting the historiography from which we can now draw, and it remains an open question as to how they can serve in the future, if they can at all. My point is that, while the initial and subsequent work of intellectuals supported by these institutions is a foundational part of historical writing about Palestine, the danger remains that the frameworks and the methodologies employed by earlier historians become the only frameworks and accepted methodologies.

In addition to the ongoing concerns for archival evidence and documentation, the historiography of the Nakba also took a sharp methodological turn in the second generation of historians toward a reliance on oral history. Of note in this turn is the Destroyed Villages Series produced by the Birzeit University Research Center. It was first framed as classic anthropological inquiry by Sharif Kanana and later through a historical lens led by Salah Abdul-Jawad, among others. The series relies on oral evidence in, at first, the reconstruction of village life before the villages' destruction in the Nakba War; later, moving from traditional ethnography to traditional history, the series focused more on the actual Nakba War as an inquiry into the war's military destruction. The series, while not the only project in its contemporary era, has become a classic means by which to read the historiographical turn toward people's testimonies in Palestinian studies. The erasure of Palestinian voices in the Zionist archives and subsequent historiography of the war turned inward toward a recovery project. While formed through fieldwork that was meant to record a history that would challenge settler archives, the Birzeit University Destroyed Villages Series continued with the frames first presented through the lost paradise paradigm and later through the countering methodology modality to fill voids left by settler archives and their inherent erasure of Palestine and Palestinians.

Working to explain the history of the Palestinian Nakba, scholars turned to oral testimony, oral history, and ethnography to counter the violence of erasure, from the archive to the land. In her groundbreaking work with Palestinian refugees, Rosemary Sayigh stands as a pillar in the intersection between anthropology and oral history in Palestine studies. In her book *The Palestinians*, Sayigh's framing of oral history among refugees in Lebanon as revolutionaries signaled a change (in terms of methodology) and a continuum (in terms of political and cultural intersections).[52] Sayigh has been writing and researching for nearly five decades and has produced a wealth of literature not only on refugees but on the history and historiography of the Nakba, as well as interrogations of how researchers perform in terms of intellectual and political production.[53] Her career has also spanned fundamental changes in the political context from what can perhaps best be described as the long odyssey of the PLO, its ultimate shame in 1982's retreat from Lebanon and its eventual transformation (and death) in the form of the Palestinian Authority in the time since the Oslo Accords. Sayigh's delineation of the generations of Palestinian refugees remains a steadfast foundation for conducting interviews and reflects work done with the post-1948 generations. Specifically, she describes the first three generations that experienced the Nakba: the first, the "generation of Palestine," who were born and married in Palestine; the second, the "generation of disaster," who were born in Palestine and grew up in exile; and the third, the "generation of revolution," who were born in Lebanon (primarily) and grew up after the liberation of Palestinian refugee camps in 1969.[54] While Sayigh's generational analysis grew out of her research among Palestinian refugees in camps in Lebanon, it has had traction for researchers of Palestinian refugees elsewhere. Her profound work forges an exploration of not only what it meant to be a refugee but also how the Nakba went well beyond the generation that directly experienced the violence of forced expulsion from a homeland. That generation carried lived memories that they have managed to maintain, cherish, and impart to subsequent generations.

To counter the tendency to individualize memory, Sayigh's work among refugees in the camps offers an alternative in her claim that "camps are communities of memory." In response to an academic trend that treats refugees as victims of trauma, she argues that, rather than focus on transgenerational trauma as a pathologized disease, "I propose that recording Palestinian historians can be a tool to establish claims to 'peoplehood' and 'cultural property' as well as to involve young camp intellectuals, and to mobilize cultural resources to resist the forces of fragmentation and demoralization that are particularly strong in a period of national leadership cooptation." As such, Sayigh is directly intervening in the history of the Nakba or, more specifically, historical research methodologies on the historical event. Critical of how it has been written about and researched, she argues that, "in conceptualizing the Nakba, I extend its temporality from the expulsions of 1948–49 up to the present day." Here we see Sayigh amending historical writing to include fieldwork among multiple generations into a more holistic inquiry of the ongoing

Nakba. This work toward a reconceptualization of the Nakba, in addition to challenging a certain kind of politics about refugee research, is also a direct call for what history can be: "History work should not only be about the past . . . oral history is adapted to registering stories told by camp Palestinians as well as what they want from history." In other words, Sayigh asserts that history is a political project and, specifically, the stories that she refers to about the Nakba are "an element of 'peoplehood' and a kind of 'cultural property' that needs to be recorded."[55] Fieldwork, here, is not only about recording or collecting people's experiences but also about understanding why these kind of collections matter politically—and to whom. This approach to oral history expands research about the Nakba conceptually beyond the confines of the historical events of the expulsions into a collection of testimonies about all that happened in the expulsions and since, as displacement was a state of being that followed through the generations of refugees.

Contending with violence and trauma, approaching people and their oral testimony can be wrought historiographically. While there is a difference in disciplinary approaches between social history and cultural anthropology, people's oral stories—and, specifically, the stories of Lifta between December 1947 and April 1948 (the time of settler expulsion)—might present a particular opportunity to change our approach to Palestinian history. As the violence of settler colonialism in the form of the ongoing Nakba has in many ways structured a historic timeline, the year 1948 is the catastrophe and also a watershed moment. Before and since, always defined by the moments of expulsion that were the foundation for the settler nation-state, ours is a timeline of loss and history of ongoing devastation. As Ahmad Sa'di and Lila Abu-Lughod explain, "we believe that Palestinian memory is particularly poignant because it struggles with and against a still much contested present."[56] But the past is also contested, and I want to ask how we can engage the past differently as we charge through time—from past to present to future. That is, how is thinking about remembering (and not only memory) an ongoing tool in how we navigate out of settler formations and into an otherwise way of remembering?

Memory, or Remembering?

Given the long legacy of intellectual production described in the previous section, the work of a contemporary historian delving into the world of Nakba studies is rich, albeit complicated. It should always be acknowledged that if not for those that came before us, we would neither have the space nor the tools to approach Nakba studies with a critical eye. Moving away from the foundational methodologies and frameworks of previous generations is not an act of rejection but rather an appreciation that their legacy and words have gifted us this space to think otherwise. Likewise, understanding the work of memory in historical writing in Palestine is fraught with difficulties. In particular, we face historical timelines that are set in a strictly linear frame where the memory of the Nakba as a moment of expulsion and violent dispossession necessarily colors all that came before and after it. The people of Lifta, like the rest of Palestine, experienced a series of enormous and violent attacks at the hands of Zionist militias and the nascent state's army, so it follows that the challenge of remembering seems mediated, if not imprisoned, by and through this violence. Moreover, if the violence is interpreted within the conceptual confines of trauma, how it is documented over time is also filtered through the resonance of trauma as a category. If the violence is recorded as the remains of a vanishing (or vanished) history, then memory is nothing but a memory of loss and memory is itself entirely lost. If the violence is documented as a testimony to what once was, then memory is nothing more than a proof of former presence and understood as a mourning and lamentation of a paradise that can never be recovered. The existential trap for Palestinians, then, is choosing between a memory of loss or a loss of memory. If these methodologies and frameworks blend into our present, they also determine how we see ourselves and record not only the violence previous generations endured but also the violence we continue to endure. Shall we always be confined to a vanishing past and present? Does the necessary work of documenting settler colonial violence somehow prevent us from examining other ways to approach our history? Worse, through this method of recording testimonies, are we contributing to our own confinement to the very prison walls that trap us?

Memory studies is not new to the study of Palestine. Memory is a distinct subject of inquiry within the disciplines of history and anthropology. Particularly since the 1980s and the historiographical turn to oral history, rumination on memory has become a more common research tool and topic of inquiry.[57] Anaheed Al-Hardan's valuable work on the "right of return" movement among Palestinians in Syria shows us the complicated relationship with Nakba memory and its institutionalization among generations of Palestinians.[58] Moreover, taking the work of Rosemary Saiygh as a foundation, the Palestinian Oral History Archive at the American University of Beirut also questions the generational aspect of memory and how PLO-institutionalized memory has in some ways alienated all subsequent generations.[59] Certainly not exclusive to explorations on the Nakba, memory work on Palestine has produced literature on social, popular, or collective memory as a different way of exploring the past beyond the positivist approaches of traditional history. In her survey of memory studies in the Middle East, Sune Haugbolle considers Ted Swedenburg's *Memories of Revolt* as an early example of how memory work traveled into Palestinian studies.[60] Swedenburg's work is notable in how he did not attempt to reconstruct the story of the revolt, but instead investigated through his interviews how the past affected people's narration of the present.[61] Using both theories related to Maurice Halbwachs's approach to collective memory, as well as the work of the Popular Memory Group, Swedenburg's anthropological approach did not concern itself with the event of the revolt in history as much as how he used people's memories about it to see how they narrate their present.[62]

The present that Swedenburg worked to explore was one of the First Intifada, which began in late 1987, and its longer resonance in Palestine. Though *Memories of Revolt* cannot be considered a thesis on Palestinian resistance, Swedenburg did, nevertheless, show how the idea of the revolt lasted well beyond the generation that lived the revolt. While the use of memory and the memory of a revolt in the colonial mandate era in Palestine as a means to understand how nationalism is a consummate part of Palestinian identity was an important development, Swedenburg was certainly not the first to explore memory in Palestine. Even within the confines of "oral history" or "ethnography," this book was not a first for Palestinian studies. One can easily argue that Ghassan Kanafani's famous thesis about the Arab Revolt of 1936–39 has had far greater resonance culturally and politically.[63] Swedenburg's work is, nevertheless, part of a development that uses both the language and the frameworks offered by memory studies on Palestine, past and present. This kind of investigation of memory—well embedded in assumptions grounded in an attachment to European modernity, in particular, and the institutional thesis Halbwachs argued for within a nation-state backdrop, generally—has a specific trajectory in the scholarship of post–World War II Europe. Likewise, another major genre of memory studies also relates to remembering the trauma of the war in the European context.[64]

The Eurocentric origins of memory studies present an obstacle in terms of both literal and cultural translation. Oral history as a tool, and memory studies as a frame, have been presented by many as methodological means toward constructing a counternarrative to the hegemonic Zionist narrative. Nevertheless, the act of countering through the methodology of testimony has in many ways itself hindered the value of local stories. We are once again put into a reductive framework of proving that settler colonial violence happened rather than finding our own ways through and beyond it. Even within this overdetermined framework, we are still not believed without supporting evidence from settler sources or archives.[65] Be it archives, oral history, or memory studies, we have been burdened as Palestinians with frameworks that reproduce the material work of settler violence: erasure. Why must we remain contained to be heard? Instead, how can we draw on the rich legacies of three generations before us to remove ourselves from this epistemic and methodological confinement? Again, the question remains: While we survive the violence, how can we imagine otherwise ways of remembering? Stories and all the ways we have to tell, listen to, and share them are—outside any kind of conversation with settlers or the epistemological limitations forced on us through settler anxieties (even those mediated through implicit lamentations on modernity)— the invitation to journey as Palestinians *through* and *with* the past, present, and future. Can we not search for a methodology that finally places the burdens of settler anxieties where they belong and thus work to free ourselves from the implications of legibility and a politics of recognition?

No one confronts, toys with, or challenges countering memory like the Palestinian poet Mahmud Darwish. The quintessential Palestinian storyteller, Darwish seems to take a new position regarding the position of countering a narrative not his own by simultaneously rejecting, mocking, and embodying the act of counternarrating. Long before he worked with his version of the Homeric epic in his later career, he wrote epically about a day of his life under the Israeli military siege of Beirut in Lebanon in 1982:

> Bread sprang from the soil and water gushed from the rocks. Their rockets dug wells for us, and the language of their killing tempted us to sing, "We will not leave!" We saw our faces on foreign screens boiling with great promise and breaking through the siege with unwavering victory signs. From now on we have nothing to lose, so long as Beirut is here and we're here in Beirut as names for a different homeland, where meanings will find their words again in the midst of this sea and on the edge of this desert. For here, where we are, is the tent for wandering meanings and words gone astray and the orphaned light, scattered and banished from the center.[66]

A master of language and a chronicler of Palestinian time, Darwish confronts the affects of violence on storytelling not by turning his voice away from violence but instead in its direct line. In his poetics, he accepts the challenge of telling an Indigenous story that relates the violence but is not defined by it. In the midst of the unspeakable brutality of the Israeli invasion of 1982, one episode in a long line of ongoing invasions since 1948, Darwish ponders,

> Is history not bribable? And why, then, would many places—lakes, mountains, cities—bear the names of military leaders but that they had mouthed an impression when they first beheld them, and their words became the names still used today? "Oh, rid!" (How beautiful!) That's what a Roman general cried out when he first saw that lake in Macedonia, and his surprise became its name. Add to this the hundreds of names we use to refer to places previously singled out by some conqueror, where it has since become difficult to disentangle the identity from the defeat. Forts and citadels that are no more than attempts to protect a name that does not trust time to preserve it from oblivion. Anti-forgetfulness wars; anti-oblivion stones. No one wants to forget. More accurately, no one wants to be forgotten.[67]

Since history is written through the pen of conquest, it goes without saying that it is also written to undermine and forget the oppressed. Why, then, attempt to work within this paradigm to claim our people's unforgettableness? The settler state negates both the people and the people's belonging to their land. Darwish understands that "between these two negations this generation [born after 1948] was born defending the spirit's bodily vessel, onto which they fasten the fragrance of the country they've never known. They've read what they've read, and they've seen what they've seen, and they don't believe defeat is inevitable. So they set out on the trail of that fragrance."[68] To set out in this way, the task of the storyteller is front and center. Setting forth to create a new way of being—not based on countering violence but rather coming through it to resist it—becomes the basis of creating the language for storytelling. The struggle in the context of Palestine is thus between being negated or simply being. Abdul-Rahim Al-Shaikh, while contemplating the (mis)use of archive in telling the tales of history as a manipulation of memory, subtly invites us to consider Darwish's legacy to free ourselves from the constraints of proving death as a means to prove worth of life.[69] As Sinan Antoon succinctly notes, "It crystallizes the dynamics of death and destruction unleashed by military might and the human will to resist and to live: 'To be, or to be' as Darwish writes. This is an old plot, to be sure, but one performed with exceptional barbarism in the last few decades."[70] Memory in Palestine and for Palestinians need not be about not forgetting, nor need it be confined to narrating the past as something that has passed. Rather, memory is narrating the past for and through the present toward a future, a way of being that endures the violence, but it is, again, not willing to be defined by it.

In approaching the practice of memory, and not memory studies, in Palestine, in relation to an anticolonial praxis as well as the rich history of the poetic use of memory in Arab culture, an Indigenous understanding of storytelling is born. The result of several years of listening to shared stories and walking among all who lived and shared stories, this book walks out of the structures of historical limitations. It is not based on settler archives, nor does it rely on oral history as a science and it has little to do with memory studies as an established field of knowledge. Through walking, listening, and sharing this is, in part, a critical examination of memory under construction and the art of remembering under settler colonial conditions. This is not even an exhaustive interrogation of the politics of memory, or how history remembers, but rather how we continuously remember to survive in our ongoing return.

Ongoing Return: The Shift from Settler Colonial to Return; Stories, Not Testimony

Settler colonialism is a structure. Settler invasion is a not an event.[71] The Nakba is ongoing. These three points are a lived phenomenon in our conceptual understanding of the Nakba. It is important to understand that events do occur, these events obviously can be incorporated into various kinds of historical records, and they can thus make for a linear narrative that follows events over the epoch of invasions. That is not the point of understanding settler colonialism structurally, nor does it preclude a basic understanding of the long stories that cover decades (and, now, more than a century) of events in Palestine.

As many have argued from various geographies, an exclusive focus on settler colonialism (as an analytic, structure, and system) without engaging or even accounting for Indigenous peoples, cultures, and histories reproduces the erasure endemic in settler colonial violence. Such work is rich and has a long legacy in Native and Indigenous studies, and it resonates profoundly in Palestine. Robert Warrior of the Osage people has written extensively on the tension and potentially generative conversation between settler colonial and Native studies.[72] Warrior's conceptualization of "Indigenous intellectual sovereignty" offers Palestinians a generative means of thinking outside settler logics.[73] In addition, J. Kēhaulani Kauanui of the Kanaka Maoli people argues for the concept of "enduring indigeneity" and shows how attentiveness to Indigenous peoples is a necessary aspect in writing about settler colonialism "in terms of both cultural and political struggles, one of the tenets of any claim to indigeneity is indigenous sovereignty." Kauanui rightly states that "to exclusively focus on the settler colonial without any meaningful engagement with the indigenous . . . can (re)produce another form of 'elimination of the native.'"[74] As such, Indigenous sovereignty has become a conceptual grounding for how we think about ourselves and our ways of being—not only in reaction to settler colonialism but in a holistic sense of how we engage the past and present in our ongoing efforts to forge futures. As Joanne Barker of the Lenape people notes, critical Indigenous studies, in its multivalent iterations over geographies and peoples, shows us in part how political, cultural, and intellectual mobilizations work in a decolonial praxis: "Indigenous peoples have taken on decolonization projects that include their minds and bodies in the remembrance and reform of their relations and responsibilities to the lands and ecosystems in which they live and to the other beings to whom they are related."[75] Here we can understand that the decolonial is not an attempt to return to a precolonial past presented as a paradise lost or a world before settlers; rather, it is both a continuity and a dismantlement: It is a practice and process toward understanding the past through a praxis that both refuses to be defined by settlers and rejects their temporality. The means, methods, and peoples engaged in an ongoing practice of relationality, in this sense, is a core element in how we engage knowledge and experience as inherently related and indistinguishable from each other.

In the context of Palestine and for Palestinians, the conversation of how to avoid re-centering settlers as we employ various aspects of settler colonial analytics also has a rich legacy.[76] *Indigenous* as a category has its historical specificities in each site of settler colonial invasion, and Palestine is as fraught a terrain as any. Building on the literature offered by Indigenous and Palestinian scholars, I want to argue here that though both settler colonial studies and Indigenous studies have held a place for the Palestinian context, it is incumbent on us to foster a conversation across these fields, though not without a deep appreciation of the specificities of Palestine and our own intellectual legacies. Though they are not exceptional contexts (as Zionist mythology attempts to claim), Palestine and Palestinians do have certain specificities that might be shared across geographies but may also be particular. Through attentiveness to both the commonalities and the particularities we can potentially nurture further instructive conversations across geographies and offer a complement to the concept of *enduring Indigeneity*.

Toward this end, I am attempting here to differentiate between Indigenous as an identity or category and an Indigenous methodology as a way of knowing (i.e., modes of being and modes of living). Learning from and employing Indigenous methodologies has been a grace for my own ways of knowing as I try to connect with ʿArifa. Perhaps this can be a contribution toward sharing a different kind of approach to the stories of Palestine. That is, in Palestine, "Indigenous" as a claim of ownership or as a category of identity often elides the rich historical tapestry of the land and its people that holds far more than just the recent history of Zionist settler colonial violence.[77] Moreover, even while cognizant of the destructive and reductive power of identity politics, we cannot entirely avoid the question of who is Palestinian in the conversation about how we practice being Palestinian. Positionality combines a practice and praxis of what it means to be Palestinian and can be a methodology not only for a return to the land but a way of knowing as an ongoing return. This discussion is obviously tricky in terms of the politics of belonging because of the contestation of who is the rightful owner of the land, especially given the Orientalist legacy of biblical fantasies, and it is fraught by the constant navigation of staying.[78]

Ownership and property rights have distinct limitations in thinking about ongoing return because a return to the land that is based on property in terms of commodity and ownership, while born of a far longer colonial and capitalist legacy than Zionism, still reduces Palestinian positionality into a framework of colonial capitalism and an exclusivist politics of recognition.[79] Moreover, since the advent of Zionism as an ideology and since the first Zionist settlements in Palestine, a discussion of strict sense of property rights as ownership (while logical for a people dispossessed) has nevertheless imposed a kind of competition between Zionist settlers and Palestinians. Capital modernity has a longer history in Palestine, one that Zionism, like other forms of settler colonialism, manipulated toward its settlers' ends.[80] Within the logic of capital modernity, moreover, pontifications of "rightful ownership" connect with a core feature in Zionist mythology of a Zionist connotation of Jewishness. That is, even within the framework of rights to place based on prior occupancy, Zionists' claim of "Jewish belonging" translates into "Jewish ownership" of land based on their settler claims to Jewish identity as ownership. Succumbing to this framework, Palestinians employing Indigeneity as an identity proven through a strict capitalist sense of land as property, participate in a game of settler logics whereby we are made to work to prove our belonging through the very means that violently displaced us from the land. As a village that remains partially unoccupied by settlers (empty struc-

tures), Lifta is a test, because if we imagine return through a means of capitalist commodification, we may eventually reproduce another kind of Palestinian
displacement through contestations of belonging as property rights. Rather, I
ask, what if we no longer work to "recover" history as lamentations of a paradise lost or even property stolen but instead explore the richness of the past
of how we have, do, and will foster and nurture our ever-changing belonging?
What if we free belonging from rumination of proper ownership and think
otherwise? In this sense, Indigeneity as a process/praxis/practice (as Indigenous methodology) opens up a world of possibilities. We return to the statement that, in part, holds this book together: Palestine does not belong to us;
we belong to Palestine.

Listening to 'Arifa: Storytelling, Listening, and Sharing

In Arabic, *'itiraf* has confession and acknowledgment embedded in it. It
comes from the etymological root for all things related to knowledge and
knowing. How do I know my grandmother? My maternal grandmother,
'Arifa Abdul Rahman Siam Abutaah, is someone I never "knew." But I know
her name and endlessly seek out her stories. 'Arifa was born in Lifta, a village
that is part of Jerusalem, and through her, we all belong to Lifta. Before 1948
she married and began making a family for herself there.

'Arifa's name also shares the etymological root with the word *m'arifa*
(knowledge). In Arabic, knowledge has a guide. 'Arifa literally means "she
who is the knower." My knowledge of Lifta in my work and in my life comes
with and through 'Arifa. She is the knower and what I seek to know. Her stories frame this book and are contained throughout it. I have learned to hear
'Arifa and all the voices that lead me to her to find that my own voice is worth
listening to. In 1948, Zionist military units forced 'Arifa and the rest of the
Lifta villagers out of their homes and out of the life they had always known.
Erasure and silencing are intrinsically connected forms of violence. Walking
and listening, as I try to describe them throughout this book, are the tools of
being Palestine/Palestinian. Indigenous methodologies help us forge this
way out of settler frameworks.

This journey toward knowing is not dependent on settler colonial knowledge; it is also not a counter to it.[81] This journey of knowing is a path of return, and return is divorced from the ontological power of settlers. In the
colonial present and the violence that comes with it, this divorce is the disor-
der of decolonization that Franz Fanon described with a keen eye into what
may come of systemic resistance to colonial power.[82] Undoing the ontological

structures of settlers requires the centering of Indigenous critiques of those structures. Eve Tuck and K. Wayne Yang explain this as "unsettling" settler power. They argue that the "ethic of incommensurability" requires unsettling settler anxieties, performances of innocence, and a need for reconciliation. "Decolonization is not a metaphor," and neither is Palestine. And, therefore, Palestine is not about fitting into a settler narrative and most certainly not about rescuing a settler future.[83] In Palestine decolonization moves away from the mediation of preserving a static past within a settler present. It moves away from the settlers' needs to rescue their future. It moves instead into a different temporality, where the barrier between the past, present, and future are constantly being liberated from colonial ontologies. It moves into an ongoing process of Palestinian return that navigates and connects our ways of being and various ways of living.

Walking through history on the land, and the layers of memory it holds for the people in and on Palestine, is a kind of knowing that is inseparable from the knowers and she who seeks to know. Walking through history is about stories: seeking stories, telling stories, listening to stories, sharing stories, and liberating ourselves from settler logics to hold on to these stories.[84] The journey here is return—not only the physical return to the land (though it most certainly is that) but also the ways of being that we are and become in and through return, including our ways of knowing and how we engage knowledge of the past, present, and future toward repairing our ways of living. This is the epistemological journey toward the ontological imperative of returning to Palestine.

How do we act within this kind of knowing? As Gloria Anzaldúa warns, "We can't transcend the dangers, can't rise above them. We must go through them." She reminds us, "We are not reconciled to the oppressors who whet their howl on our grief."[85] We are, however, the constant target of settler colonial violence as our bodies in relation to our land are the constant danger from which settler futures need to be rescued. Searching for and with ʿArifa through our conceptions of time moves us away from relations with settlers into our relations with the land and each other. We cannot transcend the dangers of settlers; we endure their violence on our land and on our bodies, but the violence does not define our land nor our bodies. This effort to not be defined by settlers—their logic, their anxieties, and their violence—is a daily battle for Palestinians and is neither a clean nor always clear path. Given the utterly endless, relentless, and unyielding violence that seems to increase every day, week, month, and year over the course of the last century, generations of

Palestinians have written through the violence. This book is me writing, with all the voices that hold the words together, through the violence.

Back to Lifta

Lifta is the legacy my grandmother bequeathed me. Lifta has, over the generations, become a people's symbol of Palestine more broadly. As I try to show in this book, Lifta, as it once was, reveals the meaning of "museumification." Lifta—as it is and as we allow ourselves to imagine what it will be—is a place of possibility that reveals the hope inherent in remembering divorced from the anxieties forced on us through settler colonial violence.

This book is thus divided into two parts, moving from history into reflections with the past. In chapter 1, I argue that many historians have conceptually framed Palestine within a narrow version of a quasi-national Palestinian narrative as I focus on the men who represent it. Though its formation and boundaries lie squarely within a settler colonial framework, this political history is a necessary Arab, Palestinian, and third world context for these fourth world inquiries. I begin with the political life of Yasser Arafat and the intellectual lives of Edward Said and Mahmud Darwish to show how we cannot nor should not ignore all the legacies from which we emerge. While this history is fraught with a politics of recognition that has burdened Palestinians more than it has offered a path toward liberation, it remains important to understand the PLO in order to understand the complications of an Indigenous comparison for Palestine and Palestinians.

With this critique in mind, and with a focus on Lifta, chapter 2 then interrogates the conceptual understanding and production of "museumification." By placing Palestine within a comparative Indigenous studies framework, both in methodological and epistemological terms, I argue that the past and present in Palestine can break away from the settler colonial museum. The place of Lifta has, over time, become a focus for a settler narrative of preservation, as well as a Palestinian narrative concerning historical heritage. This symbolic resonance represents how Palestine has been treated within the politics of heritage over the course of the last century. Here Lifta represents the site of a potential settler museum of a long-lost Palestinian past that, if it can even be remembered, must be resigned to only exist in the past. Heritage preservation is a bind that can be read as a false opportunity presented by settlers that is actually nothing more than an ending and a forced negotiation with destruction.

How do we tell a story that is not a retelling of settler violence? This question shapes the second part of this book. In spite of the always imminent destruction of "what remains" of Lifta, and through the struggles of stories, I want to invite myself and our people on to another path: a collective and ongoing return. This invitation remains wrought with presence, absence, and a lingering politics of recognition under the violence of the ongoing Nakba. I work to plot our way out of ruins and into return. After walking through the hesitations of modernity in chapters 1 and 2, in chapter 3 we walk across a bridge of sorts to attempt to enact a reconceptualization of space. In the second part of the book, in chapter 4 we begin to feel the possibilities of ongoing return that is not only a negotiation with destruction.

By chapter 5, I begin to ask, How can we return Lifta to an Indigenous articulation of Palestinian history? How can that restoration facilitate a different sort of return, one of Palestinians to Lifta as part of a collective right to a decolonized Palestine, a decolonized future through ongoing return? Turning away from a complete reliance on traditional archives, this journey is embedded within a deeply personal and local story of Lifta. I argue that storytelling, listening, and sharing, and the beauty and pain involved in searching through the radical inconceivability of dispossession, reveal a new understanding of the Nakba. In a way, I am turning away from history to be able to walk into the past. Walking through memory by telling, listening to, and sharing stories teaches us that return is not a singular journey nor even a straight line. Return is ongoing, and it requires us to break with the idea of a narrative arc controlled by beginnings and endings; looking for beginnings and searching for endings is to miss the point of the flow.[86] Following this flow connects the fabrics of memory and the stories they hold, and it teaches us how stories can guide us through time.

Layers of memories in the world of imagination connect me to 'Arifa through the flow of the fabric of her *thob* (dress). In chapter 5, I explore how the fabric of 'Arifa's *thob* envisions return and lets us see how imaginations are triggered by storytelling. Telling, listening to, and sharing stories allows us to grasp the ongoing of Palestinian return. Herein lies the power of 'Arifa—as the knower and as the destination of my journeys.

CHAPTER ONE

A Historical Intervention

Palestine, the Palestine Liberation Organization, and "Red Indians"

By the time we reached Ard al-Samar, otherwise known as French Hill, I was late and found Abu Nasser in the small garden waiting for me. He is a kind man and a Lifta elder. We went together to Muhammad's home, only a short walk up the hill in the small neighborhood. While I walked with Abu Nasser, his youthful energy did not reflect his age or the life he had led since he was forced to leave home in Lifta as a child. As we ascended the hill, Abu Nasser began sharing stories. "Ard al-Samar was actually a part of Lifta. Walking up this hill is like walking the valley, but in Lifta it is all green and we used to breath better." Ard al-Samar is a refuge haven for many Lifta families. Since my own family similarly grounded their refugee life in another Jerusalem neighborhood, as he spoke, I wondered about 'Arifa and imagined walking with her.

Muhammad Abu Layl, Abu Nasser, and I sat in Muhammad's salon. Before I even had a chance to ask a question, Muhammad began a long and solid history lesson, and made it clear to me that I was there to listen. He performed as professor and elder as he talked about the Palestine Liberation Organization (PLO), for he seemed to be certain that I needed to learn what he wanted to teach me: a solid and classic nationalist soliloquy. Yehia Hamouda, a son of Lifta, framed the focus of his speech. He spoke of the PLO in both the present and past tenses.

I had prepared for an "interview" as Abu Nasser requested. Sitting with two imposing men from my grandmother's generation proved instructive. I was not there to ask questions, I was there to listen. As if the script had already been written, it seems the methodology of oral history left a mark. It would be several years before I would begin to understand the massive weight of "history as testimony." At the time, I sat amazed by the insistence on reading Lifta into the PLO. Yehia Hamouda did not hold a strong place in the history of the PLO, as he was no more than an interim head before Yasser Arafat's effective takeover. But I also naively wondered how the PLO could still be relevant in a post–Oslo Accords world. Then I discovered the omnipresence of ghosts of Palestine who have for better or worse framed the last half century of political history: the PLO.

The PLO might have begun with the son of Lifta, Yehia Hamouda, as Liftawis like to remind us, but Hamouda was a mere preface for the major figures that came after him. For several generations the PLO represented the umbrella under which the often rhetorical and sometimes material claim of the ongoing revolution were made in the name of the Palestinian struggle. Since this book is located at the intersection of Palestine studies and Indigenous studies, covering the history of the PLO sheds necessary light on the idiosyncrasies of Indigenous comparisons. This book will not cover the question of who is Indigenous, for that is a broader debate and one that obfuscates the richness of exploring relationality with the people of the land, the Palestinians. Rather, I draw on methodologies of Indigenous studies while remaining grounded in Palestine. But the politics of this intersection cannot be taken for granted. To read Palestine through Indigenous studies brings many things to the fore. It also raises an imperative for Indigenous studies: to learn the terrain on which it walks toward enfolding Palestine into the realm of Indigenous and fourth world liberatory thought. This means engaging the history of Palestinian thought and struggle, including its most prominent international actors, through which aspirations for sovereignty were mobilized, fought for, averted, and argued—including speeches, essays, and poetry. In this chapter, I thus follow an almost singular thread that has become a major trope in this tapestry: the fate of the "red Indian" in comparison with and to Palestine.

While the PLO as a revolutionary entity is almost inconceivable in a twenty-first-century imagination, the promise of liberation through revolution was once the dominant Palestinian narrative that the PLO claimed to represent. In fact, the events of 1948 can easily be considered a disruption of this revolutionary trajectory of twentieth-century Palestinian politics. The break that the Nakba War (1947–49) created between Palestinians and the land of Palestine is the shadow that hovers over Palestinian peoplehood and our individual and collective relationality to the land. Describing the Nakba as an event, however, confines our understanding of life and survival under the brutality of settler colonial violence that is atmospheric, structural, and ongoing. It follows, then, that the historiography of modern Palestine can be considered as a kind of archive of both the *ongoing Nakba* and the *ongoing revolution* as conceptual frames for understanding settler colonial violence and Palestinian survival and resistance. At the height of its power, the PLO represented this historical narrative, and, in particular, three men dominate it: Yasser Arafat as the politician, Mahmud Darwish as the poet, and Edward Said as the intellectual. These three men, from wildly different paths, came together in—and then departed from—the PLO. In an effort toward not repeating this narrative, neither to vilify nor sanctify, this chapter will present parts of their stories in an effort to show how understanding these men is simply not enough but also very much necessary. The chapter is an attempt to provide context for those who do not know the history of the PLO or for those who have chosen to ignore it.

In two distinct and oft-quoted instances, Yasser Arafat, the leader of Palestinians as the head of the PLO, denied Indigenous peoples their present and future. As the chairman of the PLO, Arafat made his statements through a claim that distinguished between the future (or lack thereof) of other Indigenous peoples with that of the Palestinians. Arafat's claims have, in part, framed the possibilities (and tensions) in a Palestinian-Indigenous comparison. Moreover, both Darwish and Said, in their particular and far more complicated styles, gave Arafat's claims intellectual, political, and cultural contexts that are distinctly Palestinian. Exploring historic consistencies and contradictions, and investigating the history of the PLO and the men who have come to represent its past, might be an instructive—albeit tricky—task. Since this book is an effort to explore that other ways of thinking are possible, this is an effort toward forging a path that does not repeat or reify patriarchy and structures of power but acknowledges them and the power they have wielded (and eventually yielded) over time. We all belong to this history, however tenuously. A slight look at the longer history of the PLO can help contextualize the consistencies and ruptures of nationalism in Palestine and work to see these in relation to both Indigeneity and Indigenous comparisons.

While pondering these political and conceptual specificities, it might be useful to begin to consider the possibilities in a decolonial approach toward internal Palestinian structures and, in particular, the PLO—that is, considering the conceptual and political difference between dismantling structures of power versus preserving them to assume the helm of whatever power they offer, however compromised or limited. The PLO hovered between the two (dismantling power and assuming power) before and since the advent of the "peace process" in a history that traces back to the mid-1960s.[1] Conceptually and politically, therefore, Palestine is instructive in understanding the difference between postcolonial states and decolonization. Here we have to think a bit about the relationship between nationalism and the nation-state in an Arab and Palestinian context. Nationalism in this context did not begin with the formation of the PLO in 1964, nor has it ended with the absurdity of the PA (Palestinian Authority) as a replacement for the PLO in the mid-1990s. Nevertheless, following the history of the PLO is useful in understanding how nationalism and the nation-state merged politically, intellectually, and culturally into one idea and goal through the PLO and then morphed into the PA. Likewise, it is helpful to think about how the PLO, in its various itera-tions, also diverged from the nation-state.

Since one of the main questions posed in this book is about belonging, in ad-dition to understanding Lifta within this wider context, this chapter also ex-plores how the PLO dominated the rhetoric and discourse of Palestinian belonging for three decades (1964–94). If we see this mergence/divergence in the past, the question then becomes, Can nationalism work within a liberatory framework in spite of the colonial history of the nation-state? To investigate this question concerning the possibilities of nationalism, we can ask how national-ism works in relation to Indigeneity in Palestine and among Palestinians. For decades Palestinian peoplehood was read through the prism of, first and fore-most, the Nakba and, thus, the framing of Zionist settler colonialism and settler colonial claims to the land. In response, the Palestinian national liberation move-ment under the politics of the PLO represented a struggle toward sovereignty within the frameworks of what was denied Palestinians in the post–World War I era and solidified with international recognition of the settler state of Israel in 1948. Between denial and destruction, then, there was frozen time, where what was denied—sovereignty in the form of an imperially recognized nation-state—informed what was being sought. Needless to say, Palestinian studies has ex-plored these issues and questions for more than three generations. What follows is a humble attempt to pose these questions in a Palestinian context that can be in relation to an Indigenous methodology and ongoing return.

Yasser Arafat and the "Red Indians"

In 2004, in his final interview before leaving the Israeli-imposed siege in his compound in Ramallah, en route to a hospital in France, where he would soon later die, Yasser Arafat, chairman of the PLO and president of the PA, stated emphatically, "We have made the Palestinian case the biggest problem in the world. . . . One hundred and seven years after the Basel Conference [the formal foundation of the Zionist movement], 90 years after the Sykes-Picot Agreement [the World War I imperial agreement for the division of the Levant and Mesopotamia], Israel has failed to wipe us out. We are here, in Palestine, facing them. We are not red Indians."[2] Not at all subtle, Arafat, ar-guably the largest Palestinian political figure of the twentieth century, put forth a qualified comparison, as other Palestinian politicians and intellectuals over the course of the last several decades had done. That is, his declaration relied on the comparison between the foundations of Israel and the United

States as two settler nations. By claiming a "case" and thus a cause, Arafat, like others before him, adhered to a structural analysis claiming both Israel and the United States as settler nations, but presented one (the United States) as a "finished" story of Indigenous elimination, while holding on to the claim that the other (Israel) was prevented from achieving its inevitable settler goal of Indigenous elimination. In his battle cry, the difference for Arafat lay in how he qualified Palestinians as Indigenous. That is, unlike other Indigenous peoples, he claimed the success of the PLO lay in its power as having proven its case to "the modern world" to prevent final elimination. In response to Arafat's historical rendering of the "red Indian" as a relic that no longer exists in the present, Audra Simpson, an anthropologist and a Kahnawà:ke Mohawk, challenged this Palestinian reading of Indigenous peoples by insisting, "We are still here."[3] While Simpson's statement is an important response to Palestinian exceptionalism, Arafat's red Indians cannot be understood outside the long history of the PLO and the contemporary context of Palestinian survival. Simpson does, however, point to an important contradiction in Palestinian claims. It can arguably be said that Arafat wanted a different fate for Palestinians because of how he saw himself as guiding the Palestinian cause's successful entry into the "modern world," in spite of all of the colonial and imperial efforts to the contrary. Additionally, this claim relied on how the politics of the PLO and the subsequent politics of the PA perceived success and failure as visibility and invisibility—through the nation-state. Over the long history of settler violence against Palestine and Palestinians, Arafat's people fought for recognition that, given the framework of the PLO, would prevent elimination. This equation of recognition to prevent elimination deserves some further interrogation.

In 2004, when Arafat gave this interview, the PLO was but a shadow of its former self. The PA, the governing structure resulting from the so-called Oslo peace process, was lying under the rubble of yet another Israeli military attack, part of the long story of the ongoing Nakba. The military siege trapped Arafat in his headquarters in Ramallah (in a building that had once been a prison under British colonial rule) under the strain of several years of growing isolation from regional and international powers. After less than a decade of the implementation of the Oslo Accords, whatever false promises of Palestinian self-determination the peace process offered lay in the rubble of newly invaded cities and towns under Israeli occupation. By emphasizing "we are not red Indians," Arafat appeared to be defiant in what looked to many like defeat. Yet one must ask the question, Why were red Indians his marker for defiance or defeat?

Several scholars have mentioned Arafat's statement, including Nick Estes of the Kul Wicasa / Lower Brule Sioux, Joseph Massad and, as mentioned, Audra Simpson.[4] In her keynote address to the Seventh International Conference of Critical Geography (convened in Ramallah, in occupied Palestine), Simpson used Arafat's red Indian as an opportunity to think about the "global illegibility of Indigenous struggle."[5] Massad follows a similar thread, albeit in a different direction, as he connects Arafat's red Indian back to his historical reading of the "capacious umbrella of self-determination."[6] As for Estes, he reads the intention of Arafat's red Indian as indicative of the "different stages of settler colonialism" that both Native peoples in North America and Palestinians experienced, subsequently affecting different stages in the struggle against settler colonialism.[7] Reading Arafat's final declaration—in a political life full of declarations—as clearly provocative opens up questions for how we can read Arafat, Palestine, and Palestinians in relation to other Indigenous geographies and peoples. Yet, as Simpson noted regarding "illegibility," it is useful to provide a legible context for this declaration and the history that bore it. As Massad explains, Arafat's red Indian is an opportunity to understand how the stages of the history of Palestinian liberation movements were in relation to Palestinian notions of sovereignty and self-determination. Likewise, the implication of the disappearance of the red Indian serves as an implicit adherence toward a particular reading of modernity that embraces the nation-state as a final goal. In the context of third world movements, then, the PLO was an independence movement, whereby "liberation," as Yazid Sayigh argues, moved from emancipation into a confined definition of an independent and internationally recognized nation-state.[8] But Palestinians also belong to a fourth world reading of history. How can the possibilities of two readings—third and fourth worlds—both hold conceptualizations of a Palestinian past and present? Arafat's proclamation, then, was a product of a complicated and quite contradictory history, at the center of which lies the PLO.

In 1981, more than two decades before his declaration in 2004, Arafat gave an interview where he mentioned this Native comparison.[9] This was a very different moment for the PLO and for Arafat, as its leader, from the PLO base in Beirut. Though the PLO was still not entirely politically and militarily defeated in Lebanon, the situation must have seemed bleak, with constant Israeli invasions in the south of the country. Though more than six years into the war in Lebanon, and in spite of the political and material toll it had taken, Arafat still represented an earlier kind of rhetoric of the PLO, less conciliatory than in later years. Several months after this 1981 interview, Arafat and the PLO leadership were forced by another imperial intervention, this time sponsored by the United States, supporting another Israeli invasion to negotiate an exit from Lebanon and embark on another exile for the movement. He might have already been in the thick of this possibility (of exile yet again) during the interview and was clearly dealing with the disastrous consequences of PLO planning in Lebanon.[10] The armed struggle, on which he built his entire political rhetoric, was under attack from several directions as the Israeli settler military pounded southern Lebanon and was clearly inching its way toward the capital city of Beirut; the PLO leadership was at yet another crossroads.[11]

When prompted by the interviewer to discuss the Indigenous comparison Arafat responded, "People sometimes compare our fate with that of the American Indians, but we are living in a different age and a different civilization."[12] In response to a question about his thoughts regarding not receiving a visa to the United States to speak at the United Nations (UN) in New York City, Arafat proclaimed that Palestinians would not suffer the same fate as the red Indians. He was also responding to the US-brokered talks at Camp David between the Egyptian and Israeli regimes, which began in 1979 and effectively divided the Arab world's once united stand (at least rhetorically) against Zionism and its settler colonial aggression in Palestine.[13] He and the PLO had been boxed out, ignored, and were under fire, and Arafat was again defiant in what seemed like inevitable defeat. His defiance in this context was a refusal of the "same fate" of elimination that he implicitly assigned to Indigenous peoples in the US context. As in his later statements, Arafat adhered to an imperial reading of Native disappearance by once again connecting the settler projects in Israel and the United States but reading the latter as completed and the former as incapable of completion. Here, again, Palestinian defiance rightfully relies on a structural understanding of settler nations but elevates Palestinians as a cause that had not yet "ended." As in his later statements, Arafat evoked a sense of Palestinian exceptionality within this Indigenous comparison, once again bringing to the fore why Arafat and the PLO were so intent on being exceptional.

By end of the 1970s the PLO, as "the sole representative of the Palestinian people," received global support for the Palestinian cause as a third world anticolonial movement.[14] As the PLO was embraced by (and located itself centrally within) third world independence movements (particularly in Africa and Latin America), the PLO gained access to formal sites of global power—in particular, in the UN. In spite of this kind of recognition, Palestinians continued to endure constant settler violence, and the PLO remained under the ongoing threat of imperial and settler elimination. As the head of the PLO and the face of the Palestinian national liberation movement, Arafat represented the Palestinian people, or claimed to, and received international recognition to do so. Unlike in 2004, in 1980–81 Arafat still enjoyed support as a leader and the PLO was still the widely recognized representative of the Palestinian people, locally, regionally, and internationally. That level of support was the consequence of over two decades of work beginning officially in 1964, but with a history that goes even farther back—a history with several lines of political planning that vacillated between third world revolutionary movements and superpower diplomacy. That Arafat could, throughout his career, embody such seemingly opposite trends is itself a part of the contradictions of this history and a window into how he thought about Palestinians and the fate of the red Indians. Given the disparity of conditions between these two eras of the PLO, is the specter of the red Indian a consistency?

Indigenous erasure is a primary tool of settler violence, both in terms of people on the land and people and their historical memory. This erasure is ongoing and is as insidious in its use as it is in its consequences. In Palestine the political resonance of forgetting has been an affect of the "years of defeat" of the PA (after 1993) that followed the "years of revolution" in the PLO (the early 1970s), though we should remain skeptical of these categories because of how married they are to settler frameworks.[15] Specifically, the version of Palestine and the Palestinian people that the Oslo Accords attempted to construct was built on a necessity to forget all that came before it.[16] This is a product of the years of PLO diplomacy that preceded the Oslo Accords and is also a consequence of how playing the game of the global politics of recognition destroyed the PLO, arguably under Arafat's leadership and certainly after his death. A brief look at the literature on Palestine over the last two decades reveals a keen obsession with the truncated version of Palestine that resulted from the Oslo Accords, so much so that the history of everything before 1992 has been regulated to a new kind of "before," similar to 1948.[17] Part of our current challenge is to work to understand why these moments have dominated how we think about Palestine and Palestinians as settler colonial impositions as we work to complicate and perhaps eventually do away with them. In the case of Arafat's proclamations about red Indians, it can be helpful to examine the details, complications, complexities, and contradictions of the PLO woven into a longer Palestinian narrative. While there is much to say with regard to using this kind of methodology in terms of the long narratives of the PLO generally, here I want to focus on one part of the larger story of nation-state building and its relationship with a people: the land and self-determination. Important to note here is that over the years, as I have presented different threads of what has now become this book, I often face the assertion—by (mostly) Palestinians—of "Yes, but we are different." This is a reference to, and refusal of, a potential Indigenous comparison. Obviously, there is a set of contradictory complications here, often rendered through questions of demography and relations to nationalism via the PLO. Instead of ignoring these complications, I have chosen to try to live with them.

To return to Arafat and his complicated red Indian comparisons of 1980–81 and 2004, embracing the contradictions allows for the complications to gain color and clarity. In 2004, pounded by direct Israeli violence against him in his ever-shrinking political and physical space, Arafat was, quite literally, slowly being killed. Since the start of the al-Aqsa Intifada (the Second Intifada) in 2000, less than a decade after the establishment of the PA in occupied territories (1994–95), the Israeli Army unleashed massive and sustained violence throughout Palestine, including the occupied West Bank. Army tanks took over the streets and fighter planes and helicopters invaded the skies. The settler military isolated and eventually trapped Arafat in his Ramallah compound. A myriad of forces that included the Israeli-US alliance and their clients in the Arab world worked to make him politically irrelevant and expendable. Like the ongoing Nakba, the history of Palestinian resistance is also an ongoing story. Though a profound moment because of the destructive capacity of Zionist violence, 2004 is but one year in a century of resistance. Because al-Aqsa Intifada is retrospectively marked by the abundance of literature that covers it as a moment of miscalculated violence on the part of the PA and the Palestinian people under occupation, it has been isolated from this longer history as a means to punctuate the loss of the promise of independence of a Palestinian state. That is, the paucity of literature on al-Aqsa Intifada is part of the obfuscation of the longer Palestinian story of ongoing resistance and refusal. Removing the moment from the history of the resistance does the work of settlers by removing it from all that came before to justify all that came after.[18] As such, 2004 must be read as a part of this long narrative and not as an exceptional moment. Likewise, in 1981, Arafat as a leader of the PLO was mired in a war in Lebanon as the movement was on the verge of yet another Zionist-designed expulsion, which would come in 1982, driving the PLO leadership from Beirut to Tunis. The journey from 1981 and 2004, and many dates in between and after them, are marked by the changing political translation of self-determination within the PLO. In fact, it speaks to what might be called an ongoing translation of the meaning and substance of self-determination.[19] The historical transformations that led to the contemporary era are understandably overshadowed by the violence in the present. The long and complicated journey of the PLO into the PA, and how Arafat was at the helm during the journey, can perhaps offer insight into his intentions regarding his proclamations regarding "red Indians." There is a long story embedded in these complications that begins with a great contradiction: How can an entity represent the Palestinian people after the Nakba War (1948), its continuation in 1967, and in the midst of the ongoing Nakba? Implicit in this question lies the obvious: Zionist settler colonial violence and its ongoing attempts at eliminating Palestinians as a people and the Palestinian cause in its various interpretations on the world's stage.

The PLO: Erased History and a Negotiated Presence

Understood exclusively within the confines of the modern nation-state, the history of the PLO, as described by Yezid Sayigh, is the story of a "search for a state" in the past and the present.[20] At the turn of the new millennium, this search, as well as the state, seemed to foreclose a future. Though this book argues toward another kind of engagement with the past for Palestine, it is nevertheless useful and perhaps necessary to remember the local historical context of the PLO and the nationalist discourse that dominated that context. Again, if a comparative analysis within Indigenous studies does not account for this central aspect of Palestinian life and all of the cultural, political, and intellectual engagement around it, the nuance of what "sharedness" across Indigenous contexts can mean is lost. Moreover, and more important, it is necessary to also read how the PLO and leading politicians and thinkers within it contextualized and sometimes denied the potential richness of this Indigenous sharedness, almost always rendered through a lamentation about Palestinian statelessness.

More than two decades into the twenty-first century, and nearly three decades after the start of the Oslo Accords that fundamentally altered the structures and function of the PLO, a critique of nation-state nationalism is common and almost pedestrian. The late 1960s to the late 1980s, however, were a far different context in terms of nationalism, the nation-state, and the PLO. The initial emergence of the PLO in 1964 occurred within an Arab nationalist context, but by 1968, its reemergence came out of an Arab context of profound defeat after the June War in 1967. The conceptual framing of this period as "defeat" has been a hegemonic tool for reading Palestinian history after 1948 and modern Arab history after 1967.[21] Ironically, by 1968 the PLO can be read within a framework of Indigenous resurgence, but it must be couched within the wider Arab context, making for a paradoxical mix between Palestinian resurgence and Arab defeat. That is, "defeat" here refers to the hegemonic cultural and political frameworks as a material reality after a series of settler wars.[22] The years 1948 and 1967 occupy the main signposts for the emergence and subsequent political centrality of describing Zionist settler colonialism as a "successful" project of imperialism forcibly imposed on Palestine and Palestinians.[23] The result was the full occupation of Palestine and a highly militarized state in the heart of the Arab world, thereby isolating Palestine and Palestinians from the historical and cultural context of the larger Arab world.[24] Simply stated, intellectuals and politicians defined "defeat" after the 1967 war as the loss of the land of Palestine and lost opportunity to enter modernity through achieving an internationally recognized nation-state. Loss, and not erasure (the difference between active and passive verbs), therefore, is the defining feature in this kind of culture and politics of defeat, and it is one that was expressed within Arab politics and culture, of which Palestine is a part. With loss came an imposed isolation from this Arab cultural and political context.[25] In the Palestinian context, resurgence entails a kind of return to culture by refusing isolation and removal not only from the land but also from the context of Arab culture and history. While the PLO initially represented a refusal of defeat after 1968, by the early 1990s it came to represent ultimate defeat and abandonment of the methods of resistance and armed struggle it once embraced.

In other Indigenous contexts, resurgence is transformative in how we think about the past and work intentionally in the present toward a kind of recovering of what had been lost and denied through the violence of settler colonialism. *Grounded normativity*, and its inherent call for centering relationality to the land and each other as people of the land, is a way of describing both a return to who we are and a return to the land. In Palestine, this approach has methodological and epistemological possibilities, within the specificities of peoplehood and relationality to place and land. Nevertheless, refusing isolation and erasure places these possibilities within the context of the larger Arab world—that is, a return to the Arab context. The exceptionality of Palestine in this vast, colonized geography is that of settler colonialism. As Bashir Abu Manneh explains, what makes Palestine unique is that "no other Arab people faced both imperialism and settler colonialism (as distinct and emerging forces)."[26] While there remain specificities for Palestinians, the Arab context (as a formidable part of the third world) must always be considered both in cultural and political trajectories. For Palestinians, resurgence and ongoing refusal of the Nakba can be a helpful means of conceptualizing return, but these are not new. The history of Palestinian political mobilization for the last sixty years has been, in large part, a history of the PLO. Resurgence, here, is connected to changing notions of "cultural recovery" and/or resistance to settler colonial erasure (understanding isolation as a form of erasure) and the multivalent practices of this kind of resistance. Neither as an attempt to romanticize the PLO nor as a means to demean it, mercifully reading the PLO as part of the longer and wider history of Palestinian peoplehood can clarify ongoing return and Palestinian nationalism as both potentially within and outside Indigeneity and Indigenous methodological possibilities.

In the context of the PLO, the quite deliberate self-identification with armed struggle was absorbed (and unified) into the organization's raison d'être. In fact, early iterations of the armed struggle/resistance were already a major component in political mobilization well before the establishment of the settler state of Israel, but by the late 1960s it was the vehicle that led to the dominance of the PLO. The history of resistance in Palestine is obviously a far bigger and longer story than the history of institutionalized armed struggle within the PLO. Nevertheless, with its reemergence in 1968 the PLO— through its various structures and through the intellectual production of the people and political parties supported by it—managed to consolidate this history under a PLO-defined sense of armed struggle.[27] By the late 1960s, the PLO was the political home where these tactics, strategies, and political trajectories were widely discussed among people, factions, and various parties. The PLO's leadership transformed both the rhetorical and practical valences of resistance into their nearly exclusive domain, which had historical resonance for decades. Ironically, by the middle of the first decade of the twenty-first century, armed struggle was actively demonized by some of these same people, factions, and parties. Many of those who once strongly advocated for the methodology of armed struggle had by the second decade of PA (post–Oslo Accords) rule become tools in the hands of those same oppressors through control of the various agencies of "security" set up by the PA within imperial and settler control.[28] Given this complicated context, methodological tools of Indigenous resurgence might guide the historian outside the reductive frameworks of defeat that frame this history—certainly in terms of the post-1948 era but also in terms of the political timeline thereafter. Unlearning defeat is an invitation to look at the Palestinian past differently.

The PLO: Consistencies and Ruptures

Another potential of unlearning defeat relies on our need to examine the difference between the *cause* and the *case* of Palestine. As a "case" in the international context, read through the resolutions that followed the war in 1967 (particularly, UN Security Council Resolutions 242 and 336), there is a focus on the occupation of Palestinian territories of the Gaza Strip, the West Bank, and East Jerusalem as the only remaining land of Palestine open to Palestinian possibilities. More specifically, "territories" are a key component in this framework. The use of territories and the use of the plural negates the point of land as a homeland for a people, thereby further confining the Palestinian cause inside a settler colonial framework. Moreover, these territories as the sole consideration for eventual political negotiation severely limited future Palestinian possibilities. Defining Palestinian possibilities through these two UN resolutions converted the cause of Palestine—or, in Edward Said's terms, the "question of Palestine / Palestinian question"—into one primarily under consideration by the minutiae of international law. As Noura Erakat deftly argues, this is how land became territories, and territories became the only ground for politics.[29] In this construct, Palestine was transformed into a formula of territories to be negotiated in what eventually became the basis of the peace and recognition process among Arab states, then directly with Palestinians, and with the Israeli state, all the while mediated and controlled by the United States. Imperial powers imposed this formula on Palestinians, and it was eventually accepted by the leadership of the PLO. By the late 1970s "occupation" replaced the then obfuscated "settler colonialism" within these formulations. These maneuvers seem like a game in political compromise. The aftermath of 1967, then, changed a great deal, but other complementary and contradictory changes followed.

From a cause to a case, much did change in the PLO over the late decades of the twentieth century, and it is useful to explore the ruptures and consistencies. About a decade after the armistice agreements with surrounding Arab states in 1948–49, in the early era of decolonization (particularly in Egypt), the relatively new formations of independent Arab states put reconstituting a Palestinian body politic on their agenda. Under the auspices of Gamal Abdel Nasser's leadership in Egypt, punctuated by his version of Arab nationalism, emerged the first version of the PLO with the promulgation of its National Charter in 1964. Arab nationalism in this era was driven by two main rhetorical trends: Nasser's Egypt and the Ba'ath Party in Iraq and Syria. Nasser was also a prominent figure in the third world movement. Later, after

Nasser's death, Arafat assumed the role of a third world revolutionary leader. In his political treatise *The Philosophy of Revolution* Nasser contextualized his understanding of the loss of Palestine as imperial design.[30] As such, he articulated the fight for Palestine as a central rhetorical ploy in his popular version of Arab sovereignty. For Nasser, sovereignty and dignity were key concepts in his leadership agenda, but this translated in his political agenda to confining Palestine to an Arab issue that should fall under his direct leadership. As such, he held great political control over this early constitution of the PLO. While deeply embedded in regional Arab politics, the political mobilization of Palestinians in the 1950s and 1960s, in particular among the Arab Nationalist Movement is of great significance in terms of third world Marxist ideology and the wildly active modes of mobilization among Palestinians across the geographies and political movements of the Arab world.[31] Historians are actively working through this era in defiance of narratives of defeat and breakage in 1948.[32] While Arab nationalism in this era is often read from the top down, in terms of state leadership, it is also very important to recognize the history of people's political and social mobilization. After 1949 the forced exile by Zionist forces of nearly three quarters of the Palestinian people from the land of Palestine meant that the political body of the people and their relation (and access and lack thereof) to the land changed dramatically, affecting political mobilization.

In June 1967, another settler war resulted in the occupation of all of the land of what had been Mandatory Palestine. The war also resulted in the proverbial end of the era of Nasser-style Arab nationalism and Palestine's place within this regional context. Only months after the end of the war of 1967, the PLO reconstituted itself through armed struggle in the Battle of Karama in March 1968 and the passing of the newly amended PLO Charter approved by the Palestinian National Council (PNC) of the PLO in July of that year.[33] After Israel occupied the West Bank in June 1967, al-Karama, a town near the border (and ceasefire line) between newly occupied territory and Jordan turned into a major battle site between the Palestinian fedayeen and the Israeli military.[34] As al-Karama became a major base for the fedayeen from various parties and factions within the PLO, it quickly became an Israeli target and the battle ensued.[35] Both events, the Battle of Karama and the amended PLO Charter, are foundational for two reasons: First, it is clear in the text of the charter how resistance (in the form of armed struggle as represented, in part, by the Battle of Karama) was articulated as a core part of liberation and, second, it is clear in the charter's text that liberation was defined within the frameworks of self-determination for Palestinians *by* Palestinians. This was a departure from the previous iteration of self-determination through Nasser's influence of Arab sovereignty under the umbrella of Egypt. While the 1964 charter was the basis for this newly amended text, 1968 was a formative moment, as it was born out of the military defeat of Arab regimes in the war in 1967, the rise of Palestinian armed struggle, and the culmination of how the PLO envisioned and practiced forms of self-determination.

Article 9 is the core of the charter, for after defining homeland and the rights of the Palestinian people to determine their own destiny, article 9 states, "Armed struggle is the only way to liberate Palestine. That it is the overall strategy, not merely a tactical phase. The Palestinian Arab people assert their absolute determination and firm resolution to continue their armed struggle and to work for an armed popular revolution for the liberation of their country and their return to it. They also assert their right to normal life in Palestine and to exercise their right to self-determination and sovereignty over it."[36] The charter is also a sort of introduction of the Palestinian people into the world of nation-states, or how the PLO framed this move in its quest to achieve international recognition as the sole representative of the Palestinian people (and, therefore, the official Palestinian entity that would speak for all Palestinians regarding the case and cause of Palestine). There are direct and indirect references to self-determination and sovereignty throughout the text, with a direct engagement in article 24: "The Palestinian people believe in the principles of justice, freedom, sovereignty, self-determination, human dignity, and in the right of all peoples to exercise them."[37] Several other articles explicate further, including article 18's mention of a restoration of "national sovereignty" for the Palestinian people, as well as article 3, which establishes the "legal right" of the Palestinian people to their homeland.

Throughout the thirty-three articles in the charter, the PNC worked to establish a number of national principles (*thawabit wataniya*), including a definition for the land of Palestine (articles 1, 2, and 19); a definition for the identity of the people of Palestine within an Arab national and cultural context (articles 4, 5, 6, 7, 11, 15, 28, and 29); a definition for liberation (articles 9, 10, 13, 17, 18, and 21); and definitions for Zionism, colonialism, and imperialism (articles 19, 20 and 22). There is one reference to Palestine as the Holy Land, and this, too, was framed through national liberation; as article 16 notes, "The liberation of Palestine, from a spiritual point of view, will provide the Holy Land with an atmosphere of safety and tranquility, which in turn will safeguard the country's religious sanctuaries and guarantee freedom of worship and of visit to all, without discrimination of race, color, language, or religion. Accordingly, the people of Palestine look to all spiritual forces in the world for support." That is, there is a recognition of the land as the Holy Land, but only insofar as national liberation of Palestine (by the Palestinian people's participation in the armed struggle) was a guarantee of safety and openness to the land for all. Notably, under the auspices of establishing democratic principles, in addition to a definition of Palestinian as a genealogical legacy, the charter also explained that all the people then residing in the land of Palestine (including settlers) would have a place of citizenship in the eventual nation-state of Palestine. This kind of formulation changed dramatically in the subsequent decades. It is important to also note that the seeds of "seeking international recognition" are also visible in the text, albeit through a less exclusionary notion of nation-state than would prevail in succeeding decades.

The events of 1968, in lieu of all of the subsequent changes in the politics and rhetoric of the PLO, might seem a bit like aberrations, but they were actually a result of many forces, including popular mobilization. It is also important to note that—while the PLO abandoned this politics (in form and substance)—the will fueling the mobilizations still exists among Palestinians, as resistance remains ongoing. The 1968 version of the PLO is still widely influential in how the history of resistance is read among Palestinian people. The PLO and its leadership prior to 1968 (in the first three PNC meetings) did not emphasize armed struggle as the primary strategy for liberation (and complementary guerrilla tactics, which were later the fodder for great contestation). Moreover, prior to 1968, Palestinian representation was not overly emphasized (as it was thereafter), for the PLO was under the hands of the Arab League and under the control of Gamal Abdel Nasser. The year 1968 was a revolutionary moment for the PLO as it was a change globally in terms of third world movements. Palestine began to hold a primary position internationally in terms of anticolonialism and "third world revolution," and the PLO grew in its status as the "sole and legitimate representative of the Palestinian people."[38] If 1968 is the height of the rhetorical power of the PLO, the subsequent decade witnessed the height of its political power. In spite of all the Israeli-US efforts against it, the PLO internationalized the question of Palestine in the 1970s and, as such, it took on various forms across the globe.

The PLO was an organization and leadership in exile in the 1970s. Driven from Jordan after the events of Black September in 1970, the PLO made Lebanon its home.[39] This era, often referred to as the revolutionary period, was the first formative era of institution building after 1948 and was (at first) based on the vision set forth for liberation in the 1968 charter. Rosemary Sayigh documents Palestinian refugees in Lebanon in her classic text *From Peasants to Revolutionaries*; the book's title repeats a mantra of this era for the PLO, as displacement meant that Palestinians went from being peasants working the land to fedayeen (revolutionaries) fighting for return to the land. This was certainly an epoch, and one dominated by both the material and rhetorical reality of armed struggle and the prolific cultural production of people and political parties sponsored by and housed within the PLO. In the Beirut years, the PLO built a significant infrastructure and bureaucracy. The PLO as an institution was both about state building and liberation and was, therefore, full of contradictions and complexities. In his book *The Hundred Years' War on Palestine*, Rashid Khalidi presents the dilemmas for the leadership in this period when the PLO had international attention and even, albeit frugal, international recognition.[40] Nevertheless, the room to maneuver in terms of Palestinian futures remained narrow.

While liberation was clearly put on the agenda in 1968, the succeeding decade was actually defined by Arafat's and other PLO leaders' calculated moves toward diplomacy (as opposed to or in relation with armed struggle, opinions within the PLO ran the entire spectrum) and state building (as opposed to liberation of the land). Khalidi argues that while the decisions taken by PLO leadership left much to be desired, the actual lost opportunity of this period was for and by the Israelis. He notes that, over the course of two decades, and leading directly to the Madrid Peace Conference (1991), the Israelis refused to acknowledge the tremendous compromises of Palestinian leadership and, as a result, scripted their own role as permanent warden of an apartheid prison ruled exclusively through violence. Though Khalidi reads the failure of diplomacy valiantly, the Zionist project, built on violence, was committed to this violence as a settler colonial state in a permanent state of frontier settlement.[41] Whether the Israelis could accept compromise is not my point nor my concern, for settler anxieties have received far too much attention in Palestinian studies, but it is interesting to understand that failures in diplomacy were not Palestinian as much as they were Israeli. I do not intend to dwell on this rich period other than to help position and contextualize how Arafat and the PLO engaged the Indigenous comparison through the specter of the red Indian. The National Charter of the PLO in 1968 represented a somewhat utopian vision for the liberation of Palestine; it was certainly not the only political trajectory for Palestinians, but it was an umbrella for many. However seemingly utopian, it also had its limitations because it remained well embedded in colonial modernity, the politics of recognition and the nation-state. Nevertheless, it also included a return to the land, an end to the project of Zionism, and equal citizenship for all on the land, a kind of utopia that was articulated within nation-state terminology, albeit using a grammar that was more inclusive than that used in subsequent eras.

As the PLO entered the international sphere and began to seek and then gain further recognition, the national agenda of 1968 began to change. By 1974 a new version of the charter was voted on by the PNC; in the PLO's Ten Point Program, state building found a new and central role in lieu of liberating the entirety of the land of Palestine. The goal was now establishing sovereignty on any part of Palestine. The subtle language of 1968 and inclusive notions of citizenship and belonging changed, as did the notion of what would later be referred to by Edward Said as "Palestinianness," a new kind of exclusive rendition of Palestinian identity that has, in part, reinforced the complications of Indigenous comparisons. This iteration of Palestinian identity has actually, over the course of the thread of "seeking a state" in the PLO and PA, reduced the possibilities in comparisons as it has rendered a kind of exceptionality in Palestinian identity that is almost exclusively in relation to Zionism and the Israeli state in a two-state formulation. Chiefly, the new version of the charter called for the establishment of "national authority over every part of Palestinian territory that is liberated." With the introduction of the notion of "parts" of Palestine, we can begin to trace a more focused, fragmented, and exclusionary notion of state building and a confined politics of identity embedded with it. This was coupled with likening the importance of diplomacy with armed struggle as people within the PLO advocated more vocally and loudly, using the language of UN Security Council Resolutions 242 and 338, thus implicitly beginning the process of accepting two states in the land of Palestine. By 1974 Arafat gained such prominence that he was invited to speak for Palestine at the UN General Assembly. A few months later, the Arab League proclaimed the PLO as the "sole legitimate representative of the Palestinian people in any Palestinian territory." This recognition further solidified the PLO's status as a state in waiting to build its national authority in any part of Palestine, a liminal status that Palestinians occupy to this day.

Even in the height of the revolutionary years of the 1970s, the PLO leadership's representation of Palestinian nationalism was growing closer to ever-shrinking versions of a state. This was in no small part due to a civil war raging in Lebanon. The PLO, however, as a big political umbrella, held together a wide array of political positions and perspectives and continued to employ the language and strategy of armed struggle and liberation. By 1988, at the height of the First Intifada being fought in the land of Palestine (in the occupied territories), the PNC convened in Algiers and Arafat declared an independent Palestinian state. The Palestinian Declaration of Independence contained an explicit nod to the Israeli state, effectively giving formal notice to the world that Arafat and the PLO he represented were fully on board with a two-state solution. While it had its complicated historical trajectory, this declaration was also a source of tension among Palestinians, as the PLO leadership outside Palestine feared the power of internal leadership that had fueled the Intifada in its earlier days in 1987–88.[42] Both his speech in 1974 and this 1988 declaration were written by a number of men within the official orbit of the PLO. From 1968 until 1988 the PLO represented Palestinians and Palestine through the uneasy formula of revolution, representation, and recognition. This journey was not Arafat's alone, though he led it. It is at this time that we see the emergence of two of Palestine's most influential minds: Edward Said and Mahmud Darwish.

The PLO from Within: From M'ana al Nakba to The Question of Palestine

The political maneuvers of the PLO basically summarize the political trajectory of Palestinian mobilization since the 1960s, but these maneuvers were also held together through intellectual writings. Arafat is but one piece of this larger tapestry. While his proclamations regarding the fate of the red Indian were Arafat's audacity, reflecting on the futility of comparison, one should seek out the intellectual grounding of Palestinian mobilization. Here we find the intellectuals who, well before the formation of the PLO, played a key role in advocating for Palestine not only as a cause but also as a key impetus in forging potential paths toward liberation. While often independently prolific, many intellectuals found a home in the PLO and institutions that were close to the politics of the organization. In fact, as Sherene Seikaly astutely points out, the *Journal of Palestine Studies*, as part of the Institute for Palestine Studies, can be read as an archive for how intellectualism is politics within this orbit of the PLO.[43] As we have done with Arafat, it is useful to focus on one intellectual, Edward Said, to read the translation of Palestine through his widely popular intellectual and political production, though he certainly was not the only intellectual of his time. Rather than take on his entire oeuvre, the goal here is to simply return Said to his intellectual base in his early career: the PLO.

Just as Constantin Zureiq had done decades earlier in his *M'ana al Nakba* (The meaning of disaster), Edward Said wrote *The Question of Palestine* to offer a certain lexicon that has since framed how we think about Palestine. Said described his book as a "political essay" and offered the frame "question of" for several reasons, most notably that "Palestine is . . . a much debated, even contested, notion."[44] While Zureiq's book was written in the midst of war and as a battle cry for Palestine, Said's was one of advocacy. Writing in English, Said focused on an Anglo-American audience as he explained the historical and contemporary issues of Palestine—in his words, as "an idea and an interpretation." In the late 1970s Said published two books that would change how we think about knowledge production, colonialism, and imperialism: *Orientalism* and *The Question of Palestine.* While *Orientalism*'s scholarly resonance is well known, the same cannot be said for *The Question of Palestine,* though the two are quite complementary texts. In fact, Said's prominence as a cultural critic of empire and as an advocate for the Palestinian cause are so well connected and ingrained in each other that these texts are best read together.

According to Bashir Abu-Manneh's astute reading of Said's genealogy, Said's work was dramatically changed by the war in 1967. The complete occupation of Palestine and the profound defeat of Nasser's Arab nationalism triggered Said; only after the war did he "become a political critic and public intellectual committed to Arab and Palestinian freedom and self-determination."[45] Said began regularly writing about Palestine after 1967, and by the time of the publication of *The Question of Palestine* he had established himself as both a prolific public intellectual in the US context and an interlocutor among Palestinian intellectuals within and in close proximity to the PLO and its leadership. In his own words, "Having allowed myself gradually to assume the professional voice of an American academic as a way of submerging my difficult and unassimilable past, I began to think and write contrapuntally, using the disparate halves of my experience, as an Arab and as an American, to work with and also against each other. This tendency began to take shape after 1967, and though it was difficult, it was also exciting. What prompted the initial change in my sense of self, and of the language."[46] As Said explains in the introduction to *The Question of Palestine,* he offers "a Palestinian interpretation to a Palestinian experience." He notes how Palestinians after the defeat of Arab nationalism in 1967 began "to construct a political identity and will of our own; we have developed a remarkable resilience and an even more remarkable national resurgence."[47] Said wrote these words as a Palestinian American scholar who was, as he describes it, thinking about Palestine as he was writing *Orientalism.* He also went about presenting the question of Palestine to an English speaking audience from within the PLO. Indeed, he played this role until the Oslo Accords were announced, after which he became one of the harshest critics of the PLO leadership.

While it is well known that Said, along with many other Palestinian intellectuals, was involved politically with the PLO and served on the PNC until 1991, the point here is actually not just about Said's positionality, but also about what the PLO actually was (and represented) after 1968 until the late 1980s. Said's involvement in the PLO both as an insider and as a kind of "translator" brought the PLO and the representation of its politics to a wider audience. Said forefronts his argument with his description of a political awakening of his people and himself: Palestinians, through the PLO, "have gained the support of all the peoples of the Third World; above all, despite the fact that we are geographically dispersed and fragmented, despite the fact that we are without a territory of our own, we have been united as a people largely because the Palestinian idea (which we have articulated out of our own experience of dispossession and exclusionary oppression) has a coherence to which we have all responded with positive enthusiasm."[48] Herein lies the contradiction and complexities of the PLO: Said wrote this in the late 1970s, contextualizing "the resurgence of Palestinian nationalism" that was born out of the 1968 and 1974 moments, in relation to the third world, and distinctly not in relation to the fourth world or even the longer history of colonialism and settler colonialism in Palestine. He was writing about this kind of nationalism at the same time that he grew in fame for his poetic writings on exile.[49] That is, the connections that Said and the PLO nurtured in this period were with postcolonial states and peoples and were about asserting a very specific kind of sovereignty and self-determination defined by the nation-state. At the same time, he also wrote through exile in ways that resonate beyond any kind of statism, an art produced through a tragic embrace of exile and statelessness.

Said later explained that this was an exciting time because of how Palestinians worked to "repossess their history and politics" and how this had to do with a "rise in regional and international visibility of the PLO." But in the same breath he also explained that from the moment of his own self-described awakening, he was under "the apprehension that as a people we still had no sovereignty over any part of the land of Palestine."[50] Said worked to give Palestinians a presence through the forced absence that Euro-American Orientalism and Zionist settler colonialism imposed, in his words, "a permission to narrate."[51] In fact, in his own descriptions of his post-1967 politicization, he "felt that I had been fashioning a self who revealed for a Western audience things that had so far been either hidden or not discussed at all." Thus, for Said, this urgent need to claim a presence was inherently connected to the lack of his interpretation of sovereignty in the land of Palestine and the drive to advocate for Palestinian self-determination through the politics of representation. This framework that works toward the recognition of the nation-state of Palestine made sense to Said because "do many people now believe that the gypsies or the Native Americans can get back what they lost?"[52] A sentiment, not surprisingly, later echoed by Arafat.

As he did in terms of reclaiming and thereby defining Palestinianness (that is, what it is to be Palestinian after exile and through a political praxis) through interpretation, the PLO was also a space to practice this interpretation.[53] As such, Said infused his own understanding of what the PLO could be into his work. This kind of political philosophy, from the time of *The Question of Palestine*, was in some ways about moving away from the rhetoric, emphasis and practice of the armed struggle and into the Euro-American defined version of state-based sovereignty. Embodying a kind of PLO-held contradiction, Said was also, in his own words, "very critical of the use of slogan-clichés like 'armed struggle' and of the revolutionary adventurism that caused innocent deaths and did nothing to advance the Palestinian case politically."[54] The fight among Palestinians and within the PLO regarding different visions of a Palestinian future and a strategy toward achieving it was an internal discussion that, for Said, had worldly implications. Quite deliberately and under his definition of secular humanism, Said's version of exile often mirrored that of European Jewish exilic thinking prior to Zionism and the establishment of the state of Israel.[55]

Like others embedded in the PLO, the postcolonial context was of paramount importance for Said. The PLO, then, represented, in Said's formulation, an anticolonial independence movement in a postcolonial context. According to Said, "whereas Israel and its history have been celebrated without interruption, the actuality of Palestinians, with lives being led, small histories endured, aspirations felt, has only recently been conceded an existence." To counter Zionist mythology of return, Said emphasizes Palestinian presence: "We must understand the struggle between Palestinians and Zionism as a struggle between a presence and an interpretation, the former constantly appearing to be overpowered and eradicated by the later." This thread of Palestine as an idea and interpretation takes up a great deal of space in Said's exploration, but in doing so he also reifies that Palestine is also "an act of sustained popular will."[56]

In his commitment to the question, Said highlights the dehumanization of Palestinians and records the relentlessness of Zionist settler violence. According to Said, "the Jewish state is built on negation of Palestine and the Palestinians," for he long understood that Palestinian elimination was the ultimate goal of settler colonialism.[57] It can easily be argued that Said's major and long-lasting contribution was speaking this truth to that power, as he explained it. But *The Question of Palestine* does more than this. In it Said presents a certain kind of Palestinian future—a state-centered future that would salvage Palestinian sovereignty on parts of historical Palestinian land. In doing so, this will save Palestine from the fate of Arafat's red Indian; redemption would only come through recognition of a state for Palestinians. Though Said is well known as a critic of European colonialism and, after 1993, an outspoken critic of Arafat and PLO leadership, it was he who had earlier helped translate and promote a kind of understanding of Palestine and the "question" that was both implicitly and quite explicitly grounded in the kind of self-determination that a modern nation-state and colonial modernity represented.[58]

Said also offers the basis for a dynamic comparative analysis by distinguishing between settler comparisons and comparisons of the colonized. In terms of Zionism, the ideology's European origins position the movement within a colonial and Orientalist logic. That is, Zionism fits into this rhetoric but did not invent it. According to Said, the land of Palestine was "controlled, in the Western mind, not by its present realities and inhabitants but by its glorious, portentous past and the seemingly limitless potential of its (possibly) just as glorious future, Palestine was seen as a place to be possessed anew and reconstructed." Zionists present their ideology and movement as a means by which to accomplish these Orientalist goals because "Palestine has always played a special role in the imagination and in the political will of the West. . . . Palestine is a place of causes and pilgrimages . . . the prize of the Crusades." Grounded in biblical mythology, Orientalist visions of the Holy Land fit into the ideology of Zionism as a return to this imagined past of European invention. As Said explains, the Orientalist expert "believed that only he could speak (paternally as it were) for the natives and primitive societies he had studied—his presence denoting their absence—so too the Zionists spoke to the world on behalf of the Palestinians" as the rightful "original inhabitants of the land."[59] While the political and cultural roots of the Zionist movement emerged from Europe in the nineteenth century, settler colonial legacies had a longer historical trajectory across the globe. This lucidity in placing Orientalism and Zionism on the same register has had long-lasting implications.

Though Said uses his own interpretation of "imperialism" (which he describes in full in *Orientalism*) more often than "settler colonialism" in his description of the question of Palestine, he does describe Zionism as a settler colonial movement. When read through his own sense of loss as a Palestinian,

Said's work places great emphasis on erasure, disappearance, and absence. One of his main objectives in writing *The Question of Palestine* is to clearly show how, in spite of all the violent efforts of Zionist and imperial powers, Palestinians have not disappeared. Elsewhere he describes this existential imperative: "'There are no Palestinians,' said Golda Meir in 1969, and that set me, and many others, the slightly preposterous challenge of disproving her, of beginning to articulate a history of loss and dispossession that had to be extricated, minute by minute, word by word, inch by inch, from the very real history of Israel's establishment, existence, and achievements. I was working in an almost entirely negative element, the non-existence, the non-history which I had somehow to make visible despite occlusions, misrepresentations, and denials." Though preposterous in its implication and cruel in its necessity, this was the tone of much of his work and that of the PLO in the 1970s, disproving a negative through the frameworks and language available to become visible to the international community. However famously Said is known for his individual work and intellectual production, this collective position that he championed was held together and represented by the PLO and, until the time of the Oslo Accords, his politics were those of the PLO: "There was an existential as well as a felt political need to bring one self into harmony with the other, for as the debate about what had once been called 'the Middle East' metamorphosed into a debate between Israelis and Palestinians, I was drawn in, ironically enough, as much because of my capacity to speak as an American academic and intellectual as by the accident of my birth. By the mid-seventies I was in the rich but unenviable position of speaking for two diametrically opposed constituencies, one Western, the other Arab."[60]

As a Palestinian in the United States, Said describes how the June War in 1967 was a watershed moment for him, one that drove him into his role as a public intellectual. *The Question of Palestine* is both a culmination of this and a living document of how Said worked to frame Palestine. A readily accessible part of this is his consistent use of *exile* as a conceptual frame. The irony, of course, is that Said's exile is in another geography of settler colonial erasure, the United States—a point he distinctly does not emphasize in his framing of exile as a Palestinian. The frame is about his Palestine, as well as his work to make Palestine readable to his audience, and he did this work claiming legibility, again, from within the PLO. In terms of Palestine and Palestinians, Said explains, "We Palestinians are clearly struggling for our self-determination but for the fact that we have no place, no agreed-upon and available physical terrain on which to conduct our struggle." The PLO was a movement without a place; its members were visitors in the places they occupied outside Palestine. This was true of the organization, as well as of Palestinians: "Every Palestinian community must struggle to maintain its identity on at least two levels: first, as Palestinian with regard to the historical encounter with Zionism and the precipitous loss of homeland; second, as Palestinian in the existential setting of day-to-day life, responding to the pressure in the state of residence."[61] Exile and erasure, in this sense, require a political program that is centered on a national identity and an anticolonial praxis for Palestinians in relation to land of Palestine. How that praxis works in Said's framework, as in the framework of the PLO, is part of the complexity of the era. That is, reconstituting the political body is to be performed, as Said performs it, in conversation. The question lingers: With whom were Said and the PLO in conversation?

In spite of the codification of the demands of liberation set forth in the 1968 charter, some in the PLO, including some in leadership positions, quite quickly began to move away from the focus on armed struggle and guerrilla tactics to diplomatic advocacy for recognized nation-state sovereignty in parts of the land of Palestine. As Joseph Massad explains, these efforts culminated in the amended charter of the PLO in 1974, moving from a delineated manifesto of liberation through realization of self-determination (1968) toward a more internationally accepted version of "limited" self-determination based on post-1967 UN resolutions and a state (implicitly accepting the two-state framework).[62] Though both ends of this "spectrum of self-determination," nevertheless, relied on structures of a nation-state formation and an invitation into the world of nations, they diverged significantly in terms of tactics and goals. Of course, these contradictory trends existed within the PLO throughout the decades. That is not the point here; rather, how the PLO held all of these contradictions (and certainly not without protest or internal rebellion) as a state in formation is. Moreover, it is important to see how these sets of contradictions led to the formation of the PA and the continuation of the armed struggle (no longer embraced by the official line of the authority, and eventually actively criminalized by the PA by 2004–5). Within certain political iterations of the PLO and, later, the PA, it becomes clear why the specter of the red Indian loomed. Said's version of the question of Palestine is in its parts and in its totality a generative summary of this work of the PLO in terms of a specific kind of narration of the history of Palestinians. This narrative includes the ideological and political connections between Zionism and the history of colonialism—in particular, with the United States. Drawing these connections would prove invaluable for later explorations concerning settler colonial connections and Indigenous sharedness or generative Indigenous comparisons across various geographies, in spite of the tensions of this comparison. At the same time, Said also advocates for Palestinians' fight toward self-determination as a nation-state fully married to the grammar of the modern world order of nation-states.

The work of the PLO in this era was to represent Palestinians through their representation of the Palestinian cause (*al-qadiya al-Falastinya*) and case. Said's explanation for his use of the word "question" related to his translation of Palestine into a Euro-American context related to the so-called Jewish question within this same context.[63] In Arabic, the translation for *qadiya* is "cause," and the PLO brought the case and the *qadiya* to the world stage. It did so as a national liberation movement that, by the end of the 1970s, fully embraced a nation-state model. But because the watershed moment of 1968 propelled the PLO into being (however the official rhetoric changed, and however Arafat, as the face of the PLO, adhered to this politics of recognition), liberation was and would continue to be a demand and a fluid concept, one that continues to be practiced and debated among Palestinians today. The current irrelevance of the PLO notwithstanding, the contradictions for Said and his writing stand as primary source material for a wide spectrum of political trajectories among Palestinians and other Indigenous peoples. Even though the state-centered formula for liberation through recognition came to define the PLO (in no small part due to Said's influence), the fluidity of representation outside this politics of recognition existed and continues to exist. On this fertile ground, we build these notions of Indigenous sharedness.

It is certainly not my intention to romanticize this era, and certainly not the PLO, but when approaching a comparative analysis, it helps to situate and contextualize this history. We can thus move from the static specter of the red Indian into the more dynamic possibilities of Indigenous solidarities, commonalities, and comparisons. Because the politics of the 1990s and beyond, and the creation and implementation of the PA, has made the history of the PLO a distant shadow, it is important to remind ourselves of how people were thinking and acting in their times, even if we do so critically. The PLO and those within it were, after all, a part of these moments and the movement. What has emerged since has enabled a kind of forgetting of the details and complexities of the PLO's past. Edward Said, arguably more than anyone else in the Anglo-American milieu, translated Palestine to the English-speaking world, and after the early 1990s his rage and unadulterated anger at Arafat allow us to forget his and others' fundamental connections and contributions to the PLO.[64] In his now famous piece, "The Morning After," first published in 1993, after the signing of the Oslo Accords between Israel and the PLO, Said offered us a name for this new political era: "an instrument of Palestinian surrender, a Palestinian Versailles."[65] After this "morning after," Said's writings focused on how Arafat capitulated in Oslo and turned away from his own history and that of the PLO. Historically, one can easily argue that the PLO was and remained the object of destruction and elimination for the Israeli settler regime. As Said explains in *The Question of Palestine*, the mere use of the name Palestine in the US context is provocative because settler violence "transmuted [Palestine] from a reality into a non-reality, from a presence into an absence"; it was incumbent on the PLO to (re)claim the name of Palestine, but to also call Zionism what it was: colonialism.[66] It can be argued that the name Palestine is as provocative now as it was in the 1970s, and part of that narrative must include the PLO, in all of its contradictions.

Arafat at the UN: An Olive Branch and a Gun

Said aimed to render Palestine and the question of Palestine legible and recognizable to a global audience. This goal of legibility is tangible and material throughout *The Question of Palestine*, as it was throughout the work of the PLO in the 1970s. In this self-proclaimed "time of revolution," the political, cultural, and intellectual efforts of various political lines among Palestinians coalesced under the large umbrella of the PLO. While 1968 was a moment when the PLO defined itself, 1974 was the moment when the PLO defined the cause to the international community. It can be argued that the moment this all came together was during Arafat's speech to the UN General Assembly in 1974. In fact, the influence of intellectuals within the orbit of the PLO in that historic moment—when the chairman of the PLO spoke to the UN representing (translating) the Palestinian cause to an international audience— was tangible throughout the speech, as was Palestinians speaking for Palestine. This idea of listening to Palestinian representation was of paramount importance. As I noted earlier, in 1974 the PLO amended the 1968 charter, and one might argue that the amendments made a concerted effort to do as Said did: They made Palestine legible, where legibility also entailed compromise—that is, a version of that Palestinian *cause* that could fit into a kind of world order as a *case*. The moment was important in terms of the contradictions it embodied: liberation within the context of legibility decreed through Euro-American modernity.

Arafat began his historic speech proclaiming a hope for a "new world" represented by a new UN as a place where "oppressed nations, at present bent under the weight of imperialism, may gain their freedom and their right to self-determination." He urged his audience at the UN to recognize this world as the hope for "relations between nations on the basis of equality, peaceful coexistence, mutual respect for other's internal affairs, secure national sovereignty, independence and territorial unity on the basis of justice and mutual benefit." From the very beginning of his speech, Arafat framed Palestine in relation to other third world nations struggling toward independence, and he pleaded with the international community to support these movements. Providing a platform for a Palestinian leader to speak to the world was the proof of something potentially *new* in the *international* for Arafat. Since it is wildly known that Edward Said, like others in the intellectual orbit of the PLO at the time, contributed to the writing of Arafat's speech, Said's and others' echoes resonate in terms of locating Palestine as a hope for a new world, as well locating Zionism within an old world of colonial and imperial oppression: "We live in a time of glorious change. An old world order is crumbing before our eyes, as imperialism, colonialism, neocolonialism and racism, the chief for of which is Zionism, ineluctably perish. We are witnessing a great wave of history bearing peoples forward into a new world which they have created. In that world, just causes will triumph. Of that, we are confident."[67] Echoes of Antonio Gramsci aside (a common rhetorical tool for Said), it is clear that Arafat is offering a framework for the struggle for Palestine that is both legible in international law and in revolutionary third world movements—both a *case* and a *cause*.

Arafat and the PLO, after all, were accountable to a myriad of political trends within the PLO—or so it seemed at the time—that ranged from liberal advocates of diplomacy to radical stalwarts. Much has been said, and much more can be said, about this period; a reflection about the PLO in relation and opposition to the history of resistance is a key part of understanding Palestinian history well beyond the context of the red Indian presented here. Political parties and trajectories outside of and in opposition to the PLO are equally important. I do not claim to offer any new insights here, but I am simply reminding people of the history of the PLO and its big men to remind us that the past matters and its shadow looms large. Arafat at the UN was one of the biggest of men in his time and, ironically, continues to be a ghost long after his time ended:

> In addressing the General Assembly today our people proclaim its faith in the future, unencumbered by past tragedies or present limitation . . . we enlist the past in our service . . . to light our journey to the future alongside other movements of national liberation. If we return to the historical

roots of our cause we do so because the present at this very moment in our midst are those who, as they occupy our homes, as their cattle graze in our pastures, and as their hands pluck the fruit of our trees, claim that . . . we are ghosts without an existence, without traditions or future.[68]

History, the past, and all of their echoes were employed to advocate for a cause and the case of Palestine. Nation building stood as the long shadow over liberation as independence in 1974.[69]

The power of revisiting this moment and (re)reading this text lies in the seemingly contradictory framing of Palestine, but therein lies the potential in thinking through the past—that is, working to understand how the PLO, like Said, and like many of the big men in this big institution, could somehow speak to independence as liberation, as well as plead to an American sensibility in doing so. How people within and supported through the PLO offer us some of the earliest and most lucid scholarly and political definitions of settler colonialism, while also speaking to liberal Americans outside their own ongoing settler colonialism, is very much the contradiction that is Arafat and the PLO. "I cannot now," he said, "forego this opportunity of appealing from this rostrum directly to the American people, as them to give their support to our heroic fighting people. . . . I ask them to . . . recall George Washington . . . heroic Washington whose purpose was his nation's freedom and independence, Abraham Lincoln, champion of the destitute and the wretched, and also Woodrow Wilson whose doctrine of Fourteen Points remains subscribed to and venerated by our people."[70] Appealing to the sensibility of a settler nation like the United States while working to describe Zionism as a settler colonial project is clear indication of the paradox of this historical moment.

Describing Zionist ideology as "Western-style settler colonialism" and "imperialist, colonial and racist," and the Zionist movement as aligned with "world colonialism," Arafat reiterated the PLO's 1968 framework. He summarily rejected both the idea of a "conflict" or the framing of two states while emphasizing the settler colonial nature of Zionism in the very same speech that appealed to Americans under the banner of heroism. Is this irony? Perhaps, but it also contextualizes the specter of the red Indian. Legibility in both a liberal and radical context, like that of the PLO, was a nation-state sovereignty. Locating Palestine alongside postcolonial states in Africa, in particular, offers insight into how in the 1970s Arafat and the PLO envisioned the future he pleaded for throughout his speech: "As we defend a vision of the future, our enemy upholds the myths of the past."[71] Arafat employed even further nuance in a brief tangent in the speech whereby he described the difference between immigration and settlement, immigrants and settlers, while simultaneously describing the Americans fighting British colonialism as heroes, somehow neither immigrant nor settler.

This (in)consistency in diagnosis is not surprising given the context of the position of the PLO in both the third world and the "emerging" world. That is, the PLO was an interesting, albeit contradictory, state-building process. Conceptualization of self-determination as an independent nation-state in Arafat's appeals thus mirrored that of Edward Said: "In my capacity as Chairman of the Palestine Liberation Organization and commander of the Palestinian revolution, I appeal to you to accompany our people in its struggle to attain its right to self-determination . . . [to] regain our property, our land and thereafter live in our national homeland, free and sovereign, enjoying all privileges of nationhood. I appeal to you to enable our people to set up their national authority and establish their national identity in their own land."[72] While this is no excuse for Arafat's blatant erasure of Indigenous peoples beyond Palestine, it does offer context to his political thinking, that of the PLO, and that of the resonance of "searching for a state."

By the early 1990s this search culminated in secret negotiations between the state of Israel and the PLO that resulted in the Oslo Accords. This process later produced the PA, an entity that did not hold or even claim sovereignty in any part of Palestine. Over time the PA reduced self-determination to an exercise in patrimony achieved through proximity to the settler state and allowed itself to play the role of policing resistance and putting down the armed struggle. The PA as an institution is complicated in the same ways the PLO was complicated, because it is also a collection of individuals, but it also the largest employee under occupation and the only means by which people under occupation can interact with Israel, further complicating its endurance in spite of its absurdity. Moreover, it still, however ludicrously, represents the nation-state aspirations of the PLO. The Oslo process and the subsequent PA—as the representative of the settler state—also play a major role in furthering settler colonial fragmentation of the land and people of Palestine. The specter of Arafat's red Indian seemed to be the Palestinian body politic. In refusal of this formulation, and in refusal of disappearance, emerges a new era of Indigenous comparisons, the fertile intellectual ground for sharedness.

Mahmud Darwish and the Red Indian: Departing the PLO

In 1992 Mahmud Darwish gave the world his long-form poem, "Speech of the Red Indian."[73] Darwish, too, had a long relationship with the PLO. Like Said, he was in exile, though his path to exile was different. Their paths intersected in formative ways in the era of the revolution, in the late 1970s and 1980s, that later led to the years of disillusionment.[74]

Publication of his poem in 1992 was itself significant. As Darwish alluded, 1992 represented a connection among Native peoples; it commemorated five hundred years since Christopher Columbus's settler journey and invasion in 1492. It was also the beginning of something profoundly unsettling for Palestinians, for it was the year when the PLO was on the verge of accepting a new "peace treaty" with the settlers that would be, within the following year, formally signed as the Oslo Accords. A narrator of the Palestinian condition, Darwish supposedly abhorred reference to himself as Palestine's national poet. Like Said, he, too, used comparisons to render visible the question of Palestine: Darwish used metaphors and analogies that traveled from Rome to Islamic Spain to Palestine. Darwish, like Said, located Zionist ideology within a boarder framework of Eurocentric modernity and Orientalism. As Abdul-Rahim al-Shaikh meticulously argues, Darwish's poetic and political career can, in part, be described by the ever-changing power of his ability toward a constellation of analogies with Palestine that include grand civilizational intersections from Troy to Andalusia, with an ongoing thread of the Jewish exilic consciousness, as well as Native subjectivity in settler colonial contexts.[75] Given this range of analytic possibilities, Darwish, like Said, presents both the emphatic power of analogy as well as the allure of subsequent political paths it might open in terms of interconnected solidarities. To be sure, Darwish's particular journey into and then away from the PLO, like Said's, provides us with some context for his career in relation to the state of the cause of Palestine within a certain understanding of the valences this particular poem.

Darwish's intellectual and artistic oeuvre defies summary, as does his political journey. His legacy is a school of knowledge; my intention is not to attempt to enter that wildly provocative and formative world. Rather than review everything Darwish offered, I want to focus on this particular poem and how we can and cannot read Arafat's red Indians through it. Perhaps here, within the words of another (and, arguably, the last of his kind of) big man, we can see both the end of an era and an invitation into a new way of being. That is, I want to humbly zero in on this poem and see how it might have worked to move Arafat's red Indian into a new direction for Palestine and Palestinians. Told from the perspective of a "red Indian," Darwish's poem slips between a vague Indigenous identity whose past is marked by the tragedy of white settler colonialism and an Indigenous Palestinian who shares this tragic past. In his unique style of narrating the story, Darwish also reads the settlers (intentions, insecurities, and implications) through his red Indian's voice. Given his theoretical, political, and artistic range, it is interesting that Darwish's settler voice partakes in the discussion about "civilization" that permeates this poem:

> "We bring you civilization," said the stranger
> "We're the masters of time
> come to inherit this land of yours.
> March in Indian file so we can tally you.
> . . . .
> Keep marching, so the gospels may thrive!
> We want God all to ourselves
> because the best Indians are dead Indians
> in the eyes of the Lord."

As the settler makes these claims in the poem, Darwish eloquently articulates the pain of the Native: "So take your time / as you dismember God." Lamentation on loss of Indigenous land as a place of wonder is juxtaposed with the curious vacillation between lament and defiance:

> Don't write commandments
> from your new steel god for us.
> Don't demand peace treaties from the dead.

Earlier in the poem the Native warns that the settler will "need a treaty with our ghosts," and later he emphatically declares, "I refuse to sign a treaty between victim and killer." The clear protest in these lines is coupled with another kind of resistance—a metaphysical one. Darwish finds a way to describe Indigenous return, after slaughter and massacres:

> My people will return in the air
> in water
> in light . . .
>
> We were here first . . .
>
> Here strangers won
> over salt and sea mixed with clouds.
> . . . .
> Here our bodies evaporate, cloud by cloud, into space.

Darwish composes the grand scene as nature versus the modernity of warfare: "Soon you'll raise your world over ours / blazing a trail from our graveyards to a satellite." But as Darwish describes it, there is a curiosity in death, or a questionable finality:

> We'll emerge from the flower of the grave.
> We'll lean out of the poplar's leaves
> of all that besieges you, O White man,
> of all the dead who are still dying,
> both those who live and those
> who return to tell the tale.

Why does Darwish's red Indian speak for, as well as to, the settler? Perhaps this is Darwish's universalism, but perhaps it is also a rejection—like Said's before him—of the era of revolution that was wrought by unrequited political compromises. The settler is actually killing himself as well:

> O white master, where are you taking my people
> and yours?
> . . . .
> To what fathomless pit
> will you descend?

The abyss, it might be argued, is the peace treaty he returns to in the final stanza:

> O you who are guests in this place,
> leave a few chairs empty
> for your hosts to read out
> the conditions for peace
> in a treaty with the dead.

And so, through Darwish's poetics, perhaps this chapter should come to an end in one simple conclusion: The time of their revolution is our legacy, and perhaps from the third world we shall take this into a fourth world radical praxis.[76] From the audacity of Arafat's red Indian, to the heavy work of contextualizing in Said's question of Palestine, we can emerge from the invitation Darwish offers. For the poets have and shall continue to guide the path for hope through despair, analogies rather than comparisons, and forge a path toward interconnected ways of being.

CHAPTER TWO

The Museumification of Place
A Preserved Past in a Settler Present

*Every stolen opportunity I had to return to Jerusalem included a return to Lifta,
my routine of performing a pilgrimage. The first part of the journey begins on
Salah al-Din Street, a familiar location; then I walk down to Wadi al-Joz, back to
the cemetery, and into the Old City. The second part of the journey takes me back
to Lifta. Return is ongoing.*

*On a rare warm day during the winter months, my friend suggested that we
take our time and walk from the bottom of the valley up the entire incline. She understood the pilgrimage well and wanted to help me find new experiences in my
now established routine. Perfect—then we can see what others had seen when they
traveled between villages before settler barriers prevented us from seeing each other
and from sharing our spaces and time.*

*From the heart of the lower valley, the incline is sometimes steep enough to
need to stop, catch your breath, and remind yourself that we are guided by those
who came before us. The terraces and the plant life remind us that we are not
walking among ghosts. I reminded myself of this just as we were immediately
confronted with "conjured ghosts" by settlers filming near a building that had
once been a home. Infuriated by the settlers' ghostly presence, I fell silent, but my
friend went straight up to them and asked, "What are you filming here: some
kind of avant-garde film project?" We kept strolling, and soon I caught a glance
of two more settlers perched on the roof of another home with sound equipment.
Were they recording something to complement the film? It became clearer to me
how easily settlers can cling to the framework of a museum among ghosts. Could
we possibly be falling into that framework as well?*

*I know that all settlers are not the same: The people still living in the houses at
the top of the valley, near the ridge, were living there, not filming, but they are
still settlers. Others, in homes beyond the ridge, lived in rather dire socioeconomic
circumstances, but they are still settlers. They are all settlers, and we are prevented from access to, let alone life in, Lifta. They must have felt haunted—not us,
right?*

*Among the visitors on that day were tourists, some who wanted to see what Pal-
estine used to look like, and others who seemed far less concerned with the past. I
wondered why haunting seemed to overwhelm this place. Why was I made to feel as*

A path in Lifta along the village wall. Photograph by the author.

if I was walking among ruins of a distant, lost, but (partially) preserved past? What was it about the relationship between loss and preservation that dominated what I saw? How was it that I came to the conscious decision to not feel haunted by ghosts and to find solace in the steps of those who came before me? What was it that enabled me to try to change the direction of my seeing and listening that prompted this potential transformation in me? Was it actually a change, or was I finally dismantling the framework of haunting and ghosts that seemed to invade not only the space but how I experienced it? Whose narrative was I shedding in order to find my own?

My hesitation in moving through that space on that day created a kind of crisis in me. Would this hesitation be a kind of refusal? Could it be? If I refused to see how settlers tried to make me feel (for this felt utterly personal to me), was I refusing the beautiful? This is, after all, the picturesque village of Lifta—a place frozen in time and supposedly spared the violence of settler colonial destruction. For whatever their reasons, the settlers did not bulldoze and eventually decided not to occupy the homes in this part of Lifta in 1948, and it remains a real-life opportunity to see what once was. It is all that remains. What does it mean to refuse that which remains? Would such a refusal cause me to lose, or worse, forsake, even the little that remained? Or could this refusal open up an imaginative and then lived space, one not haunted by the past or a confinement to a closed past? One step at a time. We must first understand the layers before we are able to shed them.

In many ways, part of the story of Lifta is trapped within the uniqueness of the settler categorization of it as the "only abandoned Arab village in Israel not to have been destroyed or repopulated since 1948."[1] This is related to the longer history of preservation in the whole of Palestine. Palestine is both destroyed and remains: as a site of preservation, a site of past destruction, and a site of future potential destruction. It teaches us about a people whose memory has been constructed by the destruction that remains, a destruction that is ongoing. It reveals a set of knots around the role and function of preservation in a settler colonial landscape. In Palestine this landscape is further layered by forces of universal heritage and the hegemony of the so-called Holy Land narrative. Lifta is not only a static symbol of settler desires but also an active symbol of ostensible universal heritage. Lost in these settler colonial and universal "humanist" renderings are the Palestinians who perished in or survived this unending past, the ongoing Nakba. Haunting and ghosts, then, belong to the narratives of settlers and are yet another technology of disappearance and erasure.

This chapter traces the work of "museumification" in a longer history of heritage, protection, and preservation. In this chapter, by drawing on Indigenous methods, I show how Lifta unfolds the multiple ways in which protection and preservation are part of a matrix of power that is structurally premised on erasure. The current noise about "preserving Lifta" is a settler project that memorializes destruction. This form of preservation is also contingent on Orientalist imaginings of the Holy Land. How can we understand the matrix of power made possible through active and ongoing dispossession in Palestine? What can it teach us about museumification as a temporal form of settler politics? How can an Indigenous methodological intervention explain and perhaps find a way out of the dilemma of preservation and protection in Lifta? And how, in turn, can that open up possibilities for Palestine more generally?

The relationship between the ancient past and the settler present sheds light on the relationship between archeology and heritage. In settler colonial logic, heritage embodies preservation as a sustained mode of destruction, and preservation forges tenuous and always vulnerable links with an imagined ancient past while veiling the ongoing violence of the present. We can see here how excavation, archeological technologies, and preservation logics function as a way to erase history. Both sides of the Israeli debate on the logic of the preservation of Lifta reveal the imperative of erasure and the centering of the settler state's legitimacy and survival. This situation reveals how liberating refusal can be: Refuse to contest an ancient past with competing mythologies, refuse to fall for settler heritage, refuse to play a game of recognition that was invented on the basis of our destruction and erasure.[2] To show the potential in refusal, I try to show how all three of these trends have led to our confinement and our ghostly presence/absence according to the grammar of settler colonialism.

Lifta is caught in a matrix of impossibilities created by the settler present. This chapter examines what this means by delving into the dilemmas involved in confronting the obstacles that block a Palestinian historical narrative of Lifta. Let us return to the walk up from the lower valley of Lifta that I described in this chapter's opening vignette and to the settlers' use of stolen homes as a backdrop for their avant-garde project of the day. This is a harsh reality, but it is actually also an invitation, albeit one deeply grounded in emotional trauma. Here we can turn to questions regarding the politics of preservation: How does the settler exceptionality of Lifta represent history trapped in the bind of settler frameworks? More important, how can we work to dismantle these frameworks? I turn to Indigenous studies as a guide for how to approach Lifta within a Palestinian narrative removed from the confines of settler power. But first I need to explain the many layers of power shaping Zionist narratives and their imposition on history in/of Palestine more broadly.

The layers of power forced on Palestine and Palestinian history combine Zionist settler fantasy with Orientalist visions of Jerusalem as the Holy Land. Both mythologies focus on who predates whom as a claim to the land. Both mythologies create a complicated version of settler-invoked visions of history. In Zionist mythology, the settlers imagined themselves as "returning Natives." They saw the Palestinians (when they saw them) as squatters, temporary occupants subject to displacement because the land was not considered to be "rightfully" theirs. Because of this return myth, Zionist ideology claimed sovereignty over land that Jewish settlers neither possessed nor occupied, as these claims preceded the establishment of the settler state. This has been referred to by some as the exceptionality of settler colonialism in Palestine. That is, Zionism differs from other cases of settler colonial invasion because embedded in the mythology is not the making of a new people in a "new world" but rather the ideological resurrection of an ancient people in their "old world."[3] While a two-thousand-year return myth is specific to Zionism, it is not exceptional because it is one of many rhetorical tools used to justify settler colonial violence in various geographies, including forced displacement and erasure.

Palestine is subject not only to this specter of Jewish return but also to the category Holy Land, a related kind of religious mythology that has written Palestinians out of the story and the land. Orientalist and Zionist mythologies have worked over time in complementary and contradictory ways, but with the same end: Palestinian erasure. This comes together over time as a specific kind of historical manipulation, but understanding it as a distinctly settler manipulation whereby employing Indigenous methodology in its dismantlement proves useful.[4] That is, understanding culture as heritage as used in structures of settler colonial power in this context is revealing.

While some scholars in the context of Palestine have read preservation as a tool of resistance, it is important to understand how preservation of cultural heritage has a long history in settler societies. Using Elizabeth Povenelli's concept of "the invisible asterisk," Karen Engle describes the bind that Indigenous peoples are put in through heritage protection within the settler state, as well as within a global context of heritage protection: "Heritage makes the least demand on states . . . it asks states to be tolerant, but it also enables them both to appropriate and to accommodate heritage without attending to underlying economic, scholarly and political inequalities of which indigenous people generally bear the brunt."[5] Seen in relation to global Indigenous struggles, this bind is clear in Lifta. In the Palestinian context writ large, the Israeli state is not a settler exception, as it has directly attacked this relationship to the land to sever Palestinian connections to Palestine. Settler colonialism directly targets Indigenous relationality to the land, as noted in the famous equation succinctly explained by Patrick Wolfe: Settlers destroy to replace.[6] Since the Israeli settler state has worked hard to erase Palestinian presence in a myriad of violent ways, preservation in Lifta might seem exceptional. But, I propose, it is only exceptional if we ignore the Indigenous/settler binary, for how the state has incorporated Lifta—as an empty site of unique ruins—still erases Palestinian presence, even though it claims to preserve the past. Settler attempts at the incorporation of Lifta into cultural heritage makes any kind of Palestinian present, and presence, incumbent on the tolerance of the settler state. Understood in this way, settler tolerance is the low ceiling of Indigenous heritage.

History of the Present: The Israeli Court and the "Case for Lifta"

What is "unique" about Lifta's ongoing Nakba? The answer begins in the twenty-first century. In 2003 the Israel Land Authority issued a public tender for construction in the lower part of Lifta, the part of the village that surrounds the natural spring and stretches from the bottom of the valley up through Lifta's terraced hills, which are surrounded above by modern highways. Various actors within the settler state, ranging from the public municipality to private investment firms, offered up visions of how to transform this place nestled on the edge of Jerusalem into a site for urban development.[7] The contentious opening of a bidding process through the public tender sparked a conversation about urban development and preservation. Some Israeli developers sought to "preserve the houses and meticulously restore them."[8] This "meticulous" restoration included transforming remaining structures into restaurants and galleries alongside a public museum. Lifta would, in these scenarios, become a site of settler colonial fantasy par excellence.[9] According to Gabriel Kertesz, one of the Israeli architects who helped design a Lifta redevelopment plan, "There is one approach that nothing should be done, which means the disappearance of the village. Our approach is one involving preservation and revival. The plan requires the most meticulous preservation rules and permits construction only after the historic buildings are preserved and everything is done under the supervision of the Antiquities Authority and a conservation architect."[10] Kertesz describes preservation as revival—acts undertaken to bring back or prevent the final death of the place. Though he mentions preventing the disappearance of the place in this context, this settler position does not come to terms with the continuous violence of settler colonialism and the Nakba. Though rhetorically put into opposition with disappearance, the mode of preservation here actually reifies, guarantees, and attempts to finalize disappearance. Perhaps understanding how disappearance is a part of and not in opposition to preservation is important. Indigenous life, in contrast, can be understood and valued in actual opposition to erasure. Assertions of vitality— ongoing Palestine life in the past, present, and future—actively counter the operative logic of settler colonialism, what Patrick Wolfe theorizes as "the logic of elimination of the native."[11] Left out of this proposal that claims to preserve, however, is a big question: Whom does this prevention of disappearance serve, and for what ends? Kertesz avoids any mention of the very settler colonial structures that wrought the destructive violence at the heart of the process of disappearance in this context of preservation. Given the long decades of colonial violence preventing the return of the original inhabitants of Lifta, this kind of preservation rings hollow, as it is confined to engagement of a place outside history and politics.

In the context of heritage, perhaps it would be useful to find the irony in the spectrum of settler logics between erasure and preservation. The development plan for Lifta created a divide among Israelis regarding what the village represents, what and how that idea of place should be preserved, and for what purpose. An Israeli architect who opposed the development plan, Gadi Iron, envisioned Lifta as a world heritage site: "a 'Garden of Eden' of streams and fruit trees and beautiful landscapes and a site containing important Palestinian architecture."[12] Both architects ignore the destruction underlying "preservation," including the forced expulsion of the people for whom this village was and continues to be home. Here we can read preservation as a tactic of destruction premised on the disappearance of Palestinians. Herein lies the ironic spectrum of settler logics at the heart of heritage. This imperative of Indigenous disappearance, and erasure, is central to heritage work on Palestine.

Immediately after the Israel Land Authority issued its public tender for construction in Lifta, an Israeli-centered discussion and opposition ensued. The original plan (Urban Building Plan Number 6036) called for 212 luxury apartments, along with a commercial and tourist center in Lifta. Bimkom— Planners for Planning Rights, an Israeli nonprofit agency—publicly opposed the planned luxury apartment complex, arguing that preservation "should be the basis of common cultural knowledge for every element of the population of Israel."[13] Preservation went hand in hand with Israeli reconciliation with its own past and, in so doing, found ways to incorporate liminal Native presence void of Indigenous history: "It is appropriate to find ways to strengthen Arab citizens' feeling of belonging to the nation without hurting their connection to their culture and community."[14] Read in the context of the elaboration of the colonial politics of recognition (as examined by Glen Coulthard of the Yellowknives Dene people), the game at play in speaking to a Palestinian Arab history of Lifta is to safely pack history away into a past that is tolerable for the settler present, thereby consolidating settler futures in the sense that a materially preserved Lifta can serve the ongoing settler project.[15]

Even when site proposals are in opposition to the state's tender, the Israeli state remains the context in which planners approach the site. Its symbolic value is exclusively read it terms of its value for the settler state, and with this settler state as the central focus, the question is purely a settler inquiry. Here we see the liberal frame of the settler state and—at its most liberal iteration (a rare phenomenon for Zionists)—concerning how to deal with the memory of Indigenous dispossession and reconciliation with settler crimes for the benefit of sustained settler power over the site. This entire conflict is a settler-centered narrative in which memory serves the settler state's collective conscious, even within the liberal context of a form of recognition through reconciliation.[16] Even the concept of "belonging" is mediated through the settlers and their whims, reinforcing a settler state–centered form of liberal citizenship. Read within Eve Tuck and K. Wayne Yang's erudite concept of "settler moves to innocence," belonging is a central component of settler violence. As they explain, "Disruption of Indigenous relationships to the land represents a profound epistemic, ontological, cosmological violence. This violence is not temporally contained in the arrival of the settler, but is reasserted each day of occupation."[17] This settler-centered narrative is central to the relentless pursuit of control over the land. Settler positionality produces a framework in which settler rhetoric of belonging is both a narrative place and an attempt to control the land. In Lifta this narrative of place becomes a project of preserving what remains. It is simply all about settlers.

Within this framework, the opposition to the proposed development project found nominal success within the Israeli court system. In February 2012 the Jerusalem District Court issued a decision based on a court case filed by a coalition of Israeli supporters and some former Palestinian residents of Lifta and their descendants living in East Jerusalem.[18] The court decided to temporarily halt the real estate tender from proceeding, providing a minor reprieve for the historical site of Lifta. Even in this reprieve, Lifta's place in history is contingent upon the settler trope of it being "the only abandoned Arab village in Israel not to have been destroyed or repopulated since 1948." The judge issued this decision based on a few factors, the most significant of which was the dissatisfaction of the Israel Antiquities Authority with the terms of the original tender. The court decided that the Antiquities Authority should perform a preservation survey before any development plans went forward.[19] The politics of the Antiquities Authority is a foundational component in the longer history of heritage as a settler tool of power in Palestine. Sami Ershied, a Palestinian lawyer representing those in opposition to the proposal, praised the reasoning behind the court's reprieve: "Preservation isn't just preserving buildings, it's preserving heritage. . . . This is a historic opportunity because Lifta's history isn't just that of the Palestinians, it's the history of the State of Israel, for better or worse."[20] That the fate of Lifta was put in the hands of the Antiquities Authority is unsurprising, for the questions of preservation are framed as questions of historical antiquity for the settler state. Preservation is the work of museum makers.

By late 2016 the Antiquities Authority had completed its survey, which the authority lauded as unprecedented in its employment of the latest archeological technologies from the most recent to the most distant past. The survey results were widely circulated in the Israeli press as a historic breakthrough:

"Israel has never reconstructed any former village in this manner."[21] The survey included a digital reconstruction of the village over different historical periods whereby they "discovered" subterranean spaces of ancient history (dating back to the Hellenistic period). This vocabulary of discovery is central to Zionist constructions of national myths that attempt to link the settler present to the ancient past while also eliding what happened in 1948 and, thus, covering over the most radical change to the landscape.[22] Also important in this survey and in the Zionist construction of national myths more broadly is a temporal methodology. A longer historical narrative becomes the basis for measuring the value of material heritage, an equation of value that serves the settler state in terms of both history and historicization. In this sense, Lifta becomes part of a larger linear presentation of "historical development" leading to Zionist modernity. Such a linear narrative also manipulated the work of earlier scholars like Tawfiq Canaan's writings on traditional culture to present settler destruction as the inevitable force of modernity.

Development is the overarching framework of the report. But the bulk of the material presented in the actual survey concerned close architectural examination of the remaining structures in the lower part of the village. Reading through the survey is like reading the findings of an autopsy.[23] Since the official task of the survey was to present documentation "in order to bring about maximum preservation of the place in light of its high values and against the background of the approved 6036 plan," each structure was evaluated in terms of its historical value, urban value, and architectural value. The goal was to present the state with recommendations of whether or not to preserve and how best to preserve structures identified for preservation. The lexicon of value in this survey—value to whom and for what ends—forecasts the dynamic of Indigenous relationship with "heritage" under settler colonialism more broadly. Value, in this survey, was obviously determined by and for the settler state. But this designation of value also has significant consequences outside the framework of settler interests and sensibilities.

The court's temporary reprieve notwithstanding, the Israeli Jerusalem municipality continued laying the groundwork for material change in Lifta. In news coverage of the survey, it remained unclear what the reprieve meant in terms of the occupied structures—that is, the structures in which settlers continue to live on the top ridge above the valley, overlooking the slopes where unoccupied structures remain standing. These upper structures had once been symbols of wealth and expansion: Growing material wealth enabled a construction boom and, by the 1940s, Liftawis lived well beyond the lower valley. The survey did not investigate these specific structures, other than naming and mapping them, and did not at all consider the built expansion beyond them that defied the confined boundaries imposed on Lifta through the survey. It was later discovered, in 2019–20, that deals had been brokered by the state and the settlers occupying these structures on the top ridge that represented the line of building expansion into the upper plateau toward central Jerusalem. These settlers were allowed to remain, and to open up their own small boutique hotels overlooking the valley, and the structures beyond this line toward central Jerusalem were not ever considered, thereby confining the settler-recognized "border" of Lifta to only include the structures in the lower valley.[24]

The "scientific" survey largely ignored the divisions between upper and lower Lifta—that is, the older structures in the valley and the newer ones that were part of the village's westward expansion in the early twentieth century. These newer homes were mostly constructed by people in Lifta as a result of a structural boom of Jerusalem during the 1920s and 1930s Mandate of Palestine era, when families from the lower section of the village built newer and more modern structures on the lands they owned and/or purchased above the valley. By the beginning of the Nakba War (1947), construction and dwelling expanded well beyond the immediate proximity of the lower valley. By focusing exclusively on the structures in the lower valley, the survey ignored Lifta as a lived space in the past and confined the idea of Lifta to only a part of what the people of Lifta knew and experienced and have, since 1948, been denied.

In this context, the survey presented preservation exclusively of what the settlers would recognize as ancient dwellings, as another means of erasing history, preventing return, or even imagining life as it was for generations. The survey, again, akin to an autopsy of a dead body, further reinforced the pastness of Lifta: It could only be a dead entity embodied by the structures that were designated as "abandoned" and devoid of life. For example, the state immediately seized and occupied a majority of homes and structures in upper Lifta after 1948, incorporating them into the settler neighborhood of Romema, beyond those homes on the upper ridge of the valley. In neither the survey nor the Israeli conversation about preservation was specific mention made of these structures or of the expansive lands of the village. People lived in relation to the land in the past without these imposed boundaries, as Lifta was always changing, both as a village and as a people. Restricting the case to only cover the lower valley, even though relationality to land for people in Lifta expanded far beyond the valley, completely ignored people's lived experiences, including the great changes of their social and material realities in the twentieth century. Confining the survey to this lower valley was and remains alien to those who lived in Lifta and to those of us who imagine returning to Lifta. Moreover, several of the homes on the edge of upper and lower Lifta remain in a kind of nominal zone. During the 1950s and early 1960s, the young settler state placed Kurdish and Yemeni Jewish settlers in the newer homes in upper Lifta that were built to incorporate some of the style and appearance of the traditional homes of lower Lifta in a more modern affect over the years prior to 1948. This was another tool in the arsenal of the racism of the settler state: place more vulnerable and expendable settlers (in the racial hierarchy of the state, this meant Jewish settlers not from Europe) in these liminal lines drawn up by the state to create border zones.[25] Until 2020 the status of these liminal structures remained unclear regarding the tender competition for construction in Lifta. Conservationists working for the Israel Land Authority who worked on the survey and advocated for a preservation process clearly saw the value in material preservation of the older structures. But how preservation would work within or against the relatively newer structures and the plans to open the space up for building and reconstruction remained vague. This was further confirmed by the negotiations over compensation the Israel Land Authority was conducting with the descendants of the settler families who had been placed in these homes in the nominal zone between upper and lower Lifta.[26]

While the official case of Lifta remained as it stood in the court decision of 2012, in May 2021, local newspapers began reporting that the Jerusalem municipality was to open up the tender process anew for rebuilding plans in Lifta. This announcement was not based on a court decision, nor did it seem to be based on the Israel Land Authority survey. Rather, it seemed like a response to the popular uprising in Jerusalem that sparked the Unity Intifada throughout Palestine. As of this writing, it remains unclear if the court will allow the tender process to proceed, but what remains clear is that Lifta under settler occupation shall remain subject to escalating and ongoing threats of further destruction, demolition, and material erasure. In the midst of the Unity Intifada, another petition for developing the valley in Lifta was presented to the courts in June 2021 but the details and future of the petition remain unclear. Throughout these legal maneuvers, advocacy in the settler courts remains concerned with the various settler opinions regarding cultural and material heritage and preservation.

Museumification: Heritage as a Global Commodity

In this section, I put the specificities of the case of Lifta in a broader analytical frame, considering the work of culture as heritage and the work of heritage as preservation. Here it is important to maneuver through layers of power from the local to the global, from what we can call settler Orientalism into an international conceptualization of universal heritage. By working through these various and interconnected layers of power, we can better see how Palestinian institutional and individual efforts have worked to confront and overturn disappearance, have succumbed to it as a paradigm, or have somehow navigated between both tensions.

The history of discourse about cultural heritage is vast. But it is helpful to focus on the 1970s, when the notion of built heritage, in particular, dominated urban development studies. This focus was concerned mainly with European cities as a framework for work on cultural heritage in the United Nations Educational, Scientific and Cultural Organisation (UNESCO).[27] Like other aspects of historical preservation, built heritage is a realm of contestation. According to G. J. Ashworth, the work of built heritage in European cities has overwhelmingly been a political exercise of power and a contest concerning the encoding of symbolic meaning to reinforce this power.[28] To explain the changes over time concerning built heritage in European cities, Ashworth introduces the terms "eradification" and "museumification." He offers these concepts in the European context to explain changes toward built heritage. In this context, "eradification" means the destruction or disappearance of material culture (buildings, artifacts, etc.) due to political change. By "museumification" Ashworth means changes in the functional use of material culture brought about by political regimes aiming to transform meanings in a way that might better serve their political and economic purposes. This museumification in a European context since the 1970s is, according to Ashworth, mainly for economic reasons to create or increase the tourist industry.[29] The culprit here is the state and its heavy hand in both destroying and preserving heritage.[30] The main objective of museumification, according to Ashworth, is the bold imprinting of national identities through a systemic decision-making process regarding urban forms. This imprinting (or, perhaps, reworking) of national identity through material culture sets the framework for what to destroy and what to preserve, creating a specific urban landscape as material support for the state's narrative.

Museumification has been theorized in a number of European contexts. As Jean Baudrillard notes, "the museum, instead of being circumscribed as a geometric, is everywhere now, like a dimension of life." Deconstructing this kind of science of knowledge is complex: "In order for ethnology to live, its object must die; by dying, the object takes its revenge for being 'discovered' and, with its death, defies the science that wants to grasp it." Regarding the goal of symbolic and cultural extermination, Baudrillard plays with the notion of mummification in his discussion of museumification, explaining that only by forcing a kind of death on the past can the science of the present emerge: "Because mummies don't rot from worms: they die from being transplanted from a slow order of the symbolic, master over putrefaction and death, to an order of history, science, and museums, our order, which no longer masters anything, which only knows how to condemn what preceded it to decay and death and subsequently to try to revive it with science. Irreparable violence toward all secrets, the violence of a civilization without secrets, hatred of a whole civilization for its own foundation."[31] The history of modernity is thus one of active destruction, the history of conquest and colonialism brought about by European modernity. It is itself a history of death. It is no wonder, then, why the survey of Lifta read like an autopsy.

European cities were the most common urban backdrop for what has been called the "open air museum." These cities represented the studied physical place for the conceptual space of museumification as a commentary on modernity and devastation as well as postmodern epistemology. For Baudrillard this order and ordering represented a radicalized modernity that could only consider itself for itself: "It is here, everywhere, in the metropolises, in the White community, in a world completely cataloged and analyzed, then artificially resurrected."[32] The museum in this formulation sets up the world in the binaries of colonial and civilizational logics. Tightly bound within these binaries, then, the museum erases the cultural, social, and economic exchange that transgressed and challenged these racial and ethnic divisions, usually in violent ways. While the museum has potential to complicate colonial logics, the register of museumification works differently. Outside Europe, and in the context of settler colonial invasion, this register is actually existential because it entails the death of an Indigenous past to create an origin myth for the settler present and to ensure an exclusive settler future.

Museumification's emergence and sustaining popularity as a theorized concept has been in the general areas of architecture, heritage, tourism and urban studies.[33] The intersections of the use of the concept seem to flow around a basic theme: representation. In fact, Michael A. Di Giovine defines the term *museumification* as the "transition from a living city to that of an idealized re-presentation of itself, wherein everything is considered not for its use but for its value as a potential museum artifact."[34] Museums require material to exhibit, but when spaces become places for museumification, the heritage industry can overwhelm the space. Alexandra Mientjes refers to this process with skepticism and asks questions about racist and capitalist intentions.[35] Her questions concern representation and identity, in a city like Amsterdam, where the tourist industry represents the place in a very narrow and particular way. She provides the example of the 2010 appointment by UNESCO of the canal ring of Amsterdam to its World Heritage List. According to Mientjes, this triggered criticism and fears of "disneyfication" where the museumification process becomes an uncontrollable phenomenon of commodification. Having a UNESCO standing creates tourist value and capital, which can add to the museumification process. Even in a European city, a World Heritage Site is the trigger (and result) of a museumification process.

Although similar tensions regarding commodification and capitalist exploitation exist in the settler treatment of Lifta, it is just that point—the settler treatment—that infuses greater tensions into museumification; in the context of Lifta, it is another tool in the arsenal of the settler colonial state to control and erase Indigenous presence. Museumification is another violent form of settler dispossession. The ongoing nature of the Nakba becomes clearer here through museumification: Settler violence embodies both the original dispossession of 1948 and the ongoing dispossession that denies Indigenous belonging to place. Through this violence, Palestinians are, at best, only ghosts in the potential museumification of the ruins in Lifta.

In official and popular discourses about Lifta, use of the term *ruins* has become quite common.[36] But what is lost in only seeing ruins? It seems to be a trap to prevent us from seeing and living the layers of stories over time—the trap of seeing ourselves as the settlers see us, as ghosts confined to a ghostly past. In her work on the imperial formations of ruins, Ann Laura Stoler emphasizes the ongoing process of imperialism as she investigates "dissociated and dislocated histories of the present." Though Stoler does not speak to the particular structures of settler colonialism and the unending violence of the settler state, her focus on the ongoing process of ruination might nevertheless illuminate some thoughts on the making of ruins and how that process is related to the museumification of Indigenous Palestinian history. As Stoler notes, "Ruins are also sites that condense alternative sense of history. Ruination is a corrosive process that weighs on the future and shapes the present . . . the focus then is not on inert remains but on their vital refiguration." Treating Lifta as a site of ruins begs the question of whose history is being written through the various proposals for how to treat the site. More than focusing on memory formation, Stoler approaches the action of the verb form: "Attention here is on 'to ruin' as an active process, and as a vibrantly violent verb."[37] The focus on violence is key here; recognizing settler violence as ongoing can help illuminate the use of the word *ruins* in relation to Lifta rather than accepting the dominant narrative of "uniqueness," which implicitly poses it as an entity somehow independent or separate from Palestinian history. Nevertheless, the vitality referred to needs a subject: For whom, and for what purpose, is this vitality? Can vitality be used to imagine the de-ruination of Lifta?

In this treatment, the discussion of ruins seems to elide more than illuminate the ongoing violence of settler colonialism. Emerging from a particular reading of Franz Fanon's "tinge of decay" in reference to ruins, Stoler's focus on the ruins of empire "provides not a melancholic gaze, but a critical vantage point. . . . Asking how people live with and in ruins redirects engagement."[38] But what of the ruins that people are prevented from living in and that have only been given the option of preservation for settler representation of Indigenous absence? Of course, vantage point and perspective are key elements in Stoler's reflections, but within a settler colonial context the verb "to live with" requires action and access, and must be reexamined. In a settler colonial (as opposed to postcolonial) context of the kind examined by scholars like Stoler, at stake is life itself. But life for whom? And, again, what of the ruins that people are prevented from living in? An engagement over ruins cannot obfuscate that even in preservation ruins are settler representations of Indigenous absence. In this context, we see that even in Stoler's verb "to ruin," in lieu of the noun "ruin," remains centered on the settler. This does not capture the making and maintaining of Lifta's ruins. It might offer a potential path of interrogation regarding the designation of Lifta as ruins, but, even then, the noun attached to the verb is still only about settlers: the settler destroyed, and the settler named their destruction ruins. The notion of a Palestinian Lifta thriving, present and alive, challenges the very use of the word *ruins*. Unlike Stoler, Arielle Azoulay directly confronts the settler violence of Zionism in her conceptualization of ruins through the verbs *return* and *rebuild*: "it is necessary to return to what was destroyed, to the ruins and to the possibilities that were doomed to appear as 'past.' It is necessary to rebuild and resurrect them with and for the sake of those who were colonized and expelled, with and for the sake of their descendants." The juxtaposition of how to approach the story of Lifta not as preservation but rather as vitality means Indigenous return to Lifta. It is not a return to a vanished past of ghosts of what Palestinians once were but a return to the land, a return in which Palestinians live not among ruins but in the vitality of return as de-ruination.[39] It is not merely a question of grammar. At stake here is more than the passive or active voice. Even so, language is key: in a settler colonial lexicon, *ruins* belong to the settler. In a decolonizing lexicon, *revitalization* belongs to Indigenous people. Settler colonialism destroys; Indigenous methods build, through both destruction and vitality. Lifta and life are centered when we employ these Indigenous methodologies. Ghosts haunt, ancestors guide. Settlers are haunted by ghosts, and our ancestors guide us to return to the land. We are of the land and belong to it.

As ruins, Lifta is the static remains of history; it decays through the prism of the colonial settler. A museum—or, more appropriately in this sense, building a museum around ruins—promotes historiography of the past entangled with ongoing settler colonial violence of erasure. As Gerald Vizenor of the Ojibwe people rightly explains, in terms akin to this kind of settler ruination, "representations of the tribal past are more than mere man mimesis and more than the aesthetic remains of reason in the literature of dominance. . . . Simulations are new burdens in the absence of the real imposture of presence."[40] In other words, preservation should be read as a forced absence of an Indigenous presence/present. Likewise, the vocabulary of preservation that pervades campaigns (international and local) to "save Lifta" bring a settler ethos of ruins to the forefront: Settlers want to preserve something that is ruined, and that something must remain lifeless in its preservation.[41] After all, none of these plans included the very idea of life or a return to place. In Lifta, as in all of Palestine, from the river to the sea, the making of ruins is due to ongoing Israeli state destruction. Settler colonial violence continues to ravage the land and people of Palestine, for making ruins is a constant goal of the Zionist military establishment. The various manifestations of these campaigns to "save" Lifta are based on an implicit (or sometimes explicit) recognition of settler presence. They focus on arresting decay via preservation/museumification—without, of course, useful mention of the ongoing violence of Zionist settler colonialism. Preservation, as I have argued here, is incommensurate with restoration (or de-ruination). Preservation serves settlers' interests; restoration serves Indigenous interests. With restoration, Palestinians return to their village, and continue to return—repatriated to a lived space, not a symbolic museum space of a former past. What lies at the heart of this is the distinction in conceptualizing Lifta as a symbol of death rather than a living village thriving beyond museumification and preservation. Restoration as part of a decolonial praxis is the point here, but the struggle in getting there for Lifta and for Palestine begins, in part, with a process whereby we shed the layers of settler epistemic power that have confined us in traps of preservation.

Ruins in the Museum: The Politics of Heritage as Protection

In the museumification of Lifta as ruins, the national and the international are inextricable. One is centered in the United Nations (UN), mainly via

UNESCO and its politics of heritage protection. The other, again via UNESCO, is centered on the nation-states: Israel and, after 2011, the state of Palestine. Palestine's inclusion in UNESCO is related to the politics of the Palestine Liberation Organization (PLO) and its destructive metamorphosis into the Palestinian Authority (PA). In this iteration, Palestine is made to fit into the Zionist and internationally recognized "state of Palestine," based not on land, peoplehood, or questions of sovereignty but rather on a limited and "acceptable" articulation of Palestine. "Acceptable" adheres to the violence inherent in settler recognition and the international politics that created and maintains this politics of recognition. Part of the current rhetoric around Lifta is the claim that it must be preserved as a recognized site of cultural heritage. In fact, one advocacy effort of some working under the rubric of "saving" Lifta has been to pursue UNESCO World Heritage Site nomination. Moreover, it has recently been reported that UNESCO categorization might be the only path left to "save" Lifta.[42]

It might be helpful here to interrogate the notion of "saving Lifta" a bit further and within the larger context of heritage in Palestine. We will return to this concept of "saving" in subsequent chapters, including an in-depth discussion of the Coalition to Save Lifta in chapter 3. In 2021, people through social media employed the hashtag #Save from various locations in Palestine, beautifully complicating the notion and discourse of saving, but for my purposes here I shall confine saving to how it was used in reference to Lifta, before the rebellions of 2021. In this context, saving framed the local and international discourses of preservation in the context of settler colonial notions of saving ruins as the only option available for Indigenous preservation—in other words, the trap of reducing ourselves to ghosts. Nadia Abu El-Haj has meticulously examined how the archeology of Zionist settler colonialism serves the interests of mythmaking using the tools of ruins in the task of Zionist nation building. She notes how, particularly in Jerusalem, the Zionist state uses "ruins . . . to memorialize . . . histories of destruction." In the context of settler mythmaking, then, a question arises: Why is destruction memorialized, and how does preservation serve these interests? This is made more complicated by the precarious position Palestinians are placed in by the reductive choice of "saving" (preservation) as the only choice available to them and their history, most commonly articulated in terms of the narrow possibilities for Lifta. Again, the concept of the Indigenous bind describes the current conditions of Lifta's so-called remaining landscape. This is obviously motivated by the settler politics of recognition, where recognition only comes when the Indigenous people accept their defeat as price of entry into the settler historical narrative and settler present. Here I want to borrow from Abdul Rahim Al-Shaikh's language, where he, like others thinking through a post–Oslo Accords Palestinian context, observes that many fighters within the PLO went from confronting Zionist settler colonialism to negotiating a place for themselves within it. Al-Shaikh laments how cultural production not only followed the lead of these political elites but also paved their way. Using Al-Shaikh's description of this phenomenon, preservation for Palestinians translates into "preserving the moment of defeat" when "the ruined acknowledge their ruination" by being reduced to folkloric and aborted versions of their former selves (another form of museumification) as their only possible way of being.[43] Here preservation connects directly with the politics and culture of defeat that was a competing tension within the PLO (as examined in chapter 1). This ostensibly linked to the specter of "the red Indian" (see chapter 1) and their presumed fate; as proclaimed by Arafat, preservation is about seeking a nation-state and visibility in that imperial context.

And so, in this context, to be saved requires redemption by settler saviors. In other words, the saving of Lifta is bound by settler colonial confines, since only in that limited framework can it be saved. This saving requires that the preservation must be without an active people who resist: a place without a people (a construction that sounds all too familiar for those cognizant of Zionist tropes that describe Palestine as "a land without a people"). This myth was a primary justification for the violence that wreaked the devastation of the Nakba on Palestine and Palestinians. In this way, Lifta is merely a settler symbol, even if it means recognition of past crimes rather than ongoing Indigenous dispossession and ongoing Palestinian vitality. Such narrow recognition ignores the ongoing aspect of the Nakba and relegates it into a past historical event, from life to a lifeless, peopleless museum: museumification. Of course, preservation is one part of the settler colonial spectrum—the history of destruction, denial and erasure of Palestine is a long and violent narrative. My argument here is that while preservation on the surface might appear different, it is actually also a part of that Zionist history of Palestinian erasure and connected to the longer politics of heritage.

The Dilemma of Cultural Heritage: Antiquities and Settler Colonialism

Heritage (*turath*) is a tricky concept in Palestine. It is at once the fodder of a politics of settler colonialism (preservation) and at the same time a politics of cultural resistance and survival. In the Palestinian context, as in other settler colonial contexts, the violence of the ongoing Nakba and relentless targeting of Palestinian presence, as well as cultural and material heritage, can be subversive defiance. In the Arab context, as in other postcolonial geographies of the third world, cultural heritage is often a conversation related to development and responses to modernity.[44] In addition to these colonial implications and legacies, contestation of heritage in Palestine has the added layer of a "biblical" landscape whereby claims to the land and its culture are not confined simply to the reductionist notions of progress through modernity. Stories of, about, and with Lifta are an opportunity to navigate between the colonial complement as well as Indigenous contradiction of the politics of cultural heritage.

Reading Lifta through the framework of "all that remains" in terms of an entity that requires preservation highlights the limitations of cultural heritage but nevertheless explains the loss and drive toward preserving material belonging to a land that was stolen and a presence that is constantly being erased.[45] Given the relentless violence of the settler military's making of ruins in/of Palestine, one might understand the survival instincts embedded in preservation. Reading Lifta against the biblical narratives of Jerusalem, confined by universal and settler symbolisms, also offers a grounded reading of Jerusalem through Palestinian peoplehood. The history of the politics of heritage in Palestine is layered with a thick thread between Orientalist visions of the Holy Land and settler visions of Jewish claims of self-righteous ownership that serve Zionist ideology and mythology. As such, cultural heritage in the official Palestinian context (from PLO to PA) has, in part, been seen through a lens of biblical nativism that was not simply an investment in genealogical claims to the land but a strategy of preserving what was already under threat. This has often meant adopting both Orientalist and settler frameworks through either a technique of complementing or countering them with Palestinian interventions, where both complement and countering have relied on the very same Orientalist and settler frameworks. Caught in the midst of this are Palestinians—across a wide political spectrum— navigating the politics of recognition through response and refusal of this set of colonial and settler colonial claims. Given this mix of forces, political interactions with heritage—read over a long historical trajectory—reveal just how complicated and multifaceted cultural heritage has been.

Here it is important to not only see the history, discourse, and legislation of cultural heritage in Palestine but also to connect that history with the international language of cultural heritage. These histories connect and reveal how the forces of settler colonialism and imperialism have functioned over

time. To be sure, relating this historical journey is an effort to unpack the layers of power and mechanisms at play in terms of the politics of heritage in
Palestine. Very few who have written or worked in cultural heritage in Palestine use the language of Indigeneity or take into full account the context of
British colonialism and the history of Zionist settler colonial violence. In fact,
rarely do scholars working on this aspect even use the critical language of settler colonialism (though they are using the language of settlers). Palestine has
been forsaken in both the local and the global sphere of cultural heritage, in
part because the language of cultural heritage as imagined by the "international community" cannot act outside the narrow boundaries of settler
recognition and the nation-state. Moreover, much of the work of cultural
heritage in the Palestinian context focuses almost exclusively on a post-1967
political framework that has been the basis for what is described as a "two-
state solution to the Israeli/Palestinian conflict." This language and political
context are the foundation of the post–Oslo Accords PA and the inherent
cultural heritage industry that ensued. Yet the impetus of the flourishing of
the industry in the late 1990s and into the new century dates back to the British colonial period, when settler colonialism was firmly and officially implemented in Palestine.

Orientalism and settler colonialism, and the political contexts this duality
produced, informed the discourse and politics of cultural heritage since its
inception as the field of antiquities under the colonial era of the British mandate in the early twentieth century. Though presented in much of the literature as oppositional—settler versus universal—in pursuit of preservation of
heritage in Palestine, I argue that rather than seeing them in contest, it is more
useful to see them in complement. This longer history is important to understand the subsequent eras from the mandate state to the settler state and the
inherent dynamic of the politics of erasure and recognition. Through this history and the constellation of power it has produced, Palestine (including the
land and the people from the river to the sea) has been actively targeted for
destruction to be replaced by a settler-validated and universally legible version of Palestine, of Palestinian identity, of Palestinian culture, and of Palestinian history. In this sense, the UN and UNESCO mirror the politics of the
Israeli state as a settler state, as well as the PA as a governing entity trapped
within this settler matrix. Understanding the governance of UNESCO is part
of this contemporary story, but the politics of the practices of the international lexicon of heritage is part of a longer narrative in Palestine that can be
traced back to imperial intervention in World War I and direct British colonialism. Moreover, the story of tracing global heritage within the frameworks

of a settler grammar is grounded in the imperial and colonial roots of the UN (and the League of Nations before it). In the case of Palestine, this history is crucial background for contextualizing the work of UNESCO and its subsequent partnership since the mid-1990s with local nongovernmental organizations (NGOs) in the occupied territories in Palestine.

Direct imperial intervention first took the form of a "mandate structure" under the administration of the British Empire in the aftermath of World War I and postwar resolutions. Palestine was, therefore, not only affected by the imperial geography of postwar Europe but was directly ruled by it under the guise of a mandate administration, controlled by the British and accountable to the League of Nations but distinctly *not* to the people on and of the land of Palestine. While this imperial history is important generally in the Arab world (where European powers imposed a colonial map through the mandate structure), in Palestine, specifically, this imperial moment also officially introduced a formal adoption of the Zionist settler colonial project in Palestine.[46] The text of the British mandate on Palestine officially adopted Zionism as a core component of its governance by incorporating the entirety of the Balfour Declaration into the preamble of the League of Nations' Mandate for Palestine, specifically supporting the establishment of a "national homeland for the Jewish people in Palestine." The text's labeling of Palestinians as the "non-Jewish indigenous populations in Palestine" indicated their nefarious intentions toward the overwhelming majority of people actually living on the land of Palestine. According to the text, the people on the land should have their "civil and religious rights . . . protected" but were denied any mention of their national or political rights. That is, within this imperial framework, the Native people of/on the land were not recognized within the legal framework that Rashid Khalidi notes, "explicitly refrained from mentioning either the Palestinians as a people or their national self-determination. By contrast, the Jewish minority of the population was so recognized."[47] The mandate, then, did the work of settler colonialism, as it implicitly and explicitly made Palestinians disappear.

Palestinians challenged this notion of limited protection, among many other aspects of the mandate structures, as the connections between the British colonial project in Palestine with Zionist settler colonialism were obvious. The text of the mandate (officially approved by the League of Nations in 1922) married the goals of development toward an independent nation-state for the mandate entity—which the League of Nations' structures claimed to uphold—to the Zionist movement, denying those rights for the people of the land in support of the settlers on the land.[48] In addition to adopting the wording of the Balfour Declaration into the preamble of the text of the mandate, article 6 also included explicit support for promoting Jewish immigration and "close settlement by Jews on the land."[49] The mandate government was, thus, made to be in the service of a settler colonial project that informed its decisions, legislation, and governing practice. This is the moment when Indigeneity as a political praxis was born—not as a question of who was in Palestine first, and not a question of antiquities or ancient history, but about settler colonial invasion and Indigenous erasure.[50] Settler colonialism used the notion of "ancient" in Palestine to obfuscate the obvious, the Indigenous/settler binary as a product of recent modernity in the nineteenth century that was codified in the mandate. Identity claims to "being Indigenous," then, are directly related to settler colonialism. Because the politics of identity are directly related to modernity, here is an invitation to see scholarship at a crossroads: adhering to and falling within frameworks of knowledge production that are inherent to European modernity (in other words, preserving Lifta) or finding another way that is—as I argue throughout this book—an Indigenous methodology that enables us to see Palestinian peoplehood and our history outside the reductive knowledge of settlers. In this conceptualization, Indigenous methodologies help us examine the politics of identity without reproducing or reifying identity politics. In other words, belonging is not something to be proven but instead a way of being that can be nurtured.

Blending of the ancient past (antiquities) with the colonial present (preservation) has been a constant tool of settler power in Palestine. While the majority of the people of Palestine were only mentioned as "non-Jewish communities" in the text of the Mandate for Palestine, antiquities did receive significant attention in terms of legislation, designation, and protection. Even before the formal approval of their civil government under the auspices of the League of Nations, the British, while maintaining postwar military occupation of Palestine, took official charge of "oversight and protection of cultural heritage" through the Antiquities Proclamation of 1918.[51] This was one of the first legislative acts of the British in Palestine, indicating the importance they put into their control of tangible heritage: The British government's interests revolved around the material (tangible) value of their imagined Holy Land.[52] The legacy of the Ottoman laws regarding antiquities (the Ottoman Antiquities Law of 1874 and the Ottoman Law of 1884) were only partially incorporated into the British governance in Palestine. While the Ottoman laws were, in effect, introduced in the late nineteenth century to regulate European access to heritage material and sites, the British used their legal inventions toward building a bureaucracy of control through legislation. Given the symbolic significance of Jerusalem in European Orientalism, ownership of the heritage, as well as the heritage trade industry, are all threads that run through the legislative history of heritage in Palestine since the mandate period.[53] The British Empire, in the words of Lord Allenby, the leader of the military occupation of Jerusalem, proclaimed that they returned to take what was rightfully theirs, echoing the discourse of crusader history.[54]

In addition to the Antiquities Proclamation of 1918, the British also established the Department of Antiquities (DOA) in 1920 and the Palestine Archaeological Museum Antiquities Ordinance for Palestine. Establishing a central bureaucracy for the governance of heritage occurred even before the British formally established their civil government in Palestine. Moreover, through these measures, they created a system of control whereby their government in Palestine was deemed the "protector" of archeological antiquities. Significantly, the 1920 ordinance codified into law the proprietary rights of movable and immovable cultural heritage to the Civil Government of Palestine (the formal title for British rule).[55] In the sense of establishing ownership rights, this ordinance did borrow from the previous Ottoman era laws, with one huge difference: The government that codified its ownership of heritage was a colonial government that was clearly intent on making, maintaining, and owning their Orientalist version of the biblical landscape while also balancing its stated colonial duty toward establishing Zionist settler colonial power on the land.[56] The Antiquities Ordinance for Palestine also stipulated the power of the director of the DOA: Any "building or construction later than 1700 . . . the Director may, by order, declare to be an antiquity" (a previous article stated that objects from before 1700 were deemed automatically protected).[57] The newly formed colonial state set up a large and centralized bureaucracy of heritage and antiquities by establishing a system whereby a centralized power defined heritage, enabled its authority to measure the worth (value and protection) of heritage, and set up a national repository for items and procedures for the official licensing of trade in antiquities.

Article 21 of the League of Nations' Mandate on Palestine further reinforced central state power, which included the DOA's scientific rendering of the field.[58] Several years into their mandate rule, in Antiquities Ordinance No. 51 of 1929, the British also ensured that the DOA exclusively controlled access to excavations and archeological research for members of the League of Nations. This centralized bureaucracy thus legislated exclusive power over the heritage industry, including codifying and controlling the means by which items could be bought and sold and what items were exclusively owned by the state. The 1929 ordinance was thereafter the basis for domestic legislation of cultural heritage throughout the mandate period and continued into the rule of the subsequent settler state.[59]

The legacy of the mandate-era laws extended throughout the twentieth century and well into the twenty-first. In July 1948, only two months after it declared its new settler state, the Israeli government affirmed the 1929 ordinance in the Law and Administration Ordinance, adopting the principles of state ownership and control of antiquities and cultural heritage.[60] Between 1948 and 1967, under Jordanian and Egyptian rule, the West Bank and Gaza Strip, respectfully, fell under similar legislation, also based on the 1929 ordinance. Under Israeli military occupation after 1967, the West Bank and Gaza Strip were subject to military orders that also affirmed state ownership, but with a distinct change from the 1929 ordinance. Rather than issuing permits to export antiquities for each piece, the occupying power issued licenses for dealers, thereby supporting their state-sanctioned version of the heritage industry under settler rule. As Khaldun Bshara points out, this reliance on the 1929 ordinance enabled the long shadow of colonialism throughout the century and into the next: "This colonialist law poses one of the greatest dangers/challenges to architectural preservation in Palestine, since it excludes most of the architectural heritage of the last three centuries from protection."[61] By focusing on anything prior to 1700 CE as the basis for what could be deemed an antiquity, Bshara rightly points out that this was one of several tools in the arsenal of colonial archeology that worked to erase modern Palestinian history. Moreover, in a series of legislative acts after the 1948 Law and Administration Ordinance (in 1978, 1989, and 2002), Israel reinforced the control of all forms of cultural heritage under the governing power of the Israel Antiquities Authority, a centralized department within the state with the bureaucratic power to control all excavations, preservations and conversations in all of historic Palestine.[62]

Settler Colonialism and Orientalism: The Biblical Bind in Palestine

Under the highly centralized bureaucracy of British rule and the growing science of archaeological work (stratigraphic excavations), the trope of Palestine as the Holy Land dominated the imagined geography of the political landscape. The rhetorical power driving biblical archaeology of the mandate era is obviously not confined to the two decades of British colonial rule, but here we can ask the question of how this powerful rhetoric—voiced, controlled, and governed by the largest and strongest empire at the time—worked to erase (and replace) the Native narrative in Palestine. In real time during the mandate, and over time long after the establishment of the settler state of Israel, treating Palestine as a landscape trapped in biblical myths has remained a common trope. Religious mythology, as many have shown, is a powerful weapon in the arsenal of settler colonial movements. Holy Land imagery (a central component of biblical archaeology), along with the rhetoric of "the promised land" as a core function of Zionist mythology (connecting the story of the book of Exodus with Jewish return to Palestine) solidified the marriage between Orientalism and Zionism.[63] As Edward Said explains, Zionist leadership's ability to transform the equation in this imperial moment is instructive to understand the long lasting legacy of what might appear to be a contest between European Christian colonizers and European Jewish settlers over how to read the "holy landscape."[64] Again, rather than focusing on this moment as a contest between two opposing mythologies, it is useful to understand how both forces worked in complement toward Indigenous elimination, erasing Palestinians and the importance of Palestine as a lived space with the presence of a people who lived in/on the land.

Imaginative geography is a key component of Said's original conceptualization of Orientalism. He notes that "there is no doubt that imaginative geography and history help the mind to intensify its own sense of itself by dramatizing the distance and difference between what is close and what is far away." Space, image, and representation come together to make up a story and—what was and continues to be, in the case of Palestine—the forced nearness for a European empire. Herein we find the space of the Holy Land and its place in what Said refers to as a "European sensibility."[65] Over time this forced nearness provided a template that grew into the dominant narrative of narrow rhetorical boundaries for universal imaginations regarding heritage in Palestine. That is, biblical heritage occupied a primary space of rhetorical and practical importance as the cultural heritage in Palestine, imagined as distinctly not belonging to the people of the land. Because the politics of Orientalism and settler colonialism posed the question "Who does this history belong to?" as the hegemonic narrative, later Palestinian efforts often adhered to this framework in making a claim to belonging rather than refusing the entire notion of how this kind of belonging functioned.

The center of the symbolic landscape of the Holy Land was and remains Jerusalem. According to Said, "Jerusalem, a city, an idea, an entire history, and of course a specific geographical locale often typified by the photograph of the Dome of the Rock, the city walls, and the surrounding houses seen from the Mount of Olives . . . [is] too over-determined when it comes to memory, as well as all sorts of invented histories and traditions."[66] Though Orientalist and Zionist stories appear to be in conflict, because they emanated from each other, settler nearness and Orientalist nearness are actually in complement. Moreover, since Zionism was invested in killing the Oriental within and promoting a European ethos, it is a double link that has functioned over time. The imperial military conquest in the World War I in the Arab East and the subsequent mandate government enabled a (re)construction of nearness that is fundamental in understanding how Jerusalem as a symbol needed to be emptied of its Natives to be made viable for European sensibilities. That is, the many layers of the long and complicated history of place in Palestine needed to be replaced with an imagined Jerusalem as the site of European belonging and the lived city of Jerusalem needed to be erased for this to happen. This imagined Jerusalem is a trope of settler history, as Steven Salaita points out, whereby conquest/control of Jerusalem is the belonging myth of settler colonialism in various sites.[67] As Said notes, the "Orient," as a European designation, "speaks through and by virtue of the European imagination . . . it is Europe that articulates the Orient."[68] Following this logic, it is a European project that (re-)creates Jerusalem as a symbol that necessarily needs to rid itself of Palestine and Palestinians. The Holy Land imaginary reduced Palestine to a still image of Jerusalem confined to an equally imagined and still conception of time, and this imagined Jerusalem of spatial and temporal confinement remained an exclusive entity for European consumption. The ensuing conflicts of representation and control, likewise, remained a European contestation. Said explains that Jerusalem's mythological geography quickly took hold universally, even among Palestinians. That is, leaving the mythology in place, this Jerusalem went from being a European invention into a universally accepted vision. The lived space, the actual stories of people of and about Jerusalem, has been erased over time and through this adherence to mythology. To fit into this narrative and present it as a contestation of belonging, the PLO and the PA employed an eerily similar mythology of Jerusalem in the rhetoric of its place as a capital of their desired nation-state.[69] Given this construction of belonging, ongoing return to Lifta—while refusing the settler and Orientalist framing of belonging—renders this need for mythology mute. In refusing these constructions altogether, Lifta and Jerusalem tell the story of the people and how their lives changed over time, including stories related to faith, religion, symbols, and practice. Jerusalem, like Palestine, need not succumb to Orientalist or settler frames to be a land of holy sites. There is no need for mythology in the world of a lived past that is conceived and imagined through a present that nurtures hope for futures of return.

Pursing the stories of this kind of conceptualization of a lived past in Lifta completely removes us from the violent epistemic structures of Holy Land mythology. The Holy Land, in settler Orientalism, was nothing more than a desire for conquest and domination acted out through seemingly endless scenes of the erasure of lived life in Jerusalem. During the mandate era, as Said explains in *The Question of Palestine*, "Zionists made it their claim that Britain was blocking their greater and greater penetration of Palestine. Between 1922 and 1947 the great issue witnessed by the world in Palestine was not, as a Palestinian would like to imagine, the struggle between Natives and new colonists but a struggle presented as being between Britain and the Zionists."[70] The contest then became over *whose* Holy Land as a rhetorical contest between two ideologies born of each other but put into an antagonistic relationship via Zionist political prowess.[71] Palestinians were not only being erased by settler colonialism; their existence was meant to disappear into nothingness, out of history through the marriage between European Orientalism and Zionist settler colonialism.

By creating a tension between Orientalism and Zionism, despite how connected and complementary the visions remained, the heritage industry in Palestine conformed to these boundaries. The mythology of Palestine as the Holy Land and the inherent narratives it has produced has had a hold on archeological inquiries as part of the work of antiquities, as well as cultural production in terms of heritage. As Salim Tamari points out, during the mandate period, under the powerful shadow of Holy Land Orientalism, there emerged a group of men who found a niche for the work of ethnography as heritage.[72] Chiara De Cesari, relying on Tamari's historicization of heritage, asks, "How and when did peasant love and the vernacular culture of the recent past . . . turn into a cherished national heritage, the stuff of museums?"[73] The simple answer, it seems, is through the marriage of Orientalism and Zionism in the same era that antiquities took on a particular form: the mandate period. The more complicated part of this story is how local Palestinians engaged this paradigm.

Beginning in the late 1920s, a group of men, mostly from or located in Jerusalem and all from the bourgeois elite class and led by Tawfiq Canaan, began a project whereby they engaged the Holy Land trope with a distinct local mediation. According to Tamari, "this movement in Palestine was not in reaction to Orientalist discourse, but an attempt to modify that discourse in favour of finding a niche within its confines." Tamari coined the term "nativist ethnography" in his attempt to describe Canaan and his colleagues' work in terms of "establishing sources of legitimation for Palestinian cultural patrimony (and implicitly for a Palestinian national identity)."[74] Though, to be sure, neither Canaan nor his fellow writers described themselves as "nativist" (nor does it seem fair to do so given an understanding of the Indigenous bind), their work in ethnography was clearly focused on a formulation of peasant culture/society in Palestine that they claimed needed to be documented for preservation from the dangers of modernity.

By consistently publishing their work in the *Journal of the Palestine Oriental Society* over the course of the mandate period, this group of local men created a foundation for what became folklore studies in Palestine. As such, Tawfiq Canaan is, in many ways, seen as an originator.[75] Notably a core aspect of this presentation of folklore focused on what Tamari described as "biblical parallelism—that is, they believed that much of Palestinian Arab popular traditions are residual manifestations of daily life as it was described in the biblical narratives."[76] They were focused on living heritage and adopted a reductionist approach positing that by documenting their contemporary peasant culture (of which they were observers) they would preserve the accumulated ancient cultures of Palestine. Based on the assumption that the culture had not essentially changed over time, their work was driven by a fear that due to the forces of modernity in British colonialism, this culture would forever be lost. Unlike (but very much related to) the methodology of ethnographical work of foreign travelers who searched for the living Bible in peasant society and the archeologists who worked to create a local biblical landscape, Canaan gathered his folkloric material as a part of his professional medical practice, which took him all over the countryside as he traced disease patterns and documented treatment. In 1925 a contemporary of Canaan's, Stephan Stephan, published "Lunacy in Palestinian Folklore," in which he pursued his quest toward finding biblical parallels in his collection of contemporary cultural material.[77] Rather than nativism, it seems that Orientalism is a more apt description, as is clear in Canaan's introduction to his 1927 publication of *Mohammedan Saints and Sanctuaries in Palestine*: "The primitive features of Palestine are disappearing so quickly that before long most of them will be forgotten. Thus it has become the duty of every student of Palestine and the Near East, of Archaeology and of the Bible, to lose no time in collecting as fully and accurately as possible all available material concerning the folklore, customs, and superstitions of the Holy Land."[78]

Canaan was a student of Palestine and was recording the paradise that had not yet been lost but which he believed was on the verge of disappearing.[79] Tamari labeled this "biblical nativism," though again, it seems easier to understand this within the politics of antiquities of the mandate that combined an

Orientalist obsession with the Holy Land with a settler colonial movement equally obsessed with controlling (by creating) a religious landscape that would bolster its mythology of belonging. Canaan and his colleagues were obviously motivated by the Holy Land fascination, but they were also working to record and preserve a vanishing present.[80] In real time Canaan observed that the struggle for the Holy Land would exclude the people on and of the land—hence the call for preservation as the battle cry for his work. As a doctor, writer, and ethnologist, Canaan occupied a unique position, and his work (as well as the items he collected and inventoried) is a living archive of popular medicine, a practice he did not necessarily declare dead or useless. That others later used him for this purpose (among others) opens up space for generative and generational inquires. That this preservation was a local manifestation of Orientalist tropes and settler colonial incursion was a consequence of their present that, for them, seemed to foreclose a future. That is, the only refuge was to find the local niche in the hegemonic universal imagery of Jerusalem as a symbol.

Tawfiq Canaan, in particular, is an interesting historical figure because of his own hesitancy with modernity. He was, after all, a doctor who practiced modern medicine but collected material and knowledge of local medicinal and spiritual practices. His act as a collector reveals his own fascination with local practices rather than complete disregard for them as only belonging to an ancient world.[81] Later in his career his politics flourished. In the middle of June 1936, on the seventy-fifth day of the Arab general strike, Tawfiq Canaan authored "The Palestine Arab Cause," in which he describes the state of affairs in Palestine to an English-speaking audience and pleads for the case of Palestine.[82] However hesitant his modernity may have been, it is, nevertheless, painful reading Canaan nearly a century later. For how can we find a place for Palestine among those who worked to erase our very presence? And yet, Canaan tried to do so through his words and deeds.

The Price of UNESCO Recognition:
The Politics of Heritage Protection

Just as it is important to understand the narrative of the long shadow of the British mandate in Palestine, the historical legacy of the origins and mandate of the work involved in UNESCO is equally necessary to understand the formation of an "international community" and the rhetoric involved therein regarding a conceptualization of preservation as museumification. Since its inception, UNESCO has been the main instrument of global governance as far as heritage is concerned. It was formally established in the devastation of World War II and was mandated to "promote peace" through an agenda of education to promote cultural diversity. This language, in a European arena shattered by the violence of fascism, seems a logical European solution to a European problem. UNESCO actually came out of another European organization—the International Committee on Intellectual Cooperation (1936–46). Established by European cultural icons like Albert Einstein and Marie Curie, the International Committee's stated mission was to establish a "state of mind conducive to the peaceful settlement of international problems within the framework of the League of Nations."[83] Given this background, it follows that heritage in all of its forms was first defined through this narrow European framework. This was long ago, obviously, but the more recent past in terms of cultural heritage must be read through this history to understand the tensions involved in contemporary representations of Indigeneity in history.

The definition of heritage, specifically, was enshrined in UNESCO's 1972 Convention Concerning the Protection of the World Cultural and Natural Heritage. UNESCO took on the mandate of defining and protecting "natural and cultural heritage" under the dominant influence of European traditions of archaeology, art history, and architectural conservation. In fact, this moment in 1972 grew out of a kind of imperial compromise made by nation-states within the UN and, in particular, with US support. The World Heritage Convention, as a UNESCO plan, gained support under the auspices that it would be "a Red Cross for monuments, groups of buildings and sites of universal value." At its first meeting in 1977, the World Heritage Committee within UNESCO adopted its operational guidelines, which specified six criteria for the inclusion of cultural heritage sites and four for natural heritage sites on a World Heritage List. Since 1977 the committee has been the main place for decision-making regarding heritage, but—like other functions within both UNESCO and the UN in general—*only* national governments may propose sites for inclusion. That is, only when UN-recognized nation-states nominate sites can the World Heritage Committee consider which nominations to accept.[84]

While not as overtly powerful as other arms of the UN, UNESCO has long been considered the "idea factory" for the organization. Within the sphere of heritage, the World Heritage Centre was established in 1992 to be the focal point within UNESCO, including organizing the annual meeting for the World Heritage Committee and serving as the main adviser to states regarding site nomination. The committee is the actual decision-making body regarding World Heritage Sites, and only state parties hold positions and are represented on the committee (no nonstate actors are or have ever been represented, UNESCO is exclusively intergovernmental). Moreover, only states that have ratified the World Heritage Convention can nominate properties to the World Heritage List. That is, only if Indigenous people have a nation-state supporting them or representing them can their voice reach this international level.

In spite of these origins, the drive toward developing more inclusive categories within these institutions reveals the process that has led to a deeper sense of heritage resulting in the more robust criteria for World Heritage in 1992 and, later, a new bureaucratic instrument within UNESCO: the Intangible Cultural Heritage Convention in 2003. The evolution of these definitions—at least on the surface—has broadened the notion of world heritage including a more expansive definition of cultural heritage resulting in a more global(ized) heritage governance as a shift in the geography of power. This change has been described as a kind of redistribution of power within the UN: "The criteria designed in 1992 for World Heritage cultural landscapes . . . largely reflected values and ideas developed outside continental Europe: an Anglo–North American agenda conceptualizing landscapes as cultural heritage category alongside more traditional categories; and an agenda developed in the post-colonial context of post-settler states in Oceania—one designed to take account of indigenous perceptions of the past." Over the course of several decades, a balance between cultural and natural landscapes occurred within these confines. While the discussions around this issue had more to do with the argument regarding manmade beauty's place in landscape, they eventually opened up space for change in opinion regarding not only cultural landscapes but also cultural heritage. According to Aurelie Elisa Gfeller, an Australian archeologist privy to the internal conversations, "the new cultural landscape criteria were explicitly designed to create an opening for non- or under-represented, notable indigenous, cultures. This outcome resulted from the internationalization of an agenda developed in the post-colonial context of Australia: namely, the recognition of the values of Indigenous peoples in archaeological research in response to their growing political activism."[85] This level of recognition was born out of political pressure and a move to include diverse voices to expand the existing frameworks.

The turn to recognition of Indigenous presence, if not entirely Indigenous rights, was a sign of the times and the product of decades of hard activism on the part of Indigenous peoples, including the international legal recognition of the category Indigenous. The shift in UNESCO was due to a number of factors, including more attention to Indigenous issues that was a direct result of political mobilization by Indigenous peoples. This change came, in part, from Australia and was due to a growing "popularity within the discipline of 'Indigenous archeology.'" Within the Australian context, in light of a growing global trend toward the recognition of Indigenous histories, "the recognition of such systems as cultural heritage at local, state, and/or national levels was crucial to avoid misrepresenting Aboriginal heritage based on 'predominantly monumental' principles, 'conforming to our European traditions of 'heritage,' rather than the values and practices of the creating culture."[86] This recognition, notes Isabel McBryde, came about to promote "national reconciliation."[87] Reconciliation, as Glen Coulthard explains, is well embedded in settler sovereignty and not in Indigenous self-determination; therefore, the limitations of these efforts seem clear from the beginning.[88] The story of the World Heritage Indigenous Peoples Council of Experts (WHIPCOE) is a revealing saga of the efforts to achieve what McBryde describes as recognition for Indigenous participation in the nomination process for World Heritage. The story of WHIPCOE shows that efforts to include Indigenous voices into UNESCO have failed and—more than that—were meant to fail in fundamental ways given the confines and narrow politics of UNESCO.

The concept of *cultural landscape as heritage* began to take form as a shift among the "experts" in and around UNESCO. As a result of this shift, those who held the power to represent heritage identified a need for some kind of advisory body of Indigenous experts.[89] As explained by Lynn Meskell (an archeologist who was a part of the process), WHIPCOE is "a story of a radical, yet failed, attempt to craft a global Indigenous council of experts within an organization founded on nation-state sovereignty." Through the politics of action and mobilization, Indigenous rights and recognition gained momentum in the international arena, resulting in a number of initiatives within UNESCO—in particular, its Millennium Challenges. However inclusive the language sounds, the issue of sovereignty within a transnational world of nation-state agendas still clashed with Indigenous claims.[90] Indeed, the Convention for the Safeguarding of the Intangible Cultural Heritage was an attempt toward a semblance of recognition of Indigenous claims, stating that "cultural heritage does not end at monuments and collections of objects . . . an understanding of the intangible cultural heritage of different communities helps with intercultural dialogue, and encourages mutual respect for other ways of life." Described as "living heritage embodied in people" the notion of cultural heritage was expanded beyond material cultural into more a nuanced understanding of people's culture.[91] This newly formulated concept of culture within UNESCO is in line with its original liberal language of internationalism (and international law) drawing from such sources as the Universal Declaration of Human Rights (1948); the International Covenant on Economic, Social and Cultural Rights (1966); and the International Covenant on Civil and Political Rights (1966). Indigenous representation was not actually—but could be read theoretically—in any of these laws. Though the liberal language of protection and rights seems to include peoples whose lives have been devastated by colonialism, the practical application of this has remained trapped within the language of colonizers embedded in the matrix of settler recognition and the nation-state paradigm.

The failed odyssey of WHIPCOE tells this story of the colonial complications of recognition. WHIPCOE was first proposed in 2000 in Australia, where the World Indigenous Peoples' Forum was held alongside the twenty-fourth session of UNESCO's World Heritage Committee. The idea was quashed a year later in Helsinki. The formation of the committee was a response to a clear lack of involvement by Indigenous peoples in fundamental decision-making capacities regarding protection of their own knowledge and culture. As in other places and contexts related to the UN and international governance, Indigenous as a mere concept and definition was contested from the very beginning.[92] Nonetheless, the formation of a committee of Indigenous experts was actually supported by Australia, Canada, and New Zealand—three prominent settler colonial states. Though there was support for WHIPCOE, the ensuing year included a discussion within UNESCO about the potential role, mandate, and power such a group would be allotted. According to Lynn Meskell, "the ambition was to herald in a new era of relationships between traditional people and the World Heritage system."[93] Issues of state sovereignty, nevertheless, remained an obstacle to the mission. Reports were written, and members of the World Heritage Committee were consulted, but the next meeting of the committee reflected the nationalist concerns of the member states. The UN as a collection of nation-states simply trumped any attempt to involve Indigenous participants and Indigenous political and cultural concerns in the World Heritage process. Both France and the United States, in particular, stood in opposition to the proposal on the grounds of international law and the need to rely on law and state's sovereign rights to define what was Indigenous. Though the United States was not even a participating member of UNESCO between 1984 and 2003, its nuisance objections to creating a body like WHIPCOE (along with France's objections) derailed the process.

Since WHIPCOE was dead on arrival, what other form of direct relationship might exist between UNESCO's World Heritage and Indigenous
peoples? Questions and perhaps opportunities arose after the passage of the
2007 Declaration on the Rights of Indigenous Peoples, but the question of
nation-state sovereignty persists. Within these complexities, it seems that any
kind of instrumentalization of Indigenous empowerment within UNESCO
or the UN frameworks in general is circumspect. To put it in more basic
terms, the settler colonial state would have to recognize, then approve, a move
by Indigenous people toward claiming World Heritage. As such, recognition
would have to be sought by the colonized from the colonizer—thereby reproducing the binary and violence of settler colonialism. Or the settler would
appropriate the Native landscape (as we know settler colonialism works
toward), making the categorization of *heritage* a reinforcement of settler goals
of Indigenous erasure. Just as the importance of the historical genealogy of
"preservation" in Palestine described in this chapter reveals the British colonial context by which it was born, this genealogy of internationally sanc-
tioned forms of "heritage" reveals the central role of the settler state.

Palestine as Universal Heritage

In a show of indescribable settler violence during the Second Intifada, al-
Aqsa Intifada, the enormous force of the settler military (re)invaded Bethlehem (a space it already essentially controlled) in 2001, as it did other
Palestinian cities and towns throughout the West Bank. The tale of al-Aqsa
Intifada is still being told in remarkable ways, as the generation that took up
arms in that moment are now writing and telling their stories. This was the
moment when what Amani Sarahna has described as "the generation of rage"
was at the front lines of resistance to settler colonial power. As she and others
have shown, these stories of rebellion are also ongoing and are a core thread
in understanding Palestinian history as a tapestry of the multifaceted stories
of Palestine.[94] These events also reveal the complications and limitations of
preservation and heritage in Palestine. In April 2001 the Israeli Army wreaked
massive havoc throughout Palestine. With the PA leadership under military
siege in Ramallah, the army used unprecedented levels of violence, placing an
entire population under direct fire; it was a constant assault and an aggressive
military operation that lasted throughout the spring and summer.

These stories of violence are of paramount importance, but it was instead
the material destruction that caught the eye of UNESCO. In Bethlehem, Israeli Army tanks drew the world's attention because the physical destruction

had the backdrop of the biblical landscape—in particular, the Church of the Nativity. The scenes of devastation prompted the UNESCO World Heritage Committee to issue a condemnation of sorts, declaring its anguish over "the destruction and damage caused to the cultural heritage of Palestine" as it emphasized its exceptional value.[95] Immediately thereafter the committee and the director-general of UNESCO offered their direct assistance to the PA's Ministry of Tourism and Antiquities in establishing an inventory of cultural and national heritage, including offering "expert" recommendations about preservation and rehabilitation. The PA celebrated this recognition as at least a nod to Palestinian presence (however low the bar). (This was a sign of things to come less than a decade later.) That is, at least the mention of Palestine can be seen as a form of pushback against ongoing erasure, albeit a curious one. Preservation and heritage as a form of museumification in Palestine is embedded within this moment, as a preface to UNESCO's official recognition of "the state of Palestine" in 2011. The details of the tentative inventory, as well as the anguished means by which UNESCO acted on this issue, are revealing. First the concern about heritage mirrored that of the British mandate rule in Palestine, when heritage was not centrally perceived as a part of local or even Indigenous history; rather, it was connected to "world" civilization within the Holy Land trope. The World Heritage Committee emphasized the importance of cultural heritage in Palestine as a landscape of biblical history—as such, intervention was required.[96] In this way Palestinians were, at best, marginalized, as the history that was in need of preservation was not considered theirs. This was a point made more obvious by the anguish expressed about stones and material relative to the lack thereof in terms of the people on the land who were being targeted, terrorized, and murdered by the settler military.

Though heritage work had a much longer history in Palestine, well before the world witnessed Israeli destruction during al-Aqsa Intifada, the cultural heritage industry took a new turn under the guise of the "peace process." The Oslo Accords brought about a seemingly new distribution of local power and potential wealth as civil society was presented as an alternative governance model under the guise of a state-building process.[97] As Chiara De Cesari explains, "cultural heritage had grown into an important prism through which Palestinians understand their relationship to occupied land and lay claim to it" after the implementation of the Oslo Accords. She notes that, in the new century, cultural heritage transitioned into the language of international development combined with urban regeneration, and she describes how the PA and other organizations in civil society used heritage as the language by which to advance Palestinians rights, part and parcel of an internationally accepted human rights discourse. By neither deeply considering the settler colonial nor Orientalist discourse, however, De Cesari praises these efforts as what she strangely describes as "counter colonial," highlighting state building as the method of Palestinian sovereignty.[98] Since the language of governance and development was employed, what must be asked is whose notion of freedom and self-determination was at play when the goal, according to De Cesari, was a state-building project under occupation. De Cesari, like others, notes the apparent paradox involved in promoting heritage as development with a focus on tourism as the ultimate goal.

Basically, after nearly a century of settler colonial invasion in Palestine and under the weight of Orientalist iterations of the Holy Land, NGOs along with the PA joined the game. The PA-related ministries (and those in them) and the entirety of the NGO heritage industry flourished in the early decades of the Oslo Accords process, as they adopted and then reproduced the very same connections between Orientalism and settler colonialism in a UNESCO-inspired politics of heritage that relied on the Holy Land as its basis. As Khaldun Bshara explains, "the PA followed the sweeping attitudes of making the local heritage universal . . . the driving force of colonizing Palestine through biblical practices of archaeology and the universalizing of the Indigenous cultures and landscapes, laying the grounds for its 'appropriation.'"[99] Here Bshara understands the dangers of "universal heritage," a language that came to dominate the political rhetoric of the PA—that is, "official" Palestinian discourse—after the Oslo Accords. In this framework the PA allowed itself to quite literally set up a competition with Zionist mythology. Peoplehood is not about a state or its heritage industry, but rather is about our ongoing relationality to and with the land.

Though Palestine was recognized as a full member state by UNESCO in 2011, it is important to remember that this recognition came only when the ruling class of the PA was willing to accept and adopt the dominant settler narrative. This recognition also came in the context of the PA's drive toward UN recognition of a state of Palestine. Nominal sovereignty as defined by the Oslo Accords, along with agreements that followed (in particular, Oslo II, the Paris Accords), is nothing but surrender. The PA is a functioning apparatus of nongovernance under the direct instructions of settler rule. In a nutshell, the PA could rule over a population in limited ways but could not actually govern and was made devoid of self-determination. In other words, the Oslo Accords produced a local version of limited Indigenous rule under overall and ultimate power of settler sovereignty. One of the many victims of the PA has been Palestinian peoplehood, because the PA's governing structures, however compromised, have been effective in working to attack the notion of peoplehood and have worked to transform Palestinians into the very categories first invented by the British mandate. That the PA and the NGO apparatus benefiting from the industry heritage would also mirror and then adopt settler frameworks in light of this is not surprising.

Even within this criminal compromise, the PA and UNESCO's recognition still attracted violent imperial response. Immediately following UNESCO's recognition, the United States cut its funding to UNESCO (as it had done before, when UNESCO produced ideas that the US government was opposed to), and the Israelis shut down the UNESCO office in Jerusalem.[100] UNESCO, in spite of both Israel and the United States actively campaigning against it, moved forward with its own politics of recognition and in subsequent years declared various places in the West Bank as World Heritage Sites, including sites in the West Bank towns of Bethlehem (the Church of the Nativity) and al-Khalil/Hebron (the Ibrahimi Mosque); the West Bank village of Battir; and the Old City Walls in East Jerusalem.[101] The naming of Jerusalem and al-Khalil/Hebron, even more than Bethlehem and Battir, was seen as a hugely controversial act on the part of UNESCO and was greeted with great enthusiasm by many Palestinians. The decisions were clearly important moves on the part of UNESCO and show how this particular faction of the UN has been far more aware of Palestinian demands, however compromised those demands have been. Nevertheless, asserting this kind of recognition in one part of Palestine has essentially meant forgoing it in other parts. Palestinians entered the world of heritage not as a sovereign people, and recognition remains arrested within the confines of the imperial demands and settler power. Ongoing Israeli impunity and an utter lack of willingness to hold the settler state accountable for its violence render these decisions hollow. Given the kind of serious damage and continuing threat to heritage sites (as well as everything and everyone Palestinian) that the Israelis pose, many argue that having this form of UNESCO support is a kind of reinforcement for Palestinian safety and (semi)rhetorical sovereignty, albeit in only fragmented parts of Palestine. Zionist violence has proved otherwise.

Even though UNESCO formally recognized a Palestinian state, seeking this kind of international recognition still required significant compromise. Unlike in the West Bank and East Jerusalem (where UNESCO has managed to recognize a nominal if not entirely symbolic form of Palestinian sovereignty), settler colonial geography is the overriding factor in other parts of Palestine—as is the case of Lifta, which lies on the Israeli side of the green line in Jerusalem and is therefore within Israeli sovereignty as recognized by the PA, the UN, and UNESCO.[102] In this context the struggle for Indigenous recognition must be read through this framework both in terms of what recognition entails and what is so fundamentally sacrificed within it. The crucial aspect of inserting Lifta into a debate of cultural heritage regarding Indigenous peoples is therefore a multifaceted challenge, and one that often reproduces settler power. Within the world of nation-states, UNESCO adheres to the boundaries of the settler state. The geographical map in the case of Lifta and its Palestinian heritage is outside any conversation within UNESCO unless it is considered as part of Israeli heritage. Like other parts of Palestine within the green line, if Lifta or anyone claiming to represent Lifta were to seek World Heritage recognition, it would have to be through the Israeli state bureaucracy and the petition would have to be presented by Israel. This quandary of recognition by UNESCO is problematic, at best, because it means that cultural heritage is only Palestinian in certain, ever-compromised parts of occupied Palestine.

Let me return to the beginning of this story and the court case put up to "save" Lifta. Understanding this reading of cultural heritage, we can better see how settler narratives have dominated our history. Museumification is a kind of settler appropriation. It is a settler technique to produce a particular kind of historical narrative. It is a tool that silences Indigenous voices and prevents any real Indigenous presence. This is museumification: In order to save, preserve, or keep ruins, they have to be a part of an Israeli narrative and are confined to a past without return. What is preserved in this context of Zionist settler colonial power is Palestinian defeat and the defeat of Palestine. Preservation as cultural heritage is, therefore, preservation of an unrecoverable past. Even if part of this past is recognized as a crime by the criminals or those who were and are accessories to the crimes (the lessons to be learned from recognition of the crime are for the settlers and their national ethos), the Natives are decoration at best.

In the case of Palestine, we have been presented a choice, which is nothing more than a bind: to be decor for the settler narrative or fit into the universal narrative of the Holy Land. And rather than being choices, these two frameworks complement each other. The biblical landscape narrative, as described by Keith Whitelam, is "the master story of ancient Israel" and, as such, "has been allowed to dictate any construction of the past."[103] The related master story of Palestine as told by the PLO and PA put itself in alignment with and in competition with Zionism's mythologies, feebly countering rather than refusing the framework. Even in UNESCO's recognition of world heritage sites in Jerusalem and the West Bank, Palestinians remain marginalized, if not erased, in the universal call for the preservation of the Holy Land.[104]

Within the impossibilities of return produced by the preservation narrative, the ruins of Lifta are only recognized through a process of museumification where a not so distant past is preserved as a utopia (the Garden of Eden) that can, at best, only be remembered as part of our defeat. As such, the violence of settler history relegates Lifta to a static past that is, at best, about recognition within a settler reconciliation framework and, at worst, completely buried under the construction of a new modern building plan. All of the plans and debates referred to in my discussion of the court case of Lifta can only be considered as being trapped in settler colonial state frameworks that are made to appease the low horizon of settler sensibilities. What was and remains at stake, nevertheless, is the final and complete destruction of what remains of the village. For within this settler framework the only change that can be made to the oft-repeated description of Lifta is that it can either be "preserved" or moved into the category of over five hundred completely destroyed Palestinian villages from the Nakba War. Nevertheless, even with this sense of imminent destruction, one should be cautious about cultural heritage as a savior.

CHAPTER THREE

The Place of Possibilities and Return

History in the Present to Imagine the Future

The lower part of the village of Lifta lies beneath a major highway that commuters take from Jerusalem to Jaffa, on the coast. Lifta has always connected the hills of Jerusalem to the coast, long before these settler highways. Over the last several years, I have received seemingly random text messages on my phone regularly with distant photos of the valley. Friends driving by the valley of Lifta, witnessing a rare beauty of untouched nature that lies nestled in between intersections of several main highways connecting Jerusalem to the coast, send me messages that feel to me like they are saying, "I see you through seeing Lifta." Or maybe they are saying, "I see who and where you come from by bearing witness to what remains." This version of seeing Lifta is as beautiful as it is unsettling: the picturesque village, as a part of the distant past, nestled amid all of the interruptions of modern life and settler mayhem. Never really knowing what to say, I usually respond with a simple emoji. What can one really say to being seen through what might look like ruins? However they interpret what they are looking at—as ruins or as a place of return—there is, nonetheless, still something to see.

Might they see beyond the ruins? Or, even more existential, do they share what they see because they know that I, as one of the millions of Palestinians who are unable to reach Jerusalem (even while living only kilometers away), cannot see it as they can? This seems to be a common way of being in Palestinian exile, and exile is not to be celebrated. Or is it? Is this different? Is it a commemoration? Is it acknowledgment of belonging? Is it sharing a vision of the present about the past in the hope for envisioning collective futures in a form of return? Does return require we reconsider our notions of exile?

Exile is layered through a fragmented reality of Palestinian life. I have grown alienated by the concept and am wondering why. I can see more than so many others, as I can at least reach the parts of Palestine open to my wandering and wondering—feet on the land; some cannot access any part of the land, while others have more access than I do. We may be fragmented by these barriers, but need that mean that we are we forever broken as a people or doomed to reconcile with exile? Our relations with place and with each other can easily be defined by what layer of exile we exist in or with, but isn't that falling into the prison of the present? Exile can impose a feeling of never ending. Each generation has experienced displacement.

A view of Lifta in the present day. Photograph by the author.

We do not only recall the stories of our grandparents' forced exile; we have our own stories as well. In Palestine, exile is inherited and experienced, but is that where the story ends? Must it end?

Maybe this whole line of internal crisis is not a crisis at all, but rather can and should be reframed as an invitation. Can wandering with and wondering about the concept of return help? Can this transform exile into a station on the journey of ongoing return? And with a methodology of ongoing return, can we revisit the concept of exile? What does exile have to do with museumification? What does exile have to do with return as a method, an ongoing way of being?

My phone is also full of landscape photos taken from one of the highways that travel over Lifta. If not for "museumification," there would be no photos to share. But in the midst of a whole world built above a museumified landscape, it sometimes feels a bit like an aberration, more often an irony, and perhaps always a paradox. Can a photo shared with me, an experience relayed, and a visit made together constitute both participation in the museum and an attempt to consider another path—return as an ongoing process?

In this chapter, I explore the power of imagining and imagination as an Indigenous practice that can enable Palestinians to imagine Palestine beyond settlers. I show how Palestinians navigate settler colonial frameworks (while surviving settler violence on the land and militarized structures of settler power) by engaging with and often times performing Palestinian history in various ways. More specifically, I show how from the "case of Lifta" we can shift to the *stories* of Lifta—the lived and ongoing experiences of Liftawis. This chapter serves as the bridge for this journey—from the courts to the people—in order to open up the remaining parts of my journey to the world of possibilities as distant as possible from the hegemonic power of settler epistemologies. While I want to invite us to see beyond settler voices, anxieties, visions, and epistemologies, to imagine a world outside all of this, it is a struggle because so much of what we see and what we can see—in Lifta, in Palestine, and throughout geographies dominated by settler colonialism—is controlled in a myriad of ways by settler colonialism. Part of my invitation is also my struggle. This struggle, in the midst of the overwhelming violence of Zionist settler colonialism, is the underlining (and, I am afraid overwhelming) part of this work.

With a particular focus on the landscape and how the physical space of Lifta has been incorporated into these landscape imaginations—from preservation to perversion to celebration—this chapter explores the power of imagining as an ongoing practice. Indigenous methodology can potentially enable Palestinians to imagine Palestine beyond traditional preservation and into return. In particular, this chapter continues the conversation about a decolonizing turn in relation to a conceptualization of the Nakba within and held by Indigenous resurgence—specifically imagined as Palestinian ongoing return. That is, how can we imagine return and use this power of imagination as the framework for how we understand both the past and present? Here I shift to examine what *remains* in a deeper sense; Lifta's history and fate as a Palestinian place with Palestinian people who call it home is a part of the larger Indigenous narrative of the history of Palestine. The challenge remains: In restoring Lifta to an Indigenous-inspired articulation of Palestinian history, how do we, in turn, facilitate a different sort of return, one of Palestinians to Lifta as part of a collective return to a decolonized Palestine? In understanding Lifta with a focus not on its exceptionality but instead its possibilities, ongoing return is far different from the trope too often put forward in Palestinian historiography—that of "remembering not to forget."

Moving from the background of Palestinian political and cultural landscape and a critique of heritage, the hope is to reveal how work has been done to open up new spaces and geographies of possibilities. How can the contradictions of the Indigenous bind in relation to heritage become generative? That is, can we read the contradiction regarding the work of the projects discussed in this chapter as both resistance and adherence? I ask here that we not confuse normalization with survival. After all, survival and healing are key concepts for people who endure settler colonial violence; navigation and negotiation can be tactical components for everyday life.[1] If this is a methodology for the present and into the future, can it not also be a methodology about how we see the past in the present? Covering several contemporary projects that open up space for this exploration regarding the place of Lifta within the contradictions of the landscape of Palestine, I show how Lifta as a symbol can be more than the "only abandoned Arab village in Israel not to have been destroyed or repopulated since 1948" and become one of many sites of ongoing return.[2] As seen in the work of the case of Lifta, discussed in chapter 2, this chapter works to further conceptualize museumification and understand ways of being that are produced *through* and *against* museumification in the many ways of seeing the place of Lifta. This work is complicated and full of contradictions—so much so that there remains a possibility of openness through, then beyond, even museumification itself. The spatial engagement of Lifta has had several iterations since April 1948, when Liftawis were forced to leave their homes, with a focus on the landscape both as a specific case within Zionist settler colonial framings and a site of Indigenous imaginations.

Time and temporality are again part of a focus on interaction with the place. As such, Lifta has come to represent a kind of reckoning with the past in the settler narrations of history. Palestinians have succumbed to these settler colonial frameworks but also resisted them by performing Palestinian history through strategizing in the present about the future. Within this complex landscape of past and present, these questions will first be grounded in a material discussion about contemporary projects to "save Lifta." I explore the concept of *saving* through an examination of several initiatives from various geographical locations that have taken up the issue of the politics of this place and its representation. Moving from the settler Orientalist confines of "saving as preservation," this chapter is an exploration of how saving is translated into a complicated and complex Palestinian lexicon of action. From a standpoint that intentionally centers the conceptualization of return, what can "saving Lifta" even mean? How does this affect how we imagine belonging? How might one read these various cultural, political, and artistic projects within the frameworks of home and return? Imagining this Indigenous history might enable us to also imagine Palestine beyond preservation and into return.[3] Return as driven by the creative imagination is required to crack through both political discourse and settler epistemologies, as well as the relentless violence of settler colonialism—the ongoing Nakba. Ongoing return is understanding that we move from a frame of saving into one of return, intentionally defying settler time by conceptualizing return as both a process and a way of being. That is, return is not just a structure and not only an event; it is also about our ongoing relationship with the land as a place of life and living, an ongoing return.

#Save

In the spring of 2021 the hashtag #Save erupted across social media. Prompted by a campaign in and about the Shaikh Jarrah neighborhood in Jerusalem, the hashtag went viral. Both in Arabic (#Inqath) and English (#Save), Shaikh Jarrah reached the mental and political maps of people, first throughout Palestine and then across the globe. People like the el-Kurd twins, Mohammed and Muna, who had been on the front lines of family and neighborhood advocacy since their early childhood, were trending in algorithms that even the surveillance technologies of Facebook, Instagram, and Twitter could not silence, though they certainly tried.[4] The story of Shaikh Jarrah is not an anomaly in Palestine, and many, working with this hashtag, showed how the story is one of continued dispossession via the ongoing Nakba. Making that connection and vigilantly disempowering a narrative of exceptionalism, influential threads in the social media campaign centered instead on a Palestinian narrative. Settler violence is ongoing, and the tools of dispossession in Palestine are many—including so-called juridical injustice. In Shaikh Jarrah, as elsewhere where Palestinians live under settler colonial occupation, this has meant confronting a myriad of challenges presented by the Israeli state working to deprive families of their homes. As Mohammed el-Kurd explains, it is actually a terribly simple, albeit horrific, story: The state works to eliminate Palestinians in any and all ways, including notices of eviction and/or demolition.[5] Especially active in Jerusalem, this juridical state is unyielding and relentless. A protest movement in and about Shaikh Jarrah was certainly not new in 2021, as the Israeli state has targeted this neighborhood since 1967. But what was new were the kind of actions of which this hashtag was a part and, in social media, a main engine. From Shaikh Jarrah the hashtag moved to Silwan (#SaveSilwan), another village in Jerusalem under the constant targeting, surveillance, and unrelenting violence of the Israeli state. And from Silwan, the hashtag moved to Lifta. By June 18, 2021, #SaveLifta culminated in a call to descend on the village, performing an act of return.[6]

While working with the concepts of *save* and *saving* over the last several years, I had put together what I considered to be a critique of saving within a settler colonial context. Then 2021 happened. The ever-changing engine of

the ongoing Nakba in Palestine required that I step back from my writing on
Lifta and pay attention to action as a necessary critique of my own thinking.
In other words, I found myself speechless when I realized that saving, a concept I once stood outside of, in a critical position, had transformed into a
concept that provided fuel for the Unity Intifada in the summer of 2021. Part
of understanding what is ongoing, as I learned, is also about how that which
is ongoing is imbricated in critique—never still in the ongoing Nakba in Palestine. In speaking with activists—those behind the mobilization and those
who took part in it—in 2021, and in Jerusalem, in particular, I learned that the
rhetorical role of saving was inherited from a recent past, of which Lifta mobilization had been a major part. While inherited as a language, it also moved
into a new kind of vision and framework for the present. The overlapping
layers of mobilization in Jerusalem are both generational and contested. Neither looking for interviews nor testimony, I sought out what people were experiencing in real time in terms of political mobilization. What I learned
through these conversations with people who described their location as on
the ground and in the streets in Jerusalem put the framework of saving in the
context of what is ongoing. Dahoud al-Ghoul explained to me that if it had
not been for the mobilization on the steps of the Old City and the ongoing
contestations over changes that the settler state attempts to force on the
people of Jerusalem during Ramadan, saving in Shaikh Jarrah would have
looked very different.[7] Though the seeming exceptionalism of Shaikh Jarrah
was imposed from above and from the past (the generational component), it
was both taken up and refused on the ground as the mass protests quite literally moved from the Old City to the streets of Shaikh Jarrah, a few blocks
away.[8] Praxis through practice complicated our conceptualization of saving
by and through contradiction and complement between past and present in
what quickly became nationwide rebellion in Palestine.

If ongoing return is to be a concept that can encompass all of the many
lines of action and atmosphere of constant movement in Palestine and among
Palestinians, then it can and should hold all the seeming contradictions, including the hesitations and the critique of "saving." That said, I ask, why did
the hashtag #Save track as wildly as it did in 2021? A necessary complement to
this question involves the commitment to ongoing action in terms of both
continuities and ruptures. As in mobilization around Lifta, it is clear that saving is one of many components. Saving, therefore, can potentially become a
part of a larger movement. On the other hand, it is also possible to stop at a
static notion of saving, a kind of arrested state of being that adheres to being
in relation to settler sensibilities and desires. Again, survival conceptually and

politically helps us tackle the apparent contradictions inherent in this tension. There is obviously an immediacy attached to the notion of saving: In the case of Shaikh Jarrah, there are eviction notices and demolition orders tendered by the Jerusalem municipality as part of the long arm of the settler state. These orders are not mere threats but the actions of a violent state whose willingness to destroy and erase is its very modus operandi.[9] The fight for survival has, el-Kurd rightly explains, a temporal component, and the immediacy of actions in Shaikh Jarrah were "on the ground" in terms of a court fight against these orders, where saving brought together a constellation of actors, including Israelis and foreigners. The actions were also connected to (or, as el-Kurd put it, must be connected to) the general fight against settler colonial violence in all of Palestine.[10] How quickly the hashtag spread, and how applicable it was to other geographies in Palestine, is testimony to the methodology of settler colonial violence across the geographies of Palestine: from Gaza, to '48, to the West Bank, and, of course, throughout Jerusalem.[11] The campaign in Shaikh Jarrah did not stay confined to this single neighborhood in Jerusalem; by the summer of 2021, the settler military continued to ravage the whole geography of Palestine, including another war from the air and sea on the Gaza Strip.[12] All of Palestine, in this sense, is in need of "saving," but there remains the question of who is being called on in the notion of saving and what is being saved.

As seen among Palestinians (and, in particular, Liftawis who participated in the Save Lifta Coalition [SLC]), there is a broad spectrum of considerations through which to understand saving. Settler colonial violence is everywhere and is wielded against everyone; it is an omnipresent condition that manifests in a myriad of ways. The beauty of June 18, 2021, and the call to action in Lifta sent out under the hashtags #SaveLifta, #SaveSheikhJarrah, and #SaveSilwan was that political mobilization worked from within a Palestinian positionality toward return, even if that return was temporary and implicated by aspects of museumification, implicit in the temporary action of visiting only the lower valley of Lifta, the picturesque vision of what once was. The action of return to Lifta mirrored the immediacy of other parts of Jerusalem like Shaikh Jarrah and Silwan, even within the limitations of saving. Settler colonial fragmentation and settler colonial time are rejected in this move. Though people from Lifta were then in their seventy-third year of dispossession, 2021 was nevertheless an immediate and urgent concern in terms of the application of the hashtag. Time is ongoing, neither ending nor fixed in permanence. In this sense, saving can be considered to be a small but important part of the larger notion of ongoing return. To bring this matter to the forefront, the action planned for June was a call that came from both Shaikh Jarrah and Silwan, two different social and class locations for Palestinians in Jerusalem (among other virtual and actual locations), and was a collective call that included the older generation that had, in part, organized for over a decade under the umbrella of saving. Altogether, this culminated in a connected sense of action between all parts of Jerusalem (rejecting the eastern and western divisions of the Israeli state). This rejection in differentiating between East Jerusalem (where Shaikh Jarrah and Silwan are located) and the rest of the city in this action can be read as an urgent reaction confined to the historical moment. It certainly is that, as seen through the call for a national strike issued on May 18, 2021.[13] But, I would argue, it was not only a rejection (confined to a moment or historical event) but also an ongoing refusal and an assertion of Palestinian Indigenous sovereignty.[14] In Palestine this is about peoplehood—once mainly (mis)translated through the Palestine Liberation Organization (PLO)—becoming, through these actions, a revitalized sense of political mobility. One can read through these intentions that peoplehood in Palestine can transform saving from a static act into an ongoing one. In that transformation we can also find our translation of Indigenous sovereignty as ongoing return. This is most certainly not new, and constantly moving because the tools and rhetoric are always changing.[15] And understanding Lifta through this dynamic can be a central part of the process and reconceptualization toward ongoing return.

The Save Lifta Coalition

Images of the "the remains of Lifta" are as common as nearly any image from Palestine over the last century. As a picturesque scene of a village in Palestine, uninterrupted by people or life or even time, Lifta has come to represent a myriad of views on Palestine. The images here, however, capture something different. The photos tell a story—or, actually, many potential stories. The sign in the second photo—newly placed on the ground—reads Maqbarat Lifta (Lifta Cemetery). The ground is unkempt and, though the second photo does not show it, surrounded by ruins—structures of a village that once was. This is a representation of a landscape of a loss: homes, a mosque, a cemetery, collective spaces surrounding the village spring, the lower valley of a much larger village. These remnants of a former life are far more common.[16] But—as is clear in the second photo—the sign that reads Maqbarat Lifta is new, on white poster paper and written in black marker. How did a new sign marking a historic site get mixed up with the ruins of this abandoned

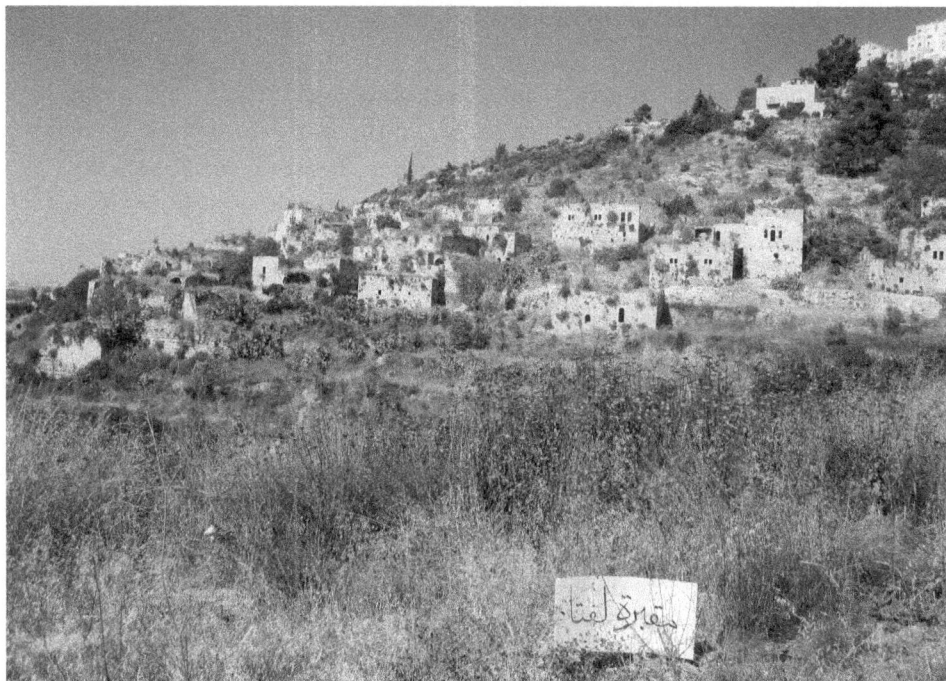

Lifta cemetery, with its handwritten sign. Photograph by Abdul-Rahim Al-Shaikh.

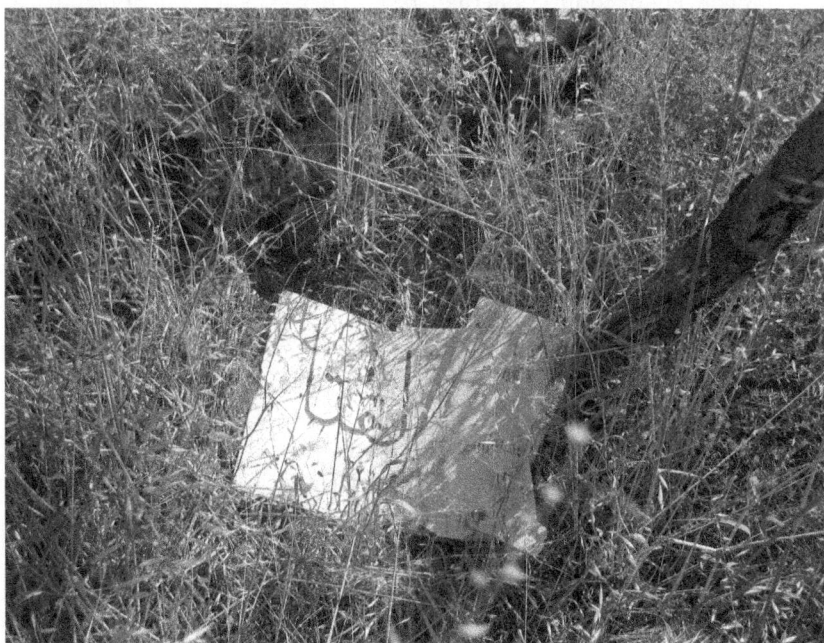

Lifta cemetery. Photograph by Abdul-Rahim Al-Shaikh.

village? How is it that one photo captures Lifta as an exception while the second can potentially release Lifta to forge and nurture connections? As the second photo shows, the sign had been knocked over, or had fallen down, and was lying in the grass; for a clearer photo (the first photo), the sign was placed upright by the photographer and remained as such as far as he knew.[17] Who had originally erected the sign, and why was it there? If it had been knocked down, who did that? The sign, it should be noted, is exclusively in Arabic; that is not the case for other signs in Lifta. These questions and the many stories that resonate from them will guide a complicated understanding of the notion of "saving Lifta."

If resisting museumification is a process embedded in ways of being that are not only inherently anticolonial but also in relation to a decolonizing praxis, then part of this exploration is a process of understanding how the present has been captured by a version of the past. The notion of an unchanging and static past prevents both a present and a future. As Leanne Betasamosake Simpson, of the Mississauga Nishnaabeg / Michi Saagiig Nishnaabeg people, asks, "What's the opposite of dispossession in Indigenous thought . . . ?" The answer, she notes, is "not possession, but connection—a coded layering of intimate interconnection and interdependence that creates a complicated algorithmic network of presence, reciprocity, consent, and freedom."[18] How can this concept of connection, then, be enacted, experienced, or planned at a site like Lifta, where ruins dominate both the actual and the rhetorical landscape? The structures and actual built heritage of lower Lifta have temporarily escaped the settler's bulldozers but still remain captured by the settler's gaze. That is, though these structures remain, they have, nevertheless, been captured in the confines of the "case of Lifta." Here I ask, How can Palestinians act on and in this space outside the settler narrative and within an ethos of Indigenous resurgence, especially in light of the exceptionality imposed on Lifta in this settler narrative? As has been clearly and extensively detailed by Indigenous scholars, settler colonialism as a violent structure denies the very idea of a future for Indigenous peoples. By actively denying a future, settler colonialism has imprisoned them in a present that can only be in relation to a settler version of the past—that is, history, essentially leaving nothing "present." Jeff Corntassel, of the Cherokee Nation, and colleagues describe this process in the introduction to their collection *Everyday Acts of Resurgence*: "Resurgence . . . entails a consciousness of being in a daily struggle to regain rebellious dignity. We are interested in how these transformational moments regenerate and invigorate Indigenous nationhood as well as our community and individual health and well-being."[19] How, then, through a regained sense of "rebellious dignity" can these ruins stop being ruins of a distant past and become something else?

In 2010 a wide range of people and organizations founded the SLC to preserve and stabilize the village. And although the people involved had different (and often competing) politics, the common goal was to prevent the Jerusalem municipality's master plan from being implemented (see chapter 2). At the time, it seemed that the only way to enable this collaboration was through temporality and contingency. Beyond stopping the development project, those involved in the coalition would not always be on the same page, for the wide umbrella of the coalition covered a spectrum of views on Lifta, from resurgent-based organizing that focused on return to recognition-based organizing that focused on static preservation. For some the final goal of the political work was to only preserve the built heritage of Lifta (herein lies the ongoing dilemma of museumification and the untenable relationship between settler desires and Indigenous presence). For others, including many of the Palestinian refugees involved, the coalition was used as a means to prevent further destruction as a first step toward return. For everyone involved, nothing was ever hard and fast in light of the urgency of further settler elimination and constant violence. Over the years, the short-term goals dominated and determined the politics of not only the coalition but work in general around the idea and space of Lifta. In Palestine we must struggle to see beyond the disastrous consequences of settler violence and not read everything through this overdetermined notion of short-term goals.

While interest and various kinds of advocacy had been present around the idea and space of Lifta for years, this particular coalition was officially formed in 2010. Actions articulating a specific "saving" narrative of Lifta circulated around the time of the announcement of the construction plan in 2005, and even before then, but the SLC represented a more organized and sustained kind of mobilization. On its website and in material distributed publicly, the coalition explains its purpose to spare the village from the construction plan (of the Jerusalem municipality) and stand against plans to demolish the village remains and replace them with a residential and commercial complex: "We believe that preserving the village structures, landscapes and environment are crucial for the future of both Lifta and Jerusalem. Our goal is to reach a steady arrangement that will ensure the preservation of Lifta as a local and universal heritage site." The SLC comprises "activists of different backgrounds, including Palestinians, Israelis and other nationalities, men and women, of different faiths and beliefs; those who lived in Lifta, their families and descendants, as well as researchers and political, environmental and social activists. All [are] people [for whom] the future of Lifta, Jerusalem and the area are dear."[20]

As the website further explains, its members may "have different views of the struggle and the future of the village, but all are united in one goal—to save Lifta from destruction and to work together to insure a better future for the beloved village."[21] Formed in earnest in light of the immediacy of the Jerusalem municipality's master plan for further destruction and total erasure of what remains of Lifta, it is no surprise that the SLC has such a wide array of views. In spite of this, the language of preservation dominates the description of the SLC and its work.

As I discussed in chapter 2, preservation and cultural heritage were not only hot political concepts for the settler juridical case of Lifta, but also concepts employed by those who intended to save the village.[22] Herein lies part of the Indigenous bind in relation to heritage and preservation, which once again begs the question, What can come of working under the low ceilings of settler-approved preservation? The SLC offers a loose framework for various people and organizations who came together over an urgent concern for the village of Lifta. The description of the coalition seems purposefully vague in its political goals and covers a wide range of opinions over what should be done with what remains. Questions of representation form the subtext in these concerns: What kind of past are they looking to represent, and for whom? Who has the authority to claim representation? Because of the immediacy of the circumstances, this kind of language serves the primary goal of preventing further change on the landscape. A glance at any photo of Lifta reveals a further immediacy: The landscape is breathtaking, a real-life image of the past made arguably more "picturesque" without large numbers of people populating the area.

Questions regarding why change should be prevented and toward what end would quite obviously produce counterproductive discussions that could severely limit the capacity of the immediate work of the SLC. In some ways, therefore, the coalition came to mirror the symbolic value of Lifta itself, where preservation meant different things to different people with one shared immediate goal: to prevent bulldozers from destroying what remained. By eliding the questions of why and for whom, preservation would continue to prevent return.

Over the subsequent decade, the SLC housed the contradictions inherent in Indigenous survival and endurance in relation to the settler state. The coalition's formation was a reaction to clear and announced plans of the settler state overtly intending further destruction and erasure. Different people who came together under the umbrella of the SLC played various roles in the advocacy for Lifta well before the coalition's formation, and they would continue to do so outside the SLC's boundaries. Many of those involved had been active regarding Lifta—albeit in often contradictory relational positions to village. Presented as a political necessity for an urgent response to the Israeli municipality's intentions, the SLC did not actually do the work of coalition building or even consensus making regarding representation or political work beyond the juridical confrontation with the settler state. It appears that urgent and narrowly conceived plans of response to the municipality's stated intentions took precedent over the contested politics of coalition building. That is, it seems that the public face of the SLC is a calculated grouping of folks from a wide spectrum meant to play the role of representational politics within a settler colonial framework rather than undertaking any concerted effort toward political mobilization and nurturing a collective sense of radical change.[23] While the coming together of this wide array of people under the umbrella of a "coalition" seemed to elide internal differences, it did include Jerusalem-based Palestinian community activists, many of whom are from Lifta and from the local chapter of the Lifta Society, based in the Wadi al-Joz neighborhood of Jerusalem. Moreover, the SLC—however porous the politics were—was a platform. It is important to not interpret the coalition as a single entity, though it might have at times presented itself and performed as such.

While the SLC is difficult to fit into one category, it has, over the years, presented a formal discourse regarding its work through publications and participation in various events about Lifta both inside and outside Palestine. For many of these events, as well as films, exhibitions, and cultural production, members of the SLC have contributed either as individuals or collectively. Given the diversity of projects in terms of politics and process, one must approach the official discourse of the SLC with great care. Nevertheless, the self-description and presentation of the SLC as a coalition is important. First, in order to present a "saving" narrative, the SLC describes what it is working to save: thousands of years of history, "at the western entrance to Jerusalem lies Lifta, the well-preserved remains of a Palestinian village that began to be built, at the latest, in the 16th century." As part of the work for the "case of Lifta," the SLC's language has in many ways been prompted by details of the ongoing court case. That is, the effort to define the historical worth and current value of the place is measured by the context of Israeli settler colonial discourse as an effort toward achieving legibility within that frame. As such, a certain kind of archeological credibility is highlighted: "Archeological and architectural remains attest to a continuity of settlement in Lifta, thousands of

years old, and the site is identified with the biblical Mey Naftoah."[24] Embedded within a well-established settler narrative, archeology—and, specifically,
biblical archeology—is taken directly from the pages of Zionist mythology.

As Nadia Abu El-Haj deftly argues in her explanation of the epistemological origins of "Jewish archeology," the value of Lifta through these kinds of
descriptions not only mirrors the discursive formula El-Haj examines but
also reproduces the narrative of their production. Jewish archeology, in this
sense, is the context and, in order for Lifta to be seen as a worthy landscape,
its origin story must fit nicely into that archeology's disciplinary frame. In this
context, El-Haj explains that the concept of Jewish archeology "highlights the
concrete transformations of the terrain that the work of archaeology brought
about, arguing that those material (-symbolic) reconfigurations are essential
to understanding both the efficacy and contours of the discourse itself and
the durability of national beliefs."[25] Thus, in this confined equation, for Lifta
to be saved, its place must not only be that of the "last abandoned village." It
must also capture a Zionist imagination regarding the ancient past, biblical
archeology based on the Holy Land narrative of settler Orientalism (see
chapter 2).

In the midst of the SLC's lawsuit to stop the Israeli municipality's building
plans, the first major intervention of the district court in Jerusalem was to issue a stay of the plans and call for an architectural, human, and environmental
survey to determine the validity of the SLC's claim regarding the uniqueness
of Lifta. Herein lies the need for creating a sense of continuity that connects
the ancient/biblical past to the more recent past, combined with a sense of
exception for Lifta to justify the need for it to be saved—hence the narrative
produced by the SLC that describes Lifta as "living testimony to the landscape that has been common in Israel for thousands of years of history and is
no more." In the cruel reality of adhering to a settler lexicon in striving for the
validity of the settlers' claim, the SLC's reference to "no more" is the implicit
articulation of the Nakba and dispossession, as well as the erasure of Palestinian presence that is embedded in the Holy Land trope. The Native, in this
instance (as much as the SLC represents the Native), is writing the end of
their own history:

> In our vision, Lifta is a tourist and research site, an open-air museum of
> the built and natural Arab cultural heritage, where one can learn about
> the ancient ways of life that developed here in the Middle East over thou-
> sands of years of history. In our vision, Lifta is a model for the search for
> paths to a shared life of peace, reconciliation and justice, in recognition of

the mutual pain and on the basis of an in-depth acquaintance with the stories, the heritage and the glorious culture of the various communities for which Lifta is a home, a dream and a history.[26]

This vision is about an open-air museum whereby the settler can work to comes to terms with a Native past. Though the historical and social context that she writes about is different, Jean O'Brien describes this kind of historical imagination as "lasting," a "composite extinction narrative that resonated everywhere and whose message was unmistakable: New England Indians had either ceased to exist, or their prospects for the future had dimmed to the vanishing point. The relentlessness of this message of extinction figured crucially in the large project of 'lasting' in which local histories participated." This is not only about the past or narrative connections from the ancient past that fold into a present understanding of everything Indigenous as the past. It is also performing a compromise with the settler vision of time in the landscape of Lifta. Adhering to the settler narrative renders the past into something that can simultaneously fit into the settler state and alleviate the anxiety of what recognition—however precarious—can mean within that state, whose very formation caused dispossession. In this framework, O'Brien explains, Natives are not only denied an actual present and presence but are likewise denied modernity. That is, in order to save a place from further destruction, the argument for saving has to elide and forgive the original destruction. To understand this O'Brien explains the power of verb tenses: "Indian history is narrated in the past tense, which places an additional burden on the possibility of Indian futures. The use of the past tense is a natural choice in historical narration, no one is prone to conclude that the non-Indian peoples whose history is being related have vanished into thin air."[27] While O'Brien is reading texts by the settlers who performed this act of lasting into their own visions of self and place, what is happening in the language of the SLC is, in part, a self-performance of lasting. The people (and Palestinian peoplehood) vanish in this scenario in order for the place—as a historical monument—to be recognizable as something worth preserving. This is part of the official discourse of the SLC, with awareness that within the settler state the tactical use of this discourse was framed by and used for the purposes of judicial advocacy. Discourse and action, of course, are not the same, as we shall see in the subsequent sections of this chapter.

Because of the porous boundaries of the SLC, the projects that engage the space and place of Lifta can almost always be traced back to elements that formed the SLC, either through individuals or concepts. Though the language of the coalition presents Lifta as a symbol resonating the language of Lifta's role as the last abandoned village, the wide spectrum of the politics of people within the SLC and the actual work of the campaign can also, perhaps, become one of many sites of return. Looking at several of the contemporary projects that have embodied these contradictions, we see how to read beyond the limitations of the work of the SLC. It is important to preface this discussion, once again, by an understanding that the coalition, though formed around the concept of saving, was not only that. The court case, of course, helped form the SLC and provided the loose framework for the events that related to the case, but people also acted in ways that did not clearly distinguish between themselves as actors (and more important, as Liftawis) or as representatives of the SLC. Therefore, the SLC's role was usefully vague, and in each of the instances discussed below, some of the same people appear in various, and sometimes, paradoxical roles.[28]

In looking at this contemporary work, I first discuss in detail the 2016 documentary film *The Ruins of Lifta* and cover how Lifta is presented and represented—to whom, by whom, and for what purposes. The SLC as a coalition appears in the film, as do individuals who act both within it and independent of it. I also cover the work of the Israeli nongovernmental organization (NGO) Zochrot, which has led several projects on the land and with the people of Lifta; in Zochrot, the SLC is again present, as are individuals. Finally, I explore the work of architects and artists in three projects (*Re:Lifta*, an architectural studio course on Lifta, and the book series *LIFTA*) to reinforce the contradictions of the work of the SLC and how its discourse is in no way seamless on the ground. While I will try to read these particular iterations of architectural experiments and landscape imaginations in relation to the SLC's work in Lifta, it is important to remain vigilantly aware of the larger context and the wide umbrella that the coalition covers. Specifically, in artistic projects imagining the future of Lifta, both the SLC (as a collective) and individuals (Liftawis) are in conversation with the architects and artists, showing just how wide a political net the SLC casts. The coalition is an amalgamation of several political discourses that are difficult to read in clear distinction from each other; there is always more than one political discourse at play at any given time, and some individuals are active in more than one discourse at a time.

Seeing Lifta for the First/Last Time: The Ruins

Building on a Palestinian complication of the notion of the "vanishing Indian" within the confines of Lifta as the last of the untouched Arab villages in

Israeli settler territory, here I examine the 2016 documentary film *The Ruins of Lifta*.[29] The timing of the film, in both its production and its release, coincided with the court case of Lifta and the work of the SLC. The official description of the film succinctly captures the tensions of the narrative of saving Lifta:

> Lifta, on the outskirts of Jerusalem, is the only Arab village abandoned in the 1948 Arab-Israeli War that has not been completely destroyed or repopulated by Jews. Its ruins are now threatened by an Israeli development plan that would convert it into an upscale Jewish neighborhood.
>
> Filmmaker Menachem Daum—an Orthodox Jew from Brooklyn—sets out to discover the story behind the headlines. He meets Yacoub, a Palestinian who was expelled from Lifta and now leads the struggle to save the haunting ruins of his village from Israeli plans to build luxury villas on the site. Learning that Lifta was once a place where Jews and Arabs got along, Menachem joins Yacoub's campaign in the hopes that Lifta can serve as a place of reflection and reconciliation. This leads to a climactic encounter between a Holocaust survivor and a Nakba refugee amidst the ruins of Lifta.[30]

Again, the repetition of the "only Arab village" and Lifta as ruins foregrounds any interaction with the place of the village. But the added complication in this film is the focus and centrality of the director and his framing of a comparative analysis between the Holocaust and the Nakba. The lens of the camera, and the eyes of the viewer, are those of Menachem Daum; therefore, his perspective is quite literally how Lifta is framed for the audience. The eyes and the footsteps, in terms of the journey, of this film are also those of Daum. He is the constant narrator; his voice describes what the viewer sees and hears throughout the film. Lifta is filtered—through these senses—via Daum and his self-narration. While this kind of deeply problematic framing is not the point of my analysis of treatments of the landscape of Lifta, it is, nevertheless, an invasion into it. In his foreword to the book that explores the limitations and extent of this kind of comparative analysis, *The Holocaust and the Nakba*, Elias Khoury frames the problematic quite well, as a direct product of and part and parcel to Zionism: "The mutual recognition of the Holocaust and the Nakba is an affront to moral sensibilities. A solid moral stance is divorced from any form of negotiation, and the interplay of moralistic mirroring is irrelevant here. In this context, it is meaningless to speak of two sides being considerate of each other, nor is empathy a relevant concept; there merely exists a perpetrator and a victim, and there is no space for equating the two."³¹ Khoury's clear rejection of the paradigm of this kind of comparison speaks to another layer of Zionist settler colonialism that distinctly builds on Nadia Abu El-Haj's argument regarding the making of archeology and the subsequent making of history. Filmmaker Daum puts the Holocaust and the Nakba in relation to each other, and the juxtaposition conceptually confines both in his own reductive and problematically overdetermined way.

Throughout the film, everything Daum covers is presented through this framework; it defines the inherent components of the film, trapping any mention of Lifta within his personal view, which is deeply devoted to Zionist ideology and mythology. Daum travels both in body and in the film throughout the sites of his conceptual journey, from New York City, to Poland (where his family escaped the horrors of the Holocaust), to Jerusalem and Lifta. Never outside the horrors of Europe, Daum presents himself as someone who travels through his own anxieties and even goes so far as to describe Lifta as an "Arab *shtetl*" (the Yiddish word for a small town or village), in direct reference to pogroms in Europe. This reference indicates the relative progress of Daum's journey, from outright denial of Palestinian presence or the right to claim a presence into an anxious internal comparison for himself. Nevertheless, it not only centers his narrative but focuses on the possibilities (albeit very limited) within Zionism to recognize Palestinians. Only in relation to the European horrors of the Holocaust can Lifta be seen in order to consider its value as something to save.

As Glen Coulthard of the Yellowknives Dene notes in the Canadian settler colonial context, the politics of recognition functions within this kind of requirement to ease settler anxieties: Recognition is presented as a goal for Indigenous peoples within the confines of the settler state and "rests on the ability to entice Indigenous peoples to identify (implicit or explicit) with the asymmetrical and non-reciprocal from of recognition—imposed or granted by the settler state and society." Though Coulthard's context is different from that of Palestine, his argument is nevertheless apt, as it clarifies the structured politics that inform *The Ruins of Lifta*, in particular, and Zionist settler colonialism in relation to Lifta as a truncated landscape in general. Because Zionism, like other settler colonial projects across the globe, shares characteristics with the settler state of Canada that Coulthard describes as having a "structure of settler colonialism [that] works toward ... dispossession and preventing self-determination," Palestinian absence is thus read as a reminder of what has passed, and this past can only be read through settler sensibilities.³²

Robbed of a sense of a Palestinian future within a settler reality, Palestinian voices are presented in the film as a Palestinian disruption to Daum's internal narrative. In spite of their limited presence in the film, Palestinian lives are shrouded in the specter of absence, and emerge as potentially *other*. In fact, while strolling down the paths of his own settler anxieties, Daum instrumentalizes Lifta and the voices of people from Lifta as part of his individual backdrop, scenery on the road to his own sense of self. Though he presents himself as riddled with unease, Daum does not allow himself to question his settler righteousness in the present and the future. Rather, his unease is easily rendered as an emotional confusion regarding the past.

The presentation of this form of settler recognition is further reinforced by the "experts" Daum consults along his journey. In the film, he interviews two Zionist historians, Hilel Cohen and Benny Morris, presenting them as interpreters for him and his audience. Both of these Israeli historians are introduced as the experts who can translate how to read through the foreignness of Palestinian presence, including Native responsibility for the violence of the past that led to their forced expulsion, a theory dutifully offered by Cohen, in the film and throughout all of his work as a historian. This fits within the settler dichotomy of denial and recognition—whereas denial is only overcome by the settlers through a kind of presentation of logics whereby the violence of settlers is justified, a classic presentation of "blaming the victims."[33] Both historians also provide the audience (Daum, and by extension, the viewer) with a logic that only a committed colonial Orientalist can produce, mirroring the logics of the settler state in relation to the Natives of the land.

The only Palestinian Daum interacts with in any significant way is Yaqub Odeh, who is a towering figure among Liftawis and is a core participant in the work of the SLC, but his undeniable stature is not because of the coalition.[34] Odeh's trajectory as an active and powerful political figure long preceded the SLC and far exceeds the court case. He is a former political prisoner and an active public figure in Jerusalem, and his familial legacy in Lifta continues to be a focal point of a great deal of local and international activism in and around Lifta. Nevertheless, all that Odeh embodies as a Palestinian from Lifta is completely flattened as the film works to present him exclusively as a Native informant to fulfill Daum's need to seek expertise to translate what Native subjectivity means on the ground. As for Daum's so-called experts, those historians who interpret the geography of Lifta for him, Daum remains committed to voices that can ease his anxieties and provide him with a structure of logic by which he can tolerate someone like Odeh (a difficult task for Daum), even as a flattened character. Once considered part of the new Israeli historians, Benny Morris is not only a historian but has a long public and scholarly legacy of strong advocacy for the Zionist project in Palestine, including as an active apologist and advocate for its violence. Cohen, only slightly more subtle than Morris in his commitment to Zionism and its logic of elimination, is also firmly placed within this broad spectrum. Both are presented in between interactions with Odeh, because the words and deeds, wants and desires of Odeh, as a refugee from Lifta, can only be filtered through Israeli expertise committed to the ideology of Zionism in Daum's view. It is not at all ironic that given how the discipline of history serves the settler narrative, these experts are both historians.

The method of what might be described as "discovering ruins" employed in Daum's film so clearly follows a settler pathology. Daum is useful as an example of settler anxieties well beyond the particularities of Zionism. Specifically, the obsessive manner in which he narrates his own emotional journey is a living text for how settler colonialism not only destroys to replace but also creates an entire pathology for the self-righteousness of settler violence. In spite of this framework, what is most interesting throughout the film are the moments of interruption that occur. For example, though the intention of "casting" Odeh as a flattened character in Daum's odyssey seems clear, the power of Odeh's voice and experience breaks through the flatness. In an early scene in the film, where Daum appears among the terraces in the lower valley of Lifta (after beginning in New York City and traveling through Poland), it seems that the intention of the imposition of Daum's narrated journey into and onto Lifta will prevail. Odeh's presence in the scene and his voice, however, punctures that moment. Odeh's loud scream of "Why?" when he narrates the story of his childhood memories of Lifta and his family's forced expulsion at the hands of Zionist violence resonates in spite of Daum's orchestration.

This scream has brilliantly unintended consequences for Daum's narrative arch, for Odeh is not only screaming in the space of Lifta, as they both stand in the village's beauty, but his voice also interrupts Daum's journey into Lifta as a beautiful protest scream to how Daum managed to finally arrive in Lifta. These kinds of interruptions continue throughout the film. Incapable of veering from his own settler narrative, however, Daum doubles down on his own privilege when he struggles with Native reckoning within the work of the SLC. He appears incapable of seeing beyond his own framework, in spite of the opportunities presented to him to do otherwise. As such, it is clear in the film that Daum wants to impose on his audience his own inability to actually see Palestinians as something other than props in his journey.

The greatest rupture occurs as a break off camera, when Odeh stands on the pathway between the hills that hold his family home. An unknown voice is heard screaming outside the lens of the camera, interrupting Odeh. It is unclear at first, but Odeh stops talking and the audience can faintly hear a male voice registering a complaint, yelling off in the distance about Odeh's intentions to return to, and not merely visit, Lifta. This is a moment in the film that is accidental, and it is not addressed. I suspect the off-camera voice is emanating from one of the lived-in houses on the upper ridge of the valley, where an unnamed and unseen settler speaks out. The camera does not pan up to catch a glimpse of the man, so he remains unseen. Though faint and unclear, the voice interrupts Odeh and speaks to the anxieties that Daum wants his audience to feel with him, the greatest of settler anxieties: Odeh's visit as a prelude to a return to Lifta. A visit, therefore, is the acceptable relation Odeh can maintain with the space of Lifta, but it is acceptable only inasmuch as it is not about a return to Lifta. Though this is an orchestrated move in the film, it is revealing, and it later feeds into the final "reflections" that Daum shares regarding his own anxieties.

After forcing a very uncomfortable and troubling "interaction between victims" between his aunt (as a survivor of the Holocaust) and Odeh (as a survivor of the Nakba War), Daum asks himself whether he has "crossed a line" in potentially favoring the Nakba narrative over those who perished in the Holocaust. This move is both clear and banal in terms of how the settler narrative forces a framework on to Palestinian survival and Palestinian voices. The audience is left with a thought far removed from the place and even the space of Lifta, rendering the scene and the voices that—even in the careful framing of Daum—disrupt the scene as a backdrop for not only settler moves to innocence but, in the Palestinian context, a blatant move to forcing a sense of Indigenous guilt on to the landscape of Palestinians' own erasure. What Daum essentially presents as a struggle is actually far removed from Lifta, reifying the tropes of settler mythology in the settler state. He suggests that either his audience recognize the horrors of the Holocaust in Europe or the horrors of the Nakba in Palestine, as if one must choose between them. This is, of course, not a choice, and not at all a part of Palestinian presence, but instead instrumentalization of one horror to excuse another and justify the violence of forced Palestinian absence. One horror excusing another is the modus operandi of the settler state of Israel.

Framed as a series of his own movements, the film follows Daum on a return visit to Lifta in order to "clean up" the cemetery. He presents the idea of work in the village cemetery as a normal part of his own journey, and connects Poland with Lifta (again reproducing his own version of the Holocaust comparison). When he does bring himself into the space of where he was told the cemetery once existed in Lifta, Daum finds himself without his Native guide. Implying on camera that though the idea of work in the cemetery is his, he complains that this work required Odeh's presence to implement. Eventually, Daum finds that the field near the mosque, the site of the old cemetery, has already been cleaned up. He and his settler companion stand, with the cleaned field as their backdrop, lamenting on the perceived lack of commitment that Palestinians generally show to Israeli willingness to engage them. The complaint, in all its absurd audacity, is registered as Palestinian obstruction to the settler journey. Immediately following this exchange, Daum confronts Odeh, and Odeh's voice once again interrupts with a scream: "Liftawis have a right to clean our own cemetery!"

Trying in vain to maintain his sense of moral superiority, Daum confronts Odeh with questions that reveal his frustrations with Odeh's unwillingness to see the profundity of his own settler willingness to recognize Lifta as a space worth preserving. While Odeh proclaims that the work in the cemetery is part of implementing a kind of connectedness to the land of their ancestors in a younger generation of Liftawis, Daum acts as if he is the one being wronged ethically: "If I understand correctly, I should back off." In spite of Daum's best efforts to make the space of Lifta the backdrop for his own settler journey, Odeh makes a countercase for instilling a groundedness in the land of Lifta for generations who were denied life there. Palestinian (self-)determination annoys Daum because it is completely outside his worldview. This begs an explicit question. In spite of all the efforts to break a relationality with the land, the most substantial inquiry one can discern from this exchange is how the people of Lifta—three generations after the forced expulsion from Lifta—remain in intimate relation to the land of Lifta. Palestinian work to nurture these relations is not only inconceivable to Daum but understood as an obstruction. While it is not at all surprising that settlers consider Native reaction to the land as a threat, the implicit question embedded in this antagonistic exchange remains, Why did Odeh even participate in such a settler fantasy? Odeh, in spite of the manipulations of the film and the politics of recognition framing every moment, is, nevertheless, an elder on the land and continues holding the land for generations to follow.

Discovering a "Post-Zionist" Middle Ground: Settler Desires for Ghosts

One of the greatest and most potentially troublesome contradictions about relation to the space and place of Lifta revolves around the idea and act of visiting the village. Within the Palestinian context, visiting is imbricated with notions of tourism, and all of their complications, as well as a *kind of*, or *temporary*, return. That is, in terms of return, presenting visiting—implicitly or explicitly—as an alternative to actual return can become an obstacle. Since dispossession is a violent break with the land, it follows that visiting can be conceptualized as a journey into the past, before the break. Return may be presented as a way to overcome this temporal barrier, but visiting necessarily complicates the possibilities of return. Nevertheless, return cannot only be a *repossession*—a reclaiming within the frameworks of settlers. Ongoing return includes physical return to the land but also invites us to conceptualize an ever-changing and ever-growing relationality to land and place. Moreover, for Palestinians, and particularly those who have experienced generational dispossession, visiting is a wrought act in and of itself. Because historical dispossession has also resulted in a lack of any kind of access to the land, visiting can be an opportunity, albeit one with grave limitations. As such, the lines between personal, intellectual, and political are blurred in the emotional turmoil of seeking any kind of physical connection to land that has long been denied. Such is the case for Palestinians in relation to their homeland.

Within the matrix of settler colonial power in Palestine, visiting—as navigating access and lack thereof—is also connected to tourism. That is, for Palestinians negotiating with settler colonial borders, one must attempt to "cross" a matrix of obstacles to be *on the land* as one of many components to being *of the land*. Return—even in the form of a visit—can potentially become part of ongoing return. After my own first "visit" to Lifta, I was personally overwhelmed by a tragic sense of confusion: How can one visit *home* when it is a *homeland* we long to return to? Though drawn to the place of Lifta, I was also overwhelmed with a sense of loss in visiting it. When I confessed my sadness to my mother, I discovered, much to my surprise, that although she was born and raised in Jerusalem, only a few kilometers from the valley of Lifta, she only visited Lifta once (in 1968). She also explained to me that her mother, my grandmother ʿArifa, choose not to "visit" the village after her and her family's forced expulsion during the Nakba War. Once I realized that ʿArifa had never visited Lifta after 1948—though, technically, she was able to at least perform the act of visiting after 1967 (as a legal resident of East

Jerusalem, according to the settler state categories). Since both my mother and grandmother had what seemed to me to be an ambivalent and melancholic relationship to visiting Lifta, I realized my feelings were not an isolated phenomenon.

However much it might bring up tensions and confusions around exile and belonging, we need to confront the contradictions of visiting. Perhaps the kind of belonging that the notion of home nurtured was prevented by the act of visiting and maybe this was untenable for 'Arifa. When I revealed my own feelings to my mother, I realized this, too, was something I inherited—from her and from her mother. I could not entirely read their unwillingness to visit Lifta as a complete refusal, for many do visit and do so for a myriad of reasons, also likely full of their own contradictions. Beyond our familial hesitations and contradictions, it also became clear to me that acts of visiting were connected to touring "the ruins of Lifta," a common settler-dominated phenomenon toward reifying museumification. In fact, among Israelis, visiting the museumified ruins of Lifta had been normalized within a Zionist ethos. Groups of schoolchildren taking trips to the village were so common that Noga Kadman included the trips she made to the wadi of the village as fundamental to the landscape of her own memory of experience in Jerusalem.[35] That is, the Israeli landscape of Jerusalem, for some, includes an "out-of-time" version of Lifta. It follows, then, that the SLC and the "case of Lifta" included and received support from Israelis from a wide spectrum of politics advocating against the proposed building plans, including those who wanted to keep Lifta a museum for their own settler fantasies.

Given the settler gaze's promotion of a museumified landscape of Lifta, how has the practice of visiting further contributed to the peopleless symbol of Lifta, and how has that affected our Palestinian understanding of Lifta and the Nakba? Through understanding museumification, the colonial logic behind preservation becomes clear, but what is the settler logic embedded in visiting, and how has that logic contributed to preventing Palestinian relationality to the land? Like the bounded preservation in museumification, settler frameworks limit the possibilities of visiting. Likewise, in doing so, these frameworks also preserve a kind of prehistory of Native life, albeit in a ghostly presence. Ghosts maintain the sense of lifelessness in places like Lifta, mirroring the peopleless landscape, representing a world that once was but can never be again. Rather than dwelling in the process of settler anxieties concerning ghosts, I wonder instead how we interact with Lifta and how visiting has, in part, incorporated settler anxieties into our own ways of being. That is, how have settlers' feelings of hauntedness actually formed or least affected how Palestinians interact with or engage Lifta? In not visiting Lifta, was 'Arifa refusing this kind of hauntedness? I came to realize that what I once considered a strange psychological phenomenon utterly embedded in a personal context was actually far more pronounced and political. Among Israelis, as among settlers elsewhere, haunting and ghostly presences are not unique. Within this settler context, then, Lifta represents a place of haunting and an opportunity for settlers to walk among ghosts.[36] While visiting ruins can be the grounds for an exploration in time that leads directly back to the event of the explosion in the Nakba War, the overall performance of visiting is both an attempt to impose a fixed temporality on Indigenous absence and an impossibility for an ongoing Indigenous presence.

The institutionalization of visiting through tours in a general sense has been a major feature of the work of the Israeli NGO Zochrot. Given the complicated symbolism of Lifta, it is not ironic that the organization was and remains a participant in the case of Lifta. Though Zochrot's participation was indirect, it was also foundational in terms of placing Lifta within a very particular frame of the Nakba. As such, its work was both informed by and helped inform the larger umbrella of the SLC. Zochrot is completely independent from the SLC, but its work in Lifta is both abundant and clearly influential in the organizational structure and ideology of the coalition. Zochrot integrates Lifta and discussions about its history and its space, in various projects, including an oral history project related to its work on Nakba remembering. What is interesting is how Zochrot, and particularly the work of Eitan Bronstein, invokes the issue of Lifta within the larger dynamic of the work of the NGO. This ethos, and the framework it informs, is in relation to a specific sort of engagement with the Nakba, on the one hand, and other actions in Lifta, on the other hand. In describing one of his many tours of Lifta, Bronstein claims, "This is a mirror that reflects who we are, where we come from, and how the State of Israel was founded on the ruins of Palestinian life which existed here."[37]

Like projects that fall within the spectrum of museumification, these tours into Lifta seem as if they are invitations to witness what remains of the past. The complicated figure of Yaqub Odeh also turns up in Bronstein's tours, as a tour guide and a voice who can tell the story of what once was. Bronstein's work is to force Israeli society to face the ghost of the Palestinian Nakba. Again, within the limitations of the politics of settler recognition, perhaps his pontifications on the battle within Israeli society to come to terms with its origins and violent past has its place. Nevertheless, Bronstein's constant use of the past tense is unnerving. Even when he describes Odeh's tour, and especially his introduction, where Odeh pierces the past to invoke a future, Bronstein quotes Odeh, who says, "Welcome to my village, to Lifta.... I hope the day is not long before I will be able to greet you in my house, which will be rebuilt here once again." Bronstein seems to record this as a kind of performance that is a test for the audience because it triggers "the fears and anxieties Jews have concerning the return of Palestinian refugees."[38] Why is a Palestinian future, even in performance, connected—always—to settler anxieties? Visits of this kind are framed through the past tense, ghosts that haunt and a society or nation struggling with its settler origins. Not at all novel to settler societies, the questions that revolve around a visit to Lifta become a series of inquiries regarding what kind of museum it can be transformed into. Museumification and the permanence of settler society are givens in this equation.

Since a main aspect of Zochrot's work is conducting these Nakba tours, there is a kind of conceptualization that has, over time, become institutionalized through the NGO's work. The question, then, becomes, Is this institutionalization of a particular mode of visiting an institutionalization of settler permanence, whereby the Palestinian can be used to temporarily disturb and then be absorbed into settler mythology and pathology? Moreover, does it work to confine—intentionally or otherwise—the violence of the Nakba, which is obviously ongoing, to the past? In an interview in *Middle East Report*, the founders of Zochrot describe visiting as foundational to its work and Bronstein describes how walking through landscapes (as in a tour) was a primary motivation in starting up the NGO:

> I initiated this project [in 2002] with Norma [Musih] and other friends, but it didn't necessarily start intentionally. I was guiding tours to Canada Park, near Latroun, which was occupied in 1967 when Israel emptied and destroyed three villages: Yalu, ʿImwas and Bayt Nuba. The Jewish National Fund founded a park in this area, but the park had no references to the three villages it was built upon. There are all kind of historical signs, but nothing about the Palestinian history. After one of these tours, I just thought it would be interesting to post some simple signs marking an ʿImwas center or the Yalu cemetery. I showed Canada Park in a critical way, how it constructed the landscape for Israelis and neglected, or silenced, the history of the Palestinians there.[39]

As the initiative grew, this kind of approach to a guided tour formed one of the main action points of the organization, in addition to other work: testimonials, a gallery about the Nakba, and a journal titled *Sedek*. In fact, the testimonial and performance components of Zochrot's work is integrated into the tours, as Bronstein explains:

> We work in villages where the former inhabitants are still living in Israel as internally displaced people. We locate people and collect testimonies. Often, our Palestinian colleagues at Zochrot do this work. On the tours, Palestinian refugees from these villages join us and share their stories. In a way, we organize the time and space for Palestinians to tell their stories in their own places of origin. Usually, but not always, their reaction is positive, with lots of emotions reacting to all the Israelis and Jews who want to hear their stories. Usually, this acknowledgement is accepted as a really great experience.[40]

Zochrot's mission, according to its website, is to "promote Israeli Jewish society's acknowledgement of and accountability for the ongoing injustices of the Nakba and the reconceptualization of return as the imperative redress of the Nakba and a chance for a better life for all the country's inhabitants."[41] Zochrot's audience is clearly demarcated as "Israeli Jewish society" and the goal is to confront Zionist national mythology about the state's origins whereby presenting Palestinian witnesses in voice and in performance during these tours is a key element toward this confrontation. While still a marginal part of the tourist industry in the region, these kinds of tours, nevertheless, have a substantial presence locally.[42]

Given the centrality of Lifta in this "pathology of visiting" in the settler colonial context of Palestine, I became interested in thinking about why. In other words, given what we have explored in terms of the symbolic weight of Lifta as "unique" in the settler sense, how does that effect how Palestinians treat Lifta? Has it contributed to our own countermythology, a tendency of performing within the settler framework? Has Lifta been used as a means by which to bring settlers and Natives into conversation? The easy answer to this question is yes. But how much of this conversation is limited to, or even defined by, settler anxieties? While it might be interesting to explore how these visits provide a means by which settler society can eventually come to terms with itself, even that exploration remains confined to the settler context and narrative and a desire for a normalized presence. Beginning and always working with the assumption that settler presence is permanent and that settler anxieties must be considered, we remain in a framework that exists to destroy us and our peoplehood. Most important, how is visiting—in this sense—part of the settler narrative move toward "reconceptualizing" return? What is more interesting is an exploration toward how our employment of

Indigenous methodologies can help distinguish between visiting and return in our Palestinian context. In the coming chapters, I will show how these methodologies help us move from a context of testimonial into one of stories and storytelling and show how Palestinians are not haunted by ghosts but instead guided by our ancestors.[43] But specifically, in this context, I want to emphasize that to ease this methodological transition we have to fully examine and dismantle our own epistemological dependence on (directly or indirectly) accounting for settler anxieties. By working to dismantle the structural confines of this framework, Palestinians can simply refuse to be haunted and refuse the framework of haunting.[44]

Reading through the material generated by Zochrot and their understanding of reconceptualization as focused on return implicates the necessity in Israeli Jewish society to come to terms with the idea of Palestinian return, if not the reality of its material implementation. Presenting return within a framework of transitional justice based on a challenge to Israeli discourse might be considered a critical move, but the critique centers and, thereby, remains dependent on the settler state and stuck within its confines. According to Norma Musih (cofounder, with Bronstein, of Zochrot), "We've spoken out quite a bit about the right of return, and we participate every year in the March of Return traditionally held by internally displaced Palestinians on Israel's Independence Day. Because we are not afraid of this issue, in some senses, we provide a model for Jews of how to engage with it."[45] The action, then, is clearly based on, as Musih says, providing their audience with an alternative way of understanding. A clear departure for an Israeli organization, dealing with all of Palestine (and not only the lands occupied in the 1967 war under the framework of occupation) has been Zochrot's major contribution to sparking a conversation among Israeli Jews about the nature of their state and the violence and destruction upon which it was founded.

The bold claim of working to provide a "model for engagement" clearly works to move the conversation among Israeli Jews away from classic Zionist tropes and toward a model of coexistence through acknowledging the atrocities of the past. This move puts the work of Zochrot in direct confrontation with the ethos of forced ignorance and the imposed invisibility of the violence of the Nakba, the common and nationally accepted practice of the settler state. Still, claiming the role of organizing "the time and space for Palestinians to tell their stories in their own places of origin" creates a different kind of tension regarding the framework of Indigenous narration. In this framework, Zochrot-organized tours with Palestinians providing personal testimony of their former lives in the destroyed villages, is a model that has rightfully received some criticism. This model is based on mutual recognition within a liberal framework, which itself works toward a kind of erasure of Indigenous sovereignty within the politics of the state.

The idea behind testimony itself is troubling, in contradistinction with a conceptual understanding of Indigenous storytelling. To whom do we testify, and why? Who is on trial, and why do we have to prove our pain? This actually sets up a framework that, while it is intended to interrupt a settler narrative or settler sensibilities, still centers the settler in the most obvious of ways.[46] What is more brilliant, albeit quite sinister, is that there is a conscious effort to hear the performance of Native voices, so even this critique of the technique of testimony and the framework of visiting, because they are so dependent on settler participation, can potentially be read as another form of silencing and erasure. The obvious contradiction embedded in this critique of testimony is our past experience and present reality of complete silencing. Voices that speak to their experiences, long denied, even with deeply problematic framing, remain important Palestinian voices, presenting another kind of Indigenous bind. Zochrot, the most prolific of the institutions and efforts that perform these kinds of visits, celebrates itself and its openness to come to terms with the violent origins of the settler state, even participating in gestures regarding return. But what is return when it is reduced to this form of performance, a gesture? From this wide scope into a tighter focus on Lifta, the exceptionality of the space in Zionist discourse described throughout this book seems to lend weight to a reductive kind of return that is framed both within the limitations of the settler state and Native testimony, even in the relatively "progressive" settler work of Zochrot.[47] Even in a celebration of the right of return, questions remains: Who is returning? How do we return? And how can a performance of return transform into a *practice* of return, if at all?

Scholarship on tourism in Palestine, like elsewhere, has explored the implications of tours of this nature in the colonial conditions of a settler state, if not explicitly challenging the notion of visiting.[48] Tourism in Indigenous geographies is a historical phenomenon of capitalist colonialism and remains a means of control and violation. As Stephanie Nohelani Teves of the Kanaka Maoli people explains in the Hawaiian context, the commodification and commercialization of the word *aloha* is a violent part of settler colonial erasure.[49] Cultural appropriation is another form of settler colonial control—as is, Teves notes, the vital role of returning to the reliance on Indigenous culture as a form of resistance. Tourism is one of many vehicles of cultural appropriation and another means of working to break relationalities with the land and its culture.

Defiance, in this context, is a return to ourselves and our land. This critique of tourism as both an industry and a means of control intersects, obviously, with the conceptualization of the role of heritage and archeology in the modern construction of national mythology. But what do we do as Palestinians when we are relegated into the confines of "touring" and "visiting" Palestine?

It is not my intention here to discuss the complicated and intimate contradictions involved in tourism in Palestine; rather, I want to simply focus in and see how Lifta can open up the space to discuss how visiting and its own complications affect relationality to place. Toward this end, a conversation regarding the notion of return is key in understanding how visiting (in its own presence and absence) is an aspect of Palestinian erasure. Scholars have focused on typology and naming in the context of Israeli state efforts to remake the landscape as a means of preventing or eventually completely breaking a relationship to place and space.[50] In particular, such literature focuses on the binary of destruction and remaking the landscape and exposes this as a primary tool of settler violence in Palestine. What the settlers have done on the land has become a well-versed narrative in Palestine, both in scholarship and in political reality. How can we understand that this kind of violence relates to an emphasis on visiting in lieu of return? Perhaps this invitation into thinking about "visiting the museum of the past" can be a generative part of this conversation and Lifta can help us in understanding all the complicated variables at play.

While a critical reading of visiting opens up different kinds of conversations, within the context of Palestine and Palestinians these discussions should be understood through the complications of accessibility and inaccessibility.[51] Belonging is a part of how we live in relation to place and space, and access and denial are harsh daily realities where the structural violence of settler colonialism can be and is enacted. As such, this is an invitation to think about how return and/or visiting vary both conceptually and politically. Though not unique to settler colonialism, the kind of violence settler-imposed borders enact on Palestinians is an integral part of this conversation. The formation of the settler state was built on the destruction of Indigenous societies; therefore, denial of access to the land of Palestine is part of ongoing Palestinian dispossession. For Palestinians this has been a century-long process of not only forced removal and massacres but the ongoing power of the Israeli settler state to actively prevent Palestinian return as it continues to also violently enact Palestinian dispossession and displacement. In this context, then, even visiting is prevented. As such, virtual tours are a supplement to temporary physical visiting.[52] Though perhaps presented as a way around the physical and often impenetrable borders of the settler state, the emancipatory notion of virtual tours is itself limited. Moreover, frameworks often remain well fixed within the visions of the settler state, though the virtual does offer a kind of relationality to space and place that would otherwise be denied. The cruelty of the ongoing dispossession remains, in part, enacted through the settler state's power of ongoing denial.[53] Relationality to land, then, is further limited, whereby visits and the politics of visiting are themselves provocative but never removed from the territorialized power of settlers. Finding a way around denial of access can perhaps be presented as a complication: Who can touch the ground and who cannot has been a formidable obstacle and contingency for Palestinians.

Thinking about Lifta, one must necessarily consider how its representational power actually affords us an opportunity to contemplate relationality even when we cannot physically reach the land. Perhaps Lifta—in all of these complications—gives us the opportunity to rethink exile through our collective challenge of the state of being as permanent. Given these Palestinian complications of relationality to the land, notions of territoriality may shed further light on my attempt to frame our history as one of ongoing return.

Deterritorialized Palestine: How to Reimagine Return

On May 15, 2011, Palestinians practiced return to Palestine. Collective actions across several geographies and coordinated among official and nonofficial channels (political parties and community mobilizations) were organized under one flag (Palestine). Palestinians came together under one unified chant: "The people want to return." In the complicated atmosphere of the revolutionary spirit in the Arab world of 2010 and 2011, Palestinian organizers in several places, including Jordan, Lebanon, Palestine, and Syria, coordinated for a day of return. This was both symbolic—as a historical demand of Palestinians—as well as real. People marched and descended on the military borders of occupied Palestine in both performance and action.

Palestinians, challenging the borders and boundaries of settler colonialism, captured a new/old imaginary in Palestinian organizing: return by any means. I have offered the conceptual invitation of *ongoing return* to hold this and other forms of thinking and action across temporal and spatial spectrums among Palestinians—that is, thinking about return as an ongoing practice within ontological implications. Even within the complications described above, visiting remains a limited and limiting framework that is confined to a relationality prescribed by and through settler violence; even if visiting is a defiance, it is not alone a practice. While the performance of return in a symbolic sense has had political and historic resonance for Palestinians, performance that happens outside practice can never become ongoing return.

While this set of actions, like all mobilizations, was born of political work and gave birth to more such work, I pause at this moment to invite us to tap into the imagination that led thousands of people to the streets and the militarized borders that are not only symbolic but also actual military fronts that actively prevent access to the land of Palestine for Palestinians and have done so since 1948. The actions that were coordinated through several channels, including Palestinian political parties, connected the work of community organizers and the larger structures of these parties. These actions were also in coordination with Palestinians inside the borders of Palestine, including actions in Haifa, Gaza, Jerusalem, Ramallah, and other towns and villages in occupied Palestine. Scenes of practicing return on the imposed borderlands in Lebanon and Syria caught media attention and propelled the movement into a much wider sphere of media representation.[54] The action tapped into a long Palestinian cultural and political ethos, historically represented by political parties both within and outside the PLO. Palestinian political mobilization after 1948 resulted in long decades of historical confrontations and contestations on all the borders of Palestine. The product of a constellation of forces on the ground in various geographies, this seemingly fleeting moment in 2011 can be considered in many ways another articulation of Palestinian peoplehood—an articulation that connects Palestinian people over time and across geographies. But it can and should also be considered as part of the larger praxis within Palestinian ways of being, a praxis that began during forced expulsion and continues today.

Though a myriad of forces and agendas were at play at the time, the overarching principle that could not be ignored, regardless of the respective political agendas, was that this was about Palestinian peoplehood in relation to the land of Palestine. That this happened in 2011, well into the outrageous political absurdity of the Palestinian Authority (PA) and the qualified death of a national political agenda, is worth noticing. While much can be written about this moment in 2011, the intention here is to simply focus on the question of relationality to the land and peoplehood in an attempt to insert an understanding of ongoing return into these particular stories of practicing return. Were these actions an aberration in light of the contemporary politics of malaise of a dying (if not dead) PLO and in light of the absurdity of political power of the PA? Were these actions an attempt to reset a revolutionary praxis in the PLO as a last-ditch effort to resurrect the PLO from the political shame that had become the PA? Was it all a ruse, conceived by the very political actors who have long worked to prevent return and destroy the very hope of return in the political playbook of the PLO? Were the actions the product of political negotiations among new political actors in the Palestinian youth movements that worked to gain visibility in light of the long and dark shadow of the PA and the inherent parties and politics of the nonsovereign state farce of a PA agenda?

I actually do not have answers to these questions, but I raise them to offer another form of inquiry in terms of Palestinian peoplehood and its relation to the land of Palestine. Under the obvious supposition that settler colonialism is about conquering land and eliminating the people of the land, Zionism functioned like other forms of settler colonialism toward negating both Palestinian peoplehood and breaking our relations to the land. Now, given this ongoing and structural violence, the question remains, How have we functioned in relation to the land in the violent atmosphere of ongoing negation and elimination? A necessary reflection in light of the tensions around "visiting," this might offer us the opportunity to open up further examinations about how we can move beyond the "case of Lifta" into the "place of Lifta" and use this journey as an opportunity to think about how settlers have attempted to prescribe a relationality to the land and how an Indigenous exploration on the theme might offer a kind of resurgence in thinking about relationality. Moreover, a practice of return, in this sense, reasserts Palestinians into the symbolics of the space of Lifta, and ongoing return empowers us toward reestablishing relationality with the place of Lifta.

From what we know of the history of the PLO, assertions of Palestinian right of return once formed the political and cultural foundations for mobilization. But as with all inquiries about the past, the stories are neither linear nor unique. The PLO acted toward achieving a state in various modes and iterations over time, but it was not an actual nation-state with the capacity to perform as one, though its bureaucracy and institutional power did attempt to work toward that direction. As such, this statist past is complicated, and various iterations of Palestinian peoplehood are part of it. A necessary complication to these stories is the various forms of social, community, and political mobilizations within and around the formal structures of the PLO (and the informal networks the organization acted in and interacted with). This is a past that is as much about confrontation as it is negotiation within and outside the PLO. Moreover, Palestinian political mobilization is also not confined to the Nakba timeline or the PLO.[55] Nevertheless, the Nakba War is a watershed moment that historically translates this practice of return as a generational question, as was the case for the PLO.

Relationality to the land is a historical continuum whose changes over time are far bigger than settler colonial practices, but violent explosion and a war of elimination, nevertheless, did change not only the basic composition of peoplehood but the relation Palestinians had and worked to maintain with the land of Palestine. After 1949 the very notion of mobilization changed because of the exile of Palestinian people, which included both those now forced to live as refugees outside their homeland and those forced to live under the structural violence of settler colonialism on the land within the homeland. By the 1950s and into the early 1960s, political organizing among refugees centrally focused on return and a political agenda that would support Palestinian return to the land of Palestine.

Over time, and employing various techniques, the PLO brought together much (though certainly not all) of the political mobilization of Palestinians. According to Mjriam Abu Samra, the General Union of Palestinian Students was one of main lifelines of mobilization that quickly fed into the subsequent evolution of the PLO.[56] It is neither ironic nor a coincidence that the politics of return have been and continue to be lead by younger Palestinians, passing on from one generation to the next. There was once a time when the PLO presented itself as the holder of Palestinian political will and desires; student mobilization and political parties were always key to this representation, as was return. The history of the PLO, however, is also not one color, as it is a mesh of various threads of community politics, student mobilizations, and guerrilla groups and their various (and often contradictory) tactics and strategies. Nevertheless, one of the main tactics of organization in the PLO was an open and constant commitment (often a singular obsession) to advancing and "protecting" Palestinian identity articulated through relations to the land of Palestine and Palestinian refugees' return to that land. That is, a kind of political and cultural engineering regarding "identity" was key, though constantly changing in all of the political iterations of the PLO and, thereafter, the PA.

This form of identity politics was not new, but the Oslo Accords framework so completely changed the playing field that the identity in identity politics was a very noticeable rupture, one that attempted to redefine the concept of return by eliminating the actual possibility of return, thereby working to change (if not altogether eliminate) Palestinian relationality to the land of Palestine. In fact, the kind of return enacted in the aftermath of the signing of the Oslo Accords and the PLO's leadership and their entourage entering Palestine (first through Gaza, and then the West Back, through Jericho) created a mechanism of entering Palestine so sullied by the politics of the Oslo Accords and the corruption of the PLO and the PA that the very defiance involved in practice of return now had a "handler" in the form of the PA. Scenes of Palestinians once relegated to a life in exile actually reaching the land Palestine in the mid- to late 1990s, albeit emotional in terms of enacting the very desire of return, were also a worrisome sign of how the practice of return, once a radical proposition of Palestinian resurgence, would now be regulated and absorbed into the corrupt and corrupting politics of the PA, which was never divorced from Zionist power or control. That is, from relationality to the land of Palestine we were now subjected to a new relationality, that of proximity or lack thereof to the newly formed PA. As the PA absorbed the politics of the PLO over time, this proximity to power grew ever more limited as the PA was also clearly nothing more than the entity that enacted and secured the whims and desires of the settler state.

The obsession with a post–Oslo Accords assertion of Palestinian identity in contemporary cultural critique rightfully laments the abandonment of sovereignty but also tends to obfuscate the historical trajectory that brought this reality into form. Because this lamentation so often reads as ahistorical and outside a cognizant history of the PLO, the scholarly and political obsession with the PA as somehow removed from the history of the PLO turns into another form of rupture. With the advent of the Oslo process and the subsequent PA, critique of the PA and the Oslo process has ironically done what the critique itself is attacking: negating the past and its many complications. The state that the PA represented was not the state that was imagined in the PLO Charter of 1968, nor the Ten Point Program of 1974, nor even the Palestinian Declaration of Independence in 1988; nevertheless, reading the PA outside the PLO's historical legacy of nation-state desires also ignores our relationship with return. That is, though the PLO built its rhetoric on Palestinian right of return, confining return in a liberal state framework into a question of rights rather than a practice paved the way for what was to come next in the form of the PA. Given this history of the PLO, this statist trajectory was not exactly new, but the devastation it brought in the form of the advent of the PA was—and remains—enormous.

Obviously, the actual presentation of "Native rule" on territory still very much under the rules, mechanisms, and violence of settler occupation is the absurdity of the Oslo Accords process. Nevertheless, the establishment of an "authority" (the PA) that borrowed from or at least benefited slightly from the overwhelming recognition the PLO had achieved in the previous three decades has meant a gigantic change in how politics function in Palestine—on the ground in the "occupied territories" and how the PA worked to actively prevent politics outside these territories.[57] Zionist violence fragmented Palestine as a space and place, and the people have often been left to fend for themselves through the breaks this fragmentation caused. In this context we can understand the conflation of visiting with return. The last three decades (the post–Oslo Accords years) have been a long, drawn out, and painful tragicomedy—with more tragedy than farce—for Palestinian peoplehood.

One of the most painful initial blows of the Oslo Accords was the attempted obliteration of Palestinian peoplehood and the inherent relationality to the land that peoplehood carried. Instead people were directed into a discussion of "citizenship" and "democracy" within the limited confines of colonial liberalism, with only one state under serious consideration: the Israeli settler state. The farce of Palestinian statehood under the Oslo Accords was nothing more than an elaborate, violent, and despicable ruse, but one that many people on the ground negotiated in various ways. The continuation of settler colonial violence did not cease; rather, it grew in elaborate and all-encompassing ways under the auspices of the PA. Fragmentation of Palestinian peoplehood has meant that those on the ground under Israeli military occupation under the guise of limited Palestinian self-rule were confined to an identity that mirrored the confines of their own (im)mobility on the ground. Meanwhile, the Oslo framework further performed the work of settler colonialism to exclude a majority of the Palestinian people, refugees inside and outside the homeland, violently prevented from being on the ground, rendering the very attempt at *grounded normativity* a seeming impossibility for Palestinians. Demographics have always been a concern of the settler state of Israel, and under the Oslo process, the supposed "demographic threat" of Palestinian existence on the land translated as a broad attempt to use the PA as an instrument in the arsenal of settler tools. *Shatat* (often translated as "diaspora") has been an integral concept in Palestinian cultural and political reality since 1948, and the Oslo framework worked to flatten the exilic identity into one of a foregone and overdetermined conclusion. In the midst of this context, spatial Palestine remains an abstract defiance while speaking of relations with the place of Palestine (that is, the land)—a proposed impossibility.

In literature and reflections of the work of the Palestinian Youth Movement (PYM; formerly the Palestinian Youth Network), it quickly becomes apparent that this kind of mobilization among Palestinians in the post–Oslo

Accords period challenged the PA's equations about Palestinianness through a reassertion of the PLO. As Loubna Qutami and Mjriam Abu Samra argue, the break from a collective commitment by the PA—which no longer considered return an option, let alone a priority—was a phenomenal rupture with all that came before it.[58] Visiting, then, takes on new dimensions because return was so severely diminished by the politics of this new era, limited as a right and altogether abandoned as a practice. Nevertheless, even the narrow possibilities embedded within "visiting" produced a whole labyrinth of power created by the settler state involving visitor permits, tourist visas, and conditional permission to travel. Visiting thus became a threshold for belonging under the weight of all this violence and, as a direct result, functioned to determine and undermine peoplehood in relation to land. Whereas the changes in the PLO over time worked to change how Palestinians existed in relation to Palestine, the PA exists to assist the settler state in a near complete break of this relationship and, even more, operates to redefine Palestinianness as having no relation to land. Visiting became embroiled in an obvious tool of settler colonial power intent on making any material form of return based on relationality to the land obsolete. Intentions and results are not the same. In spite of all of these efforts, Palestinian peoplehood was not destroyed by the Oslo framework (and neither was relationality), but, again, given this matrix of eliminatory power, we can see how visiting was manipulated. Here we see that power worked to determine people's access (and material lack thereof) to the land of Palestine.

Visiting or access, by eliding the quest of relationality to the land, reflect the structure of power and privilege of settler colonialism. Under the Oslo process, it appeared that this power was mediated through the PA, though it was clearly not determined by the PA. From here we can observe the invitation of the PYM, among other organizations, to the claim of a deterritorialized notion of Palestine, in part to challenge the intended breaks caused by access (or lack thereof). Outside and inside Palestine, absence and presence, rather than being seen as a continuum that defied settler logics, became a reinforced boundary toward peoplehood. Therefore, the PYM worked to reconceptualize Palestine: "No longer framed solely as a project of territorial, national liberation, Palestine is conceived as one of the most visible, present-day materialisations of the 'coloniality of power.'"[59] To counter the politics of the Oslo framework, movements then reasserted Palestine as a question and an analytic, echoing the work of Edward Said. Given the confinement imposed on us through the PA (and the PLO), the PYM and other organizations no longer accepted identity politics as a core part of the question; rather, they worked to dismantle the politics of identities through an articulation of the "Palestinian condition." This conceptual move enabled a reading of the PA as part and parcel of the conditions of coloniality, similar to that of other postcolonial states but still very much under direct settler colonial rule. This postcolonial colony, as Joseph Massad and others have described it, was the intended essence of the Oslo framework and the PA.[60] Nevertheless, this countering of the PA's abandonment of peoplehood and return, while preserving the space of Palestine as an abstract still attainable through conceptualization, actually limited our interactions with the place of Palestine—feet on the ground. This turn toward conceptualization is understandable in light of the limitations of Oslo. While built on the power of imagination and bold refusal, it still carries the heartbreaking reality of an exilic condition. Given these political limitations, is ongoing return—both in thought and in practice—an unrequited dream?

From bad to worse and dream to nightmare in a landscape of political suffocation, this era brought about even further devastation to Palestinian peoplehood. With an intensification of political malaise in the midst of ongoing settler invasions, a politics enforced by the PA in the occupied West Bank, the settler state imposed with mind-boggling cruelty a suffocating siege on Palestinians in the Gaza Strip, transforming it into what many called a large, open-air prison. While the concept and violence of the ongoing Nakba have been a Palestinian reality for over a century, the brutality of the siege and a series of successive genocidal wars against the small coastal strip expanded the scale and intensity of the ongoing Nakba in the new century. The level of violence that Gaza has endured in the face of the indescribable settler Zionist capacity for violence in the pursuit of utter annihilation is only equaled by the complicity of a global imperial will committed to Palestinian elimination.[61] From the settler-imposed killing fields emerged a new/old political mobilization toward Palestinian return. Distinctly separate and ideologically divorced from the subterfuge of the PA, under the governance of the Islamic Resistance Movement, Hamas, Gaza represented an expanded kind of settler carceral logic combining a brutal siege with ongoing wars waged from the air, the land, and the sea that defined anew the singular goal of settler colonialism: elimination. The expanded walls of the larger prison resembling those of the smaller prisons located throughout occupied Palestine from the sea to river were no longer metaphor, but neither was return. From this came a call to and practice of return manifested in the Great March of Return, a bold and righteous demand to practice return in 2018.

More than three-quarters of Palestinians in Gaza are refugees, and so it seems quite perfect that in the seventieth year of *shatat* (since 1948), Palestinians in Gaza marched toward the settler-constructed walls and military zones to go home. Gaza was the location for continued political organization centered on return and a major center of the actions in 2011. In 2018, this call for return echoed throughout Palestine but remained central to Gaza through mobilization across political parties, including Hamas and people from Islamic Jihad, as well as civil society organizations. In response, Palestinians marched toward return. From imagination to practice, the Great March of Return in Gaza is perhaps the most instructive and hopeful accumulation of efforts of practicing return. As Haidar Eid describes it, "The Gaza March of Return campaign has the potential to promote true national unity. . . . It has the potential to revive the concepts of national liberation and self-determination by addressing the new facts on the ground that Israel created."[62] The violence of the settler military indicates the level of existential fear the mere practice of Palestinian return represents. In 2018 the practice of return centered in and on Gaza, but it was another in a long history of Palestinians practicing ongoing return.

Even with the criminal absurdity of national politics in Palestine under the PA and even in the aftermath of stolen revolutionary spirit in the Arab world, from the epicenter of brutality toward a people under siege, a new practice of return emerged from the eastern shores of occupied Palestine in Gaza. The popular return practiced was met with even more brutal levels of settler colonial violence from the Zionist military. People marching were targeted for maiming and murder en masse by the Israel military. Settler violence against the people and place of Gaza is the greatest shame of humanity in the twenty-first century.

Telling a Story of Loss: Home (Re)Imagined or Unimagined

In 2012 Nora Akawi, a Palestinian architect and former director of Studio-X Amman—part of the global education programs of Columbia University—was contacted by members of the SLC to discuss potential work in Lifta. As she explained it to me in a conversation we had, Akawi had just finished her thesis on history and preservation in architectural design and, having spent a good part of her young life in Jerusalem, already had a relationship with the place of Lifta and the politics that it produced. As she asserted, "Lifta is a place of possibility . . . it is not easily penetrable and its topography affords it a space to hide/protect it." She was referring to the unique setting of the lower section of the village, the underbelly of a built-up landscape, now nestled between modern highways and the intersections of Jerusalem. Lower Lifta is a kind of haven in an urban landscape. But, as Akawi also pointed out, "it was also a functioning place ... people visited, hung out, et cetera and had their own specific relationship with the space in the midst of a large city." She explained that the potential in the context of Lifta was also double-edged, as the past bleeds well into the present and the space has, in her words, "a sustained potential of loss." Like others (including myself) who did work implicitly or explicitly within the arena of the SLC, Akawi was thoughtful about the complications involved in what preservation and architectural inquiries could mean in Lifta. She—along with several Palestinian architects, all locally based at the time—explored what she called the "possibilities." Akawi and her friend and colleague at Columbia University and Studio-X, Nina Valerie Kolowrat-nik, invited Palestinian architects Elias Anastas, Yousef Anastas, Victoria Dabdoub, Dima Khoury, Inas Moussa-Wa'ary, Mahdi Sabbagh, and Ahmad Wa'ary to participate in a project that would be an "exploration in how to imagine return."[63] The project resulted in the exhibition *Re:Lifta*, which opened at the Yabous Cultural Center in Jerusalem in November 2012.

The group of young architects and planners, who took the name COLLECTIVE Memory | Imaginaries | Planning, first met at the Al Ma'mal Foundation for Contemporary Art in Jerusalem's Old City to discuss potential work.[64] As Mahdi Sabbagh explains, "it was clear to us, as it is to any planner who goes through a foundational understanding of political landscapes in Palestine, that Lifta is a battleground of narratives." Having grown up in Jerusalem, Sabbagh shared Akawi's familiarity with Lifta as a space and connected that to his work in the project. He notes that "Lifta, in collective Palestinian memory, is not just a destroyed village: it symbolizes Palestinian resilience and Palestinians' relationship to their ancestral land."[65] Lifta thus embodies the entirety of Sabbagh's political trajectory on and in Palestine and his vantage point / orientation as both an artist and a local Palestinian. In the context of Palestine, the notion of lived space moves in various directions; after all, most of the refugees from Lifta neither have the daily experience of lived Jerusalem nor do they have access to experience Lifta.[66] This is not unique, as we have seen this symbolism in many other projects and approaches to Lifta. It is, nonetheless, a core part of the inquiry here regarding Lifta as a place. The challenge remained (and remains): How can the space of Lifta be imagined as a place of return?

As the initial meeting and collective exploration of the architectural minds grew into a project, *Re:Lifta* came to life. In Sabbagh's words, "our goal at Re:Lifta was to respond to [the Jerusalem municipality's Urban Building Plan] No. 6036 by conceptualizing Liftawis in a post-return Lifta rather than finding an immediate solution to the remains of the village. We were interested in collaborative work that would re-imagine Lifta as a narrated typology of return, a landscape of memories and ideas."[67] Sabbagh puts his finger on the contradiction: What to do through space in the real place under constant threat in all times—past, present, and future? For Sabbagh, saving Lifta in their project would be translated into imagining a kind of spatial return. This kind of relationship with saving is what Robert Warrior of the Osage people describes as "Indigenous subversion of one of the basic tools of settler-colonial intervention."[68] While Warrior is writing in the context of Native American studies, here Sabbagh takes one slice of that in the highly contested and complicated terrain of Lifta and turns saving on its head. Sabbagh describes a similar process: taking the idea of return and removing it from the quagmire of contemporary politics as way to articulate "saving Lifta." He explains that "to have focused solely on Lifta's current political landscapes would have prevented our minds from wondering beyond the physical and psychological barriers that define the majority of Palestinian visual culture: always in relation and reaction to its Israeli oppressor."[69] To imagine is to wonder, and it is a collective process that is grounded in the place but was not locked into a fixed conception of it. Reflecting on their work several years later, in my conversation with her, Akawi echoed a similar sentiment, recalling her unease in working against and in reaction to the immediate circumstances of the Jerusalem municipality's plan: "Our project was not about the municipality, or their proposed plans, but rather we considered it to be speculative. We refused to be forced into the confines of a *reaction to settlers*—who were simply trying to silence [what they perceived as] phantoms through their own plans of ongoing erasure; theirs was a plan of pacification, ours was one of possibilities."[70] Akawi, as the curator of this project, highlights the limitations of saving, but she does so actively: Saving need not be about the past as static but can instead be about imagining bringing life back while also understanding life never really fully left the place, which was deemed "abandoned" only by the settlers.

This sense of speculative art informs a certain politics regarding preservation. As Akawi described it, "Preservation is a spectrum ... but in preservation there is a danger of depoliticizing the space, especially spaces that are not monumental—spaces of daily life that challenge the colonizer's narrative."[71] In an interview, Jorge Otero-Pailos explains the role of the preservation artist: "There's a sense that preservation participates in estranging us from historic places, that rift is where artists come in—not necessarily to heal it, but to interrogate it and cast it in a new light. I love the idea of 'enlivening' places, because that word seems central to me." A dynamic notion of preservation as art informs Otero-Pailos's work; he asks, "What are the objects that we've inherited that help us provide new answers, think anew about these problems, and develop ideas that would not otherwise be available to us? The short of it is learning from the past."[72] Learning from the past and not reenacting it seems to be the key to this iteration of preservation as an art form. Otero-Pailos, when questioned about defining preservation art spoke of "home," mentions that one of the exciting potentials in working on preservation in this way is that people can "take a memory home." How art informs preservation is clearly a departure from other forms of preservation, but the question for this work in Lifta remains: How can memory, and memories of home, be and become a practice of return? In his work on ruins, pollution and preservation, Otero-Pailos's inquiries seem to follow along these same lines as he explores a sense of reuse and reconstruction outside the classic notion of pristine preservation or complete erasure—that is, the binary presented by the field of architectural preservation.[73] Defying this binary can be seen not only as part of preservation that defies museumification but also as an attempt to reclaim home through a practice of return. In this way, imagining home becomes part of the work of return, especially in places as contested as Lifta.

This understanding of architecture as art, and preservation as creation, provides a necessary elevation to the low ceilings of pure restoration. The site of Lifta was, nevertheless, a challenge for the small group of architects and planners. Individuals who were active in the SLC, as mentioned earlier, were also in conversation with individuals like Akawi and others about this work on Lifta. The motivations for the work were in some ways prompted by the work of the SLC, but not necessary entirely informed by it and certainly not confined to it. Therein lies the possibilities through the contradictions. In a piece titled "Silencing Conflict, Pacifying the Ruin," written after their work on Lifta, Nora Akawi and Nina Valerie Kolowratnik reflect on what working in ruins can potentially mean. First, they (like many others) understood the motivations of the settler state, "the role of the ruin . . . and how it is instrumentalized in the silencing of conflict, where Palestinian architectural heritage (erased or preserved) is to be rendered invisible within the official narrative of the state." Clearly fully cognizant of settler violence through cultural cleansing, they explain the problematic that arose from the saving narrative in Lifta: "What the ruins of Lifta have evoked amongst the Israeli left is 'liberal angst' or 'moral angst,' a term borrowed from Nadia Abu El-Haj, a sentiment leading to actions toward preserving Lifta's stones, however also risking the silencing of the village's political story and the rights of its indigenous population to return by rendering the village's value a universal heritage site, that is worth preserving due to its undeniable beauty and melancholic landscape."[74] The tensions of the combination of potentially problematic interpretation of preservation and the wide range of the politics of the SLC, along with the immediate circumstances of the municipality's intentions, posed the danger of allowing verbs to all collapse into a past tense, removed altogether from both return and home.

Well aware of the sense of potential museumification, Akawi and Kolowratnik understood that preservation was another possible weapon in the arsenal of the settlers' drive toward Indigenous elimination: "The preservation of built Palestinian fabric as a depoliticized site within Israel, in fact ends the life of a ruin as a possible source or container of memory or stage for politics." By approaching Lifta as a stage for a potential project for return, Akawi and Kolowratnik show us another kind of preservation, one defined by the practice of return. By reasserting return into the equation, they break the limited and limiting settler framework in Lifta. Rather than basing the work on fear of loss, Akawi and Kolowratnik articulate another more prevalent fear: "While erasure seemed to be the dominant approach to Palestinian quotidian and political life before Israel, today, practices of depoliticization through 'preservation' prove just as dangerous."[75] Aware that their expertise could easily be employed toward these ends, architects working in or on Lifta represent another layer of complications: resistance through imagination or succumbing to pacification through this limited sense of preservation.

Akawi and Kolowratnik are cognizant that "the appropriation of such sites into the official narrative of Israel, and their preservation as shared 'universal' heritage would lead to the inevitable silencing of the conflict they bear, and to the pacification of their political role."[76] The work of the *Re:Lifta* architects could cut either way. Akawi explained that they chose to work through these tensions and focused on the power of speculation and imagination: "Projecting scenarios and creating new narratives, imagining return . . . here the plural is important, narratives, otherwise things are locked down . . . and in my understanding of preservation as art, that [locking down] is a violent act."[77] This plural in the narratives is not about a liberal project of identity production but about breaking through the solid prison walls of a static past and the dominant settler version of "reality" into an imagined future, a practice of return. Preservation that relies on the power of imagination can then become the tools of resurgence and Indigenous rebellion.

In 2012, the Yabous Cultural Center hosted a symposium on Lifta that included several presentations (including one by myself) and was highlighted by the exhibition *Re:Lifta*. As Sabbagh describes the evolution of their work as a collective, "it . . . became clear to us that our initiative had to expand to become truly collaborative. We expanded into a socio-cognitive process to include scholars, artists, graphic designers and Liftawis whom we could reach. This generated many conversations and culminated into a body of work that had to be returned to and presented with Palestinian society."[78] This symposium actually revealed the fluidity on the issue of not only the politics of the SLC but also the contradictions well beyond that moment and its narrow legal claim. Expertise, then, took on a different form or became something entirely collective. Preservation in the sense of architecture as art was no longer to be confined in the field of their expertise; rather, it was intended to be a conversation among many, a conversation beyond form, and was intended to be culturally relevant. In the traditional sense, as in other forms of museumification, preservation in the field of architecture was about capturing a site frozen in time. Resisting museumification, in this sense, is a speculative process involving the art, culture, and imagination of an Indigenous return. Return, in this move toward the collaborative, becomes fluid, not solid. The exhibition on display at the Yabous Cultural Center, like the public talks that occurred alongside it, were works in progress with an emphasis on the fluidity of both the discussions and the imaginative production.[79] A collection of imaginary return, the projects ranged from a futuristic depiction of building atop the village in space to a project that imagined windmills throughout the landscape with the title *Green Lifta*.

Nearly immediately after the symposium, Akawi suggested to her colleagues in New York that a classroom studio focused on the space of Lifta for undergraduate students in architecture would yield very interesting results. Because politics overlap, projects blend and evolve, and people can occupy several political and social locations, those in conversation with the work of the architects (who were themselves, as noted earlier, in conversation with members of the SLC), implemented Akawi's suggestion and ran a course in the fall semester of 2013–14 on preservation and Lifta. The studio project run through the Columbia University Graduate School of Architecture, Planning, and Preservation was a research and practical skills course that followed but overlapped with the work of *Re:Lifta*. As a teaching assistant in the course, as well as a part of the teams that visited Lifta over the course of the work of *Re:Lifta*, Kolowratnik wrote about her own thinking on Lifta and the political context of settler colonialism in Palestine: "Analyzing the visible and invisible layers which shape the contemporary landscape reveals the geography of the place as a complex arena of spatial and political forces, where the Palestinian landscape has been overwritten by an Israeli present. The multiple layers of significance of today's Israeli-Palestinian geography, as well as the fact that any return will take place in a newly constructed and spatially transformed reality, mean that we must work very deliberately with the landscape that currently exists, responding to its forms and structures. The contemporary landscape must be challenged, redefined or subverted."[80] Echoes of how return was imagined in *Re:Lifta* also grounded the work of imagination in the studio-as-classroom on Lifta. Kolowratnik explains her strategy in traversing the "landscape of return," as she describes it, which both integrates the various layers of the past with a functional understanding of making a future:

> The aim should not be a reconstruction or a projection of the past, but return as an ongoing process taking place in the present. A spatial return must not be reduced to symbolic memorials, or rebuilding of old villages in their original form, which would simply ignore the history of the last 60 years and deny today's reality and the conditions pertaining to today. The layer of the past serves as an important point of reference and point of departure for return to a land which has in the meantime become strange, but the spatial practice of return must aim to ensure that the past is finally past, and that the Palestinian refugees can begin to live in the present again.[81]

As settler colonialism collapses the present into the past—while always trying to foreclose Indigenous futures—return then challenges the aim of elimination. The work of this studio class was in part based on an original architectural survey conducted on the "remains of Lifta" for the purpose of the case filed against the Jerusalem municipality by the SLC. The students also met with members of the SLC and were escorted on a hike through the ruins of Lifta. Unlike the film *The Ruins of Lifta*, the studio class opened up a line of questioning regarding not only the permanency of ruins but also the power of imagination to inform fluid notions of return. While this could have been an actual practice of return, but removed from the context of Lifta and put into the classroom, questions remained about space and place: To whom was the project accountable, and how can a spatial imagination be accountable to a grounded space and Palestinian peoplehood? That is, how can an architectural practice of return transform into practices of return or, in other words, ongoing return? Unlike *Re:Lifta*, whose work was a part of a locally based cultural project, the studio course was less tied to a community and, therefore, less accountable to the people. Even with all the complications inherent in its connections to the SLC, *Re:Lifta* was still not removed from the politics of the present and was therefore informed by Palestinian peoplehood. As described by the people involved, it challenged traditional notions of preservation as they focused their work on imagined futures.

Return Without the Land: Reimagining or Abandonment

Unpacking and disaggregating "Lifta as a symbol" from settler colonial frameworks is only part of the process of our methodological interventions regarding Lifta. The *Re:Lifta* project challenging tradition was articulated as an open invitation in thinking about Palestine through Lifta. As such, the pertinent question here remains, What is Lifta for Palestinians? More specifically, what *can* it be? Embedded deeply in this question is a tension in terms of symbols. This tension is in direct relation to the Indigenous bind, where the question is larger than what kind of symbol, and for whom, but instead why it should be a symbol. Not surprisingly, Lifta (as a space, as an idea, and as a home for us as a people) has been an interesting trigger for what can perhaps be described as "futurity" in Palestine. Though settler colonial frameworks work to deny Indigenous futures, this new iteration of imagining the future in Palestine is, like political mobilization, a political and cultural phenomenon in the new century. Not surprisingly, Lifta has a central place in this world of imagination.

Under what might at first seem like a curious title because of its wider focus on Palestine beyond the place of Lifta, *LIFTA* is a multidisciplinary platform and book series; its first volume is a compilation, *LIFTA: Future Palestine*. The project features a diverse array of material guided by the question, "How much of history, reality, and experience can we shed in the realm of the imaginary?" Curiously, only one selection in the volume directly engages Lifta as a place, in spite of (or perhaps because of) the volume's title. As a part of the architectural/artist project *Re:Lifta*, and under that same title, volume 1 of *LIFTA* features the work of AAU Anastas (the Anastas brothers) and Karim Kattan. Perhaps serving as a bridge between the two projects (*Re:Lifta* and *LIFTA*), which both ask questions in relation to the future, this piece, titled "Re:Lifta," is a design of an imaginary return to Lifta accompanied by text. In the text, the authors/artists think through "absence" and provide a provocative and even potentially infuriating take on the future in, of, and on Lifta: "The fact remains, this land so many of us so fondly refer to as our homeland was shaped by our absence. We were not here all along. . . . In truth, it was not ours in the past nine decades. We are—don't wince—settlers of a new sort." How Palestinians can be conceived as settlers in Palestine remains a perplexing question, but one that is perhaps intended to provoke new thinking about space, place, and people after settler colonialism. In their effort to imagine the future and a potential return to Lifta, they imagine themselves in a future where Palestine as a space is open to being made anew after Zionism: "What the builders of this country, the engineers and architects, have set out to do is not to reclaim an illusory pre-Israel Golden Age— rather, they venture to stage the ruin and rebirth of the Palestinian nation." By presenting their contribution as imagining Palestine in a postsettler formation, the artists present Lifta for the quandary that it is in the present and as a quandary for the future. In this way they work brilliantly to dismantle the hegemony of settler time: "Lifta, as a town in the valley of ruins, offers an unprecedented challenge: do we keep the ruins?"[82] This circles directly back to the discussion of museumification, for it is not only a tool of settlers but it shall be an inheritance in a postsettler future for Palestine. This actually makes an argument for the present through thinking about a future through the past, and with the overarching question, How do we treat the past? In this way, it is not an inheritance so much as it is a reality.

Other contributions to the first volume of *LIFTA* follow themes prevalent in the growing field of futurity studies in Palestine. In this sort of imagining, Palestine borrows from and merges with Palestinian studies as a part of Indigenous studies. With themes of survival in postapocalyptic worlds and imaginaries highly influenced by science fiction, thinking about the future among Palestinians and with Palestine is wrought with realities that clearly emerge from the present and past. The apocalypse happened already for Palestinians (in 1948), in much the same way as other Indigenous peoples endure a continuing and continuous apocalypse. But can we possibly imagine emerging from it and its unspeakable violence? In this way, "what shall we do with the ruins?" remains a layered question, grounded in the land, but it is also an invitation to imagine our relations with the land. It is also about how we imagine ourselves. Where do we go from here?

Part II

CHAPTER FOUR

A People's Memory
Ayam al-Balad, *the Days of Our Homeland*

Life before was pleasurable and dignified.
—Habiba Muhammad ʿAbdiyat

Memory: We have been listening to stories about the days of refuge since settlers first forced Palestinians to leave their homes, land, and homeland in the war that began in 1947. These are the stories that settlers and their myriad accomplices in Palestine have worked to deny. Denial and erasure of stories are methodologies of settler violence. When Zionists claimed that we did not exist, we were put into the position of having to prove our existence. When Zionists claimed that our people left because our leaders told us to leave in 1948, we worked to prove otherwise. When Zionists claimed that we were primitive terrorists, we worked to prove that resistance is our right and/or righteous. Basically, the framework of working against Zionists' claims regulated us into a methodology of countering. To counter, even to disprove, still kept us in the prisons—intellectual and otherwise—of settler power, settler epistemologies, and settler time. Palestine and Palestinians have been in a defensive modality for over a century, and the discipline of oral history has been front and center in this modality. We continue to live through this positionality and, thus, memory is a tool. In the hands of the settlers, as a forced absence, memory is a denial. In its insistence, in the minds of Palestinians, it is a modality of resistance. Memory and remembering, then, are a battlefield. It is a righteous battle indeed.

Remembering: In an ongoing Nakba, settler violence is structural and constant. Settler violence is everywhere. It is the atmosphere in which we live and through which we move in our collective and individual struggles to survive and remain. Violence is omnipresent in the past and in the present, and Zionist settler colonialism is relentless violence. But to say it is constant does not quite capture the reality of this violence. When violence in all of its forms feels never ending, memory can become a burden. Who can keep up? Who can sustain presence in the present while also working to sustain presence in the past? Violence is not only an event, or even simply a series of events or attacks. Violence is more than repetitive. It is beyond language. Violence is constant and everywhere within every moment of every day. As I compose these words, the violence is constant; as you read these words, the violence may even be worse. We cannot keep remembering because every day, every moment, is violent, and violence and survival may require a different relationship with memory.

Impossible possibilities: What if we remove ourselves from the prisons set up by settlers? What if we wrest free our capacity for memory and remembering? Can we do this? This chapter and chapter 5 will work through this challenge. So many tools of oral history have imprisoned our stories, we have to try to find a different way to share stories and storytelling. The historiography produced through oral history has also been imprisoned within settler frames. But storytelling can be different. Just as storytelling is an art form, so too can be listening to stories. After all, listening to poets gives life to the poems and the stories they tell. What lies between the battlefield of memory and remembering? Might that question give us capacity to live outside omnipresent settler violence every day? Is it possible to dream to live as such? In this in-between state, can we catch our collective breath even when breathing is next to impossible? Palestine holds these stories in the space between their narration and their reception in acts of listening. The language of poets who defy imprisonment shows us how to live beyond the words of settlers. Their stories wrest the ground and sky of possibilities from within an atmosphere of the impossible. Shall we engage our past, through our present and into our future, through the dreams of poets?

Walking through space and time as the journey of this book is the imaginative grounding for an attempt to forge a methodology that defies settler temporality and spatiality through a practice/praxis of mental walking. In this chapter and chapter 5, I address writing as life and scholarship as vitality, exploring practices of life and living as methodology. I do so as far more than an academic exercise. I do so as a praxis of survival. In their telling and in the listening, stories carve out a pathway toward living and breathing in spite of the asphyxiation of settlers and colonial violence. In truth, this entire book recounts practices of survival, written betwixt and between remaining, feet on the ground, amid the brutality of denial and forced exile, while navigating the overwhelming forms of settler violence, in a rather common Palestinian way of being.

Seen in this way, Palestinian scholarship becomes a generative space of collective possibilities, "living beyond settlers, even in the midst of their violence." Survival is a concept that Palestine illuminates and that Palestinians embody. Navigating the intensity of settler colonial violence lands us in an endless struggle for mere survival. In the face of this never-ending violence that can overcome and overwhelm, our stories are ongoing as well. Framing, imagining, and narrating our lives as ongoing helps push back the suffocating, everyday, never-ending violence.

Stories and storytelling are more than the objects of my desire; they chart a path from the personal to the collective. Storytelling is a method of living through the past in the present as we imagine the future. The stories I recount in this book are stories of the land. They are stories we carry within us as a people. In the omnipresence of settler violence, Palestinians have—over time—forged and navigated through stories and storytelling a unique relationship with the land to which we belong.

Walking, Remembering, and Imagining

Walking on the main artery of eastern Jerusalem, Salah al-Din Street, you leave the Old City behind; you enter the street from its wide opening, leading you into what was once "new" in the New City. New and old blend, as do the faces of the people bustling about as they maneuver the obstacles of settler surveillance. Look to your left; let the senses take over in order to avoid staring at the heavily fortified police compound on your right. Embrace the aroma of coffee beans roasting rather than the violence of the settler-transformed building and all of the nefariousness inside it. It was once something else; it will once again be something else. The past is present and the future opens up as you walk. Keep walking down the block from the San-douka Coffee Shop, but not so far as to the lose the smell of the roasting coffee. "Senses can guide you," my mother taught me as she showed me how to walk this street, what to pay attention to, and how to make sure I do not draw attention to myself. Her lessons were formed under one of the many layers of time this book holds. Her mother, ʿArifa, taught her other lessons, for ʿArifa found herself on Salah al Din Street "after Lifta," as one station in her life as a refugee. All of these are lessons inside me. Look around you to see how the cobblestones of the pavement reveal that lived life has always far exceeded colonial intentions. By the mid-1920s the British colonial government in Palestine intended to manifest a transformation: Jerusalem into a city planned over time to hold an Orientalist version of the ancient and the modern. More than a hundred years later, as I walk, I can discern the intentions, but I can also feel the life . . . our lives lived over time. The women selling their fruits and vegetables on the pavement reveal how time holds both change and continuity. Access to Jerusalem is an ongoing tool of settler violence: Who can be here and who cannot is a story of survival told anew for my generation. I cannot walk this street with the ease and access of those who came before me, and they could not walk it like those who came before them. But we still walk. Mostly, these days, I walk in my mind, but that emotional map is mine, one I

Peering through the gate at the entrance to the cemetery on Salah
al-Din Street, Jerusalem. Photograph by the author.

inherited and will someday be inherited by others. I inherited memories, and
I am making memories to be inherited. Presence on the ground is our lives
being lived through settler violence, over time, and through generations, but
life continues to be lived. Focus on the women selling their produce and you
can discern the intimacy of seasonal change through their products while you
no doubt note that the women that came before arrived here in very different
ways. Modernity is nothing more than a paradigm to be challenged, nuanced,
complicated, and confused by our ongoing return.

Walking blends temporalities, and you realize that we are neither ancient
nor modern, neither simply rural nor exclusively urban, for these are concepts
that cannot capture all of the layers of living. Continue walking and you catch
the glimpse of flowers on the opposite side of the street, at a flower shop on
the corner. The flowers are waiting to be picked from the metal trees the shop
owner carefully curates. Once these flowers come into view, from a distance,
you will find yourself in front of the cemetery. In the middle of this busy street
in Jerusalem, there is a large green metal gate opening up to one of the largest
cemeteries in this part of Jerusalem. A cemetery entrance in the midst of the

Inside the cemetery on Salah al-Din Street, Jerusalem. Photograph by the author.

city's bustle seems rather out of place, but this is how Jerusalem exists for Palestinians. The green gates are not always open to the public; they are routinely open on Thursdays, open on holidays for folks visiting their ancestors, and opened abruptly on the occasion of death and the need for burial. The first time I passed the green gates, my aunt Khawlah told me, "Your family is buried there; you might want to stop and say the fatiha every once in a while when you pass by." Several years later, Khawlah was to join my grandmother in her grave, along with her grandmother: three generations lie together atop the hill. And so it was, passing by the gates, over the years, I noticed myself stopping in the street, reciting the fatiha to myself, and then continuing about my day.

If the cemetery gates are closed, I recite the fatiha in front of them. If the gates happen to be open, my recitations take another kind of journey, one that creates the stories that hold space for the times I cannot make it up the hill. Walking through the gates and up the stairs of the urban cemetery is a journey full of stories of the past, through the present, and in the hopes for the future. These are acts, journeys, and stories that hold the place for other moments over and through time, beyond access and lack thereof.

After passing through the cemetery gates, you immediately encounter large cement stairs leading up from the busy street that you must ascend to behold a massive sight. At the top of the stairs, you are surrounded by gravesites; there is a walkway to guide you through the maze. If you keep going up, you will find another set of stairs. Those stairs lead to a cement-paved hill, where there is another maze of graves. Not everyone buried there is from Lifta, but enough of them are that, in time, people in Jerusalem came to commonly refer to the cemetery as "Lifta's cemetery." It is not unusual for people driven from their land to congregate—in death, as in life.

Beyond the cement-paved hill, the path leads to a summit. Once you reach the top of the hill, you can no longer see the street down below, as if you have ascended beyond, with only the faint sounds of the city breaking the silence of the somber place you have found yourself in. There you will find the grave of my grandmother, ʿArifa. Her place at the top of the hill probably had more to do with when she passed than what she wanted. Her husband, my grandfather ʿAta, is buried several meters below her, toward one side. Her mother, my mother's grandmother, Tamam, was buried in this plot on the top of the hill first, in 1954. Tamam passed on a few years after they were forced from the village, but before 1967; therefore, her family was able to bring her from Amman, Jordan, back to Jerusalem for burial. I wonder what her children wanted. Was it she who requested a resting place in Jerusalem? Some daughters in Jerusalem, and others in Amman—was it is battle among them? Maybe in 1954 they all felt a fluid kind of exile rather than the specter of permanence, where (East) Jerusalem was both accessible to all and represented a nearness to Lifta. Was return so embedded conceptually and viscerally that perhaps it did not require an actual conversation? If it did not require a conversion, did return to this cemetery spark a discussion? I wonder what they considered—a cemetery for Lifta as a complement to Lifta's cemetery? Or did they consider it a replacement, but one less harsh—internal exile as less painful than external exile?

I know from our family stories that, ʿArifa gave birth to a girl on the same day she received the news of her mother's passing. Was she relieved in her pain that her mother was returning to her, to be buried in Jerusalem? Tamam's daughter, my grandmother, ʿArifa, followed her several decades later, in 1991. Her mother's grave atop this hill in "Lifta's cemetery" was opened for her. Her eldest daughter, my Aunt Khawlah, followed more recently in the depths of winter in early 2015. Only in her last days did Khawlah make the request to be buried with her mother and grandmother. My mother tells me that she and her sisters were surprised when they learned of the request, for Khawlah was the eldest of the six daughters and did not share this desire with them until only days before her passing.

The first time I met my grandmother was in that cemetery. In retrospect, I think I began my search for her and her stories from that spot atop the remarkable hill that can't be seen from below. Maybe that is my story, one I tell myself, or maybe this is how I choose to weave together this part of our story. Maybe that is where I found storytelling. Maybe there is where I found I needed stories.

Give yourself to your senses again. From atop the hill, you can still hear and feel the city. Just as you let your senses guide you from the roasting coffee to the flowers along the street, those senses hold you, and you hold them inside you on the days you can stroll down Salah al-Din Street and on all the days you cannot. The moment from when my story became a desire for our story is neither a beginning nor an end; it is a guide rather than a timeline. Likewise, listening and learning how to hear from beyond the grave is also neither an end nor a beginning, and it might also lead us to find and accept guidance.

I met ʿArifa through all of these senses and sensibilities. This is how we learn to *move beyond*, not confined by settler spaces and settler time. And so begins this chapter: the search for a story that is the story of her, the story of me, and the stories of all of those voices that connected me to ʿArifa and my generation to our past.

The cemetery is like a microcosm of a place that exists as an idea as much as it does a reality. The idea is one built of my Indigenous imagination, and the reality is one effected by the destruction, reconstruction, and constant violent touch of settlers. I once knew where I was supposed to find things: I was told where to look as a historian, but what I found only vaguely matched up with the map in my head. Empirical evidence has its limits. When that vagueness manifests as a disconnect, I get lost. Perhaps the map—real and imagined, lived and dreamed—is only one element and the questions that we explore are those that we might not even know how to pose. So the struggle of this chapter is to capture and honor personal stories in a collective sense of storytelling. These are the stories that history cannot contain.

Before the spring of 1948, the people of the village of Lifta lived in their homes and on the homeland. Their lives, like others throughout the villages and towns in Palestine, were, in part, defined by a historical trajectory to the past, as well as by the enormous changes that came with the present. Listening to the stories of people who lived through the first part of the twenty-first century captures how they experienced this mix and also how they retrospectively describe an anticipation of the ominous future that lay ahead for them as refugees. Given these layers and complexities, their stories and how they address their lives, which were upended by Zionist settlers and their armed militias, prove difficult to comprehend. To enter into the private lives of people who exist beneath, within, and on the margins of the label *refugee* in any sense is not a light task. For Palestinians it is a line of inquiry with a long history and a harsh present. Because the historiography of the Nakba is a vast field of study that contains literature from the earliest moments of forced expulsion and continues throughout the generations that followed, many have already entered this realm as historians, anthropologists, journalists, activists, and politicians. Here, rather than recount this body of existing work and the rich focus therein on the construction of memory, remembering, testimonials, and oral history, I shall try to center the stories and ask how understanding the art of storytelling can elaborate and differ from what we were supposed to know or what we think we already knew.

Memory work has been a major aspect in the work of archive making and institutional thinking. Focusing on storytelling, however, attempts to focus more on the people who remember and the sometimes contradictory process of how they remember, as well as how—through employing methodologies of Indigeneity—we can potentially engage these memories in a different way, what I shall name here as an otherwise way. Beyond the work of archives, then, this chapter begins with the distinction between memory work and stories. As in every chapter, I present the dilemma as a product of what has already been written as history, as well as how historians and others have approached research in/on Palestine. Establishing a mode of Indigenous methodology in research and writing presents a different path—hopefully a more open path between and with the past, present, and future.

The Personal Is Political and the Intellectual Is Personal

My own personal journey in a search for an otherwise way of thinking through and about the past has been fundamentally informed by my location. That is, through professional and personal experience, I almost literally walked into a need for this methodology of imagined walking. This began anew through two distinct positions I occupied: one as a professor of history at Birzeit University (BZU), which contributed to the other, a stint as a researcher in a project informed by the "case of Lifta" for the Save Lifta

Coalition (SLC). These roles were not—and are not—mutually exclusive. Though both eventually inspired, directly and indirectly, my search for 'Arifa, that was not the case initially. My personal connections with Lifta through my maternal genealogy was initially, at best, an afterthought. In fact, because *research* in terms of Lifta had been so informed by the confining framework of history as a discipline, a framework, and a methodology, both BZU and the SLC expected that I consciously work to avoid my personal attachments and stories. In retrospect, I can now see that 'Arifa guided me into a new world and way of being because I was in dire need of walking away from an epistemology that silenced me and her through erasure.

My research work began in an archiving project under the framework (described in chapter 3) of *saving*. After having established a humble presence at BZU in the Department of History, I unknowingly became an "expert" in oral history. Having taught courses in several departments and programs that centered around the methodology of oral history and the Nakba, I came to realize that the institutional intentions of these courses were both confined and confining. That is, given the vitality and unexpected kind of knowledge exchange involved in teaching, I came to realize that disciplinary knowledge had major limitations. Settler colonial rule and settler military occupation in the West Bank (where BZU is located) is an atmosphere of unyielding violence that exposes these limitations and can create a grave alienation among students and professors alike. Courses offered through the History Department and the several graduate programs that wanted a "historical" perspective on the Palestinian Nakba presented similar challenges. Over time I came to realize that certain folks in various academic departments and programs at BZU began to consider me someone who should present the field of "refugee studies." This unexpected and rather haphazard institutional recognition in Palestine brought about a myriad of issues for me, mostly defined by the practice of "oral history as testimony." Ironically, being in Palestine among three generations of people who hone survival mechanisms as they endure the ongoing Nakba did little to break the hegemonic pedagogical concept of the Nakba as an event from the past that has long since passed. Specifically, we seem to remain confined to the framework of Nakba denial and the dire need of countering this violent erasure through the testimony of those who experienced 1948. History, as described by Samera Esmeir, is a courtroom where perpetrator testimony, along with the archival weight of the settler state, resigned Palestinians to the role of proving our victimhood.[1] We remained captive to a fear of forgetting, a fear prescribed by Zionists and subscribed to by Palestinians.

Approaching the Nakba as a singular event also produced a relationship with the past among students that was informed by a positivist methodology of historical documentation in accordance with traditional archival evidence. At its best, this approach relied on a classic understanding of "oral history" and has been translated locally as a dire need for Palestinian voices that could counter Zionist mythology. That is, students had long been exposed to the Nakba-as-event framework while also living through the ongoing Nakba. While it seems counterintuitive, this appeared to cause a dramatic break in their relationship between their own lived experiences (their own voices) and the lived experiences of past generations. That is, history confined in disciplinary forms of knowledge production (voices as "testimony" in a kind of legal framework of diagnosis and reconstruction) rendered devoid of connection and continuity between what they had been taught in classrooms (both at the secondary and university educational levels) and what they live through. This alienation that I both experienced and observed in the classroom seemed insurmountable. Well into the second decade of the new century, history courses were intended to be offered as a record of Palestine as an exclusive narrative of loss and the history of some Palestinians as permanent refugees. Neither frames offered space for the ongoing lived experiences or a practice of return— that is, a Palestinian history with a present and a future.

As anyone can attest to in an educational context, intentions (course descriptions and course plans) and what actually happens in the learning environment are very different. Exchange, sharing, and the vitality of discussions can cut through the walls of alienation. Nevertheless, the structural pressures of presenting history as a linear narrative of events with one huge break in 1948 reproduced the very frameworks that erased Palestinians in the historical annals. At BZU this approach was grounded in institutional memory and the projects of the Birzeit University Research Center's work in the 1980s and 1990s in its Destroyed Villages Series. As described earlier, this center produced a number of booklets (twenty-two in total) along with a large amount of additional material resulting from fieldwork, including records of oral testimony by people from the villages violently depopulated and destroyed by the settler state. Ironically, neither the booklets nor the work of the center was clearly archived within BZU until decades later, after much material had been misplaced or lost. After the haphazard journey of archiving and digitizing what remained of the BZU Research Center, a process that happened in several locations in different projects on campus, the work of the center is now a part of the ethnographic collections at BZU Museum as a digital collection that is organized and legible as a researchable archive. Reviewing this archive, it becomes clear that at one time the research center was of profound importance; it was among the projects that fundamentally infused people's voices, albeit confined within a certain framework, into the historical imagination. It becomes equally clear that over time its work restricted the historical imagination and grew into another potential quandary of museumification. It became obvious that we needed to generate another way of thinking about the past, through actively engaging our present, to open a future. I did not think we were in need of a new rhetoric or discourse, or even a new discipline, as much as we needed to find a way through the violence of the ongoing Nakba in celebration of love, living, and breathing. That is, the Nakba is not an event that ended, and our historical inquiries needed to expand beyond the confines of events into understand ongoing life. Not aiming for a philosophical or pedagogical breakthrough, I simply worked to make the classroom a space where we could reflect on our present and our past. In spite of the limitations of a classroom, teaching turned into a collective learning journey. It was clear that we needed to embrace a methodology that reinforced our connections rather than reproduced the disconnects and forced fragmentations that settler colonialism employs to eliminate us as a people. Even more than framing the discussions through the ongoing Nakba, we practiced a shared methodology that enabled us to see the past in the present. Because of this work, and in spite of structural constraints, BZU turned into the place where I found my way to ʿArifa. Over time it has become the place where my students walk me through Jerusalem when I cannot walk there, and it is the place where my peers have showed me that historians as storytellers can practice return because traditional historians prevented it.

The intended work for the SLC was informed by a similar static approach to the past that suffocated the university classroom. To address the needs of the legal case against the Jerusalem municipality's plans for Lifta (see chapter 2), the SLC approached me as a researcher who could help create an archive of the Nakba generation from Lifta by gathering oral histories to serve as testimony. My fieldwork extended over several months into what has now become a multiyear project delving into a multiperson journey. Initially, when I spoke with Lifta refugees in Jerusalem and Ramallah, my goal was simply to speak with survivors of the events of the Nakba War from Lifta. Their testimonies were intended to document, in part, proof of life and, in part, proof of a past. The SLC coordinated this work through Lifta Society chapters in Jerusalem and Ramallah (and, later, Amman). Through coalition members' introductions and planning, I was able to visit many people's homes and enter their lives in this semiofficial capacity to create a popular archive of those who had lived in and remembered Lifta. This framework, however, grew into something larger and more complicated for myself over the long months of listening to stories, even as I continue to maintain a commitment to honor the words of those who told me their histories.

Over the course of this long-term project, I began to think about what it actually means to create an archive and how that affects how we read and write Palestinian history. After all, performing as a researcher under the limited framework of proving that a people once existed relies on settler colonial frameworks of elimination as the basis of one's inquiry, even as it challenges the assumptions of those frameworks. While we collected stories, this framework limited our collective capacities to share, and in doing so, we seemed to reinforce an implicit disregard for people's ongoing vitality as they shaped and told their generational histories—of which we are all a part. Moreover, the context of Lifta, as a place of interest for various entities within the Israeli state, proved to be a burden as well as an opportunity to confront Zionist frameworks while not succumbing to them—that is, the contradictions embedded in the challenge of museumification. "We once existed here" is a problematic mantra but one that, nevertheless, seeps into how conversations are conducted in terms of oral history. Keeping in mind Rosemary Sayigh's call to conceptualize the ongoing Nakba from 1948–49 up to the present day, while also transforming (and being transformed by) the listening process for stories of the past in the ongoing present, offers an opportunity to focus on the power of people's voices and realize the power in storytelling (not testimony).[2] If we are no longer passive collectors, working through a methodology of sharing stories can transform us all.

Storytelling and Lifta—the Generative Possibilities of Memory

As I kept these contexts in mind, and as I engaged with a range of criticism on oral history, memory, and testimony, I eventually decided to walk with the stories Palestinians from Lifta shared with me. Through this process I discovered my personal need to find ʿArifa—not only through a feeling of responsibility to her past but also a dire need to contextualize my own present and hope for our future. Since stories of the past are told through the present, the violent dispossession Liftawis endured in the past is an obstacle to understanding their stories, as that violence has in so many ways created a hegemonic framework through which they tell them. Though this past can and should be understood as trauma and survival, how can we resist being defined only as victims of trauma? Moreover, because the people who told me their stories continue to live under occupation, they continue to endure set-tler violence and live it through their lens of the trauma of the spring of 1948. How could that not be the case? There was a major rupture in the spring of 1948 for every last person in or from Lifta. Zionists waged a war against them that drove them from their homes and into exile from their land; that war has not ended. This was a traumatic experience, and the violence of the ongoing Nakba is persistent trauma. Storytelling enables us to not be defined by vio-lence and allows us to move away from liberal frameworks of diagnosis and pathology. Their pasts in Lifta, in this context, became what was constantly described to me as *ayam al-balad* (the days of our homeland), with all that followed described as *ayam al-luj*ʾ (the days of refuge). It is important to re-spect the experience that gave birth to this framework but also to challenge it as a concrete distribution of historic time. Respect, accountability, and a deep and existential sense of responsibility account for the anxiety with which I (re-)present the stories that follow.

Toward creating a space that both respects and challenges the frameworks of people's memories, especially given the legacy of settler colonial violence on and in these frameworks, several themes emerged in the storytelling cru-cial to Lifta's refugees' experiences of the past and of the present. The primary focus in my reading of these themes in the stories is the lives of the generation that survived the dispossession of 1948, the first Nakba generation, though not all stories were exclusive to this generation.[3] Each of the following sec-tions centers on a theme that traces people's stories from birth to their life in Lifta, *ayam al-balad*. Each theme accounts for both the collective experience of village life and kinship and the individual stories of people. *Collective* and *individual* are simultaneously contradictory and complementary concepts as translated through the stories. Clearly and irrefutably, Zionists directly at-tacked the collective life of the village and its structures of kinship, forcing each person into an individual story of survival (or death) as part and parcel of the overall goal of elimination. But in the process of storytelling, it seemed as if we generated and worked to nurture another (similar) kind of collectiv-ity. As we worked outside the imposed boundaries between past and present, the new was also familiar: collective Palestinianness. Instead of centering the narrative on settler violence, focusing on storytelling seeks to capture the ten-sions and intricacies of a collective past while understanding that that past continues in the midst of ongoing settler colonial elimination. This collective past has been transformed into, in part, a narrative of longing and sorrow, but as it has become stories of the sorrow and pain of loss it has also, through a sense of hope to return, itself become a collective story.

Though memory and nostalgia often coexist, especially given the rupture and horrible dispossession that the people of Lifta endured at the hands of the Zionist forces, the power and mythical dimensions of their recollections demand respectful attention and is critical to understanding "refugee story-telling." While the memories of longing for a life in Lifta might recall a kind of sweetness of a "lost paradise" and succumb to romanticized versions of the past, these reflections are also important to understand because not only was land stolen but a way of life and living were severely disrupted or completely ended in the destruction of war and settler colonial land dispossession. In the midst of the oral history fever that began in the mid-1990s (led, in part, by the BZU Research Center), the Nakba generation were heavily targeted for interviews. As teams of researchers worked among Palestinians throughout Palestine and the *shatat*, a kind of fixed narrative arc emerged. Though the details vary, looking through the booklets produced by the BZU Research Center one can discern the broad lines of this narrative paradigm in three acts: "before 1948" slowly emerged as a dreamy version of life before modern times; "war stories of 1948" centered a kind of story of destruction exclusively told through the role of victimhood without agency, as represented by the village of Dayr Yassin, which represented *the* massacre story of 1948; and, finally, "after 1948" and the stations of refuge, which were themselves confined to a fixed timeline that ended in 1948–49.[4]

People from Lifta were no exception to this trend, but the irony of our journey from "testimony" into storytelling and listening reveals how, though many people relied on framing their lives through this established narrative arc, so much more emerged through the telling of stories. Working to nurture conversations and share stories allowed this backdrop to be the landscape for much more than a static narrative that seems eerily held in place by fear of erasure. By the third generation after 1948, I think we have come to understand that however intent Zionist settlers were and are on erasing Palestinians and Palestine, we could think and live outside the fear of disappearance as we worked to collectively understand what kind of presence we could hold, beyond the absence of presence. Nakba stories no longer only describe an event (or series of events) and are no longer confined to one niche in the narrative arc of life stories. Fixed boundaries, then, give way to and open up spaces for stories and storytelling that not only challenge but actually live outside settler time and colonial temporalities. Ironically, stories and storytelling emerge in this matter in spite of the growing intensity of the genocidal violence of settlers in Palestine. The existential question and survival have not become less intense, but our approach to knowledge, I argue, can move—and has moved—beyond the basic politics of recognition embedded in testimonials of victims.

Interview as performance in the traditional testimonial sense forces a linear timeline to account for our forced disappearance. The hard focus on the moments of expulsion, though understandable in the historiographical context of Palestine, narrows how we see the past and removes us from it. In this framework, people have been asked to provide the details of their refugee journey from the village into a kind of unknown.[5] This sort of inquiry follows a certain template that has changed little over time. But lives lived are the substance of stories that defy this kind of linear narrative. Expulsion, dispossession, walking into and from the fire of settler colonial violence are not singular events or even a series of events. The story of the settler state, from its inception and its subsequent structural formations, is one of violence. To follow this violence, even in its effects, is to tell the story of the state or, at the very least, to be trapped in the narrative arc and time of the state. Asking people in the midst of ongoing dispossession to describe their lives as a series of events, or, more specifically as one massive event to prove something or to counter a narrative is like proving a negative.

There is another parallel irony in writing about dispossession and denial. How can a people driven from their land retell a story that has not ended? How can stories of loss not become exclusively about one generation's story of massive loss? Since 1948 the Palestinian people have lived an ongoing dispossession. They are not only refugees in a specific sense, deprived access to their homes, but the entire Palestinian people in all of their fragmented geographies are in a constant state of settler violence. How can one write through dispossession and violence? To center my own writing on one event as a singular eruption also disregards this ongoing violence of settler colonialism. In the stories that follow, the longing for a life and a past that was violently denied is omnipresent, as are the details of everyday life, and therein lies the memory of life "before the Nakba." Nostalgia as a yearning for this past is not necessarily always a yearning for a romanticized past. There were constant themes among the folks of Lifta that we spoke with, but the thread that connected these themes was life and living between the present and the past. The ordinary—through storytelling, listening, and writing—becomes extraordinary in how signs of living formed the paradox between lasting memory and resistance to dispossession.

This chapter, more than all of the others in this book, reveals my own catalyst for why and how I consciously began searching for ʿArifa. Every conversation I had with the women of her generation was a conversation I wanted to have with her. And so began my own journey with the generative possibilities of contradiction. While oral history as a field of inquiry has a set of criteria for the evidence gathered in speaking with people, creating another kind of historical documentation, I needed something different, an otherwise way of relation with the past and with people. In the case of Palestine, this need for evidence is most often seen in testimonies about expulsion, and I was not sure how to account for this need while also honoring our other needs. While this chapter stays true to the words that were shared with me, I let the presence of those words open up spaces for potential stories, for every story shared with me also became the catalyst for the stories that remain untold and unwritten. While ʿArifa was once a stark absence in my life, her presence in this chapter is an attempt toward understanding history differently, not through absences, but rather through attempts at opening, finding, creating presence.

A Collective Life: The Geography of a Village

From the deep green of the valley to the slight elevations of the surrounding hills, the village of Lifta grew over time; even today, as a "village in ruins," the remains of the stone walls as terraces tell the story of this growth. But, again, a focus on the beauty of "the remains" is a betrayal of the stories of life in the village. Rather, living in these stories transforms the geography of Lifta from a land of ruins to a land of life. The center of life of the village emanates from the land through the water from the ʿayn (natural spring), as it always had. The ʿayn grounds my emotional map, just as it grounded the lives of the people in the village. Water is life. Life is people.[6] The water of the ʿayn shows us how metaphors grow from reality and feed our imaginations. The ʿayn, as a symbol of the life that it nourished and witnessed, continues to identify the village. Following water here is not some folkloric sentimentality, it is an invitation to understand how people treated their natural resources in relation to their social organization. The physical and social geography of Lifta come to life in the stories of the ʿayn. As a kind geographical focal point, the natural spring in Lifta is a marker of space. In people's stories of the distribution of space, the ʿayn was a central geographical feature, as it was the basis around which the lower part of the village grew. In these stories, home and life are narrated in relation to the spring; it is the central marker in people's mapping of Lifta. People describe the mosque, another common marker of space, as being to one side of the spring. They locate their homes and their physical life in the village in relation to the spring, just as they locate their cemetery in relation to it. The ʿayn was a centerpiece of life and has become the center of memories of and in Lifta. In both the geographical and symbolic senses, it locates people in the past and present of Lifta. It is also a location of return in the future.

Nowaf Awad remembered her family house's proximity to the ʿayn and many of her childhood memories were of the spring: "Our home, when it was on the road near the hill was close to the ʿayn. I remember that my sister and I would go to the ʿayn to retrieve cool water during Ramadan."[7] Through Nowaf's words we can walk with her and her memories through the valley of Lifta. Through her stories, the ruins are no longer only ruins, or not ruins at all. The expanse of the valley in Lifta gives way to an elevation of the hills around it, and Nowaf's words of life are no longer confined to the past. Nowaf and her sister were perhaps able to take quick trips to the ʿayn as young children because their home was close, but it also was clear that the organization of life was also due to the activities of women around this water source. The lower structures in the village relied on proximity to the water and, even as the village expanded throughout the valley and into the upper plateau, the ʿayn continued to organize life. Unlike Nowaf, Nuwara Abutaah Zitawi remembers watching her father's new bride (my grandmother ʿArifa) going to the ʿayn to fetch water from her father's house in upper Lifta: "We only had running water in the pipes for about four to five months before we were forced to leave Lifta, so your grandmother actually went down to fetch water every day since she married my father, your grandfather."[8] Nuwara, as my mother's half-sister, seemed to understand that my questions about the geography of the village were both a necessity to record history and a means for me to understand ʿArifa's movement. I suppose it was implicit to her that if I understood how ʿArifa moved through the village, I could learn how to move with her. I discerned this because in between questions Nuwara reminded me that I did not actually know my grandmother and did so with sadness—a kind of lamentation. As ʿAta's daughter from his first marriage, she is much older than my mother and understood that she was a thread that could connect me with a younger ʿArifa and so shared these stories with great detail and patience. When I explained to her that I wanted to know more about Lifta through ʿArifa, she told me that she would be happy to help because of my mother, who initiated and participated in the conversation alongside Nuwara and myself. Nearly three decades after her passing, and more than seven decades after their forced expulsion, we gathered to be with ʿArifa.

ʿArifa was the youngest of three daughters. Perhaps when she was a child, she went to the ʿayn with her sisters, like Nowaf, or perhaps, like Nuwara, she watched others make the trip. Because her sisters were significantly older, after they married ʿArifa might have, at a young age, carried the responsibility of helping her mother with water duties. Perhaps like others, a young ʿArifa navigated the village from the distance of her family home up the hills through her trips down to the *ʿayn*. She, too, married in the village, and with her new husband came his young daughter from a previous marriage (Nuwara), along with a mother-in-law, Safiya; a sister-in-law, Amouna; and the first wife, ʿIzziya, who kept their young son and Nuwara's brother, Muhammad, with her.[9] Nuwara saw her father's wife navigate the old and the new in her life—family and geography. Would ʿArifa remember the *ʿayn* with the same nostalgia as Nowaf? Would she agree with how Nuwara looked back? After all, the wife and the daughter might have been in conflict. Nuwara told her stories through love. She said that ʿArifa embraced her as a friend and comrade, but also held her as a daughter, in spite of their relative proximity in age. Listening to Nuwara, I wondered how ʿArifa would remember *ayam al-balad*.

Strolling across the upper edge of the higher terraces in upper Lifta, not far from the school, we walked down to the *ʿayn*, empowered by Nowaf's and Nuwara's memories. The past broke through the scene of ruins and transformed it into a geography of possibilities. Walking through the layers of time as told through their stories weaves the living tapestry of Indigenous time in Palestine—neither ruins nor museums, these are the means by which connections endure through time. On the warmer days, in the early morning hours ʿArifa would likely be among the women walking down from the area in upper Lifta they called *khala al-tarha* (the area of the slight decline) to fetch water for the day. Her older brother's wife, ʿAzziza, would be at her side and they would take with them large containers to fill for the day's supply of water. With sunrise and morning prayers as the backdrop, ʿArifa probably walked from the house her husband built for their family to the house of his mother, widowed young with four children, to borrow the donkey for the morning. Her mother-in-law, Safiya, was no doubt up early to milk the cows (she purchased two in the first decade after her husband's death). Selling the milk of the cows in nearby neighborhoods in Jerusalem sustained the family, so Safiya prioritized them in her daily routine. Up early for the day's work, ʿArifa must have noticed every day that her sister-in-law, Amona, remained happily sleeping through the morning. One woman's lack of a work ethic might have been a source of tension. Was it spoken about, or did it remain in the arena of the unsaid? Did it remain a tension that generations of women would navigate? Such are the meat of stories of life and their continuities: The beauty and the laziness of certain women were the tales that were told through the generations. The names might be different, but the stories are similar, and they have become part of our stories, memories come to life through speculation.

Ibrahim, ʿArifa's brother, was trouble all of his life, and ʿArifa saw her role as covering for him and smoothing over the inevitable daily disappointments he brought to their small family. Every day ʿAzziza would lend an empathetic ear on the way to the ʿayn. The path to the ʿayn took them down a winding road on a slight hill. Through the paths you can almost see the donkey, who carefully made his own way, and so led the way for all who follow. Historically these kinds of paths in Palestine were actually forged by the instinct of the donkey.[10] The path was not only a road to the ʿayn but a road through the valley of the village—a kind of marked geography of life.

How much water would be enough for a family's daily use?[11] There was water for cooking, and cleaning, and water to drink. In spite of her initial patience, Nuwara grew frustrated by my questions about the water retrieval process: "My daughter, I do not understand what you mean. We did not measure need before they returned for more water. Rather, we measured use by what they returned with."[12] The ʿayn provided the path toward sustenance.

Geography is not necessarily fixed, for it travels with us. Jamila ʿAwad recalled her family home, the place where she was born, and her location of the house also followed the natural spring: the home was "close to the ʿayn, like this house and the street [in reference to a house and street in Ramallah, where we were speaking]."[13] More than simply a geographical coordinate, the ʿayn remains the life source of memory. The spring continued to measure distance and time in stories told of the very concept of home. For Jamila, it remained her sense of distance in Ramallah, as it had in Jerusalem before that.

Sensory memory is not fixed; it lives on. In her storytelling, Amana Khalil fondly remembered the taste of the water from the ʿayn: "my God, if you drank from the water of the ʿayn, you did not feel like you drank . . . because it was so light. . . . Oh, my! How fantastic the water from ʿayn baladna was, by God."[14] Amana's voice reflected the lightness of the water she described, the joy in the memory remaining a lived experience in her senses. The ʿayn not only physically located her memory but also reflected a social and sensory experience.

Maybe ʿArifa carried the taste of the water with her like Amana, embedded within her body as much as it was within her memory. Every home that she touched that I have been in, from the one she built for her young family after her husband's sudden death in 1967, to all the homes her daughters built for themselves and their children, the clay jug, *al-sharba,* was a prominently featured decoration. *Al-sharba* is a traditional means of holding water to keep it cool and clean tasting. I grew up in the shadow of it in my own childhood home, so I notice them wherever I go even now. I once thought it strange to make a holder of water into an almost sacred object, but I have come to realize that it is the continuity of 'Arifa's daily trek to the 'ayn. It is her daughters'—and their daughters'—marker of the journey to the 'ayn, even though they never made the trip themselves. It has not passed, nor is it only in the past. The social life of the 'ayn and the material life of water is this continuity. Indigenous geographies rightfully covet water as life, each context specific to the social and environmental health of the people, as sources of water are cared for and care for the people of the land. Amana and 'Arifa are reflections of the life that the water of the 'ayn carried and continues to carry.[15]

In Palestine, these women and their words seem to echo the words of Mahmoud Darwish, or does Darwish echo their words? Either way or both ways, it creates a sense of synchronicity through water and life, for Darwish also sang of water:

> Water under these conditions comes to us like a miracle. Who says water has no color, flavor, or smell? Water does have a color that reveals itself in the unfolding of thirst. Water has the color of bird sounds, that of sparrows in particular-birds that pay no heed to this war approaching from the sea, so long as their space is safe. And water has the flavor of water, and a fragrance that is the scent of the afternoon breeze blown from a field with full ears of wheat waving in a luminous expanse strewn like the flickering spots of light left by the wings of a small sparrow fluttering low.[16]

In all of this storytelling, a listener can easily be lost between the romance of the past and the harsh longing for this past in the present. The taste of the water lives on, as does its source, the 'ayn in Lifta, which continues to feed the land. Settlers have transformed how they relate to the spot, coveting it as holy, in one of many attempts to transform the landscape. That violence cannot be ignored, but it can be put in its place, out of the center of our journeys between the past and the present. The 'ayn, the layers and generations of lives it has nourished, defies attempts of settler transformation. Lifta is unique in the sense that part of the geography of place is still material and for some who can travel into Jerusalem—it remains accessible in its (non)ruins.[17] The 'ayn was, is, and will be a location and a locater. But, currently physically accessible or not, Lifta, like Palestine, lives inside us and in our stories. This living is a path that arcs both toward the past and the future. This is ongoing return.

Lifta al-Tahta and Lifta al-Foqa: Social Structures and Modernity in the Village

Along with the memory of material and symbolic location, the geography of Lifta was also marked by the connection between the lower part of the village (Lifta al-tahta) and the upper, more newly built, part (Lifta al-foqa), as well as the intimate connection people in both the lower and upper parts of Lifta enjoyed with other parts of Jerusalem. The division of upper and lower Lifta actually had an important social and economic context, in particular, given the construction boom of the mandate period. While this change in the so-cial economy of northwestern Jerusalem is well documented,[18] people's nar-ratives reveal the intricacies, including both divisions and cohesions brought about by this kind of slow expansion.

Ibrahim Khalil spoke of the process and context that culminated in, for some, the move from lower to upper Lifta. He explained that lower Lifta was the original and, as such, older part of the village. Located in the valley, it contained the older geography of the village, including the familial division of property. As relationships with capital changed, so did the village's social landscape. Families moved from lower to upper Lifta as capital wealth ex-panded, but, according to Khalil, the expansion did not dramatically change the structural relationships families had both with each other and their land. Nevertheless, this expansion did further highlight the intimate connection people in Lifta had with other parts of Jerusalem—from al-Haram al-Sharif and regular trips there for Friday prayers to neighboring parts of Jerusalem, including Romema. Ibrahim Khalil spoke of daily visits by the men of Lifta to the café owned by Saleh Eissa, located between Romema and Lifta.[19] The café was a point of connection with other parts of Jerusalem and a vibrant social space, but it was not only a common meeting place; it also became a focus and target of political activity.

The connection of the lower and upper parts of the village also highlighted the variety of shared experiences people in Lifta had with other parts of Jeru-salem. Salima al-Baja spoke of the geography of Lifta as an intimate part of Jerusalem. But also, and with great pride, she noted that the geography of the village expanded throughout the mandate period. She spoke fondly of the vastness of the land of the village and its connection to Jerusalem: "Our vil-lage was the closest village to Jerusalem. The land of our village is vast *mashal-*

lah [praise be to God's will], extending to the land of where the Hadassa Hospital in ʿAssiywa now stands, my father-in-law used to tell me that they planted that land with wheat and barley before the hospital was built. Our village lands reached Shuʾfat, Bayt Iksa, and Nabi Samuel."[20] Because of this vast expanse, Salima al-Baja explained that many from Lifta were able to rebuild parts of their lives after 1948 in other parts of (East) Jerusalem where they owned and worked land, though it was not an entirely collective effort because of class stratification; only some families were able to rebuild in Bab al-Zahra, Shaikh Jarrah, Wadi al-Joz, and other neighborhoods in Jerusalem.

Recollections of the landscape of the village were actually interesting in how borders functioned (or, more specifically, did not function or even exist) before 1948. Muhammad Nassar recounted his own family's lands as an indication of how porous these (non)borders were in the decades before 1948: "We worked and lived in the land in lower Lifta, this land was close to the natural spring . . . but we also had land and worked in the surrounding villages—from Bayt Haninya, to Bayt Iksa, to Dayr Yassin." Once again, the discussion of upper and lower Lifta was nuanced by connections with the rest of Jerusalem. A collective kind of narrative emerged among those who lived in Lifta in the decades prior to 1948 about their relationship to the Old City of Jerusalem and its surrounding neighborhoods. Muhammad Nassar actually clearly proclaimed that "there was no real difference between Lifta al-tahta and Lifta al-foqa other than Lifta al-foqa's closer proximity to Jerusalem, perhaps in an attempt to elide the class dimension in the past."[21] ʿAbd al-Karim Zhour also described the intimacy of connection with Jerusalem, and Rifqa Odeh described her life in upper Lifta and how that enabled an organic connection with Jerusalem's center of life. She fondly recalled what life in upper Lifta meant in a structural and social sense, that it was "a part of the life in Jerusalem."[22] Each person spoke through this location and its relationship to other parts of Jerusalem as a means, it seems, toward subtly describing class stratification.

Within Rifqa Odeh's descriptions of this proximity we find a nuanced reflection of nascent relations with modernity in both an urban and a capitalist construct. In my own experiences with familial stories of Lifta, my mother and her siblings' reflections of their parents also reveal the subtleties of a cultural analysis based on class structures between upper and lower Lifta. My maternal grandfather, ʿAta Abutaah, was a teacher in local government schools in other neighborhoods of Jerusalem, and, as such, he was able to accumulate the basic capital wealth that enabled him to build a house for his young family in upper Lifta in the 1940s. Before she married, ʿArifa lived between her father's house in upper Lifta and the family's lands in lower Lifta. Over time, well after 1948, these stories became the source of a kind of familial lamentation of loss (in the sense of Lifta) and a tale of continuity (in the sense of Jerusalem) for a family who, after life in Lifta, resided in the Old City and, after the war in 1967, in the Wadi al-Joz neighborhood of Jerusalem.[23] Taha Hamouda also focused on this relationship and not only described the social connections between Lifta and Jerusalem but found Lifta to be a part of the geography of Jerusalem as he declared, "Lifta is part and parcel of Jerusalem and has always been!"[24] In fact, this point of Lifta as a part of Jerusalem was a constant theme in how people spoke of their lives before 1948 and its continuities after 1948. Like others, Ibrahim Khalil declared that Lifta was the "key to Jerusalem and its bride" both because of its location in proximity to the center of the city as well as its strategic importance as a connection between Jaffa and Jerusalem.[25]

The geography of the village was not only about the village but also about the city. Jerusalem, as such, was a city of its inhabitants, and the village of Lifta, like other surrounding villages, were often considered neighborhoods within the city. This urban logic was not exclusive to Lifta or Jerusalem, for it was the case throughout Palestine, particularly as the local economy expanded and cities were more accessible and necessary for everyday life. In the context of Lifta, though, this connection to Jerusalem is a projection of the past as much as it is a reflection of the present. An intimate connection between homeland and Jerusalem is a political as well as social and cultural reading of the past through the present. Ibrahim Khalil's sentiment about Lifta as the key to Jerusalem is a common element of the emotional map of Lifta that many shared, bridging the memories of the past with the experiences of the present and creating paths that bring the tenses together as they walk through time. The layers of life in the city reflect the layers of life in the village.

Economy of Progress: Upper and Lower Lifta and Change as Progress

Describing those who resided in upper Lifta, Muhammad Nassar said that there were people who worked their land as a primary form of income, there were those who worked in the stone quarry, and there were professionals (teachers, state employees, etc.).[26] The apparatus of the mandate state structure employed many folks in Lifta, including, as Jamila Awwad explained, her husband, who served in the Palestine Police Force.[27] Ibrahim Khalil's father was employed in the Jerusalem municipality as a plumber, and he also worked his land, where he had both olive groves and fig trees.[28] Agricultural land was mainly located in the northern and western parts of the vast landscape of the village, as the eastern parts were mostly for building, as that part of upper Lifta was basically viewed as an extension of Jerusalem's city center. Salima al-Baja, who lived in upper Lifta, explained the interaction between the economy and land: "People who worked outside the village [like those who now work directly within '48 lands] earned money and built homes [in upper Lifta], but those in lower Lifta had olive groves and many of them had farm animals like cows, whose milk they would sell in Romema."[29] Class stratification in the mandate period brought with it a kind of social capital people carried throughout their lives. As part of family folklore, my mother and her sisters held on to stories their mother, ʿArifa, told of her father. Abu Siamo— the name most often used for him in these stories, though he was actually Abu Ibrahim (Siamo is a playful take on his family name of Siam)—was famously regarded as a successful street merchant in Romema, where he sold fruits and vegetables. He apparently did not learn Hebrew or Yiddish to run his small business, except for certain key phrases, and when frustrated by the settler customers who tried to haggle over prices, he was famous for becoming angry and aggressive. In our family, to this day, when someone screams from frustration we refer to this as "performing like Abu Siamo." Though told through a kind of comedic lens, Abu Siamo's anger may have more to do with tragedy given the fragility of his and his family's economic well-being in a growing settler-dominated capital market.

The economy of trade and a lived connection between various parts of Jerusalem is also about markets. Here emerges the significance of the market in Mahane Yehuda (a common location of interest in many of these narratives) both as a place to purchase and as a place to sell fruits and vegetables during times of harvest. This further indicates how connected the parts of Jerusalem were before 1948, as well as how tenuous these connections were.[30] As Jamila Awwad explained, "I used to go back and forth to Jerusalem with my mother all the time; we went by foot . . . before they introduced the bus . . . we would go to the market in Mahane Yehuda to buy all that we needed for the house,"[31] as they did not grow fruits or vegetables of their own. The market was also very close to their home and the village and, as such, was convenient. Though Mahane Yehuda was first established in the late nineteenth century under Ottoman rule, in the 1920s, under British rule, the market grew and became a staple for Jerusalem's merchants.[32] People from Lifta frequented the marketplace, as did those from all areas around Jerusalem.

In the 1920s and 1930s, and well into the 1940s, the landscape of life was changing as the economy of Jerusalem expanded under British colonial rule. As these stories reveal, this meant various things to different people, but for many in Lifta, it obviously brought about a change in their local economy. Habiba al-'Abdiyat's father was a landowner and worked his land throughout his life, but during her youth, he had also been a construction worker. She recalled the irony of her own inability to go to the local school, even though it was a project that her father worked on before he grew ill and was unable to continue construction work.[33] The construction industry was obviously a main economic boom that brought about significant social and cultural change for families in Lifta from the 1920s to the 1940s. Muhammad Nassar explained this change as he described his own and his father's work in Lifta al-tahta and Jerusalem. His father worked as a stonemason (naqash), and did this work throughout Lifta.[34] Nassar explained that the local al-'Asi family owned the most prevalent construction company in Lifta and were actually the ones who built many of the houses in upper Lifta. The income generated from construction and the stone quarry in Lifta not only changed the economic landscape of the village but was also the impetus for major local change as families moved into upper Lifta.

Though people were clear not to necessarily describe the construction boom and its economic resonance as upward mobility, it was, nevertheless, indicative of the major changes that the three decades of the mandate period brought about. This is not exclusive to Lifta in this time period, as the economy of Palestine experienced dramatic change after World War I and throughout the mandate period.[35] Lifta was, nevertheless, a local focal point for economic opportunity because of the open geography of the place, the stone quarry, and the ability to work within an area without locally enforced borders. Taha Hamouda explained that, during the construction boom, "people were actually building [not only for themselves but] as a means of financial investment."[36] Ibrahim Khalil recalled that his father worked as an employee of the Jerusalem municipality and also on his land.[37] These stories of double-duty work were common among this generation in Lifta. As the economy changed in the form of new and different kinds of employment—in particular, with the growing bureaucracy of the government—people worked their land and other jobs.

With these kinds of organic connections between upper and lower Lifta came some tensions. Salima al-Baja described her home in the "new neighborhood" as comfortable, with modern amenities, so much so that it enabled her father to "rent space out to people from places like Hebron who worked in the British administration." She also made a distinction between lower and upper Lifta in terms of modernity and amenities: "Those of us in upper Lifta were of a slightly higher class, and those in lower Lifta relied more directly on their peasant lifestyle."[38] This language of modernity is not surprising, for it followed the changing nature of the economy of all of Palestine under British capital rule. Nevertheless, the distinction between upper and lower Lifta were not at all hard and fast. Salima, who explained the difference in lifestyle, also explained that her husband and his family lived in Lifta al-tahta and their union was not at all extraordinary. In fact, the opposite occurred with Jamila Awwad, who lived in Lifta al-tahta and, after she married, moved to Lifta al-foqa. As she explained, "Marriage between lower and upper Lifta was completely normal, it was marriage within the village."[39] Though the geography expanded through accumulated capital, it did not create a hard boundary or socially divide the village.

The geography of the village, while not unique, as many villages expanded into an upper and lower sections, tells of the ways people moved through space over time. The expansion of the built sections of the village meant that walks through Lifta were not static or unchanging before 1948 but were, nevertheless, continuous. People focused on this continuity through the change in their stories, and the mobility of 'Arifa's life in Lifta is testament to this. From the large Siam family, she had kin and land in the lower sections of the village. In her lifetime, her family moved from lower to upper Lifta and a newly built home near the upper ridge. Her daily ventures to the 'ayn, like that of others, meant walking through changes that came with time. 'Arifa's husband went into the Old City of Jerusalem daily, to his job as a teacher at the Dar al-Aytam School; her mother-in-law sold the milk and eggs she gathered daily in surrounding neighborhoods in Jerusalem. 'Arifa and her family existed in all the worlds living in these various spaces provided, and family enabled me to see these lives and all their movements and to connect the past with our present. Change has always been a factor, and the fluidity of changing life (and lifestyles) create a vital relationship between life before and after 1948. That is, we learn through these stories that there is no need to impose a kind of static version of the past in order to reveal the devastation of rupture.

The visibility of the multiple geographies can help us think about how people moved through space, always grounded in this movement by land. So, what did the land mean to people? Location and relation to land are superimposing forces in the memories expressed by the refugees. Ibrahim Khalil spoke of how important land was to his family and his memory when he declared, "Of course we had land! What is a person without land?"[40] This statement seems as much about the past as it is about all that happened since. The answer to the question is a glaring reality for people who no longer have access to or enjoy the fruits and sustenance of their land. Thus, relation to the land is about a relationship with people, land, and home, and this entire relational framework changed in the spring of 1948 when people were violently driven from their homes. Nevertheless, working to understand how people tell the stories of their lives in Lifta has revealed that forms of relational frameworks sustained themselves in the living memory of the past through the present. This became not only a core of the memory of Lifta as part of the past but also a sense of how Lifta has been divided. The differences between the upper and lower sections appear in various ways in these memories, but the overwhelming element of this divide is about how a "simple life" in the past (which was hardly simple) is imagined. Habiba al-ʿAbdiyat stated this quite succinctly: "Life was simple—believe me, my child, we were far happier than we are today."[41] Yet this longing for the simplicity of life revealed a not-so-simple story colored by the complicated relations with and connections to land. Though representations of the memories of the lifestyle in Lifta al-tahta can easily be read as nostalgia, it seems that the simplicity that people described is framed by their stories about loss and all the violence that loss has entailed over time. Embedded within these larger frames of a kind of "paradise lost" are the realities of the everyday. When reality and longing mix, they make for a complicated spectrum of memory for this first generation of refugees from Lifta, revealing the nature of nostalgia and what constitutes simplicity and unity. Strikingly, a common phrase that Taha Hamouda used in his reflections on life before dispossession was that it was a "simple life": "We were one, we were one people."[42] Obviously, the fragmentation that comes with settler violence takes a hold on people, the past, and memory. The "simple," here, is a reflection on the complications of life outside the tragedies of dispossession and displacement.

This kind of language of longing also appeared in the stories of everyday life. The early decades of the twentieth century were a time of significant change, and people's stories obviously reflect that change. Capitalist modernity was a reality in Palestine long before the violence of dispossession, and with it came the language of class and progress. Relations to land and people prior to 1948 enable people to remember the connections more than the differences. Collective experiences, even for those who resided in upper Lifta, were still very much tied to the social life of the lower village. Here we need to widen our understanding of dispossession and think about it not just as being without possessions but being forcibly removed from a complicated atmosphere of relational life. This social world that lives on in people's memories also entailed holidays and celebrations, including life events from birth to death.

Everyday Life: From the Cradle, Through School, Work, and Marriage, to the Grave

This generation of people from Lifta, as they did in their relation to land, straddled a complex relation to tradition and modernity in how they recounted the stories of their births. Notably, birth stories again reveal a great deal of the village's proximity and relationship to the city. Habiba al-ʿAbdiyat was born in a hospital in the city of Jerusalem and recalled the family story of her naming: Her mother allowed the nurses to name her. The nurses named her Mona, but when her father arrived at the hospital, he told his wife, "But she is our beloved and her name will be 'beloved'—Habiba."[43] Not all women went to hospitals to give birth but, according to Nowaf Awad (whose mother gave birth to two sets of twins after Nowaf), a majority of the women she knew of her mother's generation and younger did go to hospitals in Jerusalem by the mid-1930s.[44] The narrative of birth, for women especially, tended toward this discussion between birth in hospitals in various parts of Jerusalem or birth via midwife in Lifta. While the details of each person's birth story vary, the overwhelming sense in the stories told retain an ambivalence to modernity (as represented by hospital births). As in the stories of work and land, this ambivalence is telling, as it counters the classic linear story of modern progress. That is, the binary of the older times versus the modern times was neither obvious nor even of great consequence in how the stories were told. Rather than being a symbol of modernity, the hospital in these narratives was more about relations to and with Jerusalem.

Even more telling than the hospitals were the stories about the school in Lifta. Rifqa Odeh's stories about her childhood was literally marked by color: The fondness of her youth was defined by her schooling and her love of the blue pinstripe uniform she wore with pride every school day. Located on the road to Jerusalem, the local school served as a common marker for many. Its construction was a primary innovation in the lives of folks in Lifta, and it also deepened and continued the village's relationship with Jerusalem. People remember the stages of their lives through the framework of their education. Their education and stories of their school days, therefore, created for many in Lifta another form of continuity with Jerusalem, since, for many, furthering their education meant going to the various other schools in the center of

Jerusalem. Rifiqa Odeh recalled how she and others would walk to the local school, which was a geographical meeting- point between lower and upper Lifta (located on the ridge where the valley meets the plateau, marking the beginning of upper Lifta) until a bus was made available for the village.[45] She explained that she entered the school at age five; though she was younger than the other students, her father was so keen on her getting an education that he negotiated an earlier entry for his daughter. According to Rifqa, the sweetness of her childhood school memories remained with her throughout her life. Today the building that once housed the school still stands; though it has been occupied by settlers, it remains a lasting symbol of the formative past. The school in Lifta provided up to a fourth-grade education for girls, after which Rifqa and some other young girls in the village went on to complete their education in Jerusalem (Rifqa attended the Mamouniya School in the Wadi al-Joz neighborhood). Nuwara Abutaah Zitawi spoke of the walk from upper Lifta to the Mamouniya School with girls from various families in Lifta: "I liked it best when the weather was warm and we walked together as girls from Lifta to school. We were like all the girls there, we all knew how to walk through Jerusalem."[46]

The location of the school in Lifta, in terms of both geography and social significance, was a large component in Muhammad Abu Layle's memories of Lifta before the storm of dispossession and exile. He explained that the school was fully functioning by 1929 and quickly became a focal point not only for Lifta but for the entire region of northwestern Jerusalem. Children from surrounding areas, including adjacent villages, sent their children (mostly young men, according to Muhammad) to the school and, as such, it became a social and political meeting ground during this politically active period. He went on to describe how those who completed their primary education at the local school received their secondary education at various schools in Jerusalem. This kind of educational consistency marked this generation, as Muhammad explained, and resulted in a population that was educated and, according to him, politically aware.[47] Again, memory functions retrospectively and, as such, this sentiment not only spoke to the contemporary time of mandate-era Lifta but also to all that occurred later. Stories of education were a trope of the narrative of the past, and, almost always, a consistent thread that tied the past to the present—for knowledge is, in these stories, a part of the past and present that could not be stolen or taken away. This ethos remains as stories told about past education framed the stories about the educational prowess of subsequent generations. In particular, when in conversation with women, I would often hear that 'Arifa would be proud that her daughter's daughter is both "educated" and is an "educator." This is how I might have been seen as both an outsider and an insider—a far more complicated and intimate role than that of a mere researcher seeking historical testimony. I suppose I was also looking for a way to be a part of the past conversations and considering how 'Arifa would think of me. That must have been an omnipresent, albeit implicit, part of these conversations. I asked about her a lot.

Following in line with Muhammad Abu Layle's sentiment, the significance of education has, in time and memory, transformed into a major storytelling theme among refugees from Lifta. Talk of the school was common among people; they spoke of it with a sense of pride that connected their history in the village with their experiences as refugees, along with the importance of education, which remained an obvious consistency in their lives. Like Rifqa Odeh, Ibrahim Khalil fondly remembered attending the Lifta school as part of his intimate relationship with knowledge and as part of the overall geography of Jerusalem. He and his male classmates, after seventh grade, transferred to the Ibrahimiya School in the Bab al-Zahra neighborhood in central Jerusalem and their fondness for Lifta extended throughout Jerusalem. Ibrahim Khalil distinctly recalled walking to both schools—to further emphasize the connection between Lifta and other parts of Jerusalem and how storytelling is born of walking through emotional maps. Because of this proximity to Jerusalem and its location, Lifta's school attracted students not only from Lifta but also from the surrounding areas. According to Taha Hamouda, the smartest and most successful students from Lifta completed their education in various schools in neighborhoods in Jerusalem. In particular, many young boys from the village went to the Ibrahimiya School, as Ibrahim Khalil had done.[48] Unlike Taha Hamouda and Ibrahim Khalil, however, Nuwara Abutaah Zitawi remembered that when the simple walk to school meant walking through land mines (both figuratively and literally), her father thought it prudent to constrict her geography. After the bombing of Saleh al-Eissa's café in December 1947, her father decided that it would be best to keep her closer to home, so Nuwara took up an informal apprenticeship with a neighbor and learned how to sew in lieu of completing her education at the Mamouniya School. Her father (my grandfather) offered her this alternative as a means of continuing her relationship with knowledge. These seeds of 'Ata Abutaah were planted long ago, and as Nuwara shared her stories I came to realize how my mother carried this importance of education into my own life, creating both a connection with this past and a rupture from it. When I was a child, my mother picked a fight (in front of me) with our local school in Chicago to enroll me in spite of my young age. At the time I was young, stunned and embarrassed by my mother's force, but in reflection, I came to realize this was her planting the seed of education inside me, with some added defiance of her own. She won that battle for me and I wonder how many she lost before me. I was the youngest child in my class. Education in all of its iterations is formative, inherited, and, clearly, generational.

Education was not only a product of formal schooling; learning also came in the process living everyday life. Liftawis spoke about living and negotiating a dignified life from, on, and through the land. In some of these stories, the olive season was of primary significance. Habiba al-ʿAbdiyat's father had two wives, and because of that, her mother told her husband that the divisions from the olive harvest were to be made according to her wishes. That is, her mother had land and trees that were hers, and she would harvest and sell the oil for herself exclusively and her husband would do the same with his land and his trees. Habiba recalled going to the land they called *al-mesha* and picking olives with her mother every year. Her mother's arrangement with her father enabled Habiba's mother a level of self-sufficiency, as her trees and land provided well for her. Habiba remembered the olive trees and harvest season with great detail: "We would pick the olives and directly take them from our tress to the olive press, which was also in the village, located right next to the mosque; the whole process was local—from the tree to the press."[49] While the olive harvest was a major focus of the stories that are remembered about Lifta, agricultural life was not just about the olive harvests but about people's intimate connection with the land. Describing this connection was common throughout the villages of Palestine, and the intimacy of these details are important to understanding the phenomenal stories of Lifta's Natives.[50]

This intimacy was never more clear than in the stories about the village's communal *tawabiyn* (clay ovens). Habiba, in recalling the baking of bread in the *tabun*, and how her mother and paternal aunt shared the same oven, remembered how the smell of bread was omnipresent in the village.[51] As in the symbolic value of the ʿayn in Lifta, the trope of the *tabun* was also common—particularly in the women's stories. Making bread in this traditional way highlighted the collectivity the work involved. Many families shared a *tabun* and rotated use of it among the women, whereby it actually functioned as a public gathering place. This gathering place, together with the sensory memory of its smell, easily transforms bread into a trope for a shared past in these collective stories. As with the taste of water from the ʿayn, the senses have a way of not only remembering but continuing a story—in this case, a story of bread. In fact, the two depended on each other:

Water from the ʿayn was an essential ingredient in the dough of the bread, so from the ʿayn, to the hands of the women who made the dough, to the *tabun*, another kind of daily geography exists in past experience and ongoing memories. These sensory memories colored the stories so often that they seemed to become my own memories.

So, too, did weddings and women's descriptions of these celebrations reveal and sustain layers of the common and communal.[52] From the kind of wedding dress (a *thob* from Beit Jala with a particular embroidery stitch called ʿabu qutba), to the merchants where gold and home goods were bought (almost always from particular vendors in the Old City of Jerusalem), to the very detail of the woman from al-Tur who was the hairdresser for nearly all the brides of Lifta, these wedding stories reveal the consistencies and sweetness of life in the time of the village. The wedding celebration was what can best be described as a rite of passage among the young women of the village, and all of them told the stories of their weddings. Habiba al-ʿAbdiyat summarized it well: "This was our woman's world."[53] The sharing of these memories, as well as the memories themselves, nurture a strong sense of community, past and present. It almost stopped mattering that no one I listened to remembered the name of the hairdresser from al-Tur, because they all shared a fondness for her styling prowess.

From the Communal to the Individual

As the stories and storytelling of Lifta attest, in *ayam al-balad*, the distinction between individual stories and collective memory is often difficult to maintain. In the stories of Liftawis, the past is made up of individual memories, with sounds, smells, and colors that are one's own, but individual memories also hold communal stories and are full of the *we* of the community that was and is Lifta. The memory of resistance and one particular incident that occurred in late 1947, and all that followed in the form of heightened British colonial and Zionist settler colonial violence, is a testament to this collective form of storytelling. As the story goes (and as many related it, including both Habiba al-ʿAbdiyat and Nawaf Awwad, who remembered the story with extraordinary detail), in the cold of December 1947, a young fighter from Lifta named Ahmad al-ʿAbdiyat (Habiba's brother) attacked a settler bus, throwing a handmade bomb into it. He was most likely not alone, as this was a part of a larger framework of resistance that Palestinians enacted after the United Nations Partition Plan was announced on November 29, 1947. This incident was a point of pride in memories but it was also animated by the fear of settler violence.

As people recalled the story, the bus was bombed, and the Zionists attacked Saleh Eissa's crowded café, where armed men opened fire on the patrons. The café was located on the path that eventually leads down to the valley of the village of Lifta, and it was a meeting place for men from the village and the surrounding geographies. Men and their cafés are actually constants in Palestinian history, past and present. Walking through any town or village in Palestine one finds a café, walks by it, and catches snippets of the stories men tell. The public space of the café is a meeting place; targeting it for destruction with the intent of elimination is not unusual in Palestine, for this is what Zionists do. At first, this must seem like another trope (like other tropes discussed throughout this chapter) and, in a sense, it is. Resistance and settler violence are foundational parts of all of these stories—elements that can be conflated or ignored. As the story goes, after the attack on the café, the men in the village took it on themselves to protect the village from violent Zionist settlers (Ibrahim Khalil described this in detail),[54] who it seemed would return with more violence after the café incident. And thus, it was clear to all, the war began long before the spring of 1948.

The story of the spring of 1948 that follows is, for many readers of Palestinian history, the beginning of the story of Palestinians as refugees. For those from Lifta who recalled this time, the tone of the storytelling changed dramatically as people recounted the *when* and the *how* of the violent rupture between the past in Lifta (and all the memories of that past) and the present: their lives as refugees. While the details vary for those who left for villages in the surrounding areas, those who moved into lands in other parts of Jerusalem, or those who fled further, all left because they were forced to. And the trope in this line of storytelling is the elimination of the *we* in the stories of where people ended up. The collective, the communal, and the common stories full of individual style and detail became, after the summer of 1948, individual stories of a remembered collective: Lifta.

CHAPTER FIVE

Lifta and Life Stories as Stories of Living

I never met ʿArifa. Even if I had met her as a child, we would not have been able to speak. As a child growing up in Chicago, I did not learn to speak Arabic—the tongue of my mother but not my mother tongue. I could and did listen in Arabic, but speaking came much later. And yet, I have listened to ʿArifa all my life.

The name ʿArifa is found in no archive. No one recorded her voice or her words. But I no longer have time to linger in the *not*. So in this chapter I step away from the multitude of voices telling me, as a historian and as a Palestinian living in the violence of denial, that I must find proof of life in the archive before I can speak, and that I must have recognition before I can be heard. In this chapter, I walk with ʿArifa and invite my reader, our listeners, to walk with us, to dream together, to share our pain and our joy, and—most of all—to nurture our ability to breathe amid all this violence. May we continue to return.

My Mother's Stories

At the end of a long summer in 1967, ʿArifa rented a house in the Wadi al-Joz neighborhood of Jerusalem, just a few blocks away from the house in which she and her young family had lived since the early 1950s. There is a beautiful garden inside the courtyard walls framing the long stairs that lead up to the modest rooms of ʿArifa's third home since 1948. Now that she was a widow and her children had lost their father, it would be her last material home on earth before reaching her resting place atop the hill in the cemetery down the block.

After her husband passed, ʿArifa's life had been upended once again—in another ongoing part of the Nakba. It took my mother over forty years into my life to begin to talk about the summer of 1967. Only when I asked her about how her mother had talked to her about the spring of 1948 did my mother begin to share her stories of that fateful summer in 1967. The ongoing Nakba is marked in time by the seasons. In becoming a part of this kind of storytelling, I learned that, through listening, we unsettle conceptions of time and work to understand Nakba differently as our own variation of temporal coherence between and through the past and present.

Silence disrupted this process in terms of both listening and writing. Indeed, silence has disrupted life since 1948. Listening to silence, in spite of all the markers provided for a listener to understand that silence, remains a source of great discomfort for me.[1] Listening to my mother tell me the story of her childhood and how she broke the curfew imposed after the full occupation of Jerusalem in June and July 1967 to visit her father in the hospital, I realized that some silences will never be filled with words. Unlearning the imposed sense of a crisis of silence that results from erasure is not easy. Maybe a journey with stories can challenge the anxieties of the need to not be silent. After all, sharing stories is also sharing pain, but how can we try to share without reproducing the pain? For this I have no answer, but carrying the stories opens up the space for questions outside the crisis of settlers. That is, perhaps silence can simply be about unspoken spaces without the anxiety that settlers will occupy those spaces. Instead, we have the mutual intimacy of a shared journey toward shared storytelling.

On the morning of August 5, 1967, ʿArifa and my mother's older sister had not returned from that early-morning hospital visit. Ignoring the military curfew imposed on Jerusalem after the June War, my mother left her younger siblings behind and found her way onto a bus. Since military occupation was new to her, she must have thought through how to avoid soldiers as best as she could, flagging down the bus down the hill and through small side passageways, streets hidden in the shadow of Salah al-Din Street. Maybe she thought this could be cover for a young girl walking in the street and be a safe enough distance from the walls of the Old City.

When my mother began to tell this story, I dared not interrupt to ask her a question, because she was finally sharing this story and I knew enough to not risk any interruption. Storytelling is also about learning how to listen. She explained that, in lieu of bus fare, she had her story—her father was ill and she needed to know what was happening. More than fifty years had passed, but as she sat and told her story, I could imagine my mother as a young child in the middle of what was already the worst season of her life. Finding her way to her father was her goal and the settler military and their new occupation was the backdrop. She must have been afraid; two months has passed since their new invasion, and I already knew that my mother, in spite of her young age, was the one who carried the burden of rushing into the local markets near the Old City for needed supplies during the fleeting moments the military lifted curfew in July. Palestinian children have had to navigate the unthinkable for four generations. After sharing the story of her father with the bus driver, she repeated it at the hospital door, but much louder and with greater protest, as the guards must have been wary of letting a young girl enter.

I had spent years wanting to be a part of my mother's Jerusalem. Suddenly, I found myself listening to her tell her story, living it with her in the past and the present. Sitting in her kitchen, sharing a story that has not ended for more than five decades, she animated the body language of her younger self as she stood at the entrance to the hospital. I listened and watched, reliving it with her. In the telling of the story, she lived it anew, and in this newness she invited me to live with her, even if begrudgingly. With fear and sadness that clearly never departed her body, she suddenly grew still. What had I done by asking her to share? She was reliving a sadness that words could not hold. Unlike traditional oral history of the Nakba generation of *ayam al-balad* (the days of our homeland), this was not a performance that I had to navigate nor was this a testimony that merited any kind of intrusion.

That was when my mother stopped talking to me; the narration seemed to have ended. Though I wanted and thought I needed more words, perhaps I also needed to understand silence differently, to learn how to listen. With her words, she took me through the map of the city: from their house on Salah al-Din Street, to the bus, up the long hill toward al-Tur, and to the doors of the hospital. But neither she nor her words could take me through the hospital doors. I knew what had happened next. Her father had passed; his heart could not withstand another season of the Nakba. Some moments seem impossible to fill with words. We sat silently as I noticed the tears running down her cheeks and then noticed my own. Were my tears shared with hers, was I experiencing her loss with her, or were my tears about my mother's grief? Through words and silences, she took me on a journey; I found myself in my mother's world and there we shared a silence and a grief that existed beyond words.

My mother was not just my companion in my Lifta journey toward ʿArifa; I also wanted to journey toward my mother rather than just be with her. Silences need not be ruptures; perhaps the telling of stories need not be confined to a narrative arc imprisoned by beginnings and endings. Stories and storytelling need not end, and perhaps we need to stop seeking an end. The invitation and journey into my mother's world was a sharing that I knew well enough to let be. I stopped asking questions and shared my mother's silence as I shared her loss. She would not let the story end as she sat over morning coffee with her daughter, remembering herself as a daughter. More than fifty years after the event and thousands of miles away from Jerusalem, her story continued into our story; the locations, like time, blended into one other.

In what follows, I explore variations on these kinds of interruptions, telling stories liberated from traditional structures. I recast silences as generative openings through which to explore muted histories and imaginations. I want us to allow ourselves to find ourselves in stories, to be humble in the search and bold in the hope. This is neither an oral history account nor a traditional ethnography, although I did use and borrow and perhaps even manipulate the tools of both methodologies. Much of what follows is an invitation to belonging through the imagination of the gathered: a methodology of sharing.

My mother's narrative of 1948 is one she learned through all the time that passed beyond 1948, as is mine. Ongoing Nakba is generations of settler violence in Palestine, so Nakba stories from the war flow and connect with stories from generations of the ongoing Nakba, layers of stories, inherited and experienced. Only after living in Palestine for well over a decade and only after another violent denial of entry did my mother finally share her intimate pain and joy with me. I had to earn my mother's stories.

She was not born in Lifta, but she was born into Lifta several years after 1948. "The last time I saw my mother was when I visited home in 1991 and my mother and I relived our life stories together," she told me.[2] In the early 1990s, the First Intifada was still a part of people's daily lives, along with the ebbs and flows that come with Palestinian mass resistance against ongoing Israeli settler colonial violence. By beginning with a kind of ending, in one sentence over a sip of coffee, my mother showed me that stories do not need beginnings and that endings are never really the end. She remembers this trip as the time that she and her mother tended to the scars of the war in 1967. Her story of 1967 and her mother's story of 1948 are interwoven, as the past and the present twist into each other; they do not have boundaries, for their respective storytelling layers and weaves through time.[3]

Sometime after sharing her story of her father's passing, my mother returned to her own stories as they became our stories. Or, she let me return to them to be a part of them. I think my mother was tending to my wounds; I was unable to return to Palestine (again), and was waiting to be able to find a way to return (again). So, like a mother warrior, she did not think about a book I needed to write or a life I aspired to live. I think my mother wanted to comfort me. My simple wounds and their accumulation perhaps meant that I had earned the stories to come. Stories did not flow from my mother or her sisters easily, so when they did flow, I wondered what I had done to earn them. I knew enough not to ask why or how I earned the stories, but I did learn how to walk with them. This particular part of the ongoing conversation had been triggered when I asked my mother to take out her mother's traditional dresses (*thob*) that she had brought back with her from that trip during the First Intifada to see ʿArifa. Together we unpacked her mother's clothes, carefully wrapped in a personal, cherished archive—a chest in her bedroom closet. We brought them out and laid them on the bed and started talking. There was more than one *thob*, and as the conversation evolved, I realized that the dresses—part of our shared legacy, each in their intricate design—held the stories and guided our way into storytelling. We used the *thob* to plot the journey in the story—another kind of walking with stories.

My Grandmother's *Thob*

Of all of 'Arifa's dresses, my favorite was the one with the pear-shaped (*al-injasa*) embroidery, and it was also my grandmother's favorite design. Mom's favorite was one of her mother's wedding dresses, far more fancy and with more intricate embroidery than all of the others. "The only reason I managed to get this," she said, "was because she knew she was saying goodbye to me then and my mother knew enough to control how she was to distribute her treasure." 'Arifa passed that same year, 1991, and with six daughters who carried the complications of their relationships throughout their lives, she clearly knew that if she did not share her treasures while she was still alive, they would not be shared evenly thereafter. Nearly two decades later, when I began constructing a life of my own (or which I thought was my own) in Palestine as a professor at Birzeit University, my aunts were still talking about how my mother received the coveted wedding *thob*. Though the wedding dress was 'Arifa's prize, only worn on very special occasions, and never worn after her husband's passing in 1967, my favorite *thob* was a more common fancy.

This is the *thob* she wore in my favorite photograph of her that frames and colors the imaginations behind this chapter. I am learning how to speak to/ with the photograph and, over time, the image tells me stories. Writing a historical text often requires that we write ourselves out of the narrative. This photograph refuses that equation. I found myself doing something altogether different—writing myself into this scene and into the stories. Can we learn how to write ourselves into the stories with humility and hope?

Leaping from the photograph and onto my body, the *thob* surprised me in its length because I was often told that 'Arifa was far shorter than me, but when I put it on, at my mother's urging, it reached nearly to my ankles. "It is supposed to fall to at least your feet," Mom commented as I turned my adult self into a curious child wearing her grandmother's *thob* and spinning around in my mother's bedroom. 'Arifa wore this with a *shamla*, a wide belt made of white and blue silk tied around her waist (she would fold newspaper into the belt and iron over it to help the belt keep its shape). With *al-shamla* she was

'Arifa with Amjad. Photograph from the author's collection.

able to shorten the length of the dress, as if to keep the whole fluid for me who came after her. "Knowing you," my mom commented, "you might tie *al-shamla* around your head and accessorize in your own way."

Since it was my mother's inheritance from 'Arifa's treasure chest and came to me through my mother, 'Arifa did not gift this *thob* directly to me. I was known to my grandmother only through my mother's words and descriptions, and I know my grandmother only through her daughters' words and descriptions. The stories shared through my mother are the threads that connect generations of women in my family. The stories, storytelling, and listening continue to connect us to each other. In this way, three generations have become holders of each other's stories. In sharing the stories and in practicing storytelling and listening, we are not only connecting to each other—we also generate a different sense of time transformed into our own temporalities. The intimacies of familial stories are unique but also instructive. Storytelling need not be a fixed template; it is an art, and each story, when shared, achieves the connection between individual (storyteller) and collective (storytelling and listening). Storytelling has opened up the space for me to share these stories as a different kind of relational modality that collapses the boundaries between past and present.

My mother's trip to Palestine in early 1991 might have been a kind of farewell for my mother to her mother, for ʿArifa passed shortly thereafter. But my mother did not tell me the details of that part of the return to Jerusalem, and I knew I could not ask how she said goodbye to her mother. Not knowing what I thought I wanted or needed to know came to feel like a kind of withholding. Not content with the silence, I decided to ask, and my mother gave, but in her own way. Often, our conversations would abruptly (and temporarily) end with her yelling, "I am not a subject for your research project!" Emboldened by my own sense of curiosity, I sometimes (but not always) forgot my limitations and yelled back—an immediate boomerang that would not stop the stories but rather remind us that we remain mother and daughter and of the complications of lifelong stories that never end. And though it is not a clear equation or even a stated principle in "research ethics," I needed to learn that my own mother's reaction to curiosity exposed the potential harm that research can do to our stories and story sharing. I learned that what I *could* and *should* ask were not really the point; it became about a mutual kind of sharing, and that is the path away from the testimony burden of oral history and toward a world of possibility through stories.

If I wanted to know more, I needed to dismantle and unlearn a great deal. Setting aside beginnings and endings to learn a different way, we explore together and embrace the ongoing storytelling. Through my mother's frustrations and my perception of her need to control how she shared, conversations were not interviews. However critical I learned how to be of oral history and testimony, the structures of the discipline still lingered within me, and I could only dismantle them and unlearn their power through a journey with stories. Stories nurture; testimony extracts. My mother does not tell stories with endings—or, perhaps, the stories themselves do not end. I do not know how my mother said goodbye; I do not know *if* she said goodbye, but maybe I do not need to know. My own goodbye to ʿArifa never happened, and because it never actually happened through words, deeds, or personal contact, I could always keep searching for her in the realm of our imagination and through stories. My time with my grandmother cannot be fixed and will not end. Though this was once a source of anxious grief, I have come to learn to see it as a gift and an opportunity to open history to our imagination. Physical death, in this sense, was not a finality for my relationship with my grandmother, and this perplexing gift allowed me the space to search through love and not only through loss, though both were and are intricately intertwined.

Each piece of the *injasa thob* is an independent entity, hand stitched in self-contained pieces with intricate embroidery designs. The right and left sleeves mirror each other in the same intricate pattern that, only by investigating it closely can you see where the name comes from: the bottom-heavy oval design that repeats itself, *al-injasa* (the pear).[4] The sleeves are wide; when I stood at the mirror, they flowed out and down to my waist. The arms were slightly short on me, but I could see the worn spots in the dark fabric where ʿArifa would lift each sleeve over her shoulder and pin the sleeves behind her neck so as to make the *thob* into a short-sleeve version ready for the work of the day, like water gathering.[5] In her youth, this practice was common because, like other women in Lifta, ʿArifa would bring water from the ʿayn (spring), among other work tasks on any given day. Unlike the intricate fancy of a wedding *thob*, this was perhaps my favorite because it was what ʿArifa wore in her everyday life. Through this *thob*, and her life as a widow, I imagine her lifting the sleeves to reveal her arms as she pounded the dried *jameed* (yogurt) to make her famous *mansaf* (a dried yogurt and meat dish). Everyone in Wadi al-Joz sang the praises of ʿArifa's *mansaf* to me: "Al mansaf al-Liftawi fi Wadi al-Joz [Lifta-style dried yogurt with meat dish in Wadi al-Joz]." Perhaps the memories of her cooking were too real for those who knew her to be folklore, and in time, she is imagined and remembered often enough to become almost mythical.

Blurring the lines between the real and imagined, memory is as much a place for solace as it is that strange living contradiction of love and grief. Though I never knew ʿArifa in real life, I continue to experience her presence in my life. What seemed like a million miles away, as a child in my mother's kitchen in Chicago, I would watch as my mother put together a pan of ʿArifa's *mansaf* for dinner guests. Mom would put me in charge of roasting the *snobar* (pine nuts) and *loz* (almonds) as the final garnishes—like the *shamla* for her *thob*, *snobar* and *loz* were necessary accessories. Mom cautioned me: "Do not let them burn! Watch them intently to get to the perfect brown coloring—we have a reputation to protect!" Though worlds apart, the reputation of ʿArifa's *mansaf* is shared, and the image of her open arms revealed through the pinned-back sleeves of her *thob* hold us together. I imagine her as a colossal figure, even though I know about her short frame. Wearing her dress, I felt like I was swimming in her.

The bodice is the centerpiece of the *thob*, and the embroidery on the chest is its central identity. The humility of the pear design is not overwhelmed by the intricacy of the bodice. Nevertheless, my mirror gaze focused directly on the bodice when I had the dress on. The piece of heavy embroidery is actually sewed into the frame of the *thob*, on top of another piece of fabric, making for a kind of pocket that has a small opening near where the *thob* falls against the heart. Because this was a more common *thob* for ʿArifa to wear, she must have used this pocket often. "She always had her hand-sewn cotton handkerchief in that pocket," Mom said as she watched me sneak my fingers into the pocket. "Your fingers are longer than hers, she had small hands." A pocket near ones heart makes far more sense than anywhere else. "Remember," Mom said, "how I told you that she always sprayed her perfume on the handkerchief, so she carried the scent with her, emanating from the heart." I remembered going shopping as child with my mother and how Mom would desperately search for the perfume my grandmother had requested. My mother had introduced it to her decades ago; over time it grew harder to find the original scent. Like her daughters and her daughters' daughters, ʿArifa was stubborn—she wanted the scent she knew and so it was my task as a child to help my mother find it. My nose learned how to recognize my grandmother through years of practice. I knew how she smelled. When I want to sense her, I spray the perfume of hers that I keep in my apartment in Ramallah. I actually perform this ritual and make sure I smell like her before I go the cemetery—maybe she will know me through her scent? Funny, how I convinced myself I could be known to her through her preferred scent. And so, I became convinced that I could distinguish her scent and could then smell like ʿArifa to find a way to be with her.

There are two scents I associate with ʿArifa: her signature perfume and the smell of blooming jasmine flowers that she planted in the house of hers in Wadi al-Joz. As soon as I catch a whiff of her perfume or of jasmine, I sense ʿArifa. There is a sweetness in this sensory trigger; I feel comforted because I can travel in time and through time because of a simple smell. Like her *thob*, what I perceive as ʿArifa's smell presents a different sense of time and a very different relationship with temporality. There is a solace and hope that the scent carries; there is a promise in the sensation of comfort and familiarity, just as there is love. But the complications of love also come with a deep sense of grief, the wonder of wondering. I can be transported through a smell, and, also, remain under a barrage of "nevers" in spite of it. I wish I had known her, but in my way, I do know her.

There was only one house I knew to be hers (her last home before she passed on). It was the house she had rented, and where she made a home, after the horrible summer of 1967. I returned to this home in Wadi al-Joz until the passing of my aunts; after that it was no longer their house, as it reverted to its owners. Long before that—after 'Arifa's passing—my mother tells me, even with my aunts and uncle there, it was only a blurry version of 'Arifa's home. But it was all I knew, and I need to know more. In our ongoing return there is love and sadness that mix as we work to distinguish between a house and a home. This house was one of many refugee stations, a home 'Arifa made in a house that she did not own. I love that house and dream about that home.

As soon as you opened the gate in front of that house, if the winds and sun cooperated, the smell of jasmine would immediately greet you. The scent carried you into the home even before you descended the concrete stairs that framed her urban garden. Mine is a lifelong effort to plant jasmine wherever I myself am planted, to have that scent greet me. Mom tells me that it is not just a matter of climate (in reference to the brutally cold winters of Chicago, where my folks live, as a natural obstacle to growing her own jasmine); she says that jasmine never smells as sweet as it does in Jerusalem. Another Palestinian family lives in that house in Wadi al-Joz now; I wonder if they are taking care of 'Arifa's jasmine? I sometimes wonder if the settlers who occupied upper Lifta destroyed it. Did they replace it with something 'Arifa would not recognize? No—that sweetness is indestructible. I grow jasmine on my *barenda* (balcony) in Ramallah as reminder of our ongoing return. My mother taught me the lessons she picked up through her life in Jerusalem: "Talk to the jasmine, she needs to know you love her." And so, I share stories with the jasmine on the *barenda* and we plan together all of our returns to Lifta, to plant anew and to continue to grow.

The dark fabric as the base color of the *thob* is the perfect backdrop for the colorful threads in the embroidery. So much has been said about the *thob* as a symbol of Palestine and as a material representation of history and folklore. This is not that—or, at least, not only that. It is my grandmother's dress. She was a woman of her generation and her village. Women in Lifta wore a certain kind of *thob*, and 'Arifa was no different. But the *injasa* design was a bit more playful and a bit simpler than other designs. Unlike the wedding dress, dominated by red silk thread, the *injasa* design is colorful to enhance the simple design, like the flowers running up and down her chest. Along the collar of the front of the *thob*, above the central embroidered chest, ʿArifa preferred a more pronounced opening at the center—the lined embroidery hem did not meet in the middle, leaving a slight V-neck opening. This was where she could display her gold broach. ʿArifa liked a kind of audacious subtlety in displaying her gold, a contradiction that she embodied and we inherited. As they commented on my mother's inheritance of the wedding *thob*, my aunts also noticed that I liked wearing enough of ʿArifa's gold to make sure I could work on my own sense of subtlety through ʿArifa's and my own golden bangle bracelets. The difference between what she gave me through her daughter and what her daughter gave me as my mother combines on my wrists in an audacious, even, and indistinguishable flow. Maybe I am trying to mirror her? Or maybe this is one of the ways I hold her with me? The valence of the symbolism of gold has changed from ʿArifa's Lifta to mine, but we both, nevertheless, hold our gold in style, connected together but each distinctly our own self. The women in my family all liked playing with their treasures, and all of ʿArifa's daughters and her daughters' daughters continue the practice. Memories are held in all kinds of archives—even those made of gold.[6]

Four lines of embroidery, extended versions of those on the edge of the sleeves, break through the dark fabric of the bodice flowing into a wide A-line that extends to the ground. Each one of the four pieces, like the sleeves and the chest, were embroidered separately and then stitched together. The flowers run freely throughout each independent section, but were also carefully placed to make for a singular design. The hem at the bottom is a line with simple embroidery. The lines that flow to the hem match the center in the flowery stitch that frames the pear-like oval. As I tried to see how the pieces of the *thob* fit, inspecting how each section stitched together with the rest, Mom commented, "The over-embroidered *thob* that you sometimes see these days is a much more recent phenomenon; your grandmother preferred simplicity." Simplicity is design, but also status; the *thob* I love was the one she wore as a widow, a mother, and a grandmother who lived through the seasons of the ongoing Nakba, showing us the meaning of hope. Just as it tells us stories, this worn *thob* reveals details of the political economy of life after Lifta. What my mom called overembroidered is far more expensive as a commodity than simple designs.

Each piece of the *thob* is singular in its design and beauty. Each piece is woven into the other, separate pieces that come together as a whole. It is functional, to be worn; mythical, to be imagined; intimate, to be felt; and material, to be history. Remembering Nakba stories of Lifta can try to do the same. Each of the pieces of the spring of 1948 are both fixed in that time and relived over time, each distinct story line woven in this set of stories told through how her body wore the *thob* and that same *thob* holds my body together. The remembering and sharing of these stories can be about both the past and the future; our stories are as much about dispossession as they are about melody and substance, and they are a means of practicing return. Returning to stories in this way is a path in our ongoing return. I learned storytelling through maternal story sharing, and that ethos, the intimacy embedded in every moment of sharing, is how this chapter came together. Every man and woman from Lifta whom I sat with shared a story. Though the intimacy of mothers and daughters is unique, it can flow, and this chapter was born from this hope—guided by intimacy, story sharing, and a *thob* as parts of the map.

This cannot just be a Nakba story, or cannot only be about how Nakba stories have been treated over time and over various historical records. This part of our journey is not about undoing the past but instead about learning how to listen through fluid time. Each story is like a piece of a Palestinian *thob*, like ʿArifa's *injasa thob*, intricately embroidered as separate pieces that will hopefully thread together in the form of a dress. Personal and intimate, this is a story about searching for stories; it is both personal and collective, neither mutually exclusive nor falling into a trap of personal versus collective. Perhaps a search for beauty in all the violence is a hapless venture; perhaps it is a romantic escape. But it might also be a means to understand how remembering actually functions through the obstacles of ongoing intrusion of settler violence. After all, in a constant state of violence, it is difficult, if not impossible, to keep remembering because in some ways the choice lies between survival *or* remembering where sustaining life can only be accomplished if we do not hold on to the details of all the violence that is both relentless and unyielding. In Palestine, and for Palestinians, material violence is a series of never-ending battle zones of settler violence where so much is lost that to stop and focus on the blood and loss one can no longer live. That is, settler goals of elimination work to occupy the land and destroy our relations with the land, ourselves, and each other.

Settler violence is so oppressive that we read ourselves and our relations through it even as we struggle to read outside it. Because we are imprisoned in all the nefarious ways settlers confine—through time and space—how can we work to understand the relations that account for the violence that in so many ways occupies our past and our present? Here I suggest a return to ʿArifa's *thob*, which gives *her* the space to occupy my imagination and nurture my hope. While these traditional dresses are the makings of folklore and commodities of nostalgia, they are also what we wore, what we wear, and

what connects generations of Palestinian women who wear them. As I have
noted, the *thob* is designed in pieces—from each arm, embroidered individually; to the body, starting from the centerpiece of the chest, designed as a
piece in and of itself; to the borders that run from the bodice to the hem.
While each piece is made separately, they come together, patterns connected
and woven together to make a *thob*. Maybe as we walk through time and our
stories, each story can find a way to come together like the pieces of a *thob*.
Silences can neither be overcome nor conquered in this sense, but maybe
they should not be. Perhaps we can learn to think differently about ourselves
and our pasts, presents, and futures. This is an attempt to work through that
process through these stories, beginning, connecting, and continuing with
the story of ʿArifa and the imagination that she generates and nourishes. The
line between "what really happened" and what I imagine no longer serves the
methodology, as it is the imagination and storytelling that enable us to find
our own way through the past and present into a future—surviving violence
to not be defined by it.

Two Cows, a Treasure Chest, and Ongoing Mapping

While seeking ʿArifa in the streets she walked in Jerusalem, I fell into Safiya.
In spite of herself, my mother revealed that Safiya, her own paternal grandmother, resided next door to her young family and was a kind of foundation
for a temporary coming together in the early 1950s. ʿArifa had a complicated
relationship with Safiya, her mother-in-law, and so maybe my mother's reluctance was about a kind of commitment to her mother. Imagining the move
from their first temporary station in the Old City, I asked my mom how the
family ended up on Salah al-Din Street. It was in that story I found the legend
of Safiya. It is clear that my mother did not seek her grandmother out in the
same way I have come to seek out mine, but when we walk through time and
stories together, we find what we might not have thought to seek out.

Safiya Ihmedan Abutaah always stored her treasure chest close to herself.
The family posthumously referred to it as *al-sandouk*, "the box." The stories
of the chest are the makings of a legend, but it was a kind of hidden legend
that ʿArifa's family afforded for Safiya's memory. Storytelling is as much about
the stories shared as it is about those not shared. ʿArifa's daughters, each for
her own reason, did not leave much space for Safiya. She had gold in that
chest, it is said, for she had insisted on converting money into gold coins ever
since her husband passed in the early 1920s. Her cows and the milk they produced, as well as chickens and their eggs, were her main sources of daily

income as a widow. The family worked the land in Lifta al-tahta (lower Lifta), but the cows were her own, right next to her small home above the valley in Lifta al-foqa (upper Lifta) and near the ridge where upper and lower Lifta met. Every morning—like ritual prayer—she tended to her chickens and cows.[7] Safiya passed in 1960, and her cows passed before her—but not before they accompanied her on an extraordinary journey.

Walking through the built-up commercial district of Salah al-Din Street, you are struck by the uneven kind of growth this area experienced, as is evident in how different the storefronts are. The lack of conformity in the built landscape is obvious: some structures are slightly higher than others, and each has its own peculiar design. Between the brutality of occupation and the political obstacles in obtaining any kind of construction permit, the buildings remain rather humble. Rather than an appearance of anarchy in design, the landscape reveals how difference comes together in a kind of collective landscape as the present quickly gives way to pondering the past and the buildings seamlessly blend into each other. With the Old City walls behind you, walk up Salah al-Din Street and, when you pass the cemetery on your left, on your right you will find three commercial storefronts and a currency exchange. Though now more built up, the remnants of the once empty space still resonate in my mind: This was once Safiya's refuge. What did it look like to her, in 1948?

Up the street you find a small side street leading into Asfahani Street. Right before this turn, as you walk by the two storefronts leading up to it, you have entered the place that holds the plot of land Safiya led her cows onto in the spring of 1948. Before there were buildings on this plot of land, she landed here. In front of her empty plot was an expansive (for its time) structure housing the wives and children of Haj Sandouka, the family that owns the Sandouka Coffee Shop. Behind her were the smaller buildings that members of the Zalatimo family had rented out over the course of the previous decade. Safiya had walked from Lifta with two unmarried adult children, two cows, and a borrowed donkey that carried the treasure chest on his back. She had fled Lifta, forced to leave her home like all the others in the village because of the violence of Zionist militias and the plans of the nascent state to control the western corridor of Jerusalem. While the settler violence had forced her to flee her village, she seemed to have made the decision not to leave the Jerusalem area. Her daughter-in-law, 'Arifa, was not with her; the stories subtly reveal that Safiya took her own path and, it seems, did so on her own terms. It is a contradiction indeed—how she seemed to claim control in a moment when all control was being violently taken from her—for forced dispossession is just that: an almost indescribable form of violence. But in the midst of that violence, Safiya asserted something of her own will and perhaps a lesson for us about a promise that lies at the heart of ongoing return. It was harder for me to discover Safiya's story before she found her way to Salah al-Din Street, for the familial stories through my mother and her sisters were mostly about their own memories of her from their early childhoods and Safiya and 'Arifa's strained relationship. Both women come across in these stories as extremely strong willed, just as they both experienced great pain and grief in their lives. Alas, it seems they did not get along.

Safiya was a widow for nearly two decades prior to the spring of 1948. Her husband passed while her children were still young. This was an inherited trait in the family: A generation later, her eldest son, 'Ata (who was only twelve when his father died) passed when his children were still young. 'Ata lost his father at nearly the same age my mother was when she lost her father, 'Ata. Safiya and 'Arifa were both young widows left to raise young children on their own. Though Mom shared the story of her journey from August 1967 to the hospital on the hill in Jerusalem, I know nothing of how 'Ata experienced the loss of his father in the 1920s. Some stories might remain forever buried. Unlike my stories of 'Arifa, delving into the details of Sayifa proved nearly impossible. Maybe 'Arifa did not share with her girls the stories of her mother-in-law's life so as, perhaps, not to outshine her own. Or maybe 'Arifa's girls made the choice to not share those stories with me. Subsequent familial tales color Safiya as a sometimes oppressive and sometimes depressive secondary figure in the lives of her children, almost as if purposefully ignoring her journey in the spring of 1948. When my mother learned that I would be seeking conversations with other women from Lifta of 'Arifa's generation, she answered, "You might hear about Safiya and her cows." If not for the cows and Safiya's insistence in bringing them along with her to Jerusalem, her story might have remained untold.

In that fateful spring of 1948, Safiya's four children (three sons and a daughter) were all nearly adults. Over the course of the previous decade, and using some of the precious gold that filled her treasure chest, she helped two of her sons marry. The eldest and youngest sons married and settled with their own young families near her home in Lifta al-foqa. Her middle son was still unmarried in April and living with her along with her only daughter. Safiya's eldest son, 'Ata, married twice before 1948. 'Ata married 'Arifa in Lifta several years after he and his first wife, 'Izziya (his paternal first cousin), ended their relationship. The ending of that marriage must not have gone over well with Sayifa, for she, after all, had planned 'Ata's first marriage to 'Izziya, when he was only eighteen and 'Izziya was twenty-two. Perhaps that is why 'Arifa's daughters did not share Safiya's stories. 'Izziya was the sole inheritor of her own family's land. Her father had only one son and one daughter and the son traveled west and never returned, so the family land was all left to 'Izziya, and Sayifa made sure it would become 'Ata's. 'Ata and 'Izziya had two children, but 'Ata refused to inherit what was not his, so after he finished the education afforded him in Jerusalem, he left for a teaching position in Jaffa, thus leaving the lands 'Izziya inherited to her and their children. That, too, must not have gone over well with Safiya.

'Arifa was also the one who cared for Safiya in Jerusalem after Lifta. 'Arifa, like 'Ata, apparently only had a general sense of the contents of Safiya's treasure chest. Like 'Arifa's *thob*, packed away in my mother's treasure chest, the contents of Safiya's treasure chest holds the potential for stories, but it needs unpacking. Both Safiya and her daughter passed while my mother was still a young child, so the stories Mom held did not feature these women in any central way. I do know, however, that 'Arifa told her daughters about the treasure chest long after Safiya's passing. Each daughter had a different tale to tell and, through my (not always subtle) insistence, each relayed her tale in time. Speculation has led me to think that because 'Arifa was 'Ata's much younger second bride, perhaps loyalty to their mother fed this kind of reluctance to share stories about Safiya. (I cringe as I write this, thinking about my mother reading this line and how she may react to me bringing Safiya and 'Arfia together.) Relations between mothers and their daughters do not exist in a vacuum, and part of the wonder in seeking stories is also how stories are actually shared, or not shared. Like 'Arfia and her daughters, I too am stubborn, so I forged through silences I witnessed after I stumbled across Safiya, and I persisted in asking everyone about her.

In our family, every story was a reluctant one for my aunts and mother ('Arifa's daughters) when it came to Safiya. Nevertheless, threading the stories together, I found legend in Safiya. Or maybe I made her into a legend? Why is it that the women in my family tend to tell tales of despair mixed with empowerment, even with the stories of Safiya, whom they were clearly not invested in making into a legend. Theirs stories obviously reveal as much about themselves as they do their elders. Within the complexity of shared stories over time, Safiya was sometimes a subtle villain, sometimes an accidental queen, and often a victim, but always a secondary figure in their imaginations. In addition to my speculation about my mother and aunts, maybe I am also a part of these stories. Am I revealing my own heavy hand in storytelling, listening, and sharing by trying to collect and recount their stories? Is there an irony that in looking for 'Arifa in the streets of Jerusalem I happened on Sayifa, a name I did not even know until I began asking about the legend of the woman and her cows? However much they varied, the generational stories all focus on a particular image: Safiya as a self-sufficient woman with a unique kind of resilience whose cows were as precious to her as what they produced—gold, through their milk, which afforded Safiya a certain level of autonomy. It is no wonder that she brought the cows with her when the Zionist militias forced her to flee Lifta. Did Safiya lament having to leave the chickens behind in Lifta? Though her voice was harder for me to conjure than ʿArifaʾs, by threading together pieces of stories over time, I still was able to imagine it.

Walking through the eastern part of the New City in Jerusalem is a walk through time. I keep walking us through this neighborhood because it holds the emotional map that opens up time. As I suspect Safiya did, I again ground the map in the cemetery on Salah al-Din Street. In the early 1960s the Awqaf administration made a controversial decision to decrease the size of this cemetery—it once spanned the length of the street up to where the Islamic courthouse is located. It was in 1960 that Safiyaʾs son, ʿAta, buried his mother in this cemetery. It was in 1967 that ʿAtaʾs wife and children buried him here, right next to his mother, and it was in 1991 that ʿArifaʾs daughters buried their mother here. The remarkable aspect of this street and the city cemetery remains how seamlessly the living and the buried live among each other. Opposite the cemetery and on the stretch of road between the Old City walls and the top of the hill where Salah al-Din is met by cross streets, I walked through and with the stories of Safiya. Before she was buried in the cemetery across the street from where she planted refuge, where her son raised a family, and where that family grew into a tribe, Safiya created life for herself and a legacy for the generations who followed her. On this station of refuge, quite literally in between those streets, and metaphorically through three generations, I searched for the remnants of her cows and their treasure.

A superficial focus on the built-up merchant district on Salah al-Din Street, in the heart of Jerusalem, betrays the layers of memories that are the foundation for the neighborhood. Safiya, with a son, a daughter, and two cows, settled in the open area between Asfahani and Salah al-Din Streets. The Abutaah and Siam families from Lifta owned tracts of land here long before 1948, but neither families built on nor planted it in any significant way before 1948. Several steps walking distance from the walls of the Old City, this area in the New City was clearly a desirable location, but not the sight of planned neighborhoods as elsewhere under British rule in Jerusalem.[8] Other neighborhoods, in Jerusalem and beyond, similarly hold stories of people from Lifta. Ard al-Samar (settlers refer to it as French Hill) in Jerusalem holds the legacies of several large families from Lifta; Al-Bireh, next to Ramallah, also holds the stories of people from Lifta. Lifta is not confined to the mapping of settlers; people forged their own maps through their movement, and theirs are maps of stories that hold the refugees and connect each and all through and with Lifta. Why Safiya fled Lifta alone, why she let her daughter-in-law leave before her, and why she did not move with the others is part of the making of our family mythology. The outlines of the stories are known, can be discovered, but some details are either buried, unspoken, or made invisible. Imagination must fill in the blanks.

The land holds the stories of Safiya and those around her. At first without a roof or walls, Safiya made a temporary home in the open land. The buildings on the area between Asfahani and Salah al-Din Streets tell this story as well. Where the shops are now, how they began as shelter and morphed over time into a commercial district, also tell the story of how Safiya created new kinships with others. With help from the sons of the Sandouka family, Safiya first built a roof overhead—shelter for herself, the children, and perhaps the cows. That was right before 1950. The walls of her one-room home came later. That was before 1951. It is told she built the walls when the cows were no longer a part of her family. Did they die? Did she sell them? No two people tell the same story of the fate of the cows. With those cows, Safiya carried Lifta with her—not only symbols of a life she built but symbols of a life that was constantly being built. Neither the cows nor the gold their milk produced would last forever, but their stories carried the family from one generation of refugees into the next. Carrying stories is not a linear production, but rather one of establishing and reestablishing life. As she had in Lifta, Safiya rebuilt constantly, ritually. *After* is not a *post*-but instead one part of a larger story.

By 1954, Safiya's eldest son, ʿAta, had left his family's temporary refuge within the Old City walls to join his mother between Asfahani and Salah al-Din Streets. He lost his job as a teacher in the Dar al-Aytam School as 1948 resonated institutionally throughout Jerusalem well beyond the moment of refuge. Without a regular income, he decided to use part of the land between Asfahani and Salah al-Din Streets as a space to trade in wood, and he built a home for ʿArifa and their growing family, along with his daughter from his previous marriage, next to his mother's humble home on the same plot because he knew better than to have his mother and wife under one roof. As he returned to work as a teacher through a reinstatement at the Dar al-Aytam School and later at Khalil al-Sakakini School, he built on the space he had used to sell wood and enlarged his family home. After Lifta, ʿAta would only add to Safiya's treasure chest when he could, but even if he could not, he warned his wife and children that the contents of the chest were off-limits to them. The morsels of the shared stories reveal that Safiya collected gold but wore silver, and she kept her gold treasure well protected under lock and key. Is this why ʿArifa taught me to wear our gold? Were we meant to be different? The contents of the chest were locked away and the key remained on a heavy silver necklace around Safiya's neck. Her keys were her treasure: one for the chest and the other for the house in Lifta. Keys are not only manipulated into symbols of never returning; they are also the real material of life and the makings of ongoing return. That is the thing about folklore and symbols: However much corruption commodification causes, they are grounded in a material reality so they become symbols of contradiction, the specter of never returning and the hope of ongoing return.

The intimacy of gathering stories within familial connections formed, over time, a part of this methodology of stories. Intimacy in all of its wonder taught me to nurture conversations in spite of, outside, and beyond the pressures of performing oral history. I knew I could not exactly replicate the intimacy of connections between mothers and their daughters beyond our family lines, but I wanted to try to use my positionality as a daughter seeking stories to find another way for people to share their stories that would not be limited to the boundaries of oral testimony or even ethnography. This is where methodology moves from a research technique into a way of being. This is where Indigenous presence, as ways of being in relation to temporalities and place, can become a tool of how to remember as part of the larger constellation of how we live.[9] Perhaps the Indigeneity of this Palestinian methodology is in relation to life and the ever-changing vitality of living, grounded in the land of all of Palestine. Perhaps the Indigeneity of this methodology is also about grief and survival. Perhaps that is why return in, to, and with Palestine is ongoing. Stories—imagined through and while being told—frame the past and the present as living in relation to ourselves, each other, and the Palestine(s) to which we all belong. It is not about identity or liberal politics of the production of identity; it is about living and life and one that works to nurture sharedness. The intimacy of and with family stories as a means of understanding this methodology can help us gain a collective sense of shared intimacy in all of its layers.

Telling and Listening: Resistance Coloring the Exodus

It was cold and in the early days of winter. In Palestine, December is a month when the bitterness of cold is still in its inception phase, but in 1947, the change of the seasons came with a vengeance that ominously foretold the days ahead. That winter brought about a new phase in the internationally conceived notion of the "question of Palestine." On November 29, the United Nations (UN) revealed its Partition Plan for Palestine as a proposed "solution" to what would be transformed rhetorically by imperial powers into a "conflict"—a concept that worked to purposefully erase the settler colonial nature of the violence in Palestine and on the bodies of Palestinians. For people in Lifta, like others in Palestine, the proposed UN Partition Plan—like other declarations since the Balfour Declaration in 1917 and its subsequent incorporation into the text of the League of Nations' Mandate for Palestine in 1922—was another in a long line of imperial designs on Palestinian homeland. The announcement of the plan was far more than an international declaration; it was a lived experience and marked a distinct change for life in Lifta. Forced expulsion is not an easy story to tell or to hear. It is not clean, and it does not adhere to a clear chronology. But throughout conversations with people who were forced to flee their homes in Lifta, the story of this forced expulsion began with the backdrop of the UN Partition Plan. I suppose it might have been so for ʿArifa, because the lived experience of violence in Lifta, the violence in December 1947, forced a new beginning. People experienced the events of late 1947 and early 1948 and have remembered it since through the ongoing reminders of loss. The violence has not ended. I wonder: If ʿArifa had lived to tell me the story directly, would her words mirror those of others? How much has this story been affected by the time that has passed? How much of it is framed not only through loss but through ongoing loss and what has become a sense of never-ending grief? How much of it has somehow become a new collective? This is yet another opportunity to blur the boundaries between real and imagined, and that is, in turn, an invitation to also blur the hard and fast lines between the past and the present. It is not exactly a balance between hope and loss, but rather an understanding that, without hope, despair holds nothing but the finality of a forced ending.[10]

In remembering his family's experience in 1948, Ibrahim Khalil explained the context of what the plan brought about in terms of violence and the real lived fear of what was to come. He spoke to me in the form of a lesson, teaching me what he wanted me to know about Lifta. I asked him about fear and he explained to me,

Of course, fear was paramount; what happened was that before we finally fled the village, there were groups of young men who organized themselves in small groups who would patrol the village out of fear of potential Jewish settlers sneaking, infiltrating, into Lifta. And the incident of the bus bombing happened, and after that Jewish settlers attacked Salah Eissa's café, some attacking from the back door and others from the front, and they gunned down seven or eight people from Lifta. As a result of this attack, people were afraid and started to escape. And then the massacre at Deir Yassin happened, and then there were burials in the cemetery of our village, and then people began leaving the village; some people brought mules from Beit Hanina, and they stacked their belongings on them and they left on foot, walking, alongside the mules. We finally were among those who left, understanding that it would be a week or two and we would return. We left toward Beit Hanina. . . . Beit Hanina was on the road and on that night [when we left] we had the clothes on our backs and the next day, in the morning, we found a car and we rode in it. Yaqub had a truck, and he used it to carry people and their belongings out of the village. And at the spot of Nabi Yaqub, as we understood it was a [settler] station; we were afraid that they would start shooting at us because we knew that they were heavily armed, but we kept moving and no one stopped us. When we reached Ramallah we found the home of Fahd Hasmia, close to the Manara Circle, and we took up residence in it. There were two rooms in the place and our family, along with my sister's family, lived there. After this, people got work and were able to move out, on. . . . There were also, of course, young men in the villages who participated in the resistance, ʿAbd al-Qadir's men from the village, but I do not know what happened to them.[11]

Rather than focus only on fear, Ibrahim also wanted us to talk of resistance and perhaps provide a framework by which to read beyond an event—even as he shared the details of the events that led him and his family into a life after Lifta. Since the Nakba was not a singular event, what was ongoing in this context is held through storytelling. That is, infusing the context of violence and the nuance of resistance is a pivotal methodological tool that complicates the narrative of fear as the singular feature of flight. Rather than providing a testimony of victimhood, employing the methodology of storytelling holds the contradictions of fear and resistance. Through storytelling the nuance of resistance provides the contextual markers of both agency and longing.

The reality of the spring of 1948 cannot be distilled into a static story, let alone one solely about Palestinian victimhood. The traumatic violence of the Nakba was and is real, as is the ongoing trauma that survivors continue to experience. This remains a fundamental source of intergenerational trauma for their descendants and, with the violence of the ongoing Nakba, is a multi-layered experience. Because settler colonial violence is structural, it also feels repetitive—that is, it happened to those who came before us and is still happening to us. Removed from the individualizing science of diagnosis and pathology, through this collective method of sharing stories we can find ourselves, and we live with the personal stories that hold both the darkness of despair and the wonder of hope. Generational stories exist in the past of 1948 and the present of today, thus allowing us to read ourselves in a conceptualization of temporality that can defy settler time. Through stories we evade the potential of temporal alienation ("it happened to them, in the past"). The potential of alienation is curbed by the disorganization of temporalities; the notion of "still happening," while painfully real and urgent, also unsettles the boundedness of linearity. That is, these are the stories of elders, grandmothers and grandfathers, but through the sharing of the stories, they are also our own—collective and personal. It is through these connections and continuities that we nurture this conceptualization of what is ongoing. Listening to the stories told of the past in the present reveals how telling and listening to stories reveals nuances that testimony could never actually hold. Likewise, the stories reveal that singular testimonies of fleeing impose a timeline defined by settler violence more than Palestinian existence: Opening up the space to storytelling opens up time. Moreover, sharing stories rather than testimonies also opens up the space to go beyond acts of recording and documentation. When testimony replicates the juridical frame of autopsy, we read ourselves only as victims, ones who have been burdened with the task of proving the criminal acts done to us. Testimony mirrors the anxieties of erasure; clearly understandable under the brutality of Zionist settler colonial violence, it leaves little space for imagination and the vitality and hope of life. That is the goal of settler colonial elimination. Moreover, it leaves little space for the nuances born out of the unsettling of time and disorganization of temporalities. Simply put, testimony can work to bind us into a frame of constant erasure. While that is the reality of Palestinian life under the military occupation of Palestinian land, must it also be the case for our imaginations?

Salima al-Baja, like Ibrahim Khalil, explained that the story of leaving Lifta was one colored both by resistance and fear:

Before we fled, there were confrontations [*munawashat*] in town with the
Jewish settlers. There was a young man from our village from the al-
ʿAbdiyat family, his name was Ahmad ʿAbdiyat; he boarded a Jewish settler bus and he planted a bomb that exploded. After about a week in Salah
Eissa's café in Romema, in a lovely part of Lifta, an armed man shooting
from a Jewish settler's car sprayed bullets at the old men in the café. They
were all old and well-respected men; five of them were killed and five or
six of them were injured. After this violent incident, people were afraid
and began to leave, and my father, after this incident, piled us in a car and
sent us to Kufr Malek, where my maternal grandmother was from, and he
returned alone to Lifta.[12]

Rather than exclusively focusing the narrative on why people left, as many
historians eager to counter Zionist claims have done, these stories provide a
contextual and lived connection between fear and resistance and help us
move toward understanding belonging and longing more deeply. Free of the
need to legitimize why people in Lifta left their homes and village in the
spring of 1948, space opens up to complicate a seemingly inexplicable narrative of loss through the love of Lifta. Again, the privilege of listening to stories
carries with it the responsibility of the reminder that Lifta does not belong to
us—we belong to Lifta. Salima's stories flowed as she connected pieces of the
past:

I used to hear about a young man in my husband's family, may his soul
rest in peace, named Shihdeh ʿAbd al-Rahman, he was a fugitive from
the time of the revolution [1936?]. My father-in-law used to tell us that
many of the men of the village worked in the stone quarry . . . as part of
their work in the quarry, they used dynamite. So he would tell us stories
about how they would steal the dynamite and use it against the settlers—
they became revolutionaries and fugitives. Among them was my father-
in-law, who was imprisoned for several years [by the British], along with
his friend, Shihdeh ʿAbd al-Rahman. Their siblings and their mother
would visit them in prison. . . . The dynamite that was used to break and
cut stones and boulders was converted into tools for these revolutionaries, and that converted them into fugitives . . . in the same way it is today.
In the 1970s my husband and his brother opened a *kassara* (stone
quarry) in al-Ram, and they used to use dynamite to break the stones
and boulders. . . . And some of the young men working with them, including my sister-in-law's son, took the dynamite and blew it up near the
Jewish settlers; Nafiz [her sister-in-law's son] was captured and impris-

oned for eight years. They now live on the street where Qalendia Airport was.[13]

Listening to the consistencies between *then* and *since then* also opens up space for understanding the past as layered through time and not necessarily confined by settler time. Stories flow across time just as people move through spaces. Again, free from the burden of trying to account for why people left Lifta, and the fear of being written out of history, shifting to how people live with Lifta through time allows for us to be in and of the past and present. It is important, as well, to note the everyday logic of resistance here, common sense without a need to defend its use. People's lives, livelihoods, bodies, and land are targets of colonial and settler colonial violence; of course, people on the land worked to maintain and protect the relationality with the land that was being systemically attacked. Relying on stories in this way removes us from the need to document details through a juridical or defensive framework. Stories give breath to life.

Nowaf Awad told stories of revolutionaries in relation to Lifta. Her perspective gives a further sense of intimacy to the relationship between resistance and fear:

> The revolutionaries would protect the houses in Lifta al-foqa. . . . They were worried about attacks on the homes [up there] from Jewish settlers because they were in such close proximity to each other. . . . A young man from the Rayan family would organize the young men, and they had guns and they would fire on convoys on the road to Jaffa; these convoys were convoys of Jewish settlers, and they would pass in groups because they were too afraid to pass individually. . . . The young men would wait in the hills for the convoys, and when they approached, they would shoot a bullet or two at them and then escape back into the hills; our house was close to the Rayan home, so we would hear the sound of the shooting. Once my mother sent us to stay at our grandfather's home, and in my grandfather's home [in Lifta al-tahta] we would hear the sounds of the valley and the water. Once, all of a sudden, we heard a loud shock of sound and then we heard rattling sounds coming from outside the house. There were no men around because they were protecting other houses in the village, so the women in the house thought there were Jewish settlers attacking and were going to bomb the house, so the women began screaming, "Oh, people of Beit Iksa [a nearby village], we are being attacked by Jewish settlers!" And in the end, it turned out to be dogs in the cactus plants.[14]

Nowaf's storytelling connects the thread of fear through the context of violence in geographies of resistance. After her mother's maternal uncles were shot and killed by Jewish settlers near Mea Shearim Street in Jerusalem, Nowaf described how that event prompted her family's exit. Her grandmother was originally from the village of Beitin, so that is where they headed: "We first left the house to the street, and from the street we found a car, or small truck, and it drove us, my family and my two paternal uncle's and their families, to Beitin." Nowaf also described how she attended school pretty soon after arriving in Beitin, where they found shelter. Her father later moved his family to Amman, Jordan, in search of work. He was a stonecutter by trade, and so her family lived in Amman as he sought work there. She moved to Ramallah when she married, before 1967. She moved through all of these spaces carrying time with her.

In sharing stories about her maternal uncle, Yehia Hamouda, the first head of the Palestinian Liberation Organization, before Yasser Arafat, Rifqa Odeh framed Hamouda's national past through his support of resistance in and around Lifta: "He was arrested and sent to the Moscobiya Prison [in Jerusalem] because he was the lawyer who helped the revolutionaries in various ways, with financial support or otherwise, but he never carried arms, weapons in his life; he would go visit the fighters in the mountains."

Framing the story of forced expulsion, Rifqa explained that after the implementation of UN Partition Plan, a new wave of anger and fear erupted:

> When we left the village, we went to Deir Dibwan, where my family
> owned land . . . my maternal uncle had a Ford [truck]. Once, when re
> turning in his truck from Jerusalem, he was followed by Jewish settlers,
> who attacked him and beat him. After that we all stopped going to Jerusa
> lem. Immediately, my uncle piled us into his truck and took us to Deir
> Dibwan. . . . We did not take anything with us when we left, for they told
> us in a week or two we would return, as soon as the partition was over. . . .
> When we arrived in Deir Dibwan they called us refugees—that is what
> they called us, refugees. . . . In Deir Dibwan they did not have many
> houses for rent . . . so we stayed in a room next to the school that had a
> bathroom and a kitchen that the people of the village had made for the
> teacher who taught in the village school. In that room, we all lived to
> gether, my mother and my sisters and my uncle and his wife and
> children . . . after Lifta. My older brother worked for the Arab Bank in
> Tulkarm, so as soon he came to Deir Dibwan, he took us with him to
> Tulkarm and we lived there. Five years later, we moved to Ramallah.[15]

Again, prompted by violence and driven by fear, Rifqa told the story of leaving. Even though I did not ask why her family left, Rifaq offered her narrative as an explanation. It is telling that part of the process of collecting "oral history" has left this imprint on folks: the need to explain *why* with the implicit question "How could you leave?" The discipline of history has left this imprint. Though it was not directly stated, Rifqa spoke to the legacy of what oral history as data collection in search of a narrative to counter erasure has done. That is, even in the intimacy of conversations and storytelling, the power of the trope of "victim testimony" seeps into the discussion, as if blaming the victims has been internalized. "They called us refugees" is, in part, a legacy of this thread and one that is carried through time.

Clearly another part of the making of a coherent collective narrative of exodus, Muhammad Khalil described the café incident as his preface to the story of the spring of 1948. Like Ibrahim Khalil, Muhammad approached the conversation as an opportunity to teach me and as a lesson in how we *should* remember. Patriarchy, age, and gender clearly framed our discussion, but it went beyond us; it was a rhetorical exercise that was meant to be a people's story as told to us by the men, who alone can conceive and construct it. Like memory, this story was as much about the present as it was the past. It was about unlearning, and disconnecting from, the politics of shame. Disconnecting fear from shame, however, opens space for understanding resistance beyond the shallow politics of rhetorical dogma. The way Muhammad's story is told is a primary aspect of the story, the method perhaps even more interesting than the result, and Muhammad, like others, drew intricate pictures with details that reveal great care and his love of storytelling:

> In the café in Lifta al-foqa, there was this incident with a young Arab man, not from Lifta . . . who rode the Jewish settler bus and he planted a bomb. After the bus traveled for a bit, he pulled the bell for a stop, he pulled the bell on the road in the hills. After he descended from the bus and walked away a bit, the bomb on the bus exploded. The Jewish settlers responded to this incident by bringing a bus packed with armed men to the café. They approached the café and sprayed all the people in the café with bullets, and they killed five and injured several others. This incident was in 1947, and I was in school and old enough to remember it distinctly. After this event, there was a great panic among people in Lifta and they were afraid. The bus [with the armed men] reached the upper part of the village, but could not get to the lower part, so people were afraid that they would next bring explosives and throw them down in the valley into lower Lifta.[16]

Muhammad imparted a much longer narrative, for a few days in the spring of 1948 could not possibly tell his whole story of Lifta. He later explained, "We had many heroes in Lifta; the idea of the bus was not new, for I remember a young carpenter who often used bus routes as his chosen sites of resistance, including the bus route that carried supplies to Hadassah Hospital in al-'Assiwiya. They were careful about strategic targets. Then the café incident happened and everything changed." Muhammad also explained that though there were no direct attacks on the homes, especially those in the valley, as they were protected by the steep decline into lower Lifta, people were nevertheless afraid. They also knew that at any moment there could be attacks, as the resistance was strong and many from the village took part in it, like the Battle of Bab al-Wad in Jerusalem.[17] If one considers fear and resistance together, it becomes clear that the lives that stories hold are themselves held by people and their relationality to land and to home and to each other.

After the café incident, Muhammad Khalil noted that people began to take precautions and some even left for a respite, "Yes, people began to leave, and especially given the fighting in Qastel and Abd al-Qadir al-Hussayni's killing, people left for nearby locations like Beit Hanina or Beit Iksa, thinking they would stay away for a month or two and return when the conditions calmed down a bit, because in the previous war [World War I], people did the same, as Beit Hanina and Beit Iksa were so close, and they returned after a month. People thought this time would be like the others."[18] Again, leaving was not one event but a series journeys, often back and forth. Leaving was—and is— not a finality.

Muhammad Khalil told a horrific tale about the exodus, after explaining that his family were among the last to leave, though they feared their exit, as the road to Jerusalem was Mea Shearim Street, which was full of Jewish settlers:

> There was a man who built a fine house on the outskirts of the village (in Lifta al-foqa), his name was 'Abd Saqr. It was a heavy weight on his soul that he would have to leave, so he hired Jordanian soldiers to protect his house, he provided them with food and supplies like water and food, and his wife would bake bread for them every day. And after their supplies ran out, he contacted the closest British police station and explained to them, "I no longer have anything left, and I want to leave with my children." He had a truck, and on the road he feared the violence of the Jewish settlers. They told him, "Stay in your house, we will come and escort you," and so British jeeps came and they escorted his truck, one behind him and two

in front, and when they reached Mea Shearim Street [where the Jewish settlers were] the jeeps stopped and blocked him in, they prevented his truck from moving, and watched the Jewish settlers as they attacked him and killed him. They then dragged his wife and children to Damascus Gate in the Old City and handed them over to Arabs.[19]

Muhammad had told a fantastic tale of a man who tried to be an exception. His was a tale of doom. The implicit lesson in the story can perhaps help us understand that the relationship between resistance and fear is like the relationship between the land and its people. Fear is not divorced from resistance, and loss is not divorced from fear. Removed from the constraints of testimony and working to imagine ourselves outside the domain of countering erasure, the stories people shared were as complicated (sometimes with conflicting details) as they were ongoing. As with the nostalgia of *ayam al-balad*, memories of *ayam al-luj* (the days of refuge) remain in some ways tinged by the resonance of testimony. Storytelling as a nuanced approach to sharing and understanding can perhaps begin to create fissures in the walls built by generations of testimonies. Perhaps the investigative modality deeply embedded in colonial politics of recognition have long prevented us from having the space to share our stories free of the violence of erasure. Since providing proof is an inherent element in this sense of testimony, a testimonial approach to oral history requires that we perform as victims of unspeakable acts of violence and our stories have to become documentation of these acts.

Persistent historical denial of Palestinian presence has made these testimonies existential elements in survival. Because the violence of the Nakba is ongoing, the need for documentation is also the painfully hopeful act of the historian, however limiting it is, of preparing the annals of accountability for setter crimes. But what if tracing the geographies of expulsion through less structured means of claiming presence and documenting crimes can open spaces for other elements that work to connect the past with this present? What if we seek stories rather than testimonies? Perhaps another kind of hope can emerge, as Basil al-ʿAraj's work shows, as generations of Palestinians with shared threads in vast stories become more nuanced than victims of a theater not of their own making.[20] In this way, resistance is not divorced from hope, loss, or grief. Without the boundaries of testimony, the nuance enables hope. In listening to stories about what has been memorialized as a moment of devastation, I learned that how people share and what they share gives us colors that shine and bleed into each other beyond a moment and into a different understanding of temporalities, an otherwise way. With nuance, perhaps multifaceted and wildly complicated emotional stories can give space for memory to function in ways that resemble the threads of the *thob*. These complications—the colorful threads that tie together the intricate designs of the embroidered *thob*—do the hard work of holding the trauma of the past and the hope of the present. Fear, grief, loss, and shame are not denied, but they are also part of these multifaceted stories.

Habiba ʿAbdiyat's story shares the intimacy of love as she spoke of her brother, Ahmad ʿAbdiyat, a resistance fighter living in Lifta al-tahta with their family.[21] Habiba explained that her brother was in the Boy Scouts as a child and then later, in her words, "turned political." This "turn" that Habiba explained framed her narrative about her brother—one fraught with fear and framed by pride, one also contested by dismay and full of love. The intimacy of home and sibling life colored her brief but fully charged rendering of her brother's past as a kind of marker for both the past and the present, for the Palestinian struggle is ongoing:

> I honestly do not know details, I just know he lived with us, but he disappeared often—for days—I know he was a fighter . . . and I know there were a few men around him that were not good and betrayed him. . . .
> [I remember] when ʿAli Najjar, may God rest his soul, and Muhammad Eissa [the *mukhtar*, village head] would send us women to warn us that if there was anything around, to hide it all, for the village head knew when the English were about to invade the village in search of men and weapons.[22]

Like Nowaf, Habiba spoke of the intimacy of fear and resistance. She spoke in a coded or guarded language, but was clear enough as she was sharing this story that what they were told to hide were clearly weapons. Yet even in speaking of this distant past (distance being relative) she maintained a kind of coded language in terms of speaking of weapons and resistance, as if she were speaking of the present, for resistance is also ongoing. How Habiba narrated it, without ever using the words *guns, ammunition,* or *weapons,* but clearly getting her point across to anyone familiar with being Palestinian under settler rule, is another lesson in how time blends. She spoke of such things in the past as people speak in the present, as if the settlers were still listening. The settlers, it seems and it can be, are merely bit parts (albeit intrusive and terribly violent bit parts) in our stories. It is a language carved out through time. Habiba revealed the commonplace of such incidents: "Once ʿArif al-Najjar's daughter came to our home barefoot, running all the way from Ras Nadir, near Romema, in a panic, warning us to hide anything there may be around, for the English were about to descend on [*ikabis*] the village." As Habiba further explained, "The English violently searched homes and villages back then just as the Jewish settler army does today."[23] Time is not fixed in the past and the past has not yet passed.

The story of the incident at Salah Eissa's café has a unique twist for Habiba because her story narrated the events through her brother as the hero: "One day he boarded a Jewish settler bus and he blew it up . . . he blew the bus up and went to Salah Eissa's café and announced to the men of the villages sitting there, 'Leave, for they will come and open fire on you.' The men laughed at him. He escaped and hid and was not caught by the settlers, thank God." A sister narrating her brother's story further reveals the intimate connection between fear and resistance. Given the almost mythical level the story of Salah Eissa's café held, her placement of her brother as the hero of the tale, the resistance fighter, echoes across generations. There was no need to defend a people's right to resist, for her stories far exceeded any kind of rationalization or even theorization of the resistance and placed it and her brother within the tapestry of Palestinian life. She told a story of pride and anxiety: Her brother was not captured, but her family did eventually leave. Habiba explained that though they did not depart Lifta immediately after the incident, fear of what would come next was paramount. She explained that it was several months later that they fled in light of the Deir Yassin massacre and the months of violence that followed the incident in the café in December.

According to Jamila Awad, "when people began fleeing, people who had a place to go to left."[24] Networks were already set up for people to go to other places where they or others either had family members or owned land, places that were perceived to be "safer." As Muhammad Khalil explained, leaving for a respite was not uncommon before the spring of 1948, so it was not treated in real time as anything but a temporary move. For Jamila's small family, this journey took them to the Bab al-Wad neighborhood in Jerusalem's Old City, where her sister was living with her husband and young children. Given the proximity of this neighborhood to Lifta, it is not surprising that return to Lifta remained a lived hope and reality. A sense of permanence of exile did not seep into the life stories of people searching for safety, for it was woven into these various stories as a kind of temporary and lateral move. There also seemed to be a clear, albeit implicit, rejection of the claim that people abandoned their homes and lands. Again, sharing stories like this leaves space for interpretations and storytelling, as opposed to testimony.

Like many others, Jamila Awad framed the year of 1948 through the prism of the events that surrounded the incident at Salah Eissa's café. Jamila shared a deep intimacy of the events as she chose to include a delicate naming of the people in the café:

> So the incident happened with the bomb on the bus, and the very next day, they [the Jewish settlers] descended on the café with their guns blazing at all the men sitting in the café. They hit twelve people, five of them died and seven were severely injured. ʿAbd ʿAbdullah, [and] Abu Yamouna died immediately, and Ahmad Judeh Helwa died; another man named Bakr from Lifta died immediately, and one man, not from Lifta, who was working as a guard in the village and was sitting at the café with the other men, was also shot and killed on the spot. Others were injured, like Salah Othman and Doctor Mahmud.[25]

Like the others, Jamila remembered that the idea and act of leaving Lifta was connected to the café incident. People began saying, according to Jamila, "If we stay here, the Jewish settlers will eat us alive." She added, "My family left before I did with my husband and child, but we left about a week later . . . everyone eventually left after that incident at the café."[26]

The details of the café shooting also mixed in with the pressures of adhering to a coherent narrative contracted over time, to which Deir Yassin was central. As Jamila noted, "We knew why we were leaving; we were escaping Jewish settler violence. Remember, this was also in the midst of the massacre at Deir Yassin." As if speaking about a legend, Jamila continued: "There was one man who stayed, his whole family left, but he refused to leave . . . his sons and daughters left, but he refused; Jewish settlers went down to where he was and tore him to pieces, they killed him." Returning to the echoes of Deir Yassin, Jamila spoke of how the news spread quite quickly, and she remembered distinctly how affected people were: "Of course, fear was the immediate response: 'They will slaughter us like they slaughtered the people of Deir Yassin.'"[27] The specter of Deir Yassin has a long shadow in Palestine, as it has become in many ways a template for 1948 and all the many massacres thereafter for many decades, until Gaza. The proximity of Lifta to Deir Yassin has helped foster this kind of mythological connection, but it is also the product of how oral history has "recorded" time and Deir Yassin, through this, was *the* massacre.[28] Moreover, though the stories remained alive in the storytellers and the process of sharing them, the thread of explaining leaving—justifying it—remained and was also collective, though told in individual ways. As one thread among many, the power of testimony still held weight in these stories. Nevertheless, the unique style of listening to the stories shared, and the stories themselves, leaves space for nuance and interpretation and a more fluid sense of time. Given the various story lines and constellation of timelines, it is worth wondering about the incident at the café. Was this narrative about wresting agency back from an overwhelming structure of settler power? Was it about pride and refusing the static trope of victimhood? Or, simply, was it removed from the causality that testimony requires and, rather, telling the stories of the people on the land—with all kinds of complications that can remain open to interpretation? Unlike documentation and testimonies, stories defy categories.

Listening and Sharing: Stations of the Refugee Journey, Belonging and Longing

Family stories carry through generations. Interviews and oral testimony cannot convey or explore the intimacy of growing up and into stories. The stories change, grow with time, and evolve. Certainly not historical documents catalogued in an archive, stories live with the storytellers and the listeners. In all the stories I heard, I tried to hear ʿArifa, just as I heard Safiya's story through ʿArifa's daughters. My mother and aunts mostly heard Safiya's stories over the years from their mother, with their own childhood memories sprinkled into her fantastic stories. In particular, I listened to my own mother and my Aunt Khawlah—two very different sources on two very different continents, though both in settler colonial settings, Chicago and Jerusalem, respectively. In spite of the patrilineal kinship network at large, so many of these stories flowed through women. The common thread among all—through the generations—is our collective relations with Lifta, mediated through loss and life. Stories came to occupy the space where imagination enables and empowers the collapse of boundaries between past, present, and future through telling and listening. Safiya's cows and treasure chest and Salah al-Eissa's café, for example, take on a life of their own, because of the ongoing nature of the stories, the refugee journey, and the Nakba, and perhaps also because of the ongoing practice of return.

Since the normative and oppressive methodology of traditional historical documentation has affected and occupied the concept of storytelling, the tropes of testimony in terms of both events and logics are difficult to escape. Memories in the context of Lifta almost inevitably begin or end with a fateful journey from the village in late 1947 or 1948. Over time these stories were shaped by questions posed by researchers trying to reconstruct Palestinian exodus. As such, people's stories seem to fold into one history and one moment, almost as one story. The landscape of the political struggle has given logic to this approach. That is, in the ongoing erasure of Zionist invasion, the stories of the Nakba War as told by Palestinians have formed into a kind of national consensus of both countering Zionist mythology and adhering to a legibility in international law about the right of return. While they are understandable in terms of legibility and visibility within the confinement of settler logics and the politics of recognition, what do we lose when we confine ourselves to settler frameworks and the violence therein? The quandary remains: How can we see through this all and rediscover people's ongoing lives? How can we remain connected to a collective story while also holding space for the vibrancy and nuance of personal stories? These are not answerable questions as much as they are an invitation to reconceptualize the methodology of reading the past by listening in the present and working to keep spaces open for the stories within the stories.

Rifqa Odeh's family first landed in Deir Dibwan because that is where they had agricultural land. Deir Dibwan led them eventually to Al-Bireh and Ramallah. Muhammad Nassar and Amna Khalil walked to Beit Hanina, where they, like many others from Lifta, had agricultural land. They told the story of being the last to flee Lifta. The part of the story of being "last to leave" often punctuates the weight of the exodus narrative. Nevertheless, lines of consistency breathe life into the lines of speculation that feed the stories. Did ʿArifa see Rifaq's family as she made her way east out of Jerusalem? Did Safiya cross paths with Muhammad's family as they both traveled through Beit Hanina? In those early days in Jerusalem, did Safiya's children see Jamila Awad's in the Old City? Shared contexts breed stories that are related, almost blending into one another over time. When stories are needed to produce and sustain a certain kind of culture (and, in particular, identity production), the metanarrative over-determines and imagination and speculation fall outside a political imperative. Holding together one coherent story to counter erasure is a self-defensive mechanism for survival among Palestinians. As such, in the context of the development of oral history as a methodology in Palestine, this inaugural period of violent expulsion has, over time, transformed into the national story for a people without a state.

Here the state is replaced with "a search for a state" and quest toward building the inherent continuity of the institutions embedded within the structures of the modern nation-state that promote a national mythology.[29] After all, oral history developed over time in the Palestinian context to counter Zionist archival history and has been instrumentalized as a tool of the politics of recognition deemed necessary by many for Palestinians to "enter" the modernity of nation-state nationalism. As such, institutional memory in this context is both produced and manipulated for political ends toward creating a kind of Palestinian national mythology, but one that requires a kind of meta-story for 1948. While contextually understandable within the oppressive frameworks of settler logics, containing stories within one story (as a national mythology) confines us to these logics and loses the nuance and possibilities of imagination. Imprisoned in loss and the desire to gain legitimacy in a modern world that has waged a century-long war against Palestinian peoplehood, we may have contributed to our own sense of loss by burying our stories under the rubric of "destroyed villages." While it is politically necessary to document loss, we may have contributed to our own living paradox by focusing on loss as an exclusive lost past, foreclosing return as a very possibility, and denying ongoing return as a methodology of life and vitality. That is, by countering erasure and succumbing to settler logics, have we made our history one plagued by the static of a "paradise lost"? How can we honor the work that responds to the very discipline of history in Palestine, Nakba history, and also work to move beyond it? How can we honor the people who share stories that have no doubt been affected by the quest toward a metanarrative of righteous loss? While perhaps unanswerable, these questions are always present when we share stories. Perhaps holding space for them to remain open and intentional throughout our collective quest is a core element in the methodology of stories, and perhaps posing questions remains more powerful than offering any kind of declarative answer. Grounding ourselves in the principle that we belong to Palestine and working to free ourselves from the weight of constantly have to prove that Palestine belongs to us can perhaps mediate this sense of loss.

Othmana Hamed's family first went to Al-Bireh and later moved close by, to Ramallah, but she made the point that no one from her family bought land in Al-Bireh or Ramallah for at least a decade after Lifta. They were and remained refugees, thereby emphasizing her personal story as life within and through temporary stations. Each journey, in spite of the pressures to being folding into one journey, retains an active sense of storytelling and imaginary possibilities. We live in and through these contradictions between the static and temporary. Refusal is a conscious refusal of settler logics but also an embedded refusal of this folding into one—the everyday prevails in the present and the past. Thus, exploring the conceptual field and limitations of the "temporary" is a consistent theme in refugee and exile studies in the context of Palestine. Naema ʿAbdiyat's story of flight was also emphasized by the temporary:

"We took little with us, because we knew we would be back."[30] But embedded within the immediacy of her story, Naema also narrated the intimacy of her and her family through the fear and alienation of settler violence that had become all-encompassing from December 1947 through the spring of 1948 and have remained since then. Naema made certain to begin her story with the sound of gunshots, as it was the soundtrack of how she remembered her family's flight. During these months, the short road into and out of Lifta was not an easy one to take, as it was a constant site of resistance and colonial violence. Just as it had been earlier, in 1929 and in 1936, this road tells the multilayered stories of resistance.[31] Consistent themes in the "destroyed village" trope are victim narratives and trauma-centered narratives because early Palestinian literature on the Nakba worked to counter the settler myth that people left on orders from Palestinian leadership.[32] Palestinians were and remain victims of ongoing settler violence, but in Naema's story we can also hear an agency that an opposing metanarrative cannot hold. That is, in order to counter a blaming of victims, the victim trope took center stage and resistance was forced into the background. After all, within settler logics, resistance is the terrorism that invited settler "self-defense." To negate this self-defense trope, we rightfully focused on victimhood, but we also lost the agency involved in protecting the land. While the criminalization of resistance is not new to Palestine and Palestinians, the subtle adoption of settler anxieties in countering this trope has also rendered the stories void of agency. But, again, contradictions prevail, and even in the "destroyed villages" trope a focus on the Nakba as a war where Palestine was a battlefield and not only a site of exodus eventually prevailed. Moreover, this has, in time, also become a central aspect of Nakba literature as seen in the popularity of Khaled Odetallah's and Basil al-ʿAraj's projects to walk through the geographies of resistance.[33]

I know ʿArifa went to the village of Birzeit because of the stories of stations that others shared and the intimate connections Nuwara was to have with Birzeit, just north of Ramallah. Nuwara, ʿAta's daughter from ʿIzziya, was already engaged to Muhammad Salman from Birzeit. With the growing intensity of settler attacks across Jerusalem, it seems contingency plans were being explored by many. This may have been why Muhammad went to see his future father-in-law at Dar al-Aytam School, where ʿAta taught Arabic, because in the winter and spring months of 1948 ʿAta grew accustomed to staying overnight at the school and would go home to Lifta on his days off. ʿAta met Muhammad in the Old City of Jerusalem and told him to go to Lifta and take his wife and two young children to Birzeit. Nuwara spoke of the immediacy of the moment and how ill prepared they were to leave. ʿArifa took her two small children, and Nuwara packed supplies to sustain them for some time. They then went with Muhammad to Birzeit. Perhaps ʿArifa did not have the right kind of influence over her mother-in-law, Safiya, and so they parted ways in 1948 with others who fled Lifta, Safiya with her treasure chest into central Jerusalem and ʿArifa with her young children to Birzeit. ʿAta met ʿArifa and the children weeks later in Birzeit. I asked Nuwara why her grandmother did not leave with them. She was at first perplexed by the question, but then simply answered, "Because that is not what she wanted to do."[34] Though forced by settler violence to flee, the language of choices remained, and this vocabulary also grounds the language of stories. They were hard choices, difficult, impossible, and existential decisions, no doubt, but described as choices nonetheless.

ʿArifa, first alone with her children and stepdaughter, and then with ʿAta, stayed in Birzeit for nearly fifteen months until they made their way back into Jerusalem as refugees. I wonder if ʿArifa heard the word *refugee* in Birzeit as harshly as Rifqa did in Deir Dibwan. ʿAta, ʿArifa, and their children first lived in a small home inside the Old City, later moving to the space between Asfahani and Salah al-Din Streets where Safiya had set up her refugee home. Nuwara thinks it was only a matter of a few days after ʿArifa fled to Birzeit that Safiya packed her treasure chest and journeyed toward Beit Hanina before she found her way to Asfahani and Salah al-Din Streets. Because of the kinds of journeys others spoke about, I was able to imagine the walks both ʿArifa and Safiya took, and to imagine how kinship was broken, only to be reconstructed over time. I imagined all of this through sharing the methodology that listening to stories allows. I imagined Safiya through Habiba's words about her mother, a young widow who also seized her agency and autonomy through her choices in the midst of horror.[35] Decision-making was not new to these women I imagined, for they were real, and my imaginations are an amalgamation of their choices, their decisions made in haste and in force. They were expelled, forced to leave the homes they knew and forced to bring with them material from those homes, as well as the very idea of home. ʿArifa and Safiya—each was connected and then forced to disconnect. They walked, and I learned that walking through time and space—through the layers that storytelling, even through fragmented narratives, enables—is how the journey did not end. Time is not fixed, and the story does not follow a clear linear arc; nor is it without the need to speculate and hopefully imagine. Where the walking and the storytelling connect is in a world of stories—our own, each other's, and ours together.

Sharedness: Return, Resistance, and Refugee
Come Together as Threads to Form a *Thob*

Return is deeply and forever connected to movement and action. In a conversation that moved through the generations of people from Lifta, Loay al-Manssi focused on the very same category Rifqa Odeh had described: *refugee.* Just as Rifqa and her family encountered the label, Loay, three generations later, described its enduring nature. Between the seasons of the fall and winter of 2000–2001, as the Israeli Army expanded its level and consistency of direct violence on Ramallah and its surrounding villages during al-Aqsa Intifada, Loay and his circle of childhood friends became more directly involved in the armed resistance. As he described it, "Most of us who were fighting were refugees. In Ramallah, as refugees, we always felt like we were strangers or visitors. We had this complex that was clearly inherited from our parents and was made more material in those days of violence. All my friends were refugees. We were all refugees. This was not the case in the villages around Ramallah, but in Ramallah, we were clearly our own entity. We were visitors in this land . . . inside Palestine and still a stranger."[36] As two newly released prisoners from the same third generation of refugees from Lifta, in separate conversations with me, Bilal Odeh and Loay al-Manssi shared an emphasis on this linguistic point as descendants of Lifta. Bilal, who lives in Jerusalem, was adamant about this within his description of going back to Lifta: "I went to Lifta yesterday; I have made that journey often since being released from prison, but, unlike the trips in my childhood, I appreciate going there alone these days. But it should be clear, some of us Liftawis can physically go there; others have a much harder time, if not impossible time, given settler borders, but we do not visit Lifta, we are not strangers nor foreigners to our own land, and it should be clear in all languages, we do not visit what we belong to."[37]

Bilal in Jerusalem and Loay in Ramallah each had their own story and both were connected by Lifta. This kind of reinforcement of a conceptual point is actually a reification of Loay's point: While *refugee* is a category in the contemporary life of Palestinians, belonging is actually embedded within it and persists in its defiance, as is the journey described by Rifqa, as well as the one described by Bilal. He narrated this circular journey (to and from Lifta as a place and an idea) through *hasra* (bitter longing) that is foundational in his relationship to Lifta as a place and an idea. From a dubiously close proximity to Lifta in Ramallah, Loay al-Manssi, embodying a kind of ethos of third-generation refugee from Lifta, lives loss through the events of his young life that led him in 2020 to the conclusion that "as long as we live in our stations of exile, we will always be reminded of *being refugees* and how we are not in the place we are from, Lifta."[38] Bilal explained, "We live in fear of a disaster that has already happened. We live in hope that we will find a way to make a home. Fear and hope mix, with a backdrop of longing, of the burden of an existential loss that we have inherited and the almost irrational hope that the inheritance of belonging and the burden of loss will be our return. I have lived forty-one years of exile [his age at the time], but I carry seventy-one years of it in my body."

Both Loay and Bilal spoke with me separately in Ramallah, each of them newly released from Israeli prisons having served fifteen and eighteen years as political prisoners, respectively, for their participation in al-Aqsa Intifada. Both were born in Ramallah in the late 1970s. Bilal moved back to Jerusalem with his family in the late 1980s, to Ard al-Samar and land owned by his family from the "days of Lifta." Twice imprisoned before al-Aqsa Intifada, Bilal graduated from college and less than four months later was arrested by the Israeli military in Jerusalem. Loay was also born in Ramallah, raised, as he described it, in his grandfather's "permanent-temporary home" in Al-Bireh.[39] Through all of the rich details that resist categorization, in spite of his *refugee* category, Loay described the stations of his life as active processes of creating spaces in spite of loss. Like Bilal, Loay lived through loss: "Living the life of perpetual fugitivity, we make homes for ourselves, all the while reminded that we live a permanent temporary as long as settlers police the spaces we move through."[40] Loay was a street fighter turned *tanzim* (with the political party Fateh) leader in al-Aqsa Intifada and found refuge in various neighborhoods in Ramallah with the Israeli military actively on his trail. Eventually he found his way out of Ramallah into the neighboring villages. He did not remain in one place for more than a few months, and he was eventually captured by the Israeli Army and imprisoned:

> Prison did not end the journey; it just gave it a different backdrop. It actu-
> ally was an opportunity to come together anew; we were fighters outside
> the small prison walls, but outside, we did not meet like we did inside. . . .
> And *after prison* is another continuation of the journey; it is bitter to be
> reminded in Ramallah that we are not in [and not of] this city, but it is
> also another kind of formation of community. I never need to be, but be
> sure I am always reminded that I am from Lifta and refugees find each
> other, especially in spaces like Ramallah; we have a map of Palestine
> among, between, and through us.[41]

Neither Bilal nor Loay were yet born in the early winter months of 1948, but they have both not stopped living that temporality. Bilal explained, "When we were children, whole families would go to Lifta, sometimes busloads, sometimes just a few elders taking us children through the narrow pathways of the old village.... Their goal was to take us and tell us stories—*ayam al-balad*, the very old stories from their lives before the loss. Time melted, though, because it was as if it was yesterday. They told us stories and we listened; they were not ancient to them nor to us, it was as if it were yesterday."[42] The open wound has neither closed nor stopped bleeding. Two hours into our conversation, in which he and I built community between our disparate experiences, Bilal finally said,

> This is almost impossible to explain, but, of course, you understand; you came from oceans away to come home, you wear your wounds like we all do. Stories were told because we use stories to fight the eruption that the settlers forced on us. It was a successful operation, we inherited stories, we belong to the place, now they [our families] feel better, safer in their souls, they could not spare for us the material lives they lived in the village, so they needed us to inherit our history, and it is a responsibility and at the same time a burden, because you become a prisoner of the place. The place had and still has an undeniable beauty, and you feel safe in that beauty, but at the same time it is there and not there for you; it is what you need, but now you know you need it.[43]

Only six months after his release from prison, Bilal explained that the prison extends well beyond the cells of all the prisons: "We are also in the prisons of the memory of a place, but this poses a number of questions: Do we leave this rhetorical prison? If we choose to leave it, can we?"[44] That Bilal, like Loay, also included me in the conversation is an indication of how together we are part of a shared generation and how we have held stories through time, in very specific and particular ways, through our varied relations with the place of Lifta. Bilal and Loay are very different politically and socially, though the ties that connect them are undeniable. Each from a particular journey, three third-generation refuges from Lifta found ways toward and with each other. I sought belonging with them and they both gave it to me, each in his own way. I still often see Bilal and Loay in protests in Ramallah. Loay is now a leader in the Fateh party in Ramallah and is a part of the untenable system of the Palestinian Authority. Bilal is a scholar and writer and continues to reside in Ard al-Samar in Jerusalem. We could not be more different, but also share an existential likeness. Each of us has taken their own position in particular political and cultural positionality, but all of us acknowledge, every time our paths cross, that Lifta is in each of us. I wonder how our paths will cross in return?

Stories live inside us and our bodies become archives. The stories are never static, and they leave their marks on us. The wounds are carried through the generations, from Bilal's memory as a child being given the place of Lifta as an inherited responsibility to Ibrahim Khalil remembering going back to Lifta through his own childhood memory of being forced to leave Lifta:

> More than twenty years ago, my paternal cousin and I went to the village olive oil press that many from the village families used in the past, and when we were there, all of a sudden, a Jewish settler appeared with a gun on his side. My cousin was afraid, but he [the settler] said nothing to us. . . . The houses are worn down now; back then they were in better condition, only the holes that they [the settler army] cut into the ceilings so as to make the homes uninhabitable, but now they have been worn down by time. I did not go to my family home; it is the northern part of the village and we did not go there . . . but I know our home stands in Lifta to this day.[45]

Just as Bilal explained, we never say we "visited Lifta." We are not strangers who visit. We return to Lifta. In the language of Ibrahim, when he explained why returning to Lifta is important, "We are of the place. We cannot forget what and where we are from; it is our home. . . . My hope for the younger generation is that God gives them the protection and guidance to find their way to return, so that they can see where they are from and what they are of."[46] Though they are from different families and very different geographies, and though the conversations were years apart (Bilal in 2020 and Ibrahim in 2012), both Bilal and Ibrahim echoed each other's sentiments as carriers and bearers of stories. But rather than reproducing one static narrative, the nuances of going to Lifta reveal the layers—both connected and disparate—that ongoing return offers.

Ways of Being: Unbroken and Threaded Together

Bilal and Loay gave me the space to begin to magically thread together all of our stories—like pieces of a *thob*, each piece and section in its beauty and the whole unbroken by the threads that connect us through time and space. Our conversations were not connected to the Save Lifta Coalition nor to an archive project. I wanted to also talk to people in my generation. Like so many in our generation who grew up in the land of Palestine, they were young fighters, two former political prisoners from different ideologies, parties, and geographies. I had no idea what I would do with the conversations, but I knew I wanted to begin generational conversations and both Bilal and Loay showed me kindness and generosity. They both thought I wanted to interview them and accepted the invitation, but when the conversation began, both came to realize that I did not want testimony, I wanted to share.

Over dinner in our family home, as I prepared another return to Palestine after finding a way around the last denial of access, I told my brother, Amjad, about this project of mine that felt like it could not end until I returned to Palestine. I told him about Loay and Bilal and about how I wanted to hear their stories. Amjad did not know all the details of my journey manifested into this book, but he did know ʿArifa. I showed him the photograph that captured all my thoughts: the one of him with ʿArifa. It is color photograph taken in the late 1970s, and in it ʿArifa just glows. Her young grandchild, Amjad, sits on her lap, displaying the coin she gave him. ʿArifa is wearing her *injasa thob* while proudly holding him in her loving arms. I only then realized just how formative she was for him.

When I told Amjad about the stories Mom and I shared, he told me, "I have stories too. I know Mom does not even know these stories." Sitting in our mother's kitchen in our family home, just like he and I had throughout our lives, Amjad took what I had complicated and made it simply brilliant: "Rana, it is not never ending; it is always in the making." After impatiently listening to me explain about the stories I gathered, he explained that he too had a story to share:

> She would take me on a daily walk. The entire summer trip, every after-noon, Sitti [Grandma, ʿArifa] and I would go for a stroll through Jerusa-lem that always ended up with us going to the cemetery. Mom never knew where we went; Sitti wanted it that way, and I was happy to oblige. She made the journeys fun for a young kid coming from half a world away. She told me stories of my grandfather and how important it was for me to know his story. I was only four at the time, but I remember going and sitting on what I guess was a bench near his grave. The trip to the cemetery was always the last stop after walking down Salah al-Din Street and before going up the street behind it, where she bought me ice cream.[47]

He had told me something I never knew but had imagined all along. And so I asked my brother, "Was she wearing her *injasa thob* on these walks?"

In Lieu of a Conclusion

Where to end in the ongoing?

As I get in the taxi, I am practicing how to say Balou'—a name for a neighborhood that is evasive and reveals my foreignness. However much I practice, even I can hear the "foreign" in my enunciation. That is the peculiar part of speaking with "accents": I no longer hear my own. Over time, I hear my voice speaking Arabic like everyone around me. But every once in a while, I catch it—the awkward sound of my Chicago invading my Arabic.

I always noticed my mother's accent in English as a child. I grew to love it over time. Mom thinks my newfound love of her accent is as much about her as it is about me. "Full-circle," she would say, she with her Jerusalem-Arabic-tinged English in Chicago and me with my Chicago-English-tinged Arabic in Palestine. Mom is right; I want someone to love my own strange accent in Arabic. I live in this glorious language and worked hard to pull this off for so long. I constantly repeat the phrase, "Arabic is my mother's tongue," and I often choose to omit how it is not mine, because it should be—or maybe it is?

And, even so, my mother's accent reflects all the places she has lived in from Jerusalem to Chicago, just like her mother's accent must have reflected her own lived geographies from the village of Lifta to Salah al-Din Street and Wadi al-Joz in Jerusalem. All the places that Mom and ʿArifa knew as home. This is another aspect of the bittersweet constellation of Palestinians—*shatat*—that has imposed multiple geographies and all that comes along with this displacement. Accents do more than reveal all of our locations in *al-shatat*; accents combine to become the flow and rhythm of stories.

The threads that connect us do so through all the colors of our contexts . . . and pathways home. Return is a journey into the fantastical imagination both grounded and in flight. Stories plant and carry all of the songs of return in abundance from sweet to melancholy rhythms. Home and homeland are a part of the ongoing return that framed this story.

On this day, in that taxi, I needed to figure out how to stay a little longer to continue to return. Individual displacement—anyone's individual displacement—is a mere drop in the bloody ocean of settler colonial violence and an entire people's forced displacement, *shatat*. The settler state had still not rec-

ognized my right to residency. So for me, staying translated into a visa re-
newal. Staying was, is, about buying time: I had been told that if I left to travel,
I would never be able to enter again. Return has to be ongoing, even in
denial.

This has been my life for years. The last time I traveled to see my folks in
Chicago, the settler state would not let me return. Once again, my lawyer appealed; once again, denial of a visa continued. This time came the accusation
that I was becoming a settler! In the meantime, we found another passage for
another return. And so, eventually, one gets to borders or to the offices where
soldiers and bureaucrats decide one's fate, in little moments of unbearable
belittling. But such moments are more: They are also ways of living, of what
we do to remain living.

I enter the building and head toward the offices of those in charge of "foreigners." The settler accused me of trying to settle and the Palestinian Authority (PA) labels me a foreigner: Tragedy or comedy? The men in these
buildings impose a sense of defeat in strange ways. Is this their defeat? Is it
mine? It cannot be ours. Where are the poets when I need them? I have never
read a poem about a visa.

Balou᾽ is *the* address, because it is the location of the headquarters of the
PA's General Authority of Civilian Affairs. It is where the answers to questions about visas and ID status (the elusive gifts of permanent residency
given by the settlers) are housed, but certainly not where they are answered—
for that is a power the settlers would not bestow. It is still where we work to be
legible in a system that was created to make us disappear. It is the home of the
contradiction and the heart of the forced sense of defeat. Population registry
is the playground of those who work to destroy peoplehood and to break
both the word and the concept of *belonging*.

This is one building among so many that hold these contradictions. This is
in Balou᾽. What of the settlers' compound of misery in Jerusalem? What of
all the compounding of misery that the settlers have imposed on us in order
to destroy our peoplehood? We navigate all of these sites of despair with our
rage, which nourishes our hope. Palestinian is a positionality. It is a politics. It
is a peoplehood. All of these compounds are stations, representative of the
powers that mediate further violence: waiting lists of all kinds, for anything
you can imagine. And we use the grand scheme of a hustle to get us to an even
grander scheme, a hustle for time, for another reprieve to extend the promise
of ongoing return.

I do not trust elevators in compounds like this, but I always go too far up in
the stairwell and have to circle back. Why can I never remember the details of

this building, just as I cannot retain the details of the borders and all we need to cross them or all that happens when we are unable to cross them? We belong to Palestine. Every time is like a first time; there have been so many times. We belong to Palestine. The never-ending cycle, full of holes and obstacles, and with very little solid ground, is an aberration. We belong to Palestine. This, here, is a bureaucratic semblance, with all of the superficial edifices of government offices: too many people in the halls, the strange scent of coffee mixed with cigarettes. I do not want Balou' to be the backdrop for my stories. Without the feeling of breathlessness we cannot appreciate the act the breathing. We belong to Palestine.

The edifice of the PA is a tragic joke. The people are often honest; they too belong to Palestine. Employment in a system does not mean they believe it. They also know there is no actual, solid self-determination or sovereignty in their work. I reach the office and manage a moment with the person who submitted my file to the settlers. He is a hustler, so I have to become one too. The PA is a machine and structure that is the product of settler dreams. It made a mockery out of our revolution, but so did those who came before them. But people and our peoplehood cannot fit into categories this easily. Balou' reminds me—constantly—of this. Peoplehood is not to be found in the paper pushing or even the heartless bureaucracy of false sovereignty. The hustle keeps time, holds it in place—or, perhaps, hostage. The hustle might have an expiration date. The hustle might also lead or force you and me into exile. It is only a hustle, it is temporary, and we tolerate the temporary to get to that which is ongoing.

Lifta is easier to pronounce than Balou'. It is life. It is hope. Lifta is also the scene of a crime, of a century of crimes. *Crime* does not fit as a word or a concept to describe the kind of violence Zionist settler colonialism has raged on generations of Palestinians. Poets write of these crimes, expose them, reveal their horror. The poet explains how refugee camps, prisons, and cemeteries tell the tales of violence. That is important, necessary work. The divine work of poets.

Time is not theirs to steal; it is ours to imagine. We belong to Palestine.

LIFTA IS THEIR MUSEUM. They revel in its beauty. They walk through Lifta as if they were walking back in time. These settlers made the village into something they could possibly tolerate. But even in making a museum, the settlers could not agree. Some wanted to settle in Lifta, others wanted to make it into a monument, and still others wanted to completely destroy it and build on the ruins—to force themselves to forget. As the monsters of fascism grow, the desire to destroy becomes even more intentional and omni-present, from the river to the sea. Lifta is not an exception.

We were once worried we would forget. We did not. We have not. We will not. Verb tenses fold into each other when we listen.

'Arifa taught me that to remember is to share through walking. I imagine walking with her and my mother. I wonder how they interacted as mother and daughter. To wonder, I borrow my own relationship with my mother to perhaps try to understand their mother-daughter relationship and to feed my imagination. And so I join them, generations of mothers and daughters. This is a story of mothers and daughters. What a wonder it is to walk together through time! Perhaps we can learn how to walk *toward* each other by walking *with* each other.

I learn to imagine. I listen while others imagine. I walk with all of these voices and steps in my head. I gather them and they carry me; we have collected each other over time. Sometimes I cannot find my own voice or steps among theirs. Maybe that is the point. It is not about me. We belong to Palestine. They try to destroy us, they target the best of us, they target all of us, they cannot tolerate that we belong to Palestine.

Our stories are layered; in their shared intimacy they become collective. Through sharing stories and walking through shared landscapes, we blend into each other while we retain our selves. Those who rely only on archives of the oppressors and oppression call our imaginations absurd. But they are only absurd if you do not walk together or share. We belong to Palestine. Bruised and battered, burned and demolished, our landscape has endured the ongoing violence of settler invasion. The settlers tried to change names on the landscape to make the places their own. They filled their prisons with our people, they filled cemeteries with our martyrs, and they drew borders so impenetrable as to steal the hope of our return. And when that was not enough for them, they tried to destroy everything. They weaponized food and water and air, and they have scorched the earth and left nothing and no one untouched. With all their weapons and their endless capacity to use them and the world's endless capacity to watch, they will always be strangers to this land.

In spite of a century-long campaign against us and our belonging, the settlers have become the aberration. The settlers work for our extinction and their violence increases with every episode of their failure—our annihilation is not a metaphor for monsters. We continue to walk and to share. When we walk with our stories, when we share them, we learn the methodology of walking with stories as a way of living and a way of being. We are so much more than all their brutal and incomprehensible violence. Sharing stories is how we walk together even when we struggle to breathe; even when we struggle to be together; even when we struggle to survive the seasons of this never-ending Nakba. Our methodology is learning how to endure in order to flourish.

This story has no ending. It is ongoing. I have learned to not want it to end, as there is no "ever after" in what is ongoing. I want to walk through and with Palestine. I belong to Palestine. We belong to Palestine. I do not know how this idea began. It did not begin with me, but this book is an effort to begin anew.

I refuse to write an ending for a story that shall not end.

Notes

Introduction

1. Susan Abu Hawa, *The Blue Between Sky and Water* (New York: Simon and Schuster, 2016).

2. As many scholars have pointed out, understanding settler colonialism is as much about time and temporality as it is about space. That is, the hegemonic and subsequent normative reading of past and present is also about understanding settler colonial violence. As Mark Rifken, *Beyond Settler Time: Temporal Sovereignty and Indigenous Self-Determination* (Durham, NC: Duke University Press, 2017), suggests in terms of history, it is not complete without knowing the history of history. To confront this is to unpack this in order to move beyond it. See also Elizabeth A. Povinelli, *The Cunning of Recognition: Indigenous Alterities and the Making of Australian Multiculturalism* (Durham, NC: Duke University Press, 2002); Elizabeth A. Povinelli, "Settler Modernity and the Quest for an Indigenous Tradition," *Public Culture* 11, no. 1 (1999): 19–48; and Laura Rademaker, "A History of Deep Time: Indigenous Knowledges and Deep Pasts in Settler-Colonial Presents," *History Australia* 18, no. 4 (2021): 658–75. Moreover, as J. Kēhaulani Kauanui, "'A Structure, Not an Event': Settler Colonialism and Enduring Indigeneity," *Lateral* 5, no. 1 (2016), https://csalateral.org/issue /5-1/forum-alt-humanities-settler-colonialism-enduring-indigeneity-kauanui/, suggests, Indigeneity endures in both spatial and temporal registers. For a response to Kauanui, see Melissa Gniadek, "The Times of Settler Colonialism," *Lateral* 6, no. 1 (2017), https:// csalateral.org/issue/6-1/forum-alt-humanities-settler-colonialism-times-gniadek/.

3. Allice Legat, "Walking Stories; Leaving Footprints," in *Ways of Walking: Ethnography and Practice on Foot*, ed. Tim Infold and Jo Lee Vergunst (London: Routledge, 2016), 47–62. See also Allice Legat, *Walking the Land, Feeding the Fire: Knowledge and Stewardship Among the Tlicho Dene* (Tucson: University of Arizona Press, 2012); and Esther Fitzpatrick, "A Story of Becoming: Entanglement, Settler Ghosts, and Postcolonial Counterstories," *Cultural Studies ↔ Critical Methodologies* 18, no. 1 (2018): 43–51.

4. Vanessa Cavanagh and Peta Standley, "Walking in the Landscapes of Our Ancestors— Indigenous Perspectives Critical in the Teaching of Geography," *Interaction* 48, no. 1 (2020): 14–16; Ashlyn King Barnett, "Long-Distance Walking: An Indigenous Methodology for Resistance and Resurgence" (PhD diss., University of Colorado–Boulder, 2021). In this context walking *with* has also been complemented by walking *against* (settler knowledge); see, for example, Bryan Smith, "Walking the Stories of Colonial Ghosts: A Method of/ Against the Geographically Mundane," *Journal of Curriculum and Pedagogy* 21, no. 1 (2022): 1–25. See also the work of the project WalkingLab as an example of the implementation of a "new" methodology: Stephanie Springy and Sarah E. Truman, "Creation Walking Methodologies and an Unsettling of Time," *International Review of Qualitative Research* 12, no. 1 (2019): 85–93; and Stephanie Springy and Sarah E. Truman, *Walking Methodologies in a More-Than-Human World: WalkingLab* (London: Routledge, 2017).

5. Linda Tuhiwai Smith, *Decolonizing Research: Indigenous Storywork as Methodology* (London: Bloomsbury, 2019).

6. Raja Shehadeh, *Palestinian Walks: Notes on a Vanishing Landscape* (London: Profile Books, 2010), 16–17. See also Amanda Batarseh, "Raja Shehadeh's 'Cartography of Refusal': The Enduring Land Narrative Practice of Palestinian Walks," *Cambridge Journal of Postcolonial Literary Inquiry* 8, no. 2 (2021): 232–52.

7. Leanne Betasamosake Simpson, "Indigenous Resistance Lifts the Veil of Colonial Amnesia," *Geez*, Winter 2014, https://geezmagazine.org/magazine/article/indigenous-resistance-lifts-the-veil-of-colonial-amnesia; Lucy Taylor, "Welsh-Indigenous Relationships in Nineteenth Century Patagonia: 'Friendship' and the Coloniality of Power," *Journal of Latin American Studies* 49, no. 1 (2017): 143–68.

8. Al-ʿAraj's complete work, including letters and stories of his now infamous walking tours of the landscapes of resistance, were published after the Israeli military murdered him. See Basil al-ʿAraj, *Wajadat Ajwabti: Haktha Takalm al Shahid Basil al-ʿAraj* [The appearance of my responses: So spoke the martyr Basil al ʿAraj] (Jerusalem: Dar al Rʾabal, 2018).

9. For a fine summary and intensive inquiry into the work of Khaled Odetallah, see Khaled Odetallah, "Khaled Odetallah: Filastini min al-Quds ila Gaza" [Khaled Odetallah: Palestinian from Jerusalem to Gaza], interview by Abdul-Rahim al-Shaikh, *Majallat al-Dirasat al-Filastiniyya* 137 (2024): 61–84.

10. This question is neither new nor even provocative, as many in the field of Palestinian studies have posed it in various iterations. See, for example, Brenna Bhandar, *Colonial Lives of Property: Law, Land, and Racial Regimes of Ownership* (Durham, NC: Duke University Press, 2018); Lana Tatour, "The Culturalisation of Indigeneity: The Palestinian-Bedouin of the Naqab and Indigenous Rights," *International Journal of Human Rights* 23, no. 10 (2019): 1569–93; Brenna Bhandar and Rafeef Ziadah, "Acts and Omissions: Framing Settler Colonialism in Palestine Studies," Jadaliyya, January 14, 2016, https://www.jadaliyya.com/Details/32857; Omar Jabary Salamanca, Mezna Qato, Kareem Rabie, and Sobhi Samour, "Past Is Present: Settler Colonialism in Palestine," *Settler Colonial Studies* 2, no. 1 (2012): 1–8; Rana Barakat, "Writing/Righting Palestine Studies: Settler Colonialism, Indigenous Sovereignty and Resisting the Ghost(s) of History," *Settler Colonial Studies* 8, no. 3 (2018): 349–63; Jamil Hilal, "Rethinking Palestine: Settler-Colonialism, Neo-Liberalism and Individualism in the West Bank and Gaza Strip," *Contemporary Arab Affairs* 8, no. 3 (2015): 351–62; Magid Shihade, "Settler Colonialism and Conflict: The Israeli State and Its Palestinian Subjects," *Settler Colonial Studies* 2, no. 1 (2012): 108–23; Magid Shihade, *Not Just a Soccer Game: Colonialism and Conflict Among Palestinians in Israel* (Syracuse, NY: Syracuse University Press, 2011); Lila Abu-Lughod, "Imagining Palestine's Alter-Natives: Settler Colonialism and Museum Politics," *Critical Inquiry* 47, no. 1 (2020): 1–27; Darryl Li, "Translator's Preface: A Note on Settler Colonialism," *Journal of Palestine Studies* 45, no. 1 (2015): 69–76; Walid Salem, "Jerusalem: Reconsidering the Settler Colonial Analysis," *Palestine-Israel Journal of Politics, Economics, and Culture* 21, no. 4 (2016): 21–27; and Julie Peteet, "Language Matters: Talking About Palestine," *Journal of Palestine Studies* 45, no. 2 (2016): 24–40.

11. For a concise and foundational study about the power of endurance, see Kauanui, "'A Structure, Not an Event.'"

12. Rana Barakat, "Reading Palestinian Agency in Mandate History: The Narrative of the Buraq Revolt as Anti-Relational," *Contemporary Levant* 4, no. 1 (2019): 28–38.

13. Glen Sean Coulthard, *Red Skin, White Masks: Rejecting the Colonial Politics of Recognition* (Minneapolis: University of Minnesota Press, 2014), 13.

14. Coulthard, *Red Skin, White Masks*, 65.

15. Leanne Betasamosake Simpson, "Indigenous Resurgence and Co-Resistance," *Critical Ethnic Studies* 2, no. 2 (2016): 22.

16. Leanne Betasamosake Simpson, *Dancing on Our Turtle's Back: Stories of Nishnaabeg Re-Creation, Resurgence and a New Emergence* (Winnipeg, MB: Arbeiter Ring, 2011).

17. As Jodi A. Byrd of the Chickasaw people notes in "What's Normative Got to Do with It? Toward Indigenous Queer Relationality," *Social Text* 38, no. 4 (2020): 106, her conversation with this method led to her amplification of grounded relationality as an alternative means, among other things, of fostering a connection between Indigenous and queer studies "to hold the Indigenous and queer together and bind them through the concept of ground, not as identitarian categories to be revitalized and performed within ethnographic and linguistic records of colonial archives." Replacing normativity with relationality, for all of its useful interventions in the fields of knowledge, further empathizes the idea of being in relation. See also Jodi A. Byrd, "Weather with You: Settler Colonialism, Antiblackness, and the Grounded Relationalities of Resistance," *Critical Ethnic Studies* 5, nos. 1–2 (2019): 207–14; and Jodi A. Byrd, *The Transit of Empire: Indigenous Critiques of Colonialism* (Minneapolis: University of Minnesota Press, 2011).

18. Gerald Alfred Taiaiake, *Peace, Power and Righteousness: An Indigenous Manifesto* (Toronto: Oxford University Press, 1999); George Manual, *The Fourth World: An Indian Reality* (Toronto: Collier-Macmillan, 1974).

19. Jeff Corntassel, "Re-Envisioning Resurgence: Indigenous Pathways to Decolonization and Sustainable Self-Determination," *Decolonization: Indigeneity, Education and Society* 1, no. 1 (2012): 86–101. See also Audra Simpson, "Paths Towards a Mohawk Nation: Narratives of Citizenship and Nationhood in Kahnawake," in *Political Theory and the Rights of Indigenous Peoples*, ed. Duncan Ivison, Paul Patton, and Will Sanders (Cambridge: Cambridge University Press, 2000), 113–36.

20. Kamal Abu-Deeb, *The Imagination Unbound: Al-Adab al-ʾAjaʾibi and the Literature of the Fantastic* (London: Saqi, 2007). Within Palestine studies, Walid Daqaa has quickly emerged as a pillar in the sense of the imagined power of fugitive thinking; see Abdul-Rahim Al-Shaikh, "The Parallel Human: Walid Daqqah on the 1948 Palestinian Political Prisoners," *Confluences Méditerranée* 117, no. 2 (2021): 73–87; Abdul-Rahim Al-Shaikh, "Al-Geographiyya al-sabʾa: Al-istishadun wa al-shuda wa al-kapo fi barzikh Walid Daqqah" [The seventh geography: Martyrs and kapo in the Barzakh of Walid Daqqah], *Majallat al-Dirasat al-Filastiniyya* 139 (Summer 2024): 11–45; Farah Aboubakr, *The Folktales of Palestine: Cultural Identity, Memory and the Politics of Storytelling* (London: I. B. Tauris, 2019); and Ashjan Ajour, "Captivity, Resistance and Political Consciousness in Walid Daqqa's Prison Literature," *CLCWeb: Comparative Literature and Culture* 25, no. 1 (2025): 3.

21. Benedict Anderson, *Imagined Communities: Reflections on the Origin and Spread of Nationalism* (New York: Verso Books, 2006), 185.

22. Edward Said, *Orientalism* (New York: Vintage, 1979), 57.

23. Joan M. Schwartz, "The Geography Lesson: Photographs and the Construction of Imaginative Geographies," *Journal of Historical Geography* 22, no. 1 (1996): 16–45; Anne Godlewska, "Map, Text, and Image: The Mentality of Enlightened Conquerors; A New Look at the *Description d'Egypte*," *Transactions of the Institute of British Geographers*, n.s., 20, no. 1(1995): 5–28.

24. Salim Tamari, "Shifting Ottoman Conceptions of Palestine, Part 2: Ethnography and Cartography," *Jerusalem Quarterly* 48 (2011): 6–16.

25. The literature on what has been called Ottoman reform in the late nineteenth century is vast. Mainly focusing on social history, many historians vacillate between understanding reform outside an Arab nationalist reading and a new perspective on imperial history; this revisiting of the Ottoman past has produced a great deal of inquiry. See, for example, Salim Tamari and Ihsan Salih Turjman, *Year of the Locust: A Soldier's Diary and the Erasure of Palestine's Ottoman Past* (Berkeley: University of California Press, 2011); Salim Tamari, *Mountain Against the Sea: Essays on Palestinian Society and Culture* (Berkeley: University of California Press, 2008); Beshara Doumani, *Rediscovering Palestine: Merchants and Peasants in Jabal Nablus, 1700–1900* (Berkeley: University of California Press, 1995); Beshara B. Doumani, *Family Life in the Ottoman Mediterranean: A Social History* (Cambridge: Cambridge University Press, 2017); Ussama Makdisi, *Rethinking Ottoman Imperialism: Modernity, Violence and the Cultural Logic of Ottoman Reform* (Beirut: Orient Institut, 2002); Ussama Makdisi, *Age of Coexistence: The Ecumenical Frame and the Making of the Modern Arab World* (Berkeley: University of California Press, 2021); Judith Tucker, *In the House of the Law: Gender and Islamic Law in Ottoman Syria and Palestine* (Berkeley: University of California Press, 1998); Michael Provence, *The Last Ottoman Generation and the Making of the Modern Middle East* (Cambridge: Cambridge University Press, 2017); and Monica M. Ringer and Etienne Charrière, *Ottoman Culture and the Project of Modernity: Reform and Translation in the Tanzimat Novel* (London: Bloomsbury, 2020). In addition, the project Open Jerusalem has produced literature and an archive devoted to advocating for a cosmopolitan reading of the Ottoman past; see "Opening Jerusalem Archives," home page, Open Jerusalem, n.d., accessed June 9, 2025, http://www.openjerusalem.org/.

26. James P. Krokar, "New Means to an Old End: Early Modern Maps in the Service of an Anti-Ottoman Crusade," *Imago Mundi* 60, no. 1 (2008): 23–38. See also Tzvetan Todorov, *The Conquest of America: The Question of the Other* (New York: HarperCollins, 1985).

27. Nur Masalha, "Settler-Colonialism, Memoricide and Indigenous Toponymic Memory: The Appropriation of Palestinian Place Names by the Israeli State," *Journal of Holy Land and Palestine Studies* 14, no. 1 (2015): 3–57. Unfortunately, as in his later work, Masalha uses "indigenous" well beyond a reference as prior to settlement (settler colonial invasion); as such, it is largely a blanket term that could potentially obfuscate or confuse the binary (native/settler) as one of an essentializing identity. Nevertheless, Masalha and others document closely and carefully how the Zionist state worked toward implementing, in Edward Said's terms, their "imagined geography." It should be noted that, as an identity marker, Zionist mythology claimed Jewish return to the land and, as such, claimed biblical rights to place. See also Julie Peteet, "Words as Interventions: Naming in the Palestine-Israel conflict," *Third World Quarterly* 26, no. 1 (2005): 153–72; and Zena Agha, "Maps, Technology, and Decolonial Spatial Practices in Palestine," Al-Shabaka, January 14, 2020, https://al -shabaka.org/briefs/maps-technology-and-decolonial-spatial-practices-in-palestine/.

28. Michael Heffernan, "Geography, Cartography and Military Intelligence: The Royal Geographical Society and the First World War," *Transactions of the Institute of British Geographers* 21, no. 3 (1996): 504–33.

29. Noenoe K. Silva, *Aloha Betrayed: Native Hawaiian Resistance to American Colonialism* (Durham, NC: Duke University Press, 2004).

30. Amahl Bishara, "Sovereignty and Popular Sovereignty for Palestinians and Beyond," *Cultural Anthropology* 32, no. 3 (2017): 349–58.

31. Muhammad Hashim Musa Dawud Ghushah, *Al-Awqāf al-Islamiyah fi-l-Quds al-Sharif: Dirasa Tarikhiyya Muwathaqa* [Islamic *awqāf* (charitable endowment) in Jerusalem: A historical documentation] (Istanbul: IRCICA, 2009); Rochelle Davis, "Ottoman Jerusalem," in *Jerusalem 1948: The Arab Neighbourhoods and Their Fate in the War*, ed. Salim Tamari (Ramallah, Palestine: Institute of Jerusalem Studies / Badil Resource Center for Palestinian Residency and Refugee Rights, 1998), 10–29; Rashid Khalidi, "The Future of Arab Jerusalem," *British Journal of Middle Eastern Studies* 19, no. 2 (1992): 133–43; Michael Dumper, "Israeli Settlement in the Old City of Jerusalem," *Journal of Palestine Studies* 21, no. 4 (1992): 32–53; Michael Dumper, *Jerusalem Unbound* (New York: Columbia University Press, 2014); Salim Tamari, "Waqf Endowments in the Old City of Jerusalem: Changing Status and Archival Sources," in *Ordinary Jerusalem, 1840–1940: Opening New Archives, Revisiting a Global City*, ed. Angelos Dalachanis and Vincent Lamire (Leiden, Netherlands: Brill, 2018), 490–509.

32. Tamari, *Jerusalem 1948*.

33. Rana Barakat, "The Right to Wait: Exile, Home and Return," in *Seeking Palestine: New Palestinian Writing on Home and Exile*, ed. Penny Johnson and Raja Shehada (Northampton, MA: Olive Branch, 2013), 135–52.

34. Michael R. Fischbach, "The Implications of Jordanian Land Policy for the West Bank," *Middle East Journal* 48, no. 3 (1994): 492–509; Musa Budeiri, "Controlling the Archive: Captured Jordanian Security Files in the Israeli State Archives," *Jerusalem Quarterly* 66 (2016): 87–98; Salim Tamari, "In League with Zion: Israel's Search for a Native Pillar," *Journal of Palestine Studies* 12, no. 4 (1983): 41–56; Lisa Taraki and Rita Giacaman, "Modernity Aborted and Reborn," in *Living Palestine: Family Survival, Resistance, and Mobility Under Occupation*, ed. Lisa Taraki (Syracuse, NY: Syracuse University Press, 2006), 1–50.

35. Haneen Naamneh, "A Municipality Seeking Refuge: Jerusalem Municipality in 1948," *Jerusalem Quarterly* 77 (2019): 110–21. See also Haneen Naamneh, "A City Yet to Come: A Story of Arab Jerusalem 1948–1967" (PhD diss., London School of Economics, 2020).

36. Kamil al-ʿAsali, Ajdaduna fi thara bayt al-maqdis [Our ancestors in the soil of Jerusalem] (Amman, Jordan: Muʾassassat Aal al-Bayt, 1981).

37. The history and politics of cemeteries in Jerusalem, and settler colonial erasure of the dead, are worth noting here—in particular, how little space is left to bury the dead and how graves in cemeteries are also targets of settler colonial violence; see Nazmi Jubeh, "The Bab al-Rahmah Cemetery: Israeli Encroachment Continues Unabated," *Journal of Palestine Studies* 48, no. 1 (2018): 88–103; Asem Khalidi, "The Mamilla Cemetery: A Buried History," *Jerusalem Quarterly*, no. 37 (2014): 104–9; Aya Hijazi, "Toward Spacio-cide: Building the Museum of Tolerance over the Mamilla Cemetery," *Jerusalem Quarterly* 67 (2016): 97–109; and Abdul-Rahim Al-Shaikh, "The Palestinian Living Cemetery," *Majallat al-Dirasat al-Filastiniyya* 134 (Spring 2023): 85–120.

38. Jubeh, "The Bab al Rahman Cemetery," explains (writing in 2018) that the three main cemeteries in East Jerusalem, including Bab al-Sahira on Salah al Din Street, are overflowing and within less than five years there will be no space left to bury the dead. As it is, there have been innovative ways of burial, including in my grandmother's plot. As I will discuss in chapter 3, she shares her burial plot with her own mother and, later, two of her own children were added to the plot.

39. After 1948 many refugees from Lifta in Jerusalem buried their dead in this cemetery; some also buried their kin elsewhere in Jerusalem. For the afterlife of cemeteries, and the politics of burial through settler colonial violence, see Abdul-Rahim Al-Shaikh, "Geographica al-Sadisa: Al-Haraka al-Assirya al-Falistiniyya" [The sixth geography: The Palestinian prisoners' movement], *Majallat al-Dirasat al-Filastiniyya* 32, no. 128 (2021): 9–59. In this work Al-Shaikh refers to his ongoing research and his articulation of another geography in/for Palestine, which is cemeteries. See also Ahmad Mahmoud, "Shawahid al Qubor, Arshif Falastini" [Gravestones: A Palestinian archive], *Khazaaen* (blog), July 11, 2020, https://khazaaen.wordpress.com/2020/07/11/شواهد-القبور-أرشيف-للمجتمع-الفلسطيني/.

40. Throughout the region, and not only in Palestine, water is a means of understanding colonial capitalism; see Mark Zeitoun, Naho Mirumachi, Jeroen Warner, Matthew Kirkegaard, and Ana Cascão, "Analysis for Water Conflict Transformation," *Water International* 45, no. 4 (2020): 365–84; Mark Zeitoun, Naho Mirumachi, and Jeroen Warner, eds., *Water Conflicts: Analysis for Transformation* (Oxford: Oxford University Press, 2020); and Toby Craig Jones, *Desert Kingdom: How Oil and Water Forged Modern Saudi Arabia* (Cambridge, MA: Harvard University Press, 2010). In addition to water, sewage is a likely source of settler colonial violence in Palestine; see Sophia C. Stamatopoulou-Robbins, "Failure to Build: Sewage and the Choppy Temporality of Infrastructure in Palestine," *Environment and Planning E: Nature and Space* 4, no. 1 (2021): 28–42; and Sophia Stamatopoulou-Robbins, *Waste Siege: The Life of Infrastructure in Palestine* (Stanford, CA: Stanford University Press, 2019).

41. Water as a commodity and a tool of violence in the hands of the settlers in Palestine has a long and brutal history; see, for example, Muna Dajani, "Drying Palestine: Israel's Systemic Water War," Al-Shabaka, September 4, 2014, https://al-shabaka.org/briefs/drying-palestine-israels-systemic-water-war/; Muna Dajani, "Thirsty Water Carriers: The Production of Uneven Waterscapes in Sahl al-Battuf," *Contemporary Levant* 5, no. 2 (2020): 97–112; Zayneb al-Shalalfeh, Fiona Napier, and Eurig Scandrett, "Water Nakba in Palestine: Sustainable Development Goal 6 Versus Israeli Hydro-Hegemony," *Local Environment* 23, no. 1 (2018): 117–24; Stephen Gasteyer, Jad Isaac, Jane Hillal, and Katie Hodali, "Water Grabbing in Colonial Perspective: Land and Water in Israel/Palestine," *Water Alternatives* 5, no. 2 (2012): 450; Karen Assaf, "Water as a Human Right: The Understanding of Water in Palestine," in *Water as a Human Right: The Understanding of Water in the Arab Countries of the Middle East*, ed. Simone Klawitter (Berlin: Heinrich Böll Foundation, 2004), 136–65; Marwan Haddad, "Planning Water Supply Under Complex and Changing Political Conditions: Palestine as a Case Study," *Water Policy* 1, no. 2 (1998): 177–92; Tariq Judeh, Marwan Haddad, and Gül Özerol, "Assessment of Water Governance in the West Bank, Palestine," *International Journal of Global Environmental Issues* 16, nos. 1–3 (2017): 119–34; Muna Dajani and Michael Mason, "Counter-Infrastructure as Resistance in the Hydrosocial Territory of

the Occupied Golan Heights," in *Water, Technology and the Nation-State*, ed. Filippo Menga and Erik Swyngedouw (London: Routledge, 2018), 131–46.

42. The politics of water as a resource and as life for Indigenous communities is a rich source for exploration in terms of Palestinian relationality to it; see, for example, Melanie K. Yazzie and Cutcha Risling Baldy, "Introduction: Indigenous Peoples and the Politics of Water," in "Indigenous Peoples and the Politics of Water," ed. Cutcha Risling Baldy and Melanie K. Yazzie, special issue, *Decolonization: Indigeneity, Education and Society* 7, no. 1 (2018): 1–18; Theo Claire and Kevin Surprise, "Moving the Rain: Settler Colonialism, the Capitalist State, and the Hydrologic Rift in California's Central Valley," *Antipode* 54, no. 1 (2022): 153–73; Jules M. Bacon, "Settler Colonialism as Eco-Social Structure and the Production of Colonial Ecological Violence," *Environmental Sociology* 5, no. 1 (2019): 59–69; and Kyle Whyte, "Settler Colonialism, Ecology, and Environmental Injustice," *Environment and Society* 9, no. 1 (2018): 125–44.

43. Constantin Zureiq, *M`ana al Nakba* [The meaning of disaster] (Beirut: Dar al-'Alim al-Malain, 1948). See also Hana Sleiman, "History Writing and History Making in Twentieth Century Beirut" (PhD diss., University of Cambridge, 2021); Hana Sleiman, "The Paper Trail of a Liberation Movement," *Arab Studies Journal* 24, no. 1 (2016): 42–67; and Philip Mattar, "Constantine Zurayk," *Review of Middle East Studies* 34, no. 2 (2000): 303–4. Zureiq was obviously not alone in his battle cries, as many followed; see, for example, Muhammad 'Izzat Darwaza, *Hawla al Haraka al-'Arabiyya al Haditha* [About the modern Arab movement], Sidon, Lebanon: Al-Maktaba al-'Asriyya, 1950.

44. Rosemary Sayigh, "Silenced Suffering," *Borderlands* 14, no. 1 (2015): 1–20; Rosemary Sayigh, "On the Exclusion of the Palestinian Nakba from the 'Trauma Genre,'" *Journal of Palestine Studies* 43, no. 1 (2013): 51–60; Elias Khoury, "Rethinking the Nakba," *Critical Inquiry* 38, no. 2 (2012): 250–66.

45. Patrick Wolfe, "Settler Colonialism and the Elimination of the Native," *Journal of Genocide Studies* 8, no. 4 (2006): 387–409. See also Patrick Wolfe, "Introduction," in *The Settler Complex: Recuperating Binarism in Colonial Studies*, ed. Patrick Wolfe (Los Angeles: UCLA American Indian Studies Center, 2017), 1–24.

46. Linda Tuhiwai Smith, *Decolonizing Methodologies: Research and Indigenous Peoples* (London: Zed Books, 1999).

47. 'Arif Al-'Arif, *Al-Nakba: Nakbat Bayt al-Maqdis wa l-Firdaws al-Mafqud 1947–49* [The catastrophe: The catastrophe of Jerusalem and the lost paradise 1947–49], vol. 7 (Sidon, Lebanon: Al-Maktaba al-'Asriyya, 1959). In addition to the historical labor, many of these men, including Al-'Arif, left us their memoirs to work with; see Tarif Khalidi, "Palestinian Historiography: 1900–1948," *Journal of Palestine Studies* 10, no. 3 (1981): 59–76; and Beshara B. Doumani, "Rediscovering Ottoman Palestine: Writing Palestinians into History," *Journal of Palestine Studies* 21, no. 2 (1992): 5–28.

48. In the early generation of historians documenting the Nakba, Walid Khalidi is a prominent figure not only for his *Before Their Diaspora: A Photographic History of the Palestinians, 1876–1948* (Washington, DC: Institute for Palestine Studies, 1984), but also for what would become a canonical text: Walid Khalidi, Sharif S. Elmusa, and Muhammad Ali Khalidi, *All That Remains: The Palestinian Villages Occupied and Depopulated by Israel in 1948* (Washington, DC: Institution for Palestine Studies, 1992), published in Arabic under the interesting title *Kai La Nansa* (Lest we forget). *All That Remains* has been the basis for a

series of articles, essays, and manuscripts in which Khalidi meticulously documents Israeli violence and the Palestinian Nakba. See, in particular, Walid Khalidi, "Plan Dalet: Master Plan for the Conquest of Palestine," *Journal of Palestine Studies* 18, no. 1 (1988): 4–19; Walid Khalidi, "Why Did the Palestinians Leave, Revisited," *Journal of Palestine Studies* 34, no. 2 (2005): 42–54; Walid Khalidi, "The Fall of Haifa Revisited," *Journal of Palestine Studies* 37, no. 3 (2008): 30–58; and Walid Khalidi, "Palestine and Palestine Studies: One Century After World War I and the Balfour Declaration," *Journal of Palestine Studies* 44, no. 1 (2014): 137–47.

49. The ongoing discussion of archives in the Palestinian context is both well documented and impossible to summarize; for the most poignant contemporary observations, see Sherene Seikaly, "How I Met My Great-Grandfather: Archives and the Writing of History," *Comparative Studies of South Asia, Africa and the Middle East* 38, no. 1 (2018): 6–20; Lila Abu-Lughod, "Palestine: Doing Things with Archives," *Comparative Studies of South Asia, Africa and the Middle East* 38, no. 1 (2018): 3–5; Mezna Qato, "Forms of Retrieval: Social Scale, Citation, and the Archive on the Palestinian Left," *International Journal of Middle East Studies* 51, no. 2 (2019): 312–15; Mezna Qato, "Returns of the Archive," Nakba Files, June 1, 2016, https://nakbafiles.org/2016/06/01/returns-of-the-archive/; and Beshara Doumani and Alex Winder, "1948 and Its Shadows," *Journal of Palestine Studies* 48, no. 1 (2018): 7–15. For further study, see Rona Sela, "The Genealogy of Colonial Plunder and Erasure—Israel's Control over Palestinian Archives" *Social Semiotics* 28, no. 2 (2018): 201–29; Sherene Seikaly, "Palestine as Archive," Jadaliyya, August 2, 2014, https://www.jadaliyya.com/Details/31043; Caitlin M. Davis, "Archiving Governance in Palestine," *Journal of Contemporary Archival Studies* 3, no. 1 (2016): 2; Ann Laura Stoler, "Archiving Praxis: For Palestine and Beyond," *Critical Inquiry* 48, no. 3 (2022): 570–93; Areej Sabbagh-Khoury, "Settler Colonialism and the Archives of Apprehension," *Current Sociology* 72, no. 1 (2022): 1–23; and Seth Anziska, "Special Document File: The Erasure of the Nakba in Israel's Archives," *Journal of Palestine Studies* 49, no. 1 (2019): 64–76.

50. Nur Masalha, *The Expulsion of Palestinians: The Concept of "Transfer" in Zionist Political Thoughts, 1892–1948* (Washington, DC: Institute for Palestine Studies, 1992). See also Khalidi, *Before Their Diaspora*. Masalha also contributed to the "oral history turn" in Nakba historiography; see Nur Masalha, "Remembering the Palestinian Nakba: Commemoration, Oral History and Narratives of Memory," *Holy Land Studies* 7, no. 2 (2008): 123–56; Nur Masalha, "Decolonizing Methodology, Reclaiming Memory: Palestinian Oral Histories and Memories of the Nakba," in *An Oral History of the Palestinian Nakba*, ed. Nur Masalha and Nahla Abdo (London: Zed Books, 2018), 6–40.

51. So much can and will be said about these institutes; their history and changing role in intellectual production are in many ways their self-produced narrative. See Sabri Jiryis and Salah Qallab, "The Palestine Research Center," *Journal of Palestine Studies* 14, no. 4 (1985): 185–87; Gabi Baramki, *Peaceful Resistance: Building a Palestinian University Under Occupation* (London: Pluto Press, 2009); Sherene Seikaly, "In the Shadow of War: The Journal of Palestine Studies as Archive," *Journal of Palestine Studies* 51, no. 2 (2022): 5–26; Abdul-Rahim Al-Shaikh, "In Solidarity with Birzeit: The Black, the White, and the Gray," *Curriculum Inquiry* 52, no. 3 (2022): 351–72; Ibrahim A. Abu-Lughod, "Palestinian Higher Education: National Identity, Liberation, and Globalization," *Boundary 2* 27, no. 1 (2000): 75–95; and Abdul-Rahim Al-Shaikh, *Sirat Gabi Baramki wa Tajribah fi Jam'a Birzeit, 1929–*

2012 [Biography of Gabi Baramki and his odyssey at Birzeit University, 1929–2012] (Ramallah, Palestine: Institute for Palestine Studies, 2015).

52. Rosemary Sayigh, *The Palestinians: From Peasants to Revolutionaries* (London: Bloomsbury, 2008).

53. A prolific scholar, Rosemary Sayigh's career defines summarization; but see, for example, Rosemary Sayigh, "Palestinian Camp Women as Tellers of History," *Journal of Palestine Studies* 27, no. 2 (1998): 42–58; Rosemary Sayigh, "The Palestinian Identity Among Camp Residents," *Journal of Palestine Studies* 6, no. 3 (1977): 3–22; Rosemary Sayigh, "The Struggle for Survival: The Economic Conditions of Palestinian Camp Residents in Lebanon," *Journal of Palestine Studies* 7, no. 2 (1978): 101–19; Rosemary Sayigh, "Encounters with Palestinian Women Under Occupation," *Journal of Palestine Studies* 10, no. 4 (1981): 3–26; Rosemary Sayigh, "Sources of Palestinian Nationalism: A Study of a Palestinian Camp in Lebanon," *Journal of Palestine Studies* 6, no. 4 (1977): 17–40; Rosemary Sayigh, "Dis/Solving the 'Refugee Problem,'" *Middle East Report* 207 (1998): 19–23; Rosemary Sayigh, "Palestinians in Lebanon: (Dis)Solution of the Refugee Problem," *Race and Class* 37, no. 2 (1995): 27–42; Rosemary Sayigh, "Gender, Sexuality, and Class in National Narrations: Palestinian Camp Women Tell Their Lives," *Frontiers: A Journal of Women Studies* 19, no. 2 (1998): 166–85; Rosemary Sayigh, "A House Is Not a Home: Permanent Impermanence of Habitat for Palestinian Expellees in Lebanon," *Holy Land Studies* 4, no. 1 (2005): 17–39; Rosemary Sayigh, "Product and Producer of Palestinian History: Stereotypes of 'Self' in Camp Women's Life Stories," *Journal of Middle East Women's Studies* 3, no. 1 (2007): 86–105; Sayigh, "On the Exclusion of the Palestinian Nakba from the 'Trauma Genre'"; Sayigh, "Silenced Suffering"; Rosemary Sayigh, "Oral History, Colonialist Dispossession, and the State: The Palestinian Case," *Settler Colonial Studies* 5, no. 3 (2015): 193–204; and Rosemary Sayigh, *Too Many Enemies: The Palestinian Experience in Lebanon* (London: Zed Books, 1994). See also Beshara Doumani and Mayssun Soukarieh, "A Tribute Long Overdue: Rosemary Sayigh and Palestinian Studies," *Journal of Palestine Studies* 38, no. 4 (2009): 6–11.

54. Sayigh, "Palestinian Camp Women."

55. Sayigh, "Silenced Suffering," 11–14.

56. Ahmad H. Sa'di and Lila Abu-Lughod, *Nakba: Palestine, 1948, and Claims of Memory* (New York: Columbia University Press, 2007), 3.

57. Sune Haugbolle, "Memory Studies in the Middle East: Where Are We Coming From and What Are We Going?," *Middle East Critique* 28, no. 3 (2019): 279–88.

58. Anaheed Al-Hardan, "The Right of Return Movement in Syria: Building a Culture of Return, Mobilizing Memories for the Return," *Journal of Palestine Studies* 41, no. 2 (2012): 62–79. See also Anaheed Al-Hardan, *Palestinians in Syria* (New York: Columbia University Press, 2016).

59. "Palestinian Oral History Archive," home page, American University of Beirut, n.d., accessed June 9, 2025, https://libraries.aub.edu.lb/poha/. See also Diana Allen, ed., *Voices of the Nakba: A Living History of Palestine* (London: Pluto, 2021); and Diana Allan, *Refugees of the Revolution: Experiences of Palestinian Exile* (Stanford, CA: Stanford University Press, 2013).

60. Haugbolle, "Memory Studies in the Middle East."

61. Ted Swedenburg, *Memories of Revolt: The 1936–1939 Rebellion and the Palestinian National Past* (Fayetteville: University of Arkansas Press, 2003).

62. For more on the Popular Memory Group and its intellectual formation, see Mary Jane Kehily, "Traditions of Collective Work: Cultural Studies and the Birmingham School," in *Collaboration and Duration: A Celebration of the Research and Practice of Janet Holland*, ed. Rachel Thomson and Rosalind Edwards (London: London South Bank University, 2010), 14; and Graham Dawson, "The Theory of Popular Memory and the Contested Memories of the Second World War in Britain," in *Myths, Gender and the Military Conquest of Air and Sea*, ed. Katharina Hoffmann, Herbert Mehrtens, and Silke Wenk (Oldenburg: BIS Verlag, 2015), 205–21.

63. Ghassan Kanafani, *Thawrat 1936–1939 fi Filastin: Khalfiyyat, Tafasil wa Tahlil* [Great Revolt 1936–1939 in Palestine: Background, details and analysis] (Beirut: PFLP, 1969).

64. Memory studies, in its Eurocentric iterations in the postwar period, became a reflection of the war and its atrocities, and memory and Holocaust studies merged and overlapped in important ways. Given this genealogy, memory and Palestinian experience within memory studies reproduces a dynamic that is neither about Palestine nor about memory among Palestinians. Nevertheless, this framework has served as a kind of imposition of both language and methodology. See Marianne Hirsch and Leo Spitzer, "The Witness in the Archive: Holocaust Studies / Memory Studies," *Memory Studies* 2, no. 2 (2009): 151–70. See also Stef Craps and Michael Rothberg, "Introduction: Transcultural Negotiations of Holocaust Memory," in "Transcultural Negotiations of Holocaust Memory," ed. Stef Craps and Michael Rothberg, special issue, *Criticism* 53, no. 4 (2011): 517–21; Michael Rothberg, *Multidirectional Memory: Remembering the Holocaust in the Age of Decolonization* (Stanford, CA: Stanford University Press, 2009); and Lawrence L. Langer, *Holocaust Testimonies: The Ruins of Memory* (New Haven, CT: Yale University Press, 1993).

65. Rana Barakat, "How to Read a Massacre in Palestine: Indigenous History as a Methodology of Liberation," *Omran Journal for Social Sciences* 10, no. 39 (2022): 149–72.

66. Mahmoud Darwish, *Memory for Forgetfulness: August, Beirut, 1982*, trans. Ibrahim Muhawi (Berkeley: University of California Press, 2013), 11.

67. Darwish, *Memory for Forgetfulness*, 14–15.

68. Darwish, *Memory for Forgetfulness*, 15.

69. Gil Anijar, Abdul-Rahiim Al-Shaikh, *Against History, Against Archive: Translation and Debate in the Time of Genocide* (Jerusalem: Dara Suliman al-Halabi, 2025).

70. Sinan Antoon, foreword to Darwish, *Memory for Forgetfulness*, xvii.

71. These now famous descriptions are those of the late scholar Patrick Wolfe.

72. See, for example, Robert Warrior, "Organizing Native American and Indigenous Studies," *PMLA* 123, no. 5 (2008): 1683–91; Robert Warrior, "Robert Warrior on Intellectual Sovereignty and the Work of the Public Intellectual," in *Speaking of Indigenous Politics: Conversations with Activists, Scholars, and Tribal Leaders*, ed. J. Kēhaulani Kauanui, (Minneapolis: University of Minnesota Press, 2018), 328–42; and Robert Warrior, "Home / Not Home: Centering American Studies Where We Are," *American Quarterly* 69, no. 2 (2017): 191–219.

73. Rana Barakat, "Writing/Righting Palestine Studies: Settler Colonialism, Indigenous Sovereignty and Resisting the Ghost(s) of History," *Settler Colonial Studies* 8, no. 3 (2018): 349–63.

74. Kauanui, "'A Structure, Not an Event.'"

75. Joanne Barker, "Introduction: Critically Sovereign," in *Critically Sovereign: Indigenous Gender, Sexuality, and Feminist Studies,* ed. Joanne Barker (Durham, NC: Duke University Press, 2007), 26.

76. Two pivotal articles have, in many ways, framed the debate over the course of the last decade; see Bhandar and Ziada, "Acts and Omissions"; and Salamanca et al., "Past Is Present." While arguing from different focal points, both articles emphasize the long history of understanding settler colonial power in Palestine and among Palestinian scholars, including the work of Fayez Sayigh, Rosemary Sayigh, and Maxime Rodinson. See Fayez Sayigh, *Zionist Colonialism in Palestine* (Beirut: Research Center, Palestine Liberation Organization, 1965); Rosemary Sayigh, *The Palestinians*; and Maxime Rodinson, *Israel: A Colonial-Settler State?* (New York: Monad, 1973).

77. For example, Lila Abu-Lughod, "Imagining Palestine's Alter-natives: Settler Colonialism and Museum Politics," *Critical Inquiry* 47, no. 1 (2020): 1–27, discusses her own apprehensions in speaking of Palestinians as Indigenous subjects in comparison with other geographies ravaged by settler colonial invasion.

78. Adel Manna, *Nakba and Survival: The Story of Palestinians Who Remained in Haifa and the Galilee, 1948–1956* (Berkeley: University of California Press, 2022). Of great importance in this sense is the work of Ismael Nashif, who meticulously traces Zionist intervention into Nakba conceptualization; see Ismael Nasif, *Ruins: On Expressing al Nakba* (Beirut: Dal al Adab, 2015.

79. Many have covered the neoliberal iterations of land as property in the contemporary Palestinian condition, but here it is useful to think about its longer historical arc. See, for example, Bhandar, *Colonial Lives of Property*; and Munir Fakher Eldin, "Confronting a Colonial Rule of Property: The Al-Sakhina Case in Mandate Palestine," *Arab Studies Journal* 27, no. 1 (2019): 12–33.

80. The history of capitalism in Palestine and the ruptures of settler colonial capitalist manipulations is a very rich story. Sherene Seikaly, *Men of Capital: Scarcity and Economy in Mandate Palestine* (Stanford, CA: Stanford University Press, 2015), deftly explains how paying careful mind to distinctions of colonial capital and settler manipulations and violence reveals a tapestry of Palestinian society before and after 1948 that reveals the rich layers of destruction, as well as Palestinian resistance.

81. Manu Karuka, Juliana Hu Pegues and Alyosha Goldstein, "Introduction: On Colonial Unknowing," in "On Colonial Unknowing," ed. Alyosha Goldstein, Juliana Hu Pegues, and Manu Vimalassery, special issue, *Theory and Event* 19, no. 4 (2016): 303–14, offer the possibilities in "analyzing epistemologies of (colonial) unknowing." Specifically, they ask, "How do we understand our locations in the colonial present as we contemplate and work toward the ongoing imperative of decolonization?" See also Manu Karuka, "Black and Native Visions of Self-Determination," *Critical Ethnic Studies* 3, no. 2 (2017): 77–98; Juliana Hu Pegues, "Empire, Race, and Settler Colonialism: BDS and Contingent Solidarities," *Theory and Event* 19, no. 4 (2016); and Alyosha Goldstein, "Colonialism Undone: Pedagogies of Entanglement," in *Red Pedagogy: Native American Social and Political Thought*, 10th anniversary ed., ed. Sandy Grande (Lanham, MD: Rowman and Littlefield, 2015), 111–16.

82. Franz Fanon, "Concerning Violence," in *The Wretched of the Earth*, trans. Constance Farrington (New York: Grove, 1963), 35–106. See also Anthony C. Alessandrini, ed., *Frantz Fanon: Critical Perspectives* (London: Rutledge, 2005); and Reiland Rabaka, *Forms of Fan-*

onism: Frantz Fanon's Critical Theory and the Dialectics of Decolonization (Lanham, MD: Lexington Books, 2011).

83. Eve Tuck and K. Wayne Yang, "Decolonization Is Not a Metaphor," *Decolonization: Indigeneity, Education and Society* 1, no. 1 (2012): 3, 35.

84. Lisa King, Rose Gubele, and Joyce Rain Anderson, "Introduction—Careful with the Stories We Tell: Naming *Survivance, Sovereignty*, and *Story*," in *Survivance, Sovereignty, and Story: Teaching American Indian Rhetorics*, ed. Lisa King, Rose Gubele, and Joyce Rain Anderson (Boulder: University Press of Colorado, 2015), 3–16.

85. Gloria Anzaldúa, "Speaking in Tongues: A Letter to Third World Woman Writers," in *This Bridge Called My Back: Writings by Radical Women of Color*, ed. Cherríe Moraga and Gloria Anzaldúa (New York: Kitchen Table, 1983), 173.

86. Edward Said's notion of "beginnings" can be related to "discovery" in the settler colonial context. That is, Eurocentric mythology for composing the "beginning" fits into a certain kind of story of European modernity built as the narrative justification for colonial invasion and erasure. See Edward W. Said, *Beginnings: Intention and Method* (London: Granta Books, 1997). See also M. Labelle Maurice Jr., "On the Decolonial Beginnings of Edward Said," *Modern Intellectual History* 19, no. 2 (2022): 1–25.

Chapter One

1. Helena Cobban, *The Palestinian Liberation Organization: People, Power and Politics* (Cambridge: Cambridge University Press, 1984).

2. Yasser Arafat, "Not Red Indians," October 2004 interview by Graham Usher, *Al-Ahram Weekly*, November 4, 2004, http://www.masress.com/en/ahramweekly/18801.

3. Audra Simpson, quoted in Lila Abu-Lughod, "Imagining Palestine's Alter-Natives: Settler Colonialism and Museum Politics," *Critical Inquiry* 47, no. 1 (2020): 14. See also Audra Simpson, "'We Are Not Red Indians' (We Might All Be Red Indians): Anticolonial Sovereignty Across the Borders of Time, Place and Sentiment," paper presented at the Seventh International Conference of Critical Geography, ICCG 2015, Ramallah, Palestine, July 26, 2015, Mapping Change Logbook, https://mapping-change.labor-k.org/via-audra-simpson/.

4. Simpson, "'We Are Not Red Indians'"; Joseph Massad, "Against Self-Determination," *Humanity Journal* 9, no. 2 (2018): 161–91; Nick Estes, *Our History Is the Future: Standing Rock Versus the Dakota Access Pipeline, and the Long Tradition of Indigenous Resistance* (London: Verso Books, 2019).

5. Simpson, "'We Are Not Red Indians.'"

6. Massad, "Against Self-Determination," 1.

7. Estes, *Our History Is the Future*, 482.

8. Yezid Sayigh, *Armed Struggle and the Search for State: The Palestinian National Movement, 1949–1993* (Oxford: Clarendon Press, 1997).

9. Yasser Arafat, "A Discussion with Yasser Arafat," *Journal of Palestine Studies* 11, no. 2 (1981–82): 3–15.

10. For an astute and on-the-ground analysis of this moment, see Rashid Khalidi, *Under Siege: PLO Decision Making During the 1982 War* (New York: Columbia University Press, 2013).

11. Khalidi, *Under Siege*. For further context, see Sayigh, *Armed Struggle and the Search for State*; Salim Yaqub, *Containing Arab Nationalism: The Eisenhower Doctrine and the Middle East* (Chapel Hill: University of North Carolina Press, 2004); Rashid Khalidi, "The Palestinian Dilemma: PLO Policy After Lebanon," *Journal of Palestine Studies* 15, no. 1 (1985): 88–103; Rami Siklawi, "The Palestinian Resistance Movement In Lebanon 1967–82: Survival, Challenges, and Opportunities," *Arab Studies Quarterly* 39, no. 3 (2017): 923–37; Jaber Suleiman, "Palestinians in Lebanon and the Role of Non-Governmental Organizations," *Journal of Refugee Studies* 10, no. 3 (1997): 397–410; Yusif Al-Haytham, "Lebanon Explodes: 'Battles of Survival,'" *MERIP Reports* 44 (1976): 3–14; Sami Al-Banna, "The Defense of Beirut," *Arab Studies Quarterly* 5, no. 2 (1983): 105–15; Richard A. Falk, Eugene V. Rostow, Francis A. Boyle, W. Michael Reisman, Frits Kalshoven, and Robbie Sabel, "Problems of the Law of Armed Conflict in Lebanon," *Proceedings of the Annual Meeting (American Society of International Law)* 77 (1983): 214–41.

12. Arafat, "A Discussion with Yasser Arafat," 13.

13. Seth Anziska, *Preventing Palestine: A Political History from Camp David to Oslo* (Princeton, NJ: Princeton University Press, 2020).

14. Palestine as a cause was a core element in the anticolonial and anti-imperial movements and the making of third world international and PLO leadership were a consummate presence in the literature and political mobilizations of the movements in key sites in the "formally" colonialized states; see Vijay Prashad, *The Darker Nations: A Biography of the Short-Lived Third World* (New York: Leftword Books, 2007); and Vijay Prashad, "Remembering Histories of Third World Internationalism between India and Palestine: An Interview with Vijay Prashad," by Linda Tabar and Chandni Desai, *Decolonization: Indigeneity, Education and Society* 6, no. 1 (2017): 99–104. See also Abdel Razzaq Takriti, "Before BDS: Lineages of Boycott in Palestine," *Radical History Review* 2019, no. 134 (2019): 58–95; Samir Amin, "The Arab Nation: Some Conclusions and Problems," *MERIP Reports* 68 (1978): 3–14; Suraya Khan, "Transnational Alliances: The AAUG's Advocacy for Palestine and the Third World," *Arab Studies Quarterly* 40, no. 1 (2018): 53–72; Linda Tabar, "From Third World Internationalism to 'the Internationals': The Transformation of Solidarity with Palestine," *Third World Quarterly* 38, no. 2 (2017): 414–35; Linda Tabar and Chandni Desai, "Decolonization Is a Global Project: From Palestine to the Americas," *Decolonization: Indigeneity, Education and Society* 6, no. 1 (2017); and Evyn Lê Espiritu, "Cold War Entanglements, Third World Solidarities: Vietnam and Palestine, 1967–75," *Canadian Review of American Studies* 48, no. 3 (2018): 352–86.

15. Sayigh, *Armed Struggle and the Search for State*. There is a growing body of literature on the Arab Left and this revolutionary era; see, for example, Sune Haugbolle, "The New Arab Left and 1967," *British Journal of Middle Eastern Studies* 44, no. 4 (2017): 497–512; Sune Haugbolle, "Entanglement, Global History, and the Arab Left," *International Journal of Middle East Studies* 51, no. 2 (2019): 301–4; Ahmad Agbaria, "From Translation to Critique: The Formation of the New Arab Left in Beirut 1960s," *Global Intellectual History* 7, no. 3 (2022): 593–610; Jens Hanssen and Hicham Safieddine, "Lebanon's" Al-Akhbar" and Radical Press Culture: Toward an Intellectual History of the Contemporary Arab Left," *Arab Studies Journal* 24, no. 1 (2016): 192–227; and Karma Nabulsi and Abdel Razzaq Takriti, "The Palestinian Revolution," 2016, https://learnpalestine.qeh.ox.ac.uk/.

16. This is a play on the language of Mahmoud Darwish, *Memory for Forgetfulness: August, Beirut, 1982*, trans. Ibrahim Muhawi (Berkeley: University of California Press, 2013).

17. Summarizing the massive literature on Palestine under the confined framework of the Oslo Accords is far too big of a task for this book, but it might be useful to ponder the general framework of this literature in terms of a banal political analysis (is the PA a state?) and the more important political economy of a post–Oslo Accords situation. For a general survey, see Raja Khalidi, "Introduction: Twenty-First Century Palestinian Development Studies," in "Palestinian Economic Studies," special issue, *Journal of Palestine Studies* 45, no. 4 (2016): 7–15, and the many articles in that issue. For further inquiry, see Leila Farsakh, *Palestinian Labour Migration to Israel: Labour, Land and Occupation* (Abingdon, UK: Routledge, 2005); Leila Farsakh, "Independence, Cantons, or Bantustans: Whither the Palestinian State?," *Middle East Journal* 59, no. 2 (2005): 230–45; Jamil Hilal and Mushtaq Husain Khan, "State Formation Under the PNA: Potential Outcomes and Their Viability," in *State Formation in Palestine: Viability and Governance During a Social Transformation*, ed. Mushtaq Husain Khan, George Giacaman, and Inge Amundsen (Abingdon, UK: Routledge, 2004), 64–119; Adam Hanieh, "The Internationalisation of Gulf Capital and Palestinian Class Formation," *Capital and Class* 35, no. 1 (2011): 81–106; Adam Hanieh, "Class, Economy, and the Second Intifada," *Monthly Review* 54, no. 5 (2002): 29; and Linda Tabar and Omar Jabari Salamanca, "After Oslo: Settler Colonialism, Neoliberal Development and Liberation," in *Critical Readings of Development Under Colonialism: Towards a Political Economy for Liberation in the Occupied Palestinian Territories*, ed. Rosa Luxemburg Stiftung Regional Office Palestine (Birzeit, Palestine: Rosa Luxemburg Stiftung Regional Office Palestine / Birzeit University Center for Development Studies, 2015), 10.

18. Of note here is the enormous number of theses produced by graduate students at Birzeit University regarding the Second Intifada; see, for example Ala Dandees, "Al Kifah al Muslah al-Filastini: Fateh fi Jabal al-Khalil" [Palestinian armed struggle: Fateh and Hebron Hills/Jabal al-Khalil] (master's thesis, Birzeit University, 2017); Ahmad Izz al-Din Assad, "Al Khitab al-Filastini al-Badil: Nahwa Stratigia Tahrouriya" [Alternative Palestinian discourse: Towards a strategy of liberation] (master's thesis, Birzeit University, 2014); Amani Sarahna, "Al Asra al-Filastiniyya wa Jil al-Ghadab: Kira' Aslaniya fi al-Saida wa Taqrir al-Masir" [Palestinian prisoners and the generation of rage: An Indigenous reading of sovereignty and self-determination] (master's thesis, Birzeit University, 2020); and Jamal Hiwal, "M'areqat Jenin wa Intifada al-Aqsa" [Battle of Jenin and al-Aqsa Intifada] (master's thesis, Birzeit University, 2015).

19. Massad, "Against Self-Determination."

20. Sayigh, *Armed Struggle and the Search for State.*

21. After the battlefield defeat of Arab armies in the war in 1967, a cultural shift occurred in the Arab context whereby conceptualizations of defeat invaded cultural and political production. Of particular note in this literature is Sadek Jalal al-Azm, whose thesis on defeat was a kind of *end of a revolutionary era*, marking what he described as the defeat of Arab nationalism; see Sadek Jalal al-Azm, *Self-Criticism After the Defeat* (Beirut: Saqi Books, 2012). To understand this turn, it is important to read the military defeat as a dramatic moment in Arab history and what was essentially described as the defeat of Gamal Abdel Nasser's leadership. While difficult to summarize all the trajectories this conceptual line took over the years, it is important for the purposes here to simply state that 1967 was re-

corded as a conclusion to the war in 1948 in terms of full occupation of Palestine and the attempted removal of Palestine as a cause from its setting in the Arab world. In the colonial and imperial context, this conceptualization made room for defeatist paradigms that took Orientalist assumptions and brought them into supposed Arab political critique. This framework was made famous in Fouad Ajami, *The Arab Predicament: Arab Political Thought and Practice Since 1967* (Cambridge: Cambridge University Press, 1992). This had huge effects in Palestinian mobilization, as well as how Arab states both as regimes and as people engaged (or did not engage) the Palestinian cause and, as Edward Said has noted, served as a watershed moment for Sais and his generation and grew into his form of public intellectualism. It should also be noted that though the defeat paradigm took a strong hold on cultural production, the period after 1967 (like 1948, earlier) was also a battle cry for revolutionary thinking embodied by many among the Arab Left (among them communists, socialists, Ba'athists, and Nasserists). Most notable among the writers were Mahdi 'Amel and Ghassan Kanafani. Kanafani is a consummate figure in the Arab and Palestinian Left and, after his murder at the hands of Israeli forces in 1973, his work formed a canon for generations (first and foremost in Arabic, but also in translation) regarding third world internationalism. More recently, 'Amel's work has experienced a remarkable resurgence in English, joining Kanafani's legacy in the international canon. See Ghassan Kanafani, *'Amal al-Kamal: Stories* (Beirut: Institute of Arab Studies, 1994); Ghassan Kanafani, *Adab al-Muqawama fi Filastin al-Muhtalla* [Resistance literature in occupied Palestine] (Beirut: Dar al-Adab, 1966); and Mahdi Amel, *Arab Marxism and National Liberation: Selected Writings of Mahdi Amel* (London: Brill, 2020). See also Hicham Safieddine, "Mahdi Amel: On Colonialism, Sectarianism and Hegemony," *Middle East Critique* 30, no. 1 (2021): 41–56; Mahdi Amel and Ziad Kiblawi, "Is the Heart for the East and Reason for the West? On Marx in Edward Said's Orientalism," *Critical Times* 4, no. 3 (2021): 481–500; Nadia Bou Ali, "Mahdi Amel's Colonial Mode of Production and Politics in the Last Instance," *Critical Historical Studies* 7, no. 2 (2020): 241–69; Surti Singh, "Mahdi Amel and the Nonidentical," *Critical Times* 4, no. 3 (2021): 543–51; Sune Haugbolle and Manfred Sing, "New Approaches to Arab Left Histories," *Arab Studies Journal* 24, no. 1 (2016): 90–97; and Zeyad Jihad Hamad, "The Political Thought of the Thinker Mahdi Amel," *American Journal of Social and Humanitarian Research* 2, no. 5 (2021): 4–19. Additionally, the contemporary literary critic Faisel Darraj has in many ways offered us a means of navigating how the culture of defeat emerged and evolved. See, in particular, Faisel Darraj, *Bous al Thaqfa* [The misery of culture] (Beirut: Dar al-Adab, 1996).

22. Bshir Abu-Manneh, "Tonalities of Defeat and Palestinian Modernism," *Minnesota Review* 2015, no. 85 (2015): 56–79.

23. Azmi Bishara, *Army and Political Power in the Arab Context: Theoretical Problems* (Doha: Arab Center for Research and Policy Studies, 2022).

24. Elsewhere I write about overcoming this paradigm of triumph and defeat; see Rana Barakat, "Writing/Righting Palestine Studies: Settler Colonialism, Indigenous Sovereignty and Resisting the Ghost(s) of History," *Settler Colonial Studies* 8, no. 3 (2018): 349–63.

25. Bashir Abu-Manneh, *The Palestinian Novel: From 1948 to the Present* (Cambridge: Cambridge University Press, 2016).

26. Abu-Manneh, *The Palestinian Novel*, 19.

27. In addition to absorbing various political parties, including the Marxist-Leninist Palestinians for the Liberation of Palestine, the PLO had various mechanisms within it that held the intellectual production of defining and defending the armed struggle, including the Palestine Research Center (as discussed in the introduction to the present volume). Through the cultural production of the PLO in the 1970s, including the scholarly production of the Palestine Research Center, the PLO consolidated a great deal of power, both cultural and political.

28. This is the long and miserable story of settler maneuvers to cage self-determination for Palestinians within the small confines of the PA. Over time this has not been an easy or smooth process for the settler state, as seen through the keen navigation of political parties and personalities in the PLO, not the least of which was Yasser Arafat himself. After all, Arafat singlehandedly signed the Oslo Accords on behalf of Palestine, but he is also rightfully given credit (or blame, depending on one's outlook) for supporting the resistance in certain iterations over the course of his life, both before and after 1994. After his death in 2004, and after the concerted efforts of the imperial and settler powers, the criminalization of the resistance that had existed for Palestinians since the era of the Mandate for Palestine had a new face: the PA. People are not institutions, however, so it would be misleading to use a wide brushstroke in terms of political parties. The point here is simple: The political viability of the PA after 2004 was almost exclusively as a "security" entity for the settler state. There is a massive body of literature on the politics of the PA; for some useful examples, see Islah Jad, "The Conundrums of Post-Oslo Palestine: Gendering Palestinian Citizenship," *Feminist Theory* 11, no. 2 (2010): 149–69; Alaa Tartir, "The Palestinian Authority Security Forces: Whose Security?," Al-Shabaka, May 16, 2017, https://al-shabaka.org/briefs/the-palestinian-authority-security-forces-whose-security/; Alaa Tartir, "The Evolution and Reform of Palestinian Security Forces 1993–2013," *Stability: International Journal of Security and Development* 4, no. 1 (2015); Husam Said Zomlot, "Building a State Under Occupation: The Palestinians and the Living Legacy of Oslo," *Contemporary Arab Affairs* 3, no. 2 (2010): 180–92; and Sophia Stamatopoulou-Robbins, "Waste and the Phantom State: The Emergence of the Environment in Post-Oslo Palestine" (PhD diss., Columbia University, 2015).

29. Noura Erakat, *Justice for Some: Law and the Question of Palestine* (Stanford, CA: Stanford University Press, 2019).

30. Gamal Abdel Nasser, *Falsafat al Thwra* [The philosophy of revolution] (Cairo: Bayt al-arabi l-al-tawthiq al-'asri, 1996).

31. Mezna Qato, "Forms of Retrieval: Social Scale, Citation, and the Archive on the Palestinian Left," *International Journal of Middle East Studies* 51, no. 2 (2019): 312–15; Safieddine, "Mahdi Amel"; Amel, *Arab Marxism.*

32. Fadi A. Bardawil, *Revolution and Disenchantment: Arab Marxism and the Binds of Emancipation* (Durham, NC: Duke University Press, 2020).

33. On January 1, 1965, the Palestinian National Liberation Movement political party launched an operation on a water pumping facility that the Israelis were using to steal water from the Jordan River. This operation was the launch of the party, which would eventually be the largest contingent in the PLO and the party from which Arafat emerged. This was a precursor to the Battle of Karama. See Sayigh, *Armed Struggle.*

34. The term *fedayeen* in reference to PLO fighters was both a term and title that the PLO made famous as regarded the righteousness and necessity of armed struggle.

35. For a concise rendering of the Battle of Karama, see Michael Fischbach, "Battle of al-Karama, 21 March 1968: A Triggering Moment for the Palestinian Resistance," in *Interactive Encyclopedia of the Palestine Question,* online, ed. Camille Mansour, n.d., accessed June 11, 2025, https://www.palquest.org/en/node/165.

36. "The Palestinian National Charter," in *Basic Political Documents of the Armed Palestinian Resistance Movement,* ed. and trans. Leila S. Kadi (Beirut: Palestine Liberation Organization Research Center, December 1969), article 9, 138. It is, of course, no coincidence that the Israelis focused on article 9 and required that it be amended. In 1993 then Israeli Prime Minister Yizak Rabin stated in a letter that the articles that denied Israel's right to exist be removed. In 1996, in a piece of political theater, Arafat and his circle in Gaza used the organ of the PNC to amend the charter and forsake the articles that Israel objected to—article 9 being a core objection.

37. "The Palestinian National Charter," article 24, 141.

38. Muhammad Muslih, "Towards Coexistence: An Analysis of the Resolutions of the Palestine National Council," *Journal of Palestine Studies* 19, no. 4 (1990): 3–29.

39. After the Battle of Karama, the PLO grew in strength, making Jordan its primary base of operations for the fedayeen until the state, under the leadership of King Hussein, could not withstand the power and challenge of the PLO. Jordan essentially exiled the leadership, which moved its base to Beirut.

40. Rashid Khalidi, *The Hundred Years' War on Palestine: A History of Settler Colonialism and Resistance, 1917–2017* (New York: Macmillan, 2020).

41. Patrick Wolfe, "Recuperating Binarism: A Heretical Introduction," *Settler Colonial Studies* 3, nos. 3–4 (2013): 257–79.

42. Sari Orabi, "Tahwilat al Idilojia wa al Siiyasiya fi al Haraka al Wataniya: Al Kitabib al Toulabiya" [The ideological and political transformations of the Palestinian national movement: The Students' Battalion as a mode] (master's thesis, Birzeit University, 2014).

43. Sherene Seikaly, "In the Shadow of War: The *Journal of Palestine Studies* as Archive," *Journal of Palestine Studies* 51, no. 2 (2022): 5–26.

44. Edward Said, *The Question of Palestine* (New York: Vintage Books, 1979), 4.

45. Bashir Abu-Manneh, "Said's Political Humanism: An Introduction," in *After Said: Postcolonial Literary Studies in the Twenty First Century* (Cambridge: Cambridge University Press, 2019), 1.

46. Edward Said, "Between Worlds," in *Reflections on Exile and Other Literary and Cultural Essays* (London: Granta Books, 2013), 516.

47. Said, *The Question of Palestine,* x.

48. Said, *The Question of Palestine,* x.

49. Said, *Reflections on Exile.*

50. Edward Said, *The Politics of Dispossession: The Struggle for Palestinian Self-Determination, 1969–1994* (New York: Vintage, 1995), 26.

51. Edward Said, "Permission to Narrate," *Journal of Palestine Studies* 13, no. 3 (1984): 27–48. This famous article was penned in the wake of the massacres at Sabra and Shatila.

52. Said, "Between Worlds," 522, 523.

53. Said, *The Politics of Dispossession,* 103–12.

54. Said, "Between Worlds," 519.

55. This connection found its apex in Said's declaration of himself as the last Jewish thinker. See Said, *Reflections on Exile*.

56. Said, *The Question of Palestine*, xii, 8.

57. Said, *The Question of Palestine*, xvi.

58. The question of Palestine is Said's interpretation in relation to the so-called Jewish question, to which he often referred. See Edward W. Said, "Zionism from the Standpoint of Its Victims," *Social Text* 1 (1979): 7–58; Edward W. Said. *Representations of the Intellectual* New York: Vintage Books, 2012); and Edward W. Said, "Arabs and Jews," *Journal of Palestine Studies* 3, no. 2 (1974): 3–14.

59. Said, *The Question of Palestine*, 9, 39.

60. Said, "Between Worlds," *Reflections on Exile*, 517, 516.

61. Said, *The Question of Palestine*, 122, 121.

62. Massad, "Against Self-Determination."

63. Said, *The Question of Palestine*, 4–5.

64. One need not look beyond *Peace and Its Discontents* (which presents only a slice of his work in the era of the Oslo Accords and following them) to see how critical Said was of Arafat (whom he called "the old man") at every step—from his refusal to be present at the performance of the signing of the Oslo Accords in Washington, DC, in 1993 until Said's own death in 2003, a year before Arafat's. See Edward W. Said, *Peace and Its Discontents: Essays on Palestine in the Middle East Peace Process* (New York: Vintage Books, 2012).

65. Edward Said, "The Morning After," *London Review of Books* 15, no. 20 (1993), https://www.lrb.co.uk/the-paper/v15/n20/edward-said/the-morning-after.

66. Said, *The Question of Palestine*, 10.

67. Yasser Arafat, "Speech at the United Nations," in "Palestine at the United Nations," *Journal of Palestine Studies* 4, no. 2 (1975): 181, 183.

68. Arafat, "Speech at the United Nations," 183.

69. At various points in their careers, the first generation of Palestinian male historians of the modern era— Rashid Khalidi, Walid Khalidi, Anis Sayigh, Fayiz Sayigh, and Elias Shofani—found a home in the PLO.

70. Arafat, "Speech at the United Nations," 181, 184.

71. Arafat, "Speech at the United Nations," 187.

72. Arafat, "Speech at the United Nations," 191–92.

73. Though there exist several translations of this poem, the reading herein relies on Mahmoud Darwish, "Speech of the Red Indian," trans. Sargon Boulos, Poem Hunter, n.d., accessed June 10, 2025, https://www.poemhunter.com/poem/speech-of-the-red-indian/. See also Mahmoud Darwish, "The 'Red Indian's' Penultimate Speech to the White Man," trans. Fady Joudah, *Harvard Review* 36 (2009): 152–59; and Ahmad Qabaha and Abdel Karim Daraghmeh, "A Postcolonial Ecocritical Reading of Mahmoud Darwish's 'The Red Indian's Penultimate Speech to the White Man,'" *Arab Studies Quarterly* 45, no. 2 (2023): 111–33.

74. Abdul-Rahim Al-Shaikh has covered this and many other features of Darwish's work over the course of his research on the poet and Palestinian culture. See, for example, Abdul-Rahim M. Al-Shaikh, "Mutalazimat Darwish (I): Al-nas, al-hazima, wa al-manfi" [The Darwish syndrome I: Victory, defeat, and exile], *Majallat al-Dirasat al-Filastiniyya* 31, no. 122 (2020): 159–86; Abdul-Rahim M. Al-Shaikh, "Mutalazimat Darwish (II): Al-fikr, al-thwra,

wa al-dawla" [The Darwish syndrome II: The idea, the revolution, the state], *Majallat al-Dirasat al-Filastiniyya* 32, no. 125 (2021): 147–88; Abdul-Rahim M. Al-Shaikh, "Tahwalat al-butalah fi khitab al-thaqafi al-filastini (I)" [The transformation of heroism in Palestinian cultural discourse—I], *Majallat al-Dirasat al-Filastiniyya* 23, no. 96 (2013): 73–95; and Abdul-Rahim M. Al-Shaikh, "Tahwalat al-butalah fi khitab al-thaqafi al-filastini (II)" [The transformations of heroism in Palestinian cultural discourse—II], *Majallat al-Dirasat al-Filastiniyya* 24, no. 97 (2014): 100–118. For a comprehensive article on Darwish in English, see Abdul-Rahim Al-Shaikh, "The Political Darwīsh . . . 'in Defense of Little Differences,'" *Journal of Arabic Literature* 48, no. 2 (2017): 93–122.

75. Al-Shaikh, "The Political Darwīsh"; Al-Shaikh, "Mutalazimat Darwish (I)" [The Darwish syndrome I]. Many scholars have spent an enormous amount of time on tracing Darwish's literary journey between resistance and universal humanism. See, for example, Khaled Mattawa, *Mahmoud Darwish: The Poet's Art and His Nation* (Syracuse, NY: Syracuse University Press, 2014); Muna Abu Eid, *Mahmoud Darwish: Literature and the Politics of Palestinian Identity* (New York: Bloomsbury, 2016); Najat Rahman, *Literary Disinheritance: The Writing of Home in the Work of Mahmoud Darwish and Assia Djebar* (Lanham, MD: Lexington Books, 2008); Khaled Furani, "After Criticism: Mahmoud Darwish's Mural for Enlightenment," *Boundary 2* 47, no. 1 (2020): 145–72; Khaled Furani, *Silencing the Sea: Secular Rhythms in Palestinian Poetry* (Stanford, CA: Stanford University Press, 2020); and Erica Mena, "The Geography of Poetry: Mahmoud Darwish and Postnational Identity," *Human Architecture: Journal of the Sociology of Self-Knowledge* 7, no. 5 (2009): 111–18.

76. In the Palestinian context, perhaps through this journey we can find the complement of the anticolonial and anti-imperial politics of third world movements and the political praxis of Indigenous sovereignty that forms the backbone of a fourth world movement. See George Manuel and Michael Posluns, *The Fourth World: An Indian Reality* (Minneapolis: University of Minnesota Press, 2019). In terms of movement and mobilization, see also Subcomandante Marcos, "The Fourth World War Has Begun," in *The Zapatista Reader*, ed. Tom Hayden (New York: Thunder's Mouth Books, 2002), 270–85.

Chapter Two

1. Nir Hasson, "Israel's Last Remaining Abandoned Arab Village, Lifta, Gets Reprieve as Judge Voids Development Plans," *Haaretz*, February 7, 2012, https://www.haaretz.com /2012-02-07/ty-article/israels-last-remaining-abandoned-arab-village-lifta-gets-reprieve -as-judge-voids-development-plans/0000017f-dc3d-db5a-a57f-dc7ffi5d0000.

2. For a foundational approach regarding refusal in Indigenous studies, see Audra Simpson, *Mohawk Interruptus: Political Life Across the Borders of Settler States* (Durham, NC: Duke University Press, 2014). In her lucid presentation of ethnographic refusal, in particular, Simpson offers us a conceptual map of thinking in Palestine. Refusal is a potentially rich conceptual exploration in Palestine given the wealth of literature on resistance, but it can and should draw on the long cultural and political tradition of refusing defeat as described in chapter 1. For more, see Lisa Bhungalia, "Laughing at Power: Humor, Transgression, and the Politics of Refusal in Palestine," *Environment and Planning C: Politics and Space* 38, no. 3 (2020): 387–404; Itxaso Domínguez de Olazábal, "On Indigenous Refusal Against Externally-Imposed Frameworks in Historic Palestine," *Millennium: Journal of International*

Studies 51, no. 1 (2022): 212–36; Carol McGranahan, "Theorizing Refusal: An Introduction," *Cultural Anthropology* 31, no. 3 (2016): 319–25; Sandy Grande and Teresa L. McCarty, "Indigenous Elsewheres: Refusal and Re-Membering in Education Research, Policy, and Praxis," *International Journal of Qualitative Studies in Education* 31, no. 3 (2018): 165–67; Eve Tuck and K. Wayne Yang, "Unbecoming Claims: Pedagogies of Refusal in Qualitative Research," *Qualitative Inquiry* 20, no. 6 (2014): 811–18; and Yanira Rodríguez, "Pedagogies of Refusal," *Radical Teacher* 115 (2019): 5–12.

3. For a summary of this framing, see Raef Zreik, "When Does a Settler Become a Native? (With Apologies to Mamdani)," *Constellations* 23, no. 3 (2016): 351–64.

4. The decolonial move described here is related to the understand of the relationship between settler colonial power and enduring Indigeneity as described in J. Kēhaulani Kauanui, "'A Structure, Not an Event': Settler Colonialism and Enduring Indigeneity," *Lateral* 5, no. 1 (2016), ssalateral.org/issue/5-1/forum-alt-humanities-settler-colonialism-enduring -indigeneity-kauanui/.

5. Karen Engle, *The Elusive Promise of Indigenous Development: Rights, Culture, Strategy* (Durham, NC: Duke University Press, 2010), 143.

6. Patrick Wolfe, "Settler Colonialism and the Elimination of the Native," *Journal of Genocide Research* 8, no. 4 (2006): 387–409.

7. Master plans, as they are called in the Israeli context, are a part of urban planning in Jerusalem; Lifta is but one part of the larger story in this contemporary and historical process. For more on Jerusalem master plans, see Nur Arafeh, "Which Jerusalem? Israel's Little-Known Master Plans," Al-Shabaka, May 31, 2016, https://al-shabaka.org/briefs /jerusalem-israels-little-known-master-plans/.

8. Nir Hasson, "Israel Moves to Turn Deserted Palestinian Village into Luxury Housing Project," *Haaretz*, January 21, 2011, http://www.haaretz.com/israel-moves-to-turn-deserted -palestinian-village-into-luxury-housing-project-1.338280.

9. This methodology of treatment of Palestinian villages by the Zionist settler establishment is not unique, as it is well within the Zionist arsenal of settler colonial behavior. One example is the story of 'Ayn Hawd; see Susan Slyomovics, *The Object of Memory: Arab and Jew Narrate the Palestinian Village* (Philadelphia: University of Pennsylvania Press, 1998); and Muhmmad Abu Al-Hayja' and Rachel Leah Jones, "'Ayn Hawd and the 'Unrecognized Villages,'" *Journal of Palestine Studies* 31, no. 1 (2001): 39–49. Again, what is somewhat unique in Lifta is that this kind of methodology had not been applied to all of the empty homes and buildings, particularly in the terraced valley of lower Lifta, though it was applied to many of the existing structures of Lifta as homes were given to Jewish settlers seeking refuge from other parts of the Middle East by the Israeli state in the early 1950s.

10. Gabriel Kertesz, quoted in Hasson, "Israel Moves to Turn Deserted Palestinian Village into Luxury Housing Project."

11. Wolfe, "Settler Colonialism."

12. Gadi Iron, quoted in Hasson, "Israel Moves to Turn Deserted Palestinian Village into Luxury Housing Project."

13. Bimkom, quoted in Esther Zandberg, "The Lifta That Never Will Be," *Haaretz*, February 3, 2011. According to its website, "Bimkom—Planners for Planning Rights is an Israeli human rights organization formed in 1999 by a group of professional planners and architects, in order to strengthen democracy and human rights in the field of spatial planning

and housing policies"; Bimkom, "Our Mission," n.d., accessed June 11, 2025, https://bimkom.org/eng/our-mission/. It has produced a number of projects, including a 2014 study on neighborhood planning in East Jerusalem; see Bimkom—Planners for Planning Rights, *Trapped by Planning: Israeli Policy, Planning, and Development in the Palestinian Neighborhoods of East Jerusalem* (Jerusalem: Bimkom, 2014), https://bimkom.org/eng/trapped-by-planning/. Though under the rubric of human rights, this NGO in its description of its own work and its delineation of what spatial planning is in the Israeli context, does not engage the context as one of settler colonialism, and, therefore, their work is confined and confining in the Palestinian context.

14. Zandberg, "The Lifta That Never Will Be."

15. Eve Tuck and K. Wayne Yang, "Decolonization Is Not a Metaphor," *Decolonization: Indigeneity, Education, and Society* 1, no. 1 (2012): 1–40; Glen Sean Coulthard, *Red Skin, White Masks: Rejecting the Colonial Politics of Recognition* (Minneapolis: University of Minnesota Press, 2014).

16. This context of the reliance on the role and centrality of the settler state was challenged by others who took up the task of Lifta as part of a larger Nakba project through various organizations (as will be discussed in chapter 3), but in the contemporary context of settler violence, it should perhaps be noted that the treatment of Lifta within this context reads as less materially violent in light of the wars of destruction wrought on the Gaza Strip by the settler state from 2009 to 2024.

17. Tuck and Yang, "Decolonization Is Not a Metaphor," 5.

18. The Coalition to Save Lifta was a part of this court case. Of note here is that the Palestinians who were named were *only* those specifically recognized by the state—that is, those with Jerusalem identity cards. Many others were excluded, including refugees from Lifta outside the zones of recognition of the settler state.

19. Hasson, "Israel's Last Remaining Abandoned Arab Village."

20. Sami Ershied, quoted in Hasson, "Israel's Last Remaining Abandoned Arab Village."

21. Nir Hasson, "Paved Paradise? The Secrets of an Ancient Jerusalem-Area Village Revealed," *Haaretz*, December 20, 2016.

22. The concept of *discovery* has a long and established history in various geographies of settler colonialism; see Jean M. O'Brien, *Firsting and Lasting: Writing Indians Out of Existence in New England* (Minneapolis: University of Minnesota Press, 2010); Robert J. Miller, Jacinta Ruru, Larissa Behrendt, and Tracey Lindberg, *Discovering Indigenous Lands: The Doctrine of Discovery in the English Colonies* (Oxford: Oxford University Press, 2010); and Patrick Wolfe, *Traces of History: Elementary Structures of Race* (London: Verso Books, 2016), 141–52. In Palestine, discovery has a specific resonance within Zionist return mythology and European Orientalism regarding Palestine as the Holy Land, as will be discussed later in this chapter.

23. My thanks go to Daphna Golan, from whom I received a copy of an English translation of the survey titled *Lifta Survey—Israel Antiquities Authority 2017* in June 2021. The English version was translated through the work of the Lifta Coalition; the original Hebrew version of was published by the state under the same title.

24. Daphna Golan, conversation with the author, Jerusalem, Palestine, October 2021.

25. Oren Yiftachel explains that the politics of settling Jewish settlers from the Arab region in these frontier zones was a common feature of the early settler state. Creating these

kinds of frontier spaces was based on radicalized logic within Zionism whereby non-European Jews were placed in areas to provide a kind of bordered safety. Arab Jews (or ones considered as such by the racial categorization of the state) were settled elsewhere, creating in a kind of in-between safety zone for the more privileged white European Jewish settlers. Oren Yiftachel, *Ethnocracy: Land and Identity Politics in Israel/Palestine* (Philadelphia: University of Pennsylvania Press, 2006).

26. As of late 2016 and early 2017 these families were negotiating with the state regarding compensation. In 2020, during the Israeli construction boom in Jerusalem conducted under the cover of the COVID-19 pandemic, the Israeli state came to agreement with the occupant of one of these homes and in 2022 the state once again halted discussion of rebuilding in the valley; see Sue Surkes, "Plan Shelved to Turn Historic Arab Village at Jerusalem Entrance into Luxury Housing," *Times of Israel*, August 16, 2022, https://www.timesofisrael.com/plan-shelved-to-turn-historic-arab-village-at-jerusalem-entrance-into-luxury-housing/.

27. *Basic Texts of the 1972 World Heritage Convention* (Paris: UNESCO, 2017).

28. G. J. Ashworth, "The Conserved European City as Cultural Symbol: The Meaning of the Text," in *Modern Europe: Place, Culture and Identity*, ed. Brian Graham (London: Arnold, 1998), 261–86. See also G. J. Ashworth, *Dissonant Heritage: The Management of the Past as a Resource in Conflict* (London: Belhaven, 1996).

29. See Aspa Gospodini, "Urban Morphology and Place Identity in European Cities: Built Heritage and Innovative Design," *Journal of Urban Design* 9, no. 2 (2004): 225–48; Rose Aslan, "The Museumification of Rumi's Tomb: Deconstructing Sacred Space at the Mevlana Museum," *International Journal of Religious Tourism and Pilgrimage* 2, no. 2 (2014): 1–16; Nebojsa Camprag, "Museumification of Historical Centres: The Case of Frankfurt Altstadt Reconstruction," in *Tourism in the City: Towards an Integrative Agenda on Urban Tourism*, ed. Nicola Bellini and Cecilia Pasquinelli (Cham, Switzerland: Springer, 2017), 165–78; and Paul H. Gobster, "Urban Park Restoration and the Museumification of Nature," *Nature and Culture* 2, no. 2 (2007): 95–114.

30. In the post–World War II era, forgetting and remembering were actively practiced. This is never clearer than a state's power to manipulate the forgetting of Nazi atrocities was as (or more) powerful than the forced hand of remembering. See Sharon Macdonald, "Undesirable Heritage: Fascist Material Culture and Historical Consciousness in Nuremberg," *International Journal of Heritage Studies* 12, no. 1 (2006): 9–28; Simon Levis Sullam, "Reinventing Jewish Venice: The Scene of the Ghetto Between Monument and Metaphor," in "Cultural Representations of Jewishness at the Turn of the 21st Century," ed. Magdalena Waligorska and Sophie Wagenhofer, Working Paper EUI HEC 2010/01 (European University Institute, 2010), 13–25.

31. Jean Baudrillard, *Simulacra and Simulation*, trans. Sheila Faria Glaser (Ann Arbor: University of Michigan Press, 1994), 457, 460.

32. Baudrillard, *Simulacra and Simulation*, 461.

33. Other fields have also picked up on the concept as literary critiques have provided some of the most interesting contributions to a general understanding of the term *museumification* in reference to a literary construct as a narrative tool. See John A. Stotesbury, "The Crime Scene as Museum: The (Re)Construction in the Bresciano Series of a Historical Gibraltarian Past," *Coolabah* 20 (2016): 83–93.

34. Michael A. Di Giovine, *The Heritage-Scape: UNESCO, World Heritage, and Tourism* (Lanham, MD: Lexington Books, 2009), 261.

35. Alexandra Mientjes, "Is Amsterdam Turning Into a Museum?," Pop Up City, August 8, 2013, http://popupcity.net/is-amsterdam-turning-into-a-museum/.

36. As popular as this discourse has become, it was incorporated on the big screen as a documentary film. See Menachem Daum and Oren Rudavsky, dirs., *The Ruins of Lifta: Where the Holocaust and the Nakba Meet* (First Run Features, 2016).

37. Ann Laura Stoler, "Imperial Debris: Reflections on Ruins and Ruination," *Cultural Anthropology* 23, no. 2 (2008): 193, 194. Ruins and ruination, of course, are part of the conversation on capitalist colonialism and destruction that has direct links to how Lifta and Palestine are rendered in an imperial formulation. See Anna Lowenhaupt Tsing, *The Mushroom at the End of the World: On the Possibility of Life in Capitalist Ruins* (Princeton, NJ: Princeton University Press, 2015).

38. Stoler, "Imperial Debris," 196.

39. Rachel Busbridge, "On Haunted Geography: Writing Nation and Contesting Claims in the Ghost Village of Lifta," *Interventions* 17, no. 4 (2015): 469–87.

40. Gerald Vizenor, "The Ruins of Representation: Shadow Survivance and the Literature of Dominance," *American Indian Quarterly* 17, no. 1 (1993): 7–30.

41. Daphna Golan, Zvika Orr, and Sami Ershied, "Lifta and the Regime of Forgetting: Memory Work and Conservation," *Jerusalem Quarterly* 54 (2013): 69–81.

42. This claim has been reported in the Israeli press, but it should be noted that for it to be nominated to UNESCO in order to be considered a World Heritage Site, it would have to be submitted by Israel according to the rules of the nomination process.

43. Abdul-Rahim al-Shaikh, "Rish al Hayzima," *Arab '48*, 2008, https://www.arab48.com /%D9%85%D9%82%D8%A7%D9%84%D8%A7%D8%AA-%D9%88%D8%A2%D8%B1%D8%A7%D8%A1/%D8%B1%D8%A3%D9%8A/2010/10/31/%D8%B1%D8%B4%D8%AF-%D8%A7%D9%87%D8%B2%D9%8A%D9%85%D8%A9--%D8%AF-%D8%B9%D8%A8%D8%AF-%D8%A7%D9%84%D8%B1%D8%AD%D9%8A%D9%85-%D8%A7%D9%84%D8%B4%D9%8A%D8%AE.

44. Mahdi 'Aml, *Hazema al-Thaqafa* [The defeat of culture] (Beirut: Al Adab, 2012), 57–65.

45. Muhammad Ali Khalidi, *All That Remains: The Palestinian Villages Occupied and Depopulated by Israel in 1948* (Washington, DC: Institution for Palestine Studies, 1992).

46. Much has been written about this in mandate literature on Palestine. For a brief survey of the literature, see Rashid Khalidi, *The Hundred Years' War on Palestine: A History of Settler Colonialism and Resistance, 1917–2017* (New York: Macmillan, 2020). For an understanding of the bureaucracy and mechanisms of control, see Sherene Seikaly, "Men of Capital in Mandate Palestine," *Rethinking Marxism* 30, no. 3 (2018): 393–417; and Sherene Seikaly, *Men of Capital: Scarcity and Economy in Mandate Palestine* (Stanford, CA: Stanford University Press, 2016).

47. Rashid Khalidi, *The Iron Cage: The Story of the Palestinian Struggle for Statehood* (Boston: Beacon, 2006), 32. This point is revisited in Rashid Khalil, *The Hundred Years' War on Palestine*.

48. Seikaly, *Men of Capital*, 1–22.

49. League of Nations, Mandate for Palestine, July 24, 1922, Avalon Project, https:// avalon.law.yale.edu/20th_century/palmanda.asp.

50. Kēhaulani, "'A Structure, Not an Event.'"

51. William M. Mathew, "The Balfour Declaration and the Palestine Mandate, 1917–1923: British Imperialist Imperatives," *British Journal of Middle Eastern Studies* 40, no. 3 (2013): 231–50; Morag M. Kersel, "The Trade in Palestinian Antiquities," *Jerusalem Quarterly* 33 (2008): 21–38. See also Nur Masalha, *The Bible and Zionism: Invented Traditions, Archaeology and Post-Colonialism in Palestine-Israel* (London: Zed Books, 2007).

52. Abu El-Haj, *Facts on the Ground: Archaeological Practice and Territorial Self-Fashioning in Israeli Society* (Chicago: University of Chicago Press, 2002). See also Gregory La Cuellar, *Empire, the British Museum and the Making of the Biblical Scholar in the 19th Century* (London: Palgrave Macmillan, 2019); Neil Asher Silberman, "Power, Politics and the Past: The Social Construction of Antiquity in the Holy Land," in *The Archeology of Society in the Holy Land*, ed. Thomas E. Levy (New York: Facts on File, 1995), 9–23.

53. On Jerusalem as an Orientalist symbol, see Edward W. Said, *Orientalism* (New York: Vintage Books, 1994); and Edward W. Said, "Invention, Memory and Place," *Critical Inquiry* 26, no. 2 (2000): 175–92.

54. Masalha, *The Bible and Zionism*.

55. Kersel, "The Trade in Palestinian Antiquities."

56. Khaldun Bshara, "Heritage in Palestine: Colonial Legacy in Postcolonial Discourse," *Archaeologies: Journal of the World Archaeological Congress* 9 no. 2 (2013): 295–319.

57. AO 1920, Part I, Article 2(1)(c), "Antiquities Ordinance, 1920," *Official Gazette of the Government of Palestine* 29 (October 5, 1920): 4–16.

58. League of Nations, Mandate for Palestine.

59. Kersel, "The Trade in Palestinian Antiquities."

60. State of Israel, Law and Administration Ordinance No. 1 of 5708-1948, May 17, 1948, Hamoked, https://www.hamoked.org/document.php?dID=Documents3397.

61. Bshara, "Heritage in Palestine," 303.

62. El-Haj, *Facts on the Ground*.

63. Said, *Orientalism*.

64. In addition to this discussion in Said's *Orientalism*, see also Edward W. Said, "Invention, Memory, and Place," *Critical Inquiry* 26, no. 2 (2000): 175–92.

65. Said, *Orientalism*, 55, 101.

66. Edward W. Said, "Memory, Invention and Space," in *The Landscape of Palestine: Equivocal Poetry*, ed. Ibrahim Abu-Lughod, Roger Heacock, and Khaled Nashef (Birzeit, Palestine: Birzeit University Publications, 1999), 8.

67. Steven Salaita, *The Holy Land in Transit: Colonialism and the Quest for Canaan* (Syracuse, NY: Syracuse University Press, 2006).

68. Said, *Orientalism*, 56–57.

69. Tina Sherwell, "Jerusalem: City of Dreams." *Jerusalem Quarterly* 49 (2012): 43–53, in a reading of the Palestinian artist Sulieman Mansour, explores how Jerusalem is symbolic and representation of loss. See also Ariella Azoulay, *From Palestine to Israel: A Photographic Record of Destruction and State Formation, 1947–1950* (London: Pluto Press, 2011).

70. Edward W. Said, *The Question of Palestine* (New York: Vintage Books, 1979), 26.

71. There is a vast literature one can read to uncover the forced antagonisms mentioned here. Most notable are Gil Anidjar, *The Jew, the Arab: A History of the Enemy* (Stanford, CA: Stanford University Press, 2003); William J. Dumbrell, *The Faith of Israel: A Theological*

Survey of the Old Testament (Grand Rapids, MI: Baker Academic, 2002); Ariella Azoulay, "With Open Doors: Museums and Historical Narratives in Israel's Public Space," in *Museum Culture: Histories, Discourses, Spectacles*, ed. Daniel J. Sherman and Itit Rogoff (London: Routledge, 2004), 85–112; and Jamal Hader, "The Context of Kairos Palestine," *Ecumenical Review* 64, no. 1 (2012): 3–7.

72. Salim Tamari, "Lepers, Lunatics and Saints: The Nativist Ethnography of Tawfiq Canaan and His Jerusalem Circle," *Jerusalem Quarterly* 17 (2003): 24–43; Salim Tamari, *Mountain Against the Sea: Essays on Palestinian Society and Culture* (Berkeley: University of California Press, 2008).

73. Chiara De Cesari, *Heritage and the Cultural Struggle for Palestine* (Stanford, CA: Stanford University Press, 2019), 38.

74. Tamari, "Lepers, Lunatics and Saints," 27, 25. Unfortunately, "nativist ethnography" is a misnomer; the term typically refers to settler bids for self-Indigenization, not actual Natives doing Native work.

75. Birzeit University Museum's story of coming into being is connected to Canaan material and, to date, the Tawfiq Canaan Talismans and Amulets Collection is still the most coveted collection in the museum; see Birzeit University Museum, "Tawfiq Canaan Amulets," n.d., accessed June 12, 2025, http://museum.birzeit.edu/collections/tawfiq-canaan-amulets. The museum also has established itself as a core base for research on Canaan and folklore in this era; see Birzeit University Museum, "Research," n.d., accessed June 12, 2025, http://museum.birzeit.edu/research. See also Wisam Abduallah, ed., *Ya Kafi Ya Shafi: The Tawfiq Canaan Collection of Amulets* (Birzeit, Palestine: Birzeit University, 1998).

76. Tamari, "Lepers, Lunatics and Saints," 28.

77. Stephan H. Stephan, "Lunacy in Palestinian Folklore," *Journal of the Palestine Oriental Society* 5 (1925): 1–16; Tamari, "Lepers, Lunatics and Saints."

78. Tawfiq Canaan, *Mohammedan Saints and Sanctuaries in Palestine* (Jerusalem: Syrian Orphanage Press, 1927), quoted in Tamari, "Lepers, Lunatics and Saints," 36.

79. Khaled Nashef, "Tawfiq Canaan: His Life and Works," *Jerusalem Quarterly* 16 (2002): 12–26.

80. See Khalid al Nashif, "Tawfiq Canaan: Taqweem Jadid" [Tawfiq Canaan: A new analysis], *Majallat al-Dirasat al Filastiniyya* 50 (2002): 69–91.

81. The Tawfiq Canaan Amulet and Talisman collection held at Birzeit University Museum (BZUM), along with the archive of Canaan's meticulous collection style (in terms of accession numbering and detailed descriptions) and accompanying studies published by Cannan (also reproduced digitally at BZUM), remains a fascinating source for understanding Palestinian ethnography, popular medicine, and popular culture in the early twentieth century.

82. Tawfiq Canaan, *The Palestine Arab Cause* (Jerusalem: Modern Press, 1936).

83. Fernando Valderrama, *A History of UNESCO* (Paris: United Nations Educational, Scientific and Cultural Organisation, 1995), 3.

84. Aurelie Elisa Gfeller, "Negotiating the Meaning of Global Heritage: 'Cultural Landscapes' in the UNESCO World Heritage Convention, 1972–92," *Journal of Global History* 8, no. 3 (2013): 489, 488.

85. Gfeller, "Negotiating the Meaning of Global Heritage," 485, 396.

86. Isabel McBryde, "The Cultural Landscapes of Aboriginal Long Distance Exchange Systems: Can They Be Confined Within Our Heritage Registers?," *Historic Environment* 13, nos. 3–4 (1997): 3–4.

87. Isabel McBryde, "Travelers in Storied Landscapes: A Case Study in Exchanges and Heritage," *Aboriginal History* 24 (2000): 171.

88. Coulthard, *Red Skin, White Masks*.

89. United Nations Educational, Scientific and Cultural Organisation, *Report on the Proposed World Heritage Indigenous Peoples Council of Experts (WHIPCOE)*, WHC-2001/CONF.205/WEB.3 (Paris: United Nations Educational, Scientific and Cultural Organisation, 2001), 5.

90. Lynn Meskell, "UNESCO and the Fate of the World Heritage Indigenous Peoples Council of Experts (WHIPCOE)," *International Journal of Cultural Property* 20, no. 2 (2013): 157, 156. See also Francesco Bandarin, *World Heritage: Challenges for the Millennium* (Paris: United Nations Educational, Scientific and Cultural Organisation, 2007).

91. United Nations Educational, Scientific and Cultural Organisation, "Text of the Convention for the Safeguarding of the Intangible Cultural Heritage," November 3, 2003, https://ich.unesco.org/en/convention.

92. J. Kēhaulani Kauanui, *Hawaiian Blood: Colonialism and the Politics of Sovereignty and Indigeneity* (Durham, NC: Duke University Press, 2008).

93. Meskell, "UNESCO and the Fate of the World Heritage Indigenous Peoples Council of Experts," 163.

94. Amani Sarahna, "Al-Asra al-Filastinyya wa Jil al Ghadab: Qarah Asslaniya fi al Saida wa Taqrir al Masir" [Palestinian prisoners and the generation of rage: An Indigenous reading of sovereignty and self-determination] (master's thesis, Birzeit University, 2020).

95. United Nations Educational, Scientific and Cultural Organisation, "Protection of the Cultural Heritage in the Palestinian Territories," Decision 26 COM 6.1, June 24–29, 2002, https://whc.unesco.org/en/decisions/798/.

96. Steven Salaita, *The Holy Land in Transit: Colonialism and the Quest for Canaan* (Syracuse, NY: Syracuse University Press, 2006).

97. Rema Hammami, "NGOs: The Professionalisation of Politics," *Race and Class* 37, no. 2 (1995): 51–63.

98. De Cesari, *Heritage and the Cultural Struggle for Palestine*, 6.

99. Bshara, "Heritage in Palestine," 307.

100. Harriet Sherwood, "US Pulls UNESCO Funding After Palestine Is Granted Full Membership," *Guardian*, October 31, 2011, https://www.theguardian.com/world/2011/oct/31/unesco-backs-palestinian-membership.

101. For the formal decisions concerning all four sites, see United Nations Educational, Scientific and Cultural Organisation, "Old City of Jerusalem and Its Walls (Site Proposed by Jordan) (C 148 rev)," Decision 40 COM 7A.13, 2016, http://whc.unesco.org/en/decisions/6818/; United Nations Educational, Scientific and Cultural Organisation, "Nominations to Be Processed on an Emergency Basis—Birthplace of Jesus: Church of the Nativity and the Pilgrimage Route, Bethlehem, Palestine," Decision 36 COM 8B.5, 2012, http://whc.unesco.org/en/decisions/4776; United Nations Educational, Scientific and Cultural Organisation, "Hebron/Al-Khalil Old Town: Indicators," n.d., accessed June 12, 2025, http://whc.unesco.org/en/list/1565/indicators/; United Nations Educational, Scien-

tific and Cultural Organisation, "Palestine: Land of Olives and Vines—Cultural Landscape of Southern Jerusalem, Battir: Indicators," n.d., accessed August 17, 2017, http://whc.unesco .org/en/list/1492/indicators/. See also Morag M. Kersel, "Fractured Oversight: The ABCs of Cultural Heritage in Palestine After the Oslo Accords," *Journal of Social Archaeology* 15, no. 1 (2015): 24–44; and Chiara De Cesari, "World Heritage and Mosaic Universalism: A View from Palestine," *Journal of Social Archaeology* 10, no. 3 (2010): 299–324.

102. The so-called green line is the 1949 Armistice border and is the UN recognized division between Israel and the occupied Palestinian territories.

103. Keith Whitelam, *The Invention of Ancient Israel: The Silencing of Palestinian History* (London: Routledge, 1997), 231.

104. Fathi Shikaki, "Al-Istiqlal wa al-t'bia' fi houd al-arabi al-islami, roua' nahdwia" [Independence and political formation, from the heart of Islamic Arab culture, an enlightened perspective], *Al-Janoub: The Palestinian Journal for Liberatory Studies* 1, no. 1 (Summer 2025): 222–35.

Chapter Three

1. Rema Hammami, "On (Not) Suffering at the Checkpoint: Palestinian Narrative Strategies of Surviving Israel's Carceral Geography," *Borderlands* 14, no. 1 (2015): 1–17.

2. Nir Hasson, "Israel's Last Remaining Abandoned Arab Village, Lifta, Gets Reprieve as Judge Voids Development Plans," *Haaretz*, February 7, 2012, https://www.haaretz.com /2012-02-07/ty-article/israels-last-remaining-abandoned-arab-village-lifta-gets-reprieve -as-judge-voids-development-plans.

3. Rema Hammami, "Gender, Nakba and Nation," in *Across the Wall: Narratives of Israeli-Palestinian History*, ed. Ilan Pappé (London: I. B. Tauris, 2010), 235–68.

4. Omar Zahzah, "Digital Apartheid: Palestinians Being Silenced on Social Media," Al Jazeera, May 13, 2021, https://www.aljazeera.com/opinions/2021/5/13/social-media -companies-are-trying-to-silence-palestinian-voices; 7amleh—Arab Center for the Advancement of Social Media, "Silence of the Networks: Young Palestinians Targeted for Their Online Commentary," iFex, October 25, 2019, https://ifex.org/silence-of-the-networks -young-palestinians-targeted-for-their-online-commentary/; Mariam Barghouti, "I Am Palestinian. Here's how Israel Silences Us on Social Media," Rest of World, June 23, 2021, https://restofworld.org/2021/palestine-social-media-silence/.

5. Mohammed el-Kurd, "Tomorrow My Family and Neighbors May Be Forced from Our Homes by Israeli Settlers," *Nation*, November 20, 2020, https://www.thenation.com/article /world/east-jerusalem-settlers/; Mohammed el-Kurd, "If They Steal Sheikh Jarrah," Mada, February 16, 2021, https://www.madamasr.com/en/2021/02/16/opinion/u/if-they-steal -sheikh-jarrah/; Mohammed el-Kurd, "Speech by Mohammed al-Kurd Before the UN General Assembly," https://www.un.org/unispal/wp-content/uploads/2021/11/Speech-of -Mohammed-Al-Kurd-before-the-General-Assembly-cad.pdf.

6. Rana Barakat, "'Ramadan Does Not Come for Free': Refusal as New and Ongoing in Palestine," *Journal of Palestine Studies* 50, no. 4 (2021): 90–95.

7. Performing research during what is taking place in Jerusalem is both precarious and potentially offensive. While I wanted to learn more about what people were doing, saying, and thinking, I also knew that an inability to reach Jerusalem meant I had to rely on others

who themselves remain precarious in terms of Israeli violence. In the summer of 2021 Nadi al-Aseer, the Palestinian Prisoners' Club, recorded an unprecedented number of arrests. As such, all people mobilized under this ongoing threat are targets for settler violence. It thus felt wrong to do formal research and request ethnographic interviews; rather, we gathered in the spaces we have and had conversations.

8. Dahoud al Ghoul, conversation with the author, Ramallah, Palestine, January 27, 2022.

9. Rema Hammami, "The Exiling of Sheikh Jarrah," *Jerusalem Quarterly* 51 (2012): 49–64.

10. Mohammad el-Kurd, "Here in Jerusalem, We Palestinians Are Still Fighting for Our Homes," *Guardian*, July 28, 2021, https://www.theguardian.com/commentisfree/2021/jul/28/jerusalem-palestinians-homes.

11. The '48 is the colloquial name for the area taken by Israeli settlers in 1948—that is, land within the so-called green line.

12. Haidar Eid, *Decolonizing the Palestinian Mind* (New Delhi: LeftWord Books, 2023).

13. "The Manifesto of Dignity and Hope," Mondoweiss, May 18, 2021, https://mondoweiss.net/2021/05/the-manifesto-of-dignity-and-hope/. See also Lana Tatour, "The "Unity Intifada" and '48 Palestinians: Between the Liberal and the Decolonial," *Journal of Palestine Studies* 50, no. 4 (2021): 84–89.

14. Barakat, "'Ramadan Does Not Come for Free.'"

15. It should also be noted that the use of sovereignty in the context of Palestine and through the Arab and Islamic cultural legacies that long preceded the intrusion of European modernity and the nation-state notion of sovereignty has been a point of much local discussion in Palestine. Simply put, using *sovereignty* to describe the assertion of peoplehood liberated from the nation-state is not, I argue, anathema to local contexts and is in more organic relation to similar assertions of Indigenous peoples elsewhere. For in this context this assertion is, as in other geographies of the assertion of Indigenous sovereignty, about relationality to the land and, as seen in the summer of 2021, as a means of connecting peoplehood to our collective relationality to the land.

16. A simple search through any search engine reveals just how common these photos are—Lifta quite obviously holds aesthetic value for a myriad of reasons. See, for example, Yehudit Alayoff, "Wadi Lifta (Nephtoah)," Wikipedia, April 6, 2011, https://en.wikipedia.org/wiki/File:Wadi_Lifta_(Nephtoah).jpg; and World Monuments Fund, "Lifta," n.d, accessed June 13, 2025, https://www.wmf.org/project/lifta.

17. This was told to me by the photographer, Abdul-Rahim Al-Shaikh.

18. Leanne Betasamosake Simpson, "The Misery of Settler Colonialism: Roundtable on Glen Coulthard's *Red Skin, White Masks* and Audra Simpson's *Mohawk Interruptus*," roundtable presentation at the Annual Meeting of the American Studies Association, Toronto, October 8, 2015, https://web.archive.org/web/20180907202825/https://www.leannesimpson.ca/writings/the-misery-of-settler-colonialism-roundtable-on-glen-coulthards-red-skin-white-masks-and-audra-simpsons-mohawk-interruptus.

19. Jeff Corntassel, Taiaiake Alfred, Noelani Goodyear-Ka`ōpua, Noenoe K. Silva, Hokulani Aikau, and Devi Mucina, "Introduction," in *Everyday Acts of Resurgence: People,*

Places, and Practices, ed. Jeff Corntassel, Taiaiake Alfred, Noelani Goodyear-Ka`ōpua, No-enoe K. Silva, Hokulani Aikau, and Devi Mucina (Olympia, WA: Daykeeper, 2018), 18.

20. Save Lifta Coalition, "About," n.d., accessed June 13, 2025, http://savelifta.org/about/.

21. Save Lifta Coalition, "About."

22. I first presented the concept of "the case of Lifta" in Rana Barakat, "Lifta, the Nakba, and the Museumification of Palestine's History," *Native American and Indigenous Studies Journal* 5, no. 2 (2019): 1–15.

23. Nadine C. Naber, "So Our History Doesn't Become Your Future: The Local and Global Politics of Coalition Building Post September 11th," *Journal of Asian American Studies* 5, no. 3 (2002): 217–42.

24. Save Lifta Coalition, "About Lifta."

25. Nadia Abu El-Haj, *Facts on the Ground: Archaeological Practice and Territorial Self-Fashioning in Israeli Society* (Chicago: University of Chicago Press, 2002), 20.

26. Save Lifta Coalition, "About Lifta."

27. Jean O'Brien, *Firsting and Lasting: Writing Indians Out of Existence in New England* (Minneapolis: University of Minnesota Press, 2010), 138, 139.

28. One clear example of intersecting spaces can be seen in the makeup of the Lifta Society. Like other organizations of dispossessed refuges, the Lifta Society is both local and international, with chapters in Amman, Jerusalem, Ramallah, and cities in Europe and the United States. Even with the vast geographical range of the society's chapters, the work of the SLC and individuals—particularly those in Jerusalem—resonates. Unfortunately, they do not have a central website or a consistent online presence.

29. Menachem Daum and Oren Rudavsky, dirs., *The Ruins of Lifta: Where the Holocaust and the Nakba Meet* (First Run Features, 2016).

30. First Run Features, "The Ruins of Lifta: Synopsis," n.d., accessed June 14, 2025, https://firstrunfeatures.com/ruinsofliftahv.html.

31. Elias Khoury, "Foreword," in *Holocaust and the Nakba: A New Grammar of Trauma and History*, ed. Bashir Bashir and Amos Goldberg (New York: Columbia University Press, 2019), xv.

32. Glen Sean Coulthard, *Red Skin White Masks: Rejecting the Politics of Colonial Recognition* (Minneapolis: University of Minnesota Press, 2014), 25.

33. Edward W. Said and Christopher Hitchens, eds., *Blaming the Victims: Spurious Scholarship and the Palestinian Question* (London: Verso, 2001).

34. Yaqub Odeh, in addition to being the leading and most prolific contemporary advocate for Lifta, is active in many sites, many of his own making, bringing people to Lifta and bringing Lifta onto people's political radar. Odeh approached me to assist in the oral history archive in this capacity and facilitated the work. For more, see Yaqub Odeh, "Qisa Watan" [Story of a nation], in *Lifta: Sajil sh'ab, al-tarikh, al-turath al-thaqafi wa al nidal* [Lifta: Register of a people, history, cultural heritage and struggle], ed. Nazmi Jubeh (Beirut: Institute for Palestine Studies, 2020), 277–99.

35. Noga Kadman, *Erased from Space and Consciousness: Israel and the Depopulated Palestinian Villages of 1948* (Bloomington: Indiana University Press, 2015).

36. Rachel Busbridge, "On Haunted Geography: Writing Nation and Contesting Claims in the Ghost Village of Lifta," *Interventions* 17, no. 4 (2015): 469–87.

37. Eitan Bronstein, "Studying the Nakba and Reconstructing Space in the Palestinian Village of Lifta," working paper (European University Institute, San Domenico di Fiesole, Italy, 2005), 8.

38. Bronstein, "Studying the Nakba," 2.

39. Eitan Bronstein, quoted in "A Different Kind of Memory: Interview with Zochrot," by Meera Shah, *Middle East Report* 244 (2007): 36–37.

40. Bronstein, quoted in "A Different Kind of Memory," 37.

41. Zochrot, "Our Vision," n.d., accessed June 13, 2025, https://web.archive.org/web/20181215172921/https://zochrot.org/en/content/17.

42. There have been several iterations of this kind of touring over the past two decades, one of the first being Alternative Tours Jerusalem, as a kind of antidote to the tourist industry dominated by the hegemonic Zionist narrative of place and history. See Alternative Tours Jerusalem, "About Us," n.d., accessed June 13, 2025, https://www.alternativetours-jerusalem.com/about-us/.

43. Yaqub Odeh also appears in the context of testimonial. For a reading of his presence/rupture, see Yaqub Odeh, "Yakoub Odeh, Former Resident of Lifta," interview by Laura van Rij, May 23, 2015, Zochrot, https://web.archive.org/web/20210726011821/https://www.zochrot.org/en/testimony/54909. See also Yulia Gilichinskaya, "Vulnerable Domestic Spaces of Lifta," Zochrot, 2017, https://web.archive.org/web/20210921150805/https://zochrot.org/en/article/56491; and Laura van Rij, "It's All About People: Narratives from Lifta," Zochrot, June 2013, https://web.archive.org/web/20210616194428/https://zochrot.org/en/article/54891.

44. This is a conversation that is planted in the conceptualization and practice of archiving referred to in the introduction to the present volume.

45. Norma Musih, quoted in "A Different Kind of Memory," 37.

46. Samera Esmeir, "Memories of Conquest: Witnessing Death in Tantura," in *Nakba: Palestine, 1948, and the Claims of Memory*, ed. Ahmad H. Sa'di and Lila Abu-Lughod (New York: Columbia University Press, 2007), 229–50; Samera Esmeir, "1948: Law, History, Memory," *Social Text* 21, no. 2 (2003): 25–48.

47. Malkit Shoshan and Eitan Bronstein, "Reinventing Lifta," *Monu: Magazine on Urbanism,* January 6, 2016, 64–69.

48. See Rami Isaac, C. Michael Hall, and Freya Higgins-Desbiolles, *The Politics and Power of Tourism in Palestine* (New York: Routledge, 2015).

49. Stephanie Nohelani Teves, *Defiant Indigeneity: The Politics of Hawaiian Performance* (Chapel Hill: University of North Carolina Press, 2018).

50. Abdul-Rahim Al-Shaikh, *The Columbus Syndrome and the Veiling of Palestine: Politics of Toponymy of the Palestinian Landscape 1856–2015* (Ramallah, Palestine: Institute for Palestine Studies, forthcoming); Rowda Beshara, ed., *Judthor Baladna* [Roots of our nation] (Haifa, Israel: Mada al Karmil, 2011).

51. For a nuanced reading of tourism in Palestine, see Jennifer Lynn Kelly, *Invited to Witness: Solidarity Tourism Across Occupied Palestine* (Durham, NC: Duke University Press, 2023).

52. Meryem Kamil, "Postspatial, Postcolonial: Accessing Palestine in the Digital," *Social Text* 38, no. 3 (2020): 55–82.

53. Even before the establishment of the settler state of Israel, settler colonial manipulation of population registries and demographics rendered the land of Palestine unreachable for a majority of the Palestinian people. Today, Palestinians not "counted" as residents (in all the various settler designations that exist) can at best pass through Israeli borders as "visitors" or "tourists"—when they can pass.

54. Jamil Hilal, ed., *Al-Harakat al-Shababiya al Fialstiniyya* [The Palestinian youth movement] (Ramallah, Palestine: Massrat, 2018); Ahmad Ezzeddine, *The Sociology of Resistance and Mobilization in the Colonized Spaces of Jerusalem* (Ramallah, Palestine: Research Center—Palestine Liberation Organization, 2018).

55. Rashid Khalidi, *Palestinian Identity: The Construction of Modern National Consciousness* (New York: Columbia University Press, 1997).

56. Mjriam Abu Samra, "The Palestinian Transnational Student Movement, 1948–1982: A Study on Popular Organization and Transnational Mobilization" (PhD thesis, University of Oxford, 2020).

57. As described in chapter 1, critique of the Oslo Accords and its subsequent politics and policies has been a major factor in contemporary Palestine studies. For a general overview, see Rashid Khalidi, *The Hundred Years' War on Palestine: a History of Settler Colonialism and Resistance, 1917–2017* (Boston: Metropolitan Books, 2020); Edward W. Said, *The End of the Peace Process: Oslo and After* (New York: Pantheon, 2000); Leila Farsakh, *Rethinking Statehood in Palestine: Self-Determination and Decolonization Beyond Partition* (Oakland: University of California Press, 2021); Joseph Massad, *The Persistence of the Palestinian Question: Essays on Zionism and the Palestinians* (London: Routledge, 2006); Leila Farsakh, "Undermining Democracy in Palestine: The Politics of International Aid Since Oslo," *Journal of Palestine Studies* 45, no. 4 (2016): 48–63; Seth Anziska, *Preventing Palestine* (Princeton, NJ: Princeton University Press, 2018); Somdeep Sen, "'It's Nakba, Not a Party': Re-Stating the (Continued) Legacy of the Oslo Accords," *Arab Studies Quarterly* 37, no. 2 (2015): 161–76; Jamil Hilal, "The Fragmentation of the Palestinian Political Field: Sources and Ramifications," *Contemporary Arab Affairs* 11, no. 1–2 (2018): 189–216; and Raja Khalidi and Sobhi Samour, "Neoliberalism as Liberation: The Statehood Program and the Remaking of the Palestinian National Movement," *Journal of Palestine Studies* 40, no. 2 (2011): 6–25.

58. Mjriam Abu Samra and Loubna Qutami, "Alterity Across Generations: A Comparative Analysis of the 1950's Jeel al-Thawra and the 2006 Palestinian Youth Movement," *Revue des Mondes Musulmans et de la Méditerranée* 147 (2020): 1–17. See also Sophie Richter-Devroe, "Palestinian Refugees of the Oslo Generation: Thinking Beyond the Nation?," *Journal of Palestine Studies* 50, no. 3 (2021): 18–36.

59. Ruba Salih, Elena Zambelli, and Lynn Welchman, "'From Standing Rock to Palestine We Are United': Diaspora Politics, Decolonization and the Intersectionality of Struggles," *Ethnic and Racial Studies* 44, no. 7 (2021): 1135–53.

60. Joseph Massad, "The 'Post-Colonial' Colony: Time, Space, and Bodies in Palestine/Israel," in *The Pre-Occupation of Postcolonial Studies*, ed. Fawzia Afzal-Khan and Kalpana Seshadri-Crooks (Durham, NC: Duke University Press, 2000), 311–46.

61. Eid, *Decolonizing the Palestinian Mind.*

62. Haidar Eid, "Back to the Future: The Great March of Return," Al-Shabaka: the Palestinian Policy Network, July 24, 2018, https://al-shabaka.org/commentaries/back-to-the

-future-the-great-march-of-return/. See also Eid, *Decolonizing the Palestinian Mind*; ʿAsim Hilmi Hamad, "Great March of Return: A Report," Masarat, the Palestinian Research and Policy Center, March 25, 2019; Huthifa Fayyad, "Gaza's Great March of Return Protests Explained," Al-Jazeera, March 30, 2018, https://www.aljazeera.com/news/2019/3/30/gazas -great-march-of-return-protests-explained; and Ahmed Abu Artema, "From the Arab Spring to the Great March of Return: How the Arab Revolutions Inspired Palestinian Mobilisation in Gaza," Al-Jazeera, March 6, 2021, https://www.aljazeera.com/opinions/2021/3 /6/from-the-arab-spring-to-the-great-march-of-return.

63. Nora Akawi, conversation with the author, New York City, February 20, 2019.

64. The space and production of two local institutions are of note here: al Maʾmal Foundation for Contemporary Art and Riwaq (Center for Architectural Conservation). It is important to note that, like the SLC, these institutions were not only institutions but collectives of individuals who approached the work of preservation, restoration, and cultural production in both complementary and contradictory ways.

65. Mahdi Sabbagh, "Re:Lifta, Within the Right to Plan Is the Right to Imagine Return," Arena of Speculation, November 25, 2010, https://arenaofspeculation.org/2012/11/25/re -lifta/.

66. Mahdi Sabbagh, conversation with the author, New York City, March 8, 2019.

67. Sabbagh, "Re:Lifta."

68. Robert Warrior, "Foreword," in *Speaking of Indigenous Politics: Conversations with Activists, Scholars, and Tribal Leaders*, ed. J. Kēhaulani Kauanui (Minneapolis: University of Minnesota Press, 2018), ix.

69. Sabbagh, "Re:Lifta."

70. Akawi conversation.

71. Akawi conversation.

72. Jorge Otero-Pailos, "Preservation Arab: An Interview with Jorge Otero-Pailos," by Katherine Malone-France, *Forum Journal* 30, no. 3 (2016): 9, 12.

73. Jorge Otero-Pailos, "The Ethics of Dust: Carthago Nova," *Architectural Theory Review* 20, no. 1 (2015): 120.

74. Nora Akawi and Nina Valerie Kolowratnik, "Silencing Conflict, Pacifying the Ruin," *Volume* 40 (2014): 138, 141.

75. Akawi and Kolowratnik, "Silencing Conflict, Pacifying the Ruin," 142.

76. Akawi and Kolowratnik, "Silencing Conflict, Pacifying the Ruin," 143.

77. Akawi conversation.

78. Sabbagh, "Re:Lifta."

79. For the images that were on display, see AAU Anastas and Karim Kattan, "Re:Lifta," in *LIFTA*, vol. 1, *Future Palestine*, ed. Amira Asad, Leila Peinado, and Rashed Al Deiri (Mexico City: Lifta Volumes, 2020), 22–24; and Mahdi Sabbagh, "Mahdi Sabbagh Portfolio 2012–2015," March 23, 2015, https://web.archive.org/web/20221030155507/https://issuu .com/mahdisabbagh/docs/sabbagh_portfolio_issuu_26b43936fc64af.

80. Nina Valerie Kolowratnik, "A Landscape of Return," *Sedek: A Journal on the Ongoing Nakba Towards Return of Palestinian Refugees* 6 (2011): 2.

81. Kolowratnik, "A Landscape of Return," 2.

82. AAU Anastas and Kattan, "Re:Lifta," 22.

Chapter Four

1. Samera Esmeir, "Memories of Conquest: Witnessing Death in Tantura," in *Nakba: Palestine, 1948 and Claims of Memory*, ed. Ahmad H. Sa'di and Lila Abu-Lughod (New York: Columbia University Press, 2007).

2. Rosemary Sayigh, "Silenced Suffering," *Borderlands* 14, no. 1 (2015): 1–20. Storytelling is how I read Indigenous Palestinian history—not as a counternarrative to Zionist history but as our Indigenous methodology of telling the story of our past to understand our present and to imagine our future. See Alice Te Punga Somerville, Daniel Heath Justice, and Noelani Arista, eds., "Indigenous Conversations About Biography," special issue, *Biography* 39, no. 3 (2016).

3. Talah Hassan, Odessa Warren, and Kaoukab Chebaro, "Archiving Palestinian Oral History: A Policy Perspective," Policy Brief No. 6, American University of Beirut, 2017.

4. Nakba historiography, as described in earlier chapters in this book, adheres to the timeline created through settler violence as a way to trace that through Palestinian experience or to counter it. As researchers now return to the manuscripts of the oral narratives, we find far more nuance than what is summarized in these three acts. See the Birzeit University Museum's ethnographic collections, n.d., http://museum.birzeit.edu/search/node/ethnographic.

5. Laura van Rij, "It's All About People: Narratives from Lifta," Zochrot, June 2013, https://www.zochrot.org/publication_articles/view/54891/en?Its_all_about_people; Badil Resource Center, "Sons of Lifta," YouTube video, 10:17, posted May 20, 2013, https://www.youtube.com/watch?v=L7afYef4bSQ&t=2s.

6. Nick Estes, *Our History Is the Future: Standing Rock Versus the Dakota Access Pipeline, and the Long Tradition of Indigenous Resistance* (London: Verso Books, 2019).

7. Nowaf Awad, conversation with the author, Ramallah, Palestine, October 29, 2012. All conversations in this chapter were conducted in Arabic, and the English translations are my own.

8. Nuwara Abutaah Zitawi, telephone conversation with the author, October 11, 2019.

9. Nuwara Abutaah Zitawi, telephone conversation, August 15, 2019.

10. The British recorded how roads in Palestine were packed down, almost as if paved, by donkeys, who know how to seek water; see Penny Johnson, *Companions in Conflict: Animals in Occupied Palestine* (New York: Melville House, 2019).

11. Zitawi, telephone conversation, August 15, 2019. Though many of these observations are born out of my imagination in looking back, the grounds for these stories were gratefully and kindly provided to me over time by Nuwara Abutaah Zitawi, my mother's half sister, who lives in Amman and kindly engaged in a series of telephone conversations with me. While she appreciated how involved my imagination became over time, she also sometimes showed surprise by just how involved my existence in her past became. Nuwara, a remarkable woman, was most likely in her late teens in 1948.

12. Zitawi, telephone conversation, August 15, 2019.

13. Jamila Awwad, conversation with the author, Ramallah, Palestine, November 1, 2012.

14. Amana Khalil, conversation with the author, Ramallah, Palestine, December 1, 2012.

15. Estes, *Our History Is the Future*. See also United Nations, United Nations Declaration of the Rights of Indigenous Peoples, September 13, 2007, https://www.un.org/development/desa/indigenouspeoples/declaration-on-the-rights-of-indigenous-peoples.html.

16. Mahmoud Darwish, *Memory for Forgetfulness: August, Beirut, 1982*, trans. Ibrahim Muhawi (Berkeley: University of California Press, 2013), 9–10.

17. See Rana Barakat, "Lifta, the Nakba, and the Museumification of Palestine's History," *Native American and Indigenous Studies* 5, no. 2 (2018): 1–15.

18. See Salim Tamari, ed., *Jerusalem 1948: The Arab Neighbourhoods and Their Fate in the War* (Ramallah, Palestine: Institute of Jerusalem Studies / Badil Resource Center for Palestinian Residency and Refugee Rights, 1998).

19. Ibrahim Khalil with his wife Nowaf Awad, conversation with the author, Ramallah, Palestine, October 29, 2012.

20. Salima Al-Baja, conversation with the author, Ramallah, Palestine, November 11, 2012.

21. Muhammad Khalil Nassar, conversation with the author, Ramallah, Palestine, November 3, 2012.

22. Abd al-Karim Zhrour, conversation with the author, Ramallah, Palestine, September 23, 2012; Rifqa Odeh, conversation with the author, Ramallah, Palestine, October 18, 2012.

23. These familial anecdotes are difficult to footnote, as they are based on long discussions among the children of ʿAta and ʿArifa Abutaah including the late Khawlah Abutaah, Naima Abutaah, and Salah Abutaah and the living ʿAbla Abutaah Siam, ʿAdla Abutaah Barakat, and Dalal Abutaah Kahtib.

24. Taha Hamouda, conversation with the author, Ramallah, Palestine, November 22, 2012.

25. Ibrahim Khalil with his wife Nowaf Awad, conversation.

26. Nassar, conversation.

27. Awwad, conversation.

28. Ibrahim Khalil with his wife Nowaf Awad, conversation.

29. Al-Baja, conversation. The '48 is the colloquial name for the area taken by Israeli settlers in 1948—that is, land within the so-called green line.

30. Habiba al-ʿAbdiyat, conversation with the author, Ramallah, Palestine, December 10, 2012.

31. Awwad, conversation.

32. Michael Feinberg, "Machane Yehuda" (master's thesis, University of Waterloo, 2010).

33. Al-ʿAbdiyat, conversation.

34. Nassar, conversation.

35. Sherene Seikaly, *Men of Capital: Scarcity and Economy in Mandate Palestine* (Stanford, CA: Stanford University Press, 2015); Amos Nadan, *The Palestinian Peasant Economy Under the Mandate: A Story of Colonial Bungling* (Cambridge, MA: Harvard University Press, 2006).

36. Hamouda, conversation.

37. Ibrahim Khalil with his wife Nowaf Awad, conversation.

38. Al-Baja, conversation.

39. Al-Baja, conversation; Awwad, conversation.

40. Ibrahim Khalil with his wife Nowaf Awad, conversation.

41. Al-ʿAbdiyat, conversation.

42. Hamouda, conversation.

43. Al-ʿAbdiyat, conversation.

44. Awwad, conversation.

45. Bilal Odeh, conversation with the author, Ramallah, Palestine, February 15, 2020.

46. Zitawi, telephone conversation, August 15, 2019.

47. Muhammad Abu Layle, conversation with the author, Jerusalem, September 9, 2012.

48. Hamouda, conversation.

49. Al-ʿAbdiyat, conversation.

50. Rosemary Sayigh, *The Palestinians: From Peasants to Revolutionaries* (London: Bloomsbury, 2008), bases her generational reading of Palestinians on the relationship between peasants on their land to peasants fighting to return to the land.

51. Al-ʿAbdiyat, conversation.

52. For more on Palestinian weddings, see Penny Johnson, Lamis Abu Nahleh, and Annelies Moors, "Weddings and War: Marriage Arrangements and Celebrations in Two Palestinian Intifadas," *Journal of Middle East Women's Studies* 5, no. 3 (2009): 11–35; Islah Jad, "The Politics of Group Weddings in Palestine: Political and Gender Tensions," *Journal of Middle East Women's Studies* 5, no. 3 (2009): 36–53; Nadia Yaqub, *Pens, Swords, and the Springs of Art: The Oral Poetry Dueling of Palestinian Weddings in the Galilee* (Leiden, Netherlands: Brill, 2007); Kamal Boullata, *The Palestinian Wedding: A Bilingual Anthology of Contemporary Palestinian Resistance Poetry* (Washington, DC: Three Continents, 1982); and Abdelwahab Elmessiri, "The Palestinian Wedding: Major Themes of Contemporary Palestinian Resistance Poetry," *Journal of Palestine Studies* 10, no. 3 (1981): 77–99.

53. Al-ʿAbdiyat, conversation.

54. Ibrahim Khalil with his wife Nowaf Awad, conversation.

Chapter Five

1. Saidiya V. Hartman, *Scenes of Subjection: Terror, Slavery, and Self-Making in Nineteenth-Century America* (Oxford: Oxford University Press, 1997); Michel-Rolph Trouillot, *Silencing the Past: Power and the Production of History* (Boston: Beacon, 2015).

2. ʿAdla Nahida Abutaah Barakat, conversation with the author, Wilmette, IL, November 21, 2019. Unless noted otherwise, all conversations (including ones between me and my mother) in this chapter were conducted in Arabic, and the English translations are my own.

3. For a discussion of the generational understanding of memory and the work of Rosemary Sayigh, see the introduction to the present volume. While Anaheed Al-Hardan, *Palestinians in Syria: Nakba Memories of Shattered Communities* (New York: Columbia University Press, 2016), argues that generations were not about collective memory and that a focus on 1948 erased all that came after it, and Diana Allen, ed., *Voices of the Nakba: A Living History of Palestine* (London: Pluto, 2021), makes a similar point, the focus here is not about time as events but instead about memory as inherited and lived time.

4. The pear shape is one of many designs, whereas the rose shape is more common in contemporary reproductions of classical designs. See Widad Kawar, *Threads of Identity: Preserving Palestinian Costume and Heritage* (London: Rimal, 2011). See also Widad Kamel Kawar, "The Traditional Palestinian Costume," *Journal of Palestine Studies* 10, no. 1 (1980): 118–29; Margarita Skinner and Widad Kawar, *Palestinian Embroidery Motifs: A Treasury of Stitches, 1850–1950* (London: Melisende, 2007); Tina Sherwell, "Palestinian Costume, the

Intifada and the Gendering of Nationalist Discourse," *Journal of Gender Studies* 5, no. 3 (1996): 293–303; Jeni Allenby, "Re-Inventing Cultural Heritage: Palestinian Traditional Costume and Embroidery Since 1948," in *Silk Roads, Other Roads: Proceedings of the Eighth Biennial Symposium of the Textile Society of America, September 26–28, 2002, Northampton, Massachusetts* (Millersville, MD: Textile Society of America, 2002), 101–11; and Lisa Raye Garlock, "Stories in the Cloth: Art Therapy and Narrative Textiles," *Art Therapy* 33, no. 2 (2016): 58–66.

5. With the modern craze of *tatreez* (traditional Palestinian embroidery) being a kind of museumification of heritage in which collectors continue to refer to a *thob* as a costume, these lived realties and life stories are erased by "restoration." ʿArifa did not wear a "costume," and her daughters and daughters' daughters do not. The details of ʿArifa's life shows in the wear of the fabric. For further reading, see Omar Joseph Nasser-Khoury and Sue Jones, "'Silk Thread Martyrs': Palestinian Embroidery," *Textile* 11, no. 2 (2013): 196–201.

6. Diana Taylor, *The Archive and the Repertoire: Performing Cultural Memory in the Americas* (Durham, NC: Duke University Press, 2003).

7. Nuwara Abutaah Salman, telephone conversation with the author, August 15, 2019; Nuwara Abutaah Salman, telephone conversation with the author, October 11, 2019. Her grandmother Sayifa and her cows were a prominent part of Nurwara's childhood memories from when she moved into her father's home with his new wife, ʿArifa.

8. For more on city panning in the mandate era, see Nicholas E. Roberts, "Dividing Jerusalem: British Urban Planning in the Holy City," *Journal of Palestine Studies* 42, no. 4 (2013): 7–26; Rana Barakat, "Urban Planning, Colonialism, and the Pro-Jerusalem Society," *Jerusalem Quarterly* 65 (2016): 25–27; Falestin Naili, "The De-Municipalization of Urban Governance: Post-Ottoman Political Space in Jerusalem," *Jerusalem Quarterly* 76 (2018): 8–13; and Nadi Abusaada, "Self-Portrait of a Nation: The Arab Exhibition in Mandate Jerusalem, 1931–34" (PhD diss., Cambridge University, 2019).

9. Leanne Betasamosake Simpson, "Indigenous Resurgence and Co-Resistance," *Critical Ethnic Studies* 2, no. 2 (2016): 19–34; Jarrett Martineau, "Creative Combat: Indigenous Art, Resurgence, and De-Colonization" (PhD diss., University of Victoria, 2015).

10. Sherene Seikaly, "The Politics of Hope: 1967 and Beyond" in "Fifty Years of Occupation: A Forum (Part 3)," *Middle East Report*, June 9, 2017, https://merip.org/2017/06/fifty-years-of-occupation-3/.

11. Ibrahim Khalil and his wife Nowaf Awad, conversation with the author, Ramallah, Palestine, October 29, 2012.

12. Salima al-Baja, conversation with the author, Ramallah, Palestine, November 11, 2012.

13. Al-Baja, conversation.

14. Ibrahim Khalil and his wife Nowaf Awad, conversation.

15. Rifqa Odeh, conversation with the author, Ramallah, Palestine, October 18, 2012.

16. Muhammad Khalil Nassar, conversation with the author, Ramallah, Palestine, November 3, 2012.

17. Nassar, conversation.

18. Nassar, conversation.

19. Nassar, conversation.

20. Basil al-ʿAraj, *Wajadat Ajwabti: Haktha Takalm al Shahid Basil al-ʿAraj* [The appearance of my responses: So spoke the martyr Basil al-ʿAraj] (Jerusalem: Dar al Rʾabal, 2018).

For a fine summary and intensive inquiry into the work of Khaled Odetallah, see Khaled Odetallah, "Khaled Odetallah: Filastiniyya min al-Quds ila Gaza" [Khaled Odetallah: Palestine from Jerusalem to Gaza], interview by Abdul-Rahim al-Shaikh, *Majallat al-Dirasat al-Filastiniyya* 137 (2024): 61–84.

21. Habiba al-ʿAbdiyat, conversation with the author, Ramallah, Palestine, December 10, 2012.

22. Al-ʿAbdiyat, conversation.

23. Al-ʿAbdiyat, conversation.

24. Jamila Awwad, conversation with the author, Ramallah, Palestine, November 1, 2012.

25. Awwad, conversation.

26. Awwad, conversation.

27. Awwad, conversation.

28. Rana Barakat, "How to Read a Massacre in Palestine: Indigenous History as a Methodology of Liberation," *Omran Journal for Social Sciences* 10, no. 39 (2022): 149–72.

29. Yezid Sayigh, *Armed Struggle and the Search for State: The Palestinian National Movement, 1949–1993* (Oxford: Clarendon Press, 1997).

30. Al-ʿAbdiyat, conversation.

31. Rana Barakat, "Reading Palestinian Agency in Mandate History: The Narrative of the Buraq Revolt as Anti-Relational," *Contemporary Levant* 4, no. 1 (2019): 28–38.

32. Edward W. Said and Christopher Hitchens, eds., *Blaming the Victims: Spurious Scholarship and the Palestinian Question* (London: Verso Books, 1988).

33. Al-ʿAraj, Wajadat Ajwabti. See also Khaled Odetallah, "Malhamat al-Jabal: Mʿrakat Jabla Nabi Samual fi Harb al-ʿalamiya al-ula" [The Epic of the Mountain: The Battle of Nabi Samuel in the First World War], *Bab al-Wad* (December 22, 2020).

34. Nuwara Abutaah Salman, telephone interview with the author, December 6, 2019.

35. Al-ʿAbdiyat, conversation.

36. Loay al-Manssi, conversation with the author, Ramallah, Palestine, February 4, 2020.

37. Bilal Odeh, conversation with the author, Ramallah, Palestine, February 15, 2020.

38. Al-Manssi, conversation.

39. Odeh, conversation.

40. Al-Manssi, conversation.

41. Al-Manssi, conversation.

42. Odeh, conversation.

43. Odeh, conversation.

44. Odeh, conversation.

45. Ibrahim Khalil and his wife Nowaf Awad, conversation.

46. Ibrahim Khalil and his wife Nowaf Awad, conversation.

47. Amjad al-Din Barakat, conversation with the author, Wilmette, IL, December 24, 2019. This is the only conversation in this chapter that took place predominantly in English.

Index